MW01622922

The Southern Paiutes

Legends Lore Language and Lineage

by
LaVan Martineau

KC Publications
Las Vegas, Nevada

The Southern Paiutes

Book design by LaVan Martineau

Drawings by Jetta and Shannandoah Martineau

First Edition: First Printing 1992

Library of Congress 92-74128, ISBN 0-8871-070-X

KC Publications, Box 15630
Las Vegas, Nevada 89114

Printed in the United States of America

Dedicated to the Old People of the Paiutes,
a people whose culture taught them
that giving was more honorable than receiving.

Table Of Contents

List Of Illustrations

Plates

Acknowledgments

I would like to thank all the Paiutes who have helped me compile this work particularly the older people who offered so freely without thought of payment. To these people raised in the old way their culture was like the land, no one owned it and therefore no one had the right to sell it; it belonged to everyone. Elders took pride in sharing their knowledge with the younger generation. They felt it was their duty to preserve their culture and religion they believed was given to them by the Creator. As these elders saw their culture waning, they wanted more than ever to see their knowledge preserved and written down as they could see their children losing interest. Some of them would tell me "I wish my own kids would take as much interest as you."

When the old time Indians who still lived and retained their culture are mentioned in the Paiute language, the term Wee Noonts (Old People) is used. This term does not refer to age but to **people who lived the old ways**, and to **people who lived long ago.** It is a name of distinction and honor that no one of the present acculturated generation can fully qualify for. It was my privilege to meet individuals who I felt qualified highly for this distinction; people who still believed in and clung to many of the old ways as much as they could as it slowly eroded from beneath their feet. It is from such people that most of the information was obtained.

The number after each name is a reference number so that the reader may be able to tell who first gave me the information included with their name. Most of the information in this book was given to me by many people over the years, but I would like to show my appreciation to those who first offered it. These informants are numbered in a chronological arbitrary manner and the number in no way signifies how many informants came from a particular band, nor do the numbers indicate priority in appreciation or importance. It is to some of these **Old People** that I want to first express my gratitude: Carl Jake 1, Minnie Jake 2, Jimmy Timmican 3, Florence Kanosh 10, Seth Bushhead 38, Edrick Bushhead 8, Woots Parashont 39, Bessie Tillahash 26, Archie Rogers 5, Jim Chili 41, Minnie Kanosh and James Yellowjacket.

I would also like to thank the following individuals from the Paiute tribe who still speak the language and have retained much of their culture. They have also freely given cultural information over the years and some have even helped in going over my old notes to weed out errors. My thanks to the following: Morris Jake 4, Reuben John 6, Douglas Timmican 7, Marie McFee 9, Lyman Smokey 11, Smith Bushhead 12, Wilbur Bushhead 13, Woodrow Pete 14, Earl & Verna Pikyavit 15, Ralph Pikyavit 16, Melvin John 17, Georgey George 18, Serena Mose 19, Vera Charles 20, Deere Kanosh 22, Kenneth Charles 23, Johnny Jake 24, Tony Tillahash 25, Eunice Tillahash 27, Stewart Snow 28, Warren Bushhead 29, Ruth Benson 30,

Edurine Jake 31, Marilyn Jake 35, Mable Yellowjacket 36, Arthur Richards 37, Albert Rice 40, Hamblin John 42. Wendall John, Virginia George, George McFee, Lorraine McFee, Charley Greyman, Eleanor Tom, Roy Tom, and Harry Wall. I would also like to thank those who gave information but didn't want their names used and to anyone I might have missed.

I extend my appreciation to the following members of the various Ute Bands for the information they contributed to this work: Johnny Ioup, Charles E. Queacut (Ed Wyasket), Harriet Taveapont, Annebelle Eagle, Susan Lehi, Molly Deer, Dick McCuen Sr. Richard McCuen Jr., Francis McKinley, Ouray McCook, Glen Jenks, Russel Root, Eddie Box Sr. and Vincent Sireech.

I extend special appreciation for the many things taught me by my wife Doris Kanosh who was raised by her grandmother Florence Kanosh and consequently knew a lot of her culture. I also want to thank my daughters Jetta and Shannandoah Martineau for all the time they spent wading through my faded hand-written notes to type this material into the computer, and for the art work they created especially for this book. Without their help and encouragement this book might have never been attempted. I also want to thank my daughters Dorena, Carmen, and Rachel for their moral support, encouragement, and for all the tasks they have willingly done for me to allow me time to complete this work. Lucille Watahomigie also deserves my thanks as she has helped me in many ways that have saved me a lot of money. Thanks is given to Charlene Hunt for some footwork and acquiring an old photograph. Special thanks is extended to William F. Price Ph.D. for the time he took in editing and making suggestions in the dictionary portion of this book. Special thanks is also due my nephew James D. Richards who donated a Macintosh computer, software, and a printer to make this work much easier. Without his help this compilation might never have been accomplished.

Preface

I began accumulating the material presented in this work sometime in the 1940s. I initially wrote down whatever I heard from the Paiutes, so I wouldn't forget what I was told, with no thought in mind of writing a book. I normally asked the older people for the information since they were better informed than those of my age. This was a time when the younger Paiute generation still spoke Paiute but was beginning to lose interest in their culture.

In my early years I never dreamed that the language or the culture would ever die out. Now, decades later no one under fifty speaks the language and there are few left who know the culture and legends. The culture of the Paiute people will soon pass into oblivion along with that of numerous other tribes. Now that I see it disappearing I want to see it preserved. I have often thought that after I was gone and the culture died out someone could publish my notes as I never had the desire to be a writer. Now as I compile my faded unproofed hand-written notes I realize that it would have been difficult for someone to fully understand them. Therefore I have taken it upon myself to finish the task.

Edward Sapir acquired a good understanding of the Paiute language from Tony Tillahash, and Isabel Kelly recorded a lot of cultural material from the Kaibab Band. Yet, when I read these works, I see many things that have been omitted and some mistakes. Therefore, I thought I would make my notes available and fill in these gaps the best I could.

I am purposely designing this book to be a book of the Old People. I let them do most of the talking and try to keep everything in their wording as much as possible. I am purposely avoiding making this a book of Anglo quotations, some of which are often highly suspect because of occasional prejudice, however, I do include a few. Restricting a cultural book to Anglo quotations is a practice followed by many anthropologists and writers some of whom seek to monopolize and become the curators of that which they ridicule.

I have learned the value of Indian quotes over the years when I have sought cultural information that would be helpful in deciphering the rock writings of a certain tribe. I often had to wade through hundreds of pages of analysis and opinion made by a person who only peeked in the window and was not a part of that culture. Whenever I have been lucky enough to find a direct quote from an Indian I have felt very fortunate. As a result I have often stated: *One direct cultural statement from a knowledgeable Indian is worth a complete book analyzing that statement from an anthropologist.* This type of information directly from the Indian will be of great benefit to those who study Paiute rock writings in the future. I accept the fact that some Indian quotations might be inaccurate, but time and study can weed most of these errors out. I have not included those I know to be inaccurate.

Whenever I comment on anything in this book it will be infrequent and only for the sake of clarification. Such comments will be found in the footnotes, in parenthesis, or written in a manner that the reader will know the comment is mine. This book is basically on the people that are today called Southern Paiutes. It includes some bands that were considered Utes in the past and even today. It is difficult to draw a line between some Paiute and Ute bands. My main purpose in this book is to preserve all that I have learned from the Old People in Utah, Nevada, and Arizona so I do include some Utah Ute bands. The bulk of my information on Utes that originated in Colorado is not included in this work.

The Paiute culture, as any culture of the world, has both its good and bad aspects. In this work I include almost everything I made notes on over the years whether I believe in it or not. I do omit a few notes that would be abused if the information fell into the wrong hands. Many people have worked hard to destroy Indian cultures thinking that the Indian would be better off. In cases of superstition this may be true. However, few people realize what the loss of Indian culture has done to the spirituality and character of the American Indian. Mark Twain characterized this civilizing as "Lifting Indians down to our level." Carl Lumholtz, who studied Indians in northern Mexico near the turn of the century, made a pertinent observation of the American Indian. He stated, "Their ignorance is nearer the truth than our prejudice." Stan Steiner, a more recent student of the American Indian stated that they are "Christians whether or not they had heard of Christ." And this from the log of Christopher Columbus after his encounter with the Arawaks:

> *They are so naive and so free with their possessions that no one who has not witnessed them would believe it. When you ask for something they have, they never say no. To the contrary they offer to share with anyone.*

It was a pleasure to witness these traits lingering among some of the old Paiutes; precious traits that are dying with the culture; traits that may be extolled but seldom believed; traits that the pen may praise but not preserve.

Key To Pronunciation

This pronunciation is devised to be used on typewriters where no unusual signs are needed. I've tried to keep it as simple as possible. Words found in ***bold italic*** indicate the English interpretation of a Paiute word or phrase. Sometimes the interpretation is loose and more in the form of an explanation.

A hyphen in front of a word means that word is a suffix. A hyphen at the end of a word means that it is a prefix. Long vowels generally occur at the accent or at the end of a word. Sometimes I use the long "aw" in spelling a word in place of the shorter "a." I do this to make some words more presentable and easier to read. In such cases the long vowel may be distinguished from the shorter one by the accent mark (´). I only do this with these two vowels.

Glottal stops are abundant in the Paiute language, yet not strong, and often missed. I do show the ones that are almost indispensable in pronouncing certain words but I omit most of the minor ones. I use an apostrophe (') for a glottal stop, e.g., uh'uhng ***yes***. Do not confuse this with the accent mark (´).

Reduplication of a syllable often occurs in Paiute. In some cases it indicates ***plurality***. At other times it indicates a ***repetition, to keep doing***, or ***one after another***. For example the word tungai means ***to kick once***; tuntdung´ai means ***to kick more than once*** therefore ***kicking***.

The "r" and "l" sounds are not found in Paiute. The "l" sound sometimes occurs in Shivwits lullaby songs. The "f" sound is found occasionally only at Shivwits. The "z" sound occurs occasionally at Moapa.

VOWELS AND DIPHTHONGS

Symbol	Example
a	short as in all.
aw	long as in saw. (In some of my older publications I used "ah" for this sound.)
ah	as in bat and hat.
ai	as in aisle, and pile.
ay	as in pay and hay.
ao	a diphthong combining the half long "a" and half long "o." Not found in English.
e	half long as in event.
ee	long as in see. This long vowel usually occurs at the accent.
eh	as in bet and let.
i	as in bit and ill.
ih	same sound as "i" but a little longer in the final position.
o	half long as in obey.

oh	long as in go.
oo	as in coo and Sue. When two occur together, the second one is long.
oy	a diphthong as in boy.
ow	a diphthong as in cow.
oa	similar to oar. Not found in English.
u	as in up.
uh	as in look, cook. When two occur together, the second one is long.

Hyphens separate adjacent vowels and diphthongs that otherwise would be confused with each other. Vowels and diphthongs are to be read as given above if no hyphens occur. In the following examples the second vowel is long.

Symbol	Example
e-ee	as in se-ee´.
o-oh	as in o-ohm.
o-aw	as in o-aw´kawd.
oo-oo	as in oo-oo´noovuv.
uh-u	as in kuh-uk. Without the hyphen uhu would always be a combination of uh and u.
uh-uh	as in uh'-uhng.
o-ow)	used to distinguish "oo" and the "w".

CONSONANTS

Symbol	Example
d	as in dog at the beginning of a word.
d	slightly trilled when occurring within a word.
dd	the double "d" is rolled more than the single "d".
b	often replaced with a "v" sound and sometimes sounding half way between "b" and "v "when used within a word.
g	as in go. Often replaced with an "h".
gh	a coarse, rasping sound approaching a coarse "k".
j	as in jump.
k	as in king at the beginning of a word.
kh	a very coarse rasping "k" sound combined with "h". Not found in English.
p	as in put. Occasionally replaced with "v".
kw	as in queen. Sometimes it is interchanged with a coarse "w".
s	as in see and ice.
ts	as in beets.
ch or tch	as in match and check.
td	a combination of both the "t "and "d" sounds into one letter. Not found in English.
ng	as in king. If the "n" and "g" sounds ever occur separately they will be separated by a hyphen (n-g).

-k´w,	
-ng´w,	the "w" is unvoiced after the accent at the end of a word.
v	as in victor and love. Sometimes interchangeable with "b".
vb	not found in English. These letters sound like "v" and "b" together.
w	as in walk.
z	as in whiz.

UTE AND PAIUTE LANGUAGE DIFFERENCES

The Ute language as now spoken on the Uintah and Ouray Reservation in Utah and also the Colorado reservations, differs from Southern Paiute in the following ways:

1. The Paiute "nts" endings are replaced by "ch"among the Ute, for example ***Indian***: nengwoonts´, nengwuhch´.
2. The Paiute "nt" endings are replaced by "t" among the Ute, for example, ***silly***, or ***crazy*** saw´mekunt, saw´mekut.
3. An "r" sometimes occurs among the Ute, for example, ***skunk*** in Paiute is poa´nee and in Ute it is purnee´.
4. The "ng" sound so common in Paiute is omitted, or slurred over, by many Utes.
5. The "m" sound in many words is omitted, or slurred over, by many Utes, for example, nump would be shortened to nup.
6. The Ute language has more Spanish cognates than Paiute.

CHAPTER 1

WINTER TALES

Tookwee'nup

There are no natives on earth so wicked as those who profess Christianity.
James Russell Lowell

The Paiutes had two types of stories that they used to tell during the wintertime. (They started telling them during the pinyon nut harvest in the fall.) The first type of story might be called a legend. The Paiutes called them Tookwee'nup (Kaibab 4). These stories are strictly myth and designed to be humorous and morally instructive, much like the white-man's fairy tales. As one Shivwits informant 5 put it, "They are only jokes." Others are considered by the Paiutes to be true even though they are replete with mythical animal characters and supernatural events. An attempt is made in many of these legends to make them look true by creating analogies in the story to similarities in nature, for example, why the feathers of a bird are of a certain color or why a certain geographical feature appears as it does.

Other stories, that are considered true historical accounts, are classified as Nawduh'gwenup. As one informant puts it, "They are told by witnesses." This type of story, or history, will be found in Chapter 2 on War and Historical Stories." Since Paiutes believed very strongly in the supernatural, they believed historical and war stories that included supernatural events to be true. Sometimes it becomes difficult to distinguish between Tookwee'nup and Nawduh'gwenup. Creation stories might be considered by some to fall into the category of Nawduh'gwenup. I haven't resolved this.

Kaibab informant 4 makes the following statement about how his band acquired their legends:

> *Tookwee'nup belongs to the Shivwits People and other Paiutes to the south. They taught the Kaibab Band these legends recently. These legends are about the land to the south and not Utah and Kaibab land. Nawduhgwenup*

belonged to all the Paiutes north and east of the Shivwits. These stories are historic accounts only.

These legends and historical stories were written down the same day they were told to me with the exception of one. When I first started recording this material I seldom wrote down the date they were told. In more recent years I did include the date. I first started recording legends in about 1949 and have continued to do so until the time of this writing in 1990.

Most of the stories told to me were only fragments of once lengthy accounts, nevertheless, I include these fragments because in many cases they are all that remain. They also serve another purpose. They show the extent of the same story, or similar versions, from band to band over an extensive Southern Paiute area.

In the 1950s and '60s I recorded some on reel-to-reel tapes and then on cassettes when they became popular. I've tried to keep the wording close to that of the informants, but in some cases I have had to change them for the sake of clarity since some of the informants couldn't speak English very well. Some legends were told to me several times by the same informant, and in such cases I have lumped the information in such accounts into one story. If the informant contradicted himself I mention this in the story or in the footnotes. Some legends contradict each other but I leave them as told.

Most of this material came to me naturally. I never asked for it until in very recent years. I just recorded whatever I heard. This is one reason some of the legends are only fragments. I now regret that I didn't pursue this material aggressively when the Old People were still living. However, what I was told came from many elderly people born in the last century, or from their children.

I could have made this a popular type work on legends to please children similar to what William R. Palmer did in his legend book "Why The North Star Stands Still." I have completely avoided doing this because in reality he and his publishers have changed some of the legends to the point that they have become inaccurate.

I knew Palmer personally and he admitted some were changed to fit what the publishers wanted in the way of a popular legend book. If he hadn't done this his legends would probably have never been published. He was also noted as a "creative writer" and took the liberty of adapting the legends to his creative type of writing. He was also hard of hearing and recorded the pronunciation of many Paiute words wrong. He definitely omitted all mention of sex that most Indian legends abound in, particularly in the Coyote stories. Coyote was known as Soonungwuv, Suhnuv, and Yohovuhts. Yohovuhts means ***one who always has sex***. To the Indian, Coyote's sex escapades were what made Coyote the mischievous person he was. He wasn't entirely evil as a white man would conceive evil to be. He was only human with human desires and in trying to fulfill them and outdo his elder brother Toovuts, he got himself and sometimes the entire creation into trouble. Creation today is as it is because Coyote caused it to be this way even though it could have been much better.

Toovuts (Wolf) was the righteous one who wanted peace, love, and people to live forever. He was like unto a wolf, larger, greater, and perhaps more noble than the

smaller mischievous Coyote. Wolf thus symbolized the Creator but because of his constant compromising with Coyote the Creator's plans gave way to the selfish imagination of Coyote. This is a very accurate analogy of creation as most races and religions understand it. Mankind (acting out the part of Coyote) disobeyed the Creator and did things their own way thus interfering in Gods plans. A good example from the Christian religion is the story of Adam and Eve who fell from eternal life and a life of ease by disobeying God and seeking to become as God. As a result they brought death and labor into the world. This was exactly what Coyote did. He brought death, suffering, and labor into the world as his plans to outdo his brother backfired, and because the Indians followed Coyote's ways they must suffer as he did.

Coyote is not the devil; the Paiutes had none. He is not God or the Creator yet he is as a God and a Creator because due to his misdeeds, mankind, earth, and nature have become as they are today. Toovuts, the real Creator, who died and returned to life, has retreated to his own heavenly paradise to let Coyote and mankind pursue their own imaginations. In many Christian religions God is also thought of as in retreat, leaving men to pursue the imaginations of their own heart. Coyote, as human nature, still exists today in all of us and, as much of mankind sees a part of God within themselves, so has mankind become a Demigod, just as Coyote has become.

Because of Toovuts' withdrawal, and the ways of Coyote predominating, many Paiutes would pray to Soonungwuv. He was the initial victor as it was his ways that won. This is the way it is with much of mankind. They all profess great allegiance to the Creator yet in reality they each follow their own ways, putting their own desires above the needs of others, and suffering for it.

Palmer, as a staunch Mormon, saw the Father and the Son in Toovuts and Coyote. As a result of this belief Coyote became a God of love and peace to Palmer. He cannot be entirely blamed for this because some Paiutes and other tribes equated Coyote, or their equivalent tricksters, to Jesus. However, the Indians see this trickster as more human and subject to mistakes than the Christians see Jesus. Modern day Crees, Sarcees, and Blackfeet have told me that they equate their trickster with Jesus. Norman Sunchild, a Cree from Thunderchild, Saskatchewan carries this a little further and states: "He is also called the Indian's Santa Claus because of all the useful animals he made for the Indians."

In the midst of the falsehood contained in Indian myths they often contain many grains of truth and perhaps more insight into reality and human nature than the illusions of harmony, self glory and hypocrisy that many Christians and other world religions hide behind today.

Paiutes had but one real God, Toovuts. He was the one that was resurrected. However, Coyote was also included as with the Christian God and Jesus. Paiutes believed in ghosts, evil spirits, Tookoov, Kainuhseev and water babies whom they feared, and would sometimes try to appease. Some medicine men had spirit helpers but these were not gods. In reality the Paiute and Ute religion was one of the simplest of all Indian religions, with far fewer superstitions than most other tribes. They do not worship the wolf, nor the coyote, in animal form.

This lack of superstition among the Paiutes and Utes seemed to cause wonderment among the Navajos who witnessed them breaking many Navajo taboos without suffering any consequences. To account for this the Navajos created a legend about how an abandoned Navajo baby was raised by an owl. This baby grew up and became the father of the Utes. "That's why the Utes sound like owls when they talk." Since an owl is an evil omen among almost all tribes, the Navajos might also have thought this made the Utes exempt from the consequences of breaking many of the taboos that haunt other tribes. It was the lack of excess superstition and ceremonies that made the Utes strong and feared in warfare.

Many Indian tribes believe in a magical time that existed before mankind and the earth came to be as it is today. In that primeval time of beginning, all the animals, birds, trees, stones, reptiles, sea creatures, sun, moon, stars, and numerous other things were God-like people without the knowledge of death. Stories were created to show how and why each were changed into that creature or object that they are today and how the earth came to be shaped as it now is. As these stories unfolded to the Indian child, he soon became acquainted with the characteristics of all the creatures in his world and with many of the geographical features in the land of his birth that were associated with these legends of creation.

The evidence afforded by these magical stories was constantly before the eyes of the Indian to add strength, belief, and fear regarding the religious morals contained in these mythical stories. The legends were often inventions of men, but the morals they contained were morals known and accepted by all mankind. Many trembled at making the same foolish mistakes that Coyote made in his lust and quest for fame, or that other animals made that caused their fall from Godhood. These legends, therefore, instilled fear and belief in the hearts of the American Indian to the point that many writers have noted their religious enthusiasm. Following is just one of these quotes: "No people could be more religious than were the Indians before the advent of the white man; they had no observance, rite, or custom, which they did not believe to be God-given" (Curtin 1971, p. vii).

The purpose of Tookwee'nup was to teach children why things are as they are, and to give religious instruction in actions that struck close to home as these children grew and felt these desires arise within their own hearts. Another very important purpose of these legends was also to teach children to laugh at themselves! Any person who cannot laugh, when the laugh is on himself, will have difficulty in appreciating Indian legends, most of which are oriented to such humor. This type of person often sees himself doing that very thing so such legends offend him. Indian legends are designed for people who see themselves for what they really are with all their faults including their sexual misdeeds. They are therefore designed for people who can laugh at themselves and if a person can't do this then such legends are not for him. In all Indian languages words about sex have not been profaned, as in English, therefore they do not sound dirty. They are used in purity without shame. The ability to laugh at yourself is human nature with most Indians. They are taught this as children. When a child falls and cries, the parent's laughter turns the child's tears into joy. When the child becomes an adult he then has the ability to take calamity in stride.

The value and enjoyment of hearing Indian legends lies in how they are told. They were created by skilled story tellers and worded in a manner that brought out Indian humor to its maximum. When such legends are translated into English much of that humor becomes lost because the story teller is not as skilled in bringing out humor using the English language. In some cases Indian words have to be changed, and the white-man's idiom drawn upon, in order to retain the legends inherent value.

My Kaibab informant 4 had that ability because he was an Indian cattleman and had acquired a cowboy humor from his white associates. He knew how to ad-lib and bring out the color in a legend while using the English language. Read his legend about the Coyote and the Porcupine that was taken from a tape recording. In such examples I keep to his exact wording as much as possible to portray Indian humor more in keeping with the intent of some Indian legends.

In his legend about the Coyote and the Duck, Duck healed Coyote's son, causing Coyote to be indebted to him. The informant ended the story by having Duck tell Coyote, "That will be fo' dollars please." He even gave the word "four" a southern accent. I'm sure this wasn't in the original legend, which is the reason I omitted this statement, but yet in telling such legends in English, this is what is needed to bring out the humor created within them.

The legends that Kaibab informant 4 told me, that I didn't tape-record, lost much of his humor because I wrote them down later that day and couldn't remember his exact wording. I also hadn't yet learned to appreciate the value of his brand of humor and was more concerned with story facts.

The legends that Tony Tillahash related to Sapir are extremely dry because of the direct translation and Tony's stiffness in relating them to a scholar. Some of the legends I have recorded are also very stiff because I heard them out of context, in brief conversations, where the humor was omitted. Legends often became lengthy because of the humor built into them. Most long legends also contained numerous songs.

Some of these legends appear to have been based on some true historic happening of long ago such as *The Sack of All Tribes*, that tells of the tribes coming to this continent. Through continuous telling down through the years, historical stories were easily changed as they acquired mythical and humorous elements and began to drop the historical facts. Modern scholars who have studied similar legends have discovered some basis in fact in several legends. Compare the Greek legend of Troy, and the eventual discovery of Troy.

In the legends that follow, different versions will be noted for the same legend. In some cases this does not necessarily mean that the band versions were originally different. The differences might be due to one informant not remembering as much as another informant. However, in case they were distinct, I record them as separate versions.

Writers of Northern and Southern Ute legends often refer to the older brother Wolf as Soonungwuv, and to Coyote only as Coyote or Yohovuhts. In these legends Wolf is often given the role of trickster that is exclusively assigned to Coyote in the same legends among the Southern Paiutes and most Great Basin Tribes. Utes that I have questioned refer to Coyote as Soonungwuv or Suhnuv. This is a descrepancy that writers of the Ute legends should research in greater depth, not from published legends, but from Ute elders themselves.

WHEN COTTONTAIL PUNISHED NATURE
Kaibab 4

The story begins when Cottontail (Tawvoots) began his long journey to punish Sun because he was too hot. Sun didn't like Cottontail and got after him and burnt him on the back of the neck. That is why you see a brown spot on the back of his neck today. As Cottontail journeyed to do this, many things happened to him because other wicked and dangerous things of nature such as the trees, rocks, and water heard he was coming. Cottontail didn't like this and wanted to punish them and make them all good.

While he was on his way to punish Sun, he came upon two rabbit brothers who had been having trouble with nature. Cottontail stopped to visit with them. He knew what their trouble was so he told them to go get some wood and make a fire so they all could eat. The brothers complained that they couldn't because every time they did the trees would pop and hit them. He told them to get it anyway and it happened just as they had said, the trees popped and hit them. Cottontail then said that he would straighten the trees out, so he went over there and took out a very powerful stone that he carried with him and threw it at the trees. When the

stone hit the trees it exploded and punished them for being wicked. Ever since then the trees have been good.

He then told the brothers to go get some water. They said that every time they did, the water would rush out upon them and try to pull them in and drown them, as it did their parents. Cottontail told them to go anyway and it happened just as they said, the water rushed out upon them and tried to pull them in and drown them. Cottontail went over there and threw his stone in the pool and caused all the water to splash out. The water then became good and the brothers got water from some that ran back in.

Cottontail then told them to get some food. They said that their parents had stored some in a little cave storage house but that every time they tried to get some, the rocks would fall down upon them. The only way they could get any was to poke a long stick into the cave and twist it and pull out what stuck to it. Cottontail then asked them how their parents used to obtain food, and they said: "Father would lay upon his back, towards heaven, and pray and food would be given him from heaven." Cottontail then told them to go and do this, which they did. While they were doing this, Cottontail went over to the cave and burrowed his way under the rocks causing them to fall down. Thus he caused the rocks to be good. He told the brothers to get some food. They did and then they ate.

Bear heard that Cottontail was coming and dug two holes in the ground. One was a dead end and the other had two ways out. He challenged Cottontail to race with him into the holes hoping that he would go into the dead end hole and die. During the race Cottontail beat Bear to the hole that had two ways out while Bear went into the one with the dead end. Cottontail then hit him with his stone and killed him.

Cottontail continued on, and while he was doing so, some birds (Tuhmpee´ Keyu´soats[1]) were sitting on a ledge, laughing and making fun of him, because his blanket was dragging on the ground. These birds were considered wicked because they were making fun of him. Cottontail had another little rock with him that he rubbed between his legs, at the place where cottontails have a peculiar smell. He then tossed the rock up to the laughing birds and said, "Smell it. It's very precious, so don't lose it!" After they smelled it Cottontail told them, "Step close to the edge of the cliff and toss the stone over but watch where it lands so you won't lose it." They did this, but as they were leaning over, they leaned too far out and fell off and broke their necks. This is how they were punished.

Further along his way Cottontail encountered Bull Lizard. He always used to kill people by causing them to run down some steps off the side of a hill that resembled his back. A person had to step in each small indentation between the rough places, or the steps would cut him up and he would die. No one ever reached the bottom and so they were always killed. When Cottontail came along, Bull Lizard planned to kill him in this way. Cottontail took the test and hit every step and wasn't killed.

---

[1] The translation of this word means *"**Rock Laugher**"* This bird might be a wren.

Bull Lizard then had another plan. He hid a giant snake that would roar and swallow people. He led Cottontail to that place. When the snake roared and was about to swallow Cottontail, Bull Lizard stepped aside so he wouldn't be swallowed. However Cottontail took out his stone and hit the snake on the neck and cut his head off. He threw the snake away with his cane, off into Florida, where you may find this kind of snake today. Cottontail said that the snake could no longer come back up into this part of the country where he used to live. During his travels he also threw his powerful stone at the boulders and caused them to cease from their wickedness as they were always chasing after people.

Cottontail arrived at the place where the sun rose. He tried to lie in wait for the sun each morning so he could punish it and make it good. Sun just laughed and made fun of Cottontail as it journeyed a little beyond where Cottontail was lying in wait each day. Cottontail finally figured out that Sun rose a little further south each day so he decided to allow for Sun's movement south as he sought to ambush him. Unfortunately for Cottontail, this was the day Sun backed up and started north, as Sun does at a certain time each year. This fooled Cottontail again but he eventually figured this out and made up for it.

Before he threw his stone at Sun, he asked all the bushes if they burnt all the way to the ground. Yoowaw´unump (Match Brush) said it didn't. Cottontail planned to hide under this bush so that when he hit Sun, and it exploded, he would escape being burnt. He then threw the stone at Sun and it exploded. He ran to the bush but the heat became so great he had to run on. The whole earth began to burn and sometimes when you look at the rocks you can see where it has been burning. The heat caused the gas and oil to burn, volcanoes erupted, and you can see where they flowed out. The coal is the oil that burnt and after it burnt it turned to rock just as the lava did. The trees also burnt and turned into petrified wood. Cottontail also began to burn; his legs caught on fire and burnt off as he was running. Soon Cottontail's head rolled off and as his eyes popped from the heat . Sun then ceased burning the earth. This is how Sun also became good and was no longer wicked. (This story is incomplete and probably not in the proper order of events as originally given in the old days.)

WHEN COTTONTAIL PUNISHED NATURE
Shivwits 5

A long time ago Cottontail (Tawvoots) used to be big. He went walking down the Virgin River and decided to lie down in the shade and take a nap. Then Sun saw him and laughed at him and made Cottontail short. Later Tawvoots woke up and got mad knowing what Sun had done. That's why he came up to the north side of Castle Cliff, Utah, someplace. On the way he asked all the brush how they burnt until he found one that only burnt at the top. Cottontail wanted to blow up the sun. That's the time Sun said to him, "Oovud´unee yoowaw´hawk?" ***"Are you there waiting for me?"*** Sun said that every morning as he was rising.

Way later, Cottontail was right there in that little brush that only burns on top; he was all prepared and waiting. Also the two Mourning Dove Brothers were there. When Sun arose and said "Are you there waiting for me?" Tawvoots´ hit Sun with something. I always think it was a bomb. It blew Sun up and the whole world burnt, but cottontail was still alive, because he was under that little brush that doesn't burn clear down like the other ones. The Mourning Dove Brothers were safe also. Sun became good after that, and the world again became covered with water.

Way later, the Mourning Dove Brothers and Tawvoots´ went down to get wood but couldn't get any. They said, "We can't get wood! What's the matter with this wood right here? It gets after us all the time!" Tawvoots then replied and said, "Go get it now!" He was going to do to the wood as he did to Sun so he hid a little distance away. Then the two brothers went down to get the wood but as soon as they started picking it up, the wood got after them so they ran back a couple of feet. As soon as they did that Cottontail hit the wood from his hiding place and killed the whole thing and then the brothers had all kinds of wood.

Way later, down by Littlefield, Arizona, the two brothers were hungry. Cottontail told them, "Yes. Go get it" (pinyon nuts and all kinds of food) "I'll wait here hiding." The two brothers went and when they sang, the pinenuts and everything would just come down. I can't remember the song that was sung in this story here. However, when the pinenuts would come down they would go back up again and the two brothers could only get a little bit. When the trees did that Tawvoots hit them from his hiding place and blew them all over. The larger pinenuts, Toov, landed in Nevada and western Utah. The smaller ones, Paduh, landed in the rest of Utah, Arizona, and New Mexico. That's how the two different sizes originated. The place where Cottontail hit that food is at Littlefield, Arizona and you can still see a big rock there in the river where he kicked it. It's as big as a house and can be

seen in the Virgin River on the south side of the freeway bridge. This is not the powerful rock he hit with.

Also, the two brothers had trouble getting water in a cup. Every time they reached down for it, the water would pull back and they would only get a little bit. It would also come up and try to drown them. Cottontail also hit the water making it good.

Setting The Seasons Of The Year
Kaibab 4

One time Coyote and all the birds were having a big meeting in a cave. Coyote was the leader and had made a big fire so they could all keep warm. He was using pitch wood which makes a lot of black smoke. Crow, being the furthest back in the cave, absorbed most of the smoke and that's why the Crow is black from head to foot. You can notice in some caves how black they are in the back end.

Coyote and the birds were discussing and voting on what the length of the seasons of the year should be. Coyote wanted winter and summer to be long with six months summer, and six months winter, making the year twice as long. The birds wanted three months spring, three months summer, three months fall, and three months winter. Coyote rejected this, wanting the winter months longer. The birds all said, "No! Who could live that long? That's not right. Let's cut it down to three months for each season." If Coyote had gotten his way we would have had long winters today.

The birds and Coyote were all trying to choose which season length would be the easiest and best for them. They kept arguing and arguing and couldn't come to any agreement. Meanwhile, Coyote went after another armful of wood, and all these birds started talking among themselves. "Six months is too long! Let's set it back three months." Therefore they made the decision and set the seasons while Coyote was out gathering wood.

Then they all flew out of that cave. The last bird out was Pawnuhoytch (poor-will). As he flew out he said "paiuhm´uhoy, paiuhm´uhoy." This sound that this bird makes sounds like the Paiute words for ***"Three months"*** that the birds had set for the seasons. Coyote then knew that the birds had voted for three months instead of six. That made Coyote mad and he said "Three months isn't long. It's too short." Then he dropped his armful of wood and picked up a stick and took after that bird. He barely hit the bird as it flew off at the tail end of the flock. As he flew away, Pawnuhoytch would fly a short distance and then land. Whenever he landed Coyote took after him with that stick. He wanted to finish him off. As he approached, Pawnuhoytch took off again, flew a little distance and landed. Then he turned himself into a rattlesnake. That kind of bird has been known to do that.

While Coyote was chasing the bird he noticed that the toowoomp berries (service berries) were getting ripe. Coyote noticed the berries way up on top of the bush; they were big and juicy. There was one that was extra big and delicious look-

ing. Coyote then decided that the shorter seasons were good after all. If it was still winter he would have to wait another three months before the berries ripened. Then Coyote said to the birds, "Good! Three months is good enough! I agree to it."

I think that bird that turned himself into a rattlesnake and bit Coyote there but maybe he didn't. I think that big berry up on top fell down to the bottom. Coyote reached out for it and it went on down into the ground. Coyote started digging for it. He kept digging and after while he found some bark used for covering food that is cached within the ground. Coyote dug it all out. Somebody must have stored some meat and something down there. That's the time he said, "Three months is good enough." That's the way it is right today, three months for each season. (Compiled from a tape and an oral account given to me by Kaibab 4.)

THE MANNER OF CHILDBIRTH
Shivwits 5, 8, & Kaibab 4

One time Coyote and his elder brother Toovuts were discussing how children were to be created. Toovuts wanted a child to grow inside the arm and then when it was big enough to be born all you had to do was to flip your hand and the baby would come out of your hand without any pain.

Coyote wouldn't agree with this and said, "That isn't the place where you have intercourse! A baby should grow within the womb and it should come out from between the legs." Well, as Coyote always got his way and was the one that ruined all the good things, he also got his way this time and that's why children are born the way they are now. That's why women have to suffer so much over it because that's the way Coyote wanted it to be. If Toovuts had of gotten his way, it would have been good and they wouldn't have to suffer. (As told by Shivwits 8 and Kaibab 4.)

The following additions were given by Shivwits 5: In the beginning a woman's vagina had teeth in it and would chew just like a mouth. Coyote was told to get a deer horn and stick it in the vagina. When he did this all the teeth were broken and now a vagina has no teeth. Toovuts also wanted people to be able to return to life just by flipping the hand but Coyote didn't like this and said that when they die they should stay dead and that's how it is today.

HOW THE PAIUTES ACQUIRED FIRE
Kaibab 4

A long time ago the Paiutes in southern Utah and northern Arizona were trying to bring fire and the larger pinenuts that you find in Nevada and western Utah to their own area. They would send different animals out to steal them but they would always be followed by those Indians over there and they would take away

the pinenuts and the sparks as the animals tried to bring them here. They never did succeed in getting the pinenuts here; that's why you see the larger ones there and smaller ones here.

Finally Coyote, Roadrunner, and Jackrabbit tried to bring the sparks by relaying them. The relay was prearranged. Coyote stole the sparks and took off. When he got tired he gave the sparks to Roadrunner who was followed but escaped when he fooled his pursuers by breaking his foot up, and making his tracks look as if they were going both ways. Those following Roadrunner gave up and returned home. They then used their medicine and caused it to rain in hopes of putting out the sparks. When it started to rain Roadrunner and Rabbit got scared so Rabbit took the sparks and put them under his tail to protect them from the rain. It got very hot and burned his tail and that is why Jackrabbit has the black patch on his tail.

When the rain stopped the two then tried to get the sparks to ignite into a fire. They tried everything but failed. Rat was watching and said, "Here, take some of this bark that I use for my bed and see if you can get the sparks to start burning." They succeeded and so that is how the Indians here got the fire but not the larger pinenuts.

HOW THE PAIUTES ACQUIRED FIRE
Koosharem 7

One time the Paiutes saw ashes falling from the sky so they sent different birds up to find out where they came from. Hummingbird was the only one to make it up high enough. He could see the fire in the direction of California so the Paiutes went down there and got it.

THE FLOOD
Shivwits 5, & 9

One time, long ago, there was a flood and everyone was killed. In this story Swallow brought some mud to the people and they wondered where he got it. The only survivors were the big wood ants that are found in the mountains. They used to be humans but were turned into ants.

These ant survivors are to be found on Mount Charleston, Nevada, Mount Trumbull, Arizona, and Baker Mountain, Nevada. (I don't remember all this story. Shivwits 5.)

Shivwits informant 9 said, "You aren't supposed to kill the large wood ants that live in the mountains, nor kill sea life because they can save you when there is a flood."

THE FLOOD
Koosharem 10

The big black wood ants found high up in the mountains were the only survivors at the time the water covered the earth. They ascended the highest mountain by the name of (?) and thus they were preserved at the time of this flood.

THE MOURNING DOVE BROTHERS
Shivwits 11, & 12

The Mourning Dove Brothers had lost their mother who had been taken captive by Iron Clothes (Armadillo) to the Chemehuevi land to the south. There he married her. The two brothers asked Coyote to help them gather an army to take to the south to win her release. They started out at sunrise and passed through the cut in the black hill just west of the present town of St George. On the other side of the hill they came to a rock with water sitting in it. From St. George they went up Utah Hill and then down near Turtle Neck Hill[2] to where there is cactus in the desert.

Coyote was leading the Dove Brothers so they sat down there in the sand to rest. Sidewinder came up to them and asked "Let me go with you?" Coyote answered and said, "What could you do? You got no arms, no legs. How did you fight before?" Sidewinder replied and said, "This is what I'm going to do." Sidewinder then demonstrates biting as he does, and bites a rock and causes it to crack. Coyote then said, "Yes, you can go along." Coyote then put him in his quiver and carried him along.

---

[2] The name of this hill, Aiyu'Kodu Kaiv, ***Turtle Neck Hill,*** is a Paiute name. This hill is in the shape of a turtle and lies along the foothills just north of where Interstate 15 enters the Virgin Narrows. It can best be seen coming down old Highway 91 towards Beaver Dam, Arizona. Look directly east at the Utah / Arizona border and you will see the head of this turtle looking south with the remainder of the body north of the border.

On their way down through the desert they all became very thirsty and hungry. The Mourning Dove Brothers could fly so they said, "Let's go after water." They took off and flew by a secret way to their mother. When they landed beside their mother they told her, "We're coming after you to take you home. We have a lot of soldiers out there and they are all hungry and thirsty. We came after food and water." Their mother agreed to help them and secretly gave them water, seeds, and meat. She put the water in a cup made out of squawbush. The two brothers then took off carrying the food and water back to the weakened army.

When they returned they gave all the army a drink from that small cup. Coyote drank first figuring he would drink it all up. He drank until he was full but there was still water in the cup. No matter how much he drank the cup remained full. He couldn't drink it all so he passed it to the others and each soldier in the army drank. When everyone had quenched their thirst they recovered from their weakened condition and there was still some water left in the cup. Coyote then dumped the water out and a spring came out of the ground right there and went running straight down. That spring is still down there someplace, and is called Suhuh´ Vawts ***Squawbush Water***.

After while Coyote's army came to the guard[3] standing out in the desert guarding a place that looked like a castle where the mother of the Mourning Dove Brothers was being held. Coyote stopped right there and said, "How are we going to get her?" Coyote's soldiers were in the open, with no place to hide. Coyote was in front of them holding and waving a sagebrush in front of his face to hide himself while the rest of his naked body was left exposed.

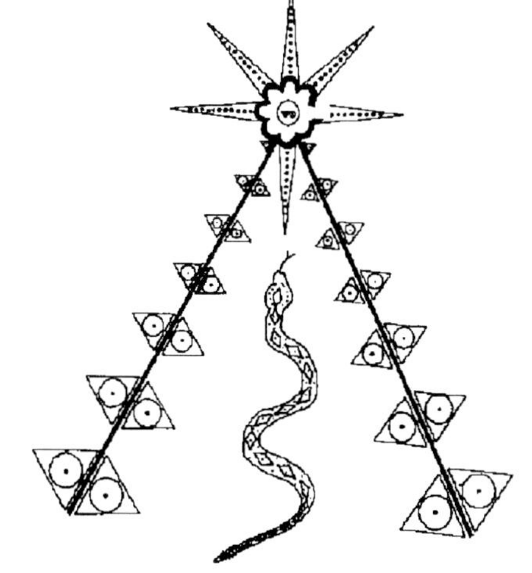

Coyote had hung his quiver, with Sidewinder in it, in a nearby tree. Coyote wanted to be the main one to get all the glory so he left Sidewinder hanging in the tree, hoping to leave him out of the upcoming battle. Sidewinder peeked out from the hanging quiver and saw the guard standing way out there. He kicked the quiver some way causing it to fall and he got out. He started towards the guard, flipping along in the manner he is accustomed to travel.[4] Sidewinder soon arrived right beneath the guard. She was a big person, standing there guarding, compared to the size of the little sidewinder.

---

[3] In Reuben John's Kaibab version this guard is Antelope. The antelope makes a good guard because of his ability to see a hunter approaching from a long way off. Few people are able to get very close when hunting them.

[4] The sidewinder is noted for its ability to travel beneath the sand. This is the manner he approached the guard in the Kaibab version. He probably did the same in the Shivwits version. The Shivwits Informant 5 said he couldn't remember the story very well.

Sidewinder then said to himself, "Where am I going to bite? Down by her vagina where she breaths? If I bite the rest of her body it wouldn't do anything. Nothing up there. Her heart beats down here where she breaths fast." He then looked real good between the spread legs and bit the guard inside her vagina.[5] When she was bitten she jumped sky high and stirred up a big cloud of dust. She then ran off towards home and died just before she entered into her house.

Coyote was about 400 yards or more away when that big cloud of dust arose. Coyote said, "I wonder what happened to cause all that dust to rise up? I'll bet that Sidewinder did that." Then Coyote went to where he had left the snake hanging and found the quiver lying there on the ground. He then went over to where the dust came from and there on the ground, in the midst of the dust, was Sidewinder sitting there with dust all over his face. Sidewinder then said to Coyote, "That's the way I do it!" That's how the war started.

Iron Clothes had two flirtatious women[6] there with him along with the mother of the Mourning Dove Brothers. Sidewinder was put in their toilet and was just sitting there waiting for Iron Clothes to come along. Early in the morning Iron Clothes came to the toilet. "Sidewinder, are you sitting in there?" he said, talking to himself and fearing Sidewinder might just do such a thing. "Are you going to do something to me and make trouble for me?" Iron Clothes said. Then he sat down low and Sidewinder bit him causing him to die. The Mourning Dove Brothers then came and retrieved their mother and returned home.

The foregoing story was translated by LaVan Martineau from a tape made by Shivwits informant 11. Shivwits informant 12 remembers a little of the story and says that at the beginning of the story, someplace, the two Mourning Dove Brothers went out hunting and killed a rabbit with an arrow. Then they threw the rabbit up in the air and shot more arrows into it while it was still in the air. When they returned home and threw the rabbit down at their mother's feet it became as many rabbits as the amount of arrows they had shot into it while in the air.

---

[5] Tony Tillahash's version given to Edward Sapir says that the "Rattlesnake" bit the Antelope between the spread hoofs. Tillahash did relate many accounts relating to sexual topics and it is doubtful that he would have omitted it here. Striking a sexual organ would be the norm in Paiute legend structure. Sapir might have misheard him, or the versions differ. Sapir did err in identifying the snake as a rattlesnake. Tony used the word "tawnukeets" which among both Kaibab and Shivwits means ***sidewinder***.

[6] Wau sawmeng is the word used here, meaning ***two sillys***. The term ***silly***, or sawmeekunt can refer to flirtatious, and sometimes nasty women. I imagine part of the story is missing here involving Coyote and these two women. These women were probably the daughters of Iron Clothes referred to by Tillahash and Reuben John.

THE MOURNING DOVE BROTHERS
(Oyov´ee Navuv´etseeng)
Kaibab 6

It was a long time ago when someone of the tribe yelled out, "Let's all go hunting and bring in meat for our families." Everyone then went hunting except Soonungwuv, the Coyote. He was very lazy and crafty so instead of going out hunting food for his family, he went out and found a large bush with berries on it. He ate berries and lay around in the sun all day long. When evening came he went home and walked among the wickiups and asked each one how many rabbits they had killed, while he himself had killed none and his family went hungry.

Now this happened every day until the berries on the bush were all eaten except for some on the very top of the bush. Coyote wondered how he was going to get these berries down when he decided to dig around the base of the bush so the bush would fall over. He found a stick and made himself a digging tool. Then he dug and dug until he was almost exhausted, when he suddenly struck a bundle. He opened it and found it full of dried meat which he immediately began to eat. Now each day he did this as he lay around in the shade.

Now this meat belonged to the family of Punu´ Tuhmpee Nahdo, ***Iron Clothes***,[7] who was chief of another tribe. Iron Clothes was a man of medicine. He had a vision in which he saw Coyote stealing his meat. He then sent his two daughters out to spy on Coyote, which they did, and they found Coyote doing just that. Now this made Iron Clothes very angry so he sent all the warriors of his tribe against Coyote's tribe. They planned a surprise attack upon Coyote's camp hoping to kill all the men.

Now in Coyotes camp there lived an old lady and her grandson. This old lady had a vision and saw Iron Clothes and his army coming upon them. She took her grandson and went down alongside the river and hid among the rocks. Iron Clothes and his army came and killed all the tribe except Coyote, who escaped. They found the old lady and her grandson among the rocks but the old lady disguised her grandson to look like a girl and so they were not harmed.

Now this boy grew up to be a young man, and one day when he was down by the river, Crane came along unseen. Now this boy felt that he was being watched but every time he turned around he saw no one. Pretty soon he bent over and looked from between his legs and saw Crane. He began to throw sticks at him. (The informant omitted a portion of the story here that can be found in the Shivwits version.)

The story was continued where Sidewinder asked to be carried along. A song is sung. These are the words: "Noneku nonee, noneku nonee" ***Carry me, carry me.***

---

[7]This Paiute word means ***Iron Rock Clothes*** referring to the ore from which metal is taken. The word punukawd can mean both ***metal*** and ***iron***. It is used in reference to the shell of the armadillo that protects it.

Sidewinder was carried in a quiver. Antelope was standing guard at Iron Clothes' camp and Sidewinder burrowed under the ground, came up beneath him and bit him.[8]

(This story was related to me one cold winter night in about 1949 in the potato cellars near Enterprise, Utah, where we were working. It was told by Reuben John of Kaibab, who said there was much more to this story.)

HUMMINGBIRD CREATES A SPRING WITH HIS CANE
Indian Peak 1

One time Moo´toonchuts the Hummingbird stuck his cane into the ground at Wah Wah Springs in western Utah. When he pulled his cane out, water also came out. That's how Wah Wah Springs came to be.

WHEN SNOW USED TO BE FLOUR
Kaibab 4

A long time ago snow used to be toohoon´ tooweev ***heavenly flour.*** It would lie in the mountains for everyone to use. Coyote was talking to his older brother Toovuts and didn't like this idea. At that time the only ones who could go up and get the flour were a newly married couple. Coyote said he didn't want it that way and that the flour should be snow and melt every spring. Coyote was always given his wish by his older brother Toovuts so that's the way it is today.

TWO PAIUTES SWALLOWED BY A FISH
Indian Peak 1, & Koosharem 7

One time two Indian men were out chasing antelope near Sevier Lake, Utah.[9] When they came to the lake they saw a whirlpool in it. One man swam out to check it out while the other stayed on shore. While the Indian in the lake was swimming out to see the whirlpool a big fish swallowed him. He was swallowed whole without being chewed up.

The man on shore saw this happen so he sharpened his knife and swam out to rescue his friend. He was also swallowed by the fish in the same manner. After the

---

[8] Kaibab informant 4 gives a note in relation to this legend. He says that the poison of the sidewinder is more deadly than that of the rattlesnake. This is the reason that Sidewinder volunteered to do the killing.

[9] I initially heard this story from Carl Jake of Indian Peak. Later, Koosharem informant 7 told me the same story, however placing the event at Utah Lake. He heard this story from Dora, the wife of Walker Ammon, the son of the renowned Chief Walker.

fish swallowed him he ended up lying right alongside his friend inside the fish's belly. He then felt around for a soft spot in the belly, and when he found it, he cut the belly open and they got out. As they got out the fish didn't move, but afterward as it was dying, it wiggled violently and splashed water all over and these two guys almost didn't get away. The bones of this fish could be seen in this lake for a long time.

HOW TOOVUTS CAME BACK ALIVE[10]
Shivwits 5, & 13

A long time ago the Paiutes were having a war with some different kind of Indians from the east. Soonungwuv killed this one man and took the dead man's

[10] The Southern Utes of Colorado tell the same legend with some variations. They combine this legend and The Sack of All Tribes into one story (Givón, 1985). In this publication Coyote is called Yohovuhts and Wolf is called Soonungwuv. I questioned Annabelle Eagle from Ignacio about this discrepancy between Paiute and Ute wherein among the Paiute Coyote is called Soonungwuv and not Wolf. She said that Coyote <u>is</u> Soonungwuv and that Givón's informant, Julius Cloud, was very old when he told the story and therefore became confused.

heart out as a souvenir and put it in a tree. It fell out of the tree and Toovuts[11] went over to grab it but it kept moving up north. He couldn't catch it so he said to it "Go after the armies," and it went. That's when they had a war, after that.

Every morning, while Toovuts (Wolf) was lying down, he told Soonungwuv to go make a lot of arrows out of mountain willows. He sang a song then (I can't remember it). Then Soonungwuv said, "Look! Big clouds and lightning are coming from the east, like rain." Toovuts already knew what was coming; it was the armies. Toovuts and Soonungwuv then started shooting arrows at the armies. When the arrows of Soonungwuv hit, they only killed a few, because his arrows were not as good as his brothers. However, when Toovuts' arrows hit, they killed many enemies.

That's the time when Toovuts got killed, because Soonungwuv said, "Whechu" signifying the ***lower leg bone***. He wasn't supposed to say that but he did and Toovuts was shot there and killed. Then the enemy hollered and came and took everything away. After Toovuts had died, Coyote would lie in his cave and cry and cry. Coyote then started looking all over this country for his brother but couldn't find him. The armies had taken Toovuts´ body[12] and clothes with them eastward, lifting them up on a pole each day and dancing around them. Way later, Soonungwuv found the enemy and planned to get Toovuts´ body back while they were dancing. Coyote went in there and grabbed Toovuts´ body and ran and the Indians chased him. Way later, over a little hill, he turned into a sagebrush. The pursuers looked for him and one said, "Maybe this sagebrush is him." It was Coyote, so he jumped up and ran away again turning into all kinds of things, including Coyote scratches, and tracks. Every time someone said, "Maybe this is him" he would jump up, run again and get way ahead of them.

Finally they lost him for good and Coyote took his brother back home to where he was killed. Coyote then looked around the spot where Toovuts was shot and found a little piece of flesh. He put it someplace and Toovuts returned to life and then went east to the ocean. From there he went up to heaven where he still lives with his good-looking wife.

Coyote followed them and stayed with them for a while. While Coyote was there he would put pine on the fire to make sparks fly so he could watch his brother make love. Toovuts then sent Coyote back home. When Coyote arrived he told everybody that when people die they will go up to heaven to their brother Toovuts. It's a good place up there. That's where everyone is, grandfathers, grand-

[11] The informant said "Toovuts" but from the context of the story he might have meant Soonungwuv. I haven't had the chance to question him on this. Toovuts is the Wolf and is considered to be God. He is the elder brother of Soonungwuv, the Coyote.

[12] Later in the story, the informant mentions that Coyote looked and found a piece of flesh belonging to Toovuts. This might indicate that the enemy only took his clothes away, in keeping with Edward Sapir's, Woodrow Pete's, and Morris Jake's versions.

mothers, brothers, and sisters. Green things grow there also, just like on earth. (This is a very long story; I don't remember it all, and left a lot out. Compiled from a tape made June 27, 1984, and an interview made May 19, 1986, with Shivwits 5.)

Following are some additions given by Shivwits informant 13: Toovuts told Coyote to go cut tuhuv´ ***serviceberry*** so Toovuts could make more arrows (a song is sung in the story here). The enemies of Toovuts were a great nation and thought that Toovuts was evil, which he wasn't. It was only Soonungwuv who was evil. As Toovuts shot one arrow in the battle that followed, hundreds would die. At the end of the story Soonungwuv was punished for his disobedience by being confined to the desert and mountains and having to howl up at the moon at nights. That is why he is still doing this.

HOW TOOVUTS CAME BACK ALIVE
Cedar City 14, and Koosharem 7

One time Toovuts and Soonungwuv were having a war with some other people. Soonungwuv was fighting them for a while and then he returned to the cave where they were living. Toovuts then told Coyote "I'll go out and fight them but don't peek out and watch me." He then went out and fought. After while Soonungwuv couldn't bear not looking out to see his brother fight, so he peeked. When he did, Toovuts was killed.

Coyote then began to look through his belongings in the cave to see if he could find something that would bring his brother back to life again. He found a little bag and opened it. When he did, it became dark and Coyote couldn't see a thing. Coyote tried to bring back the light by shooting arrows into the sky. He tried many types of feathers on his arrows. When he used the feathers of the flicker his arrow finally penetrated the red zone of light. That is why the tip of the flicker feather is black, and the rest of it red. Finally he used a magpie feather, which was the right kind of feather, and it reached the white light and let it down through the darkness to brighten up the land again. That's why you see white in the feathers of the magpie.

Coyote then followed the tracks of his enemies who had killed his brother Toovuts. When he caught up to them he changed himself to appear as a woman. The enemies were dancing around the clothes of Toovuts which were hanging upon a cross. Coyote went and danced with them until around midnight. He then floated up and grabbed Toovuts´ clothes and ran away with them. His enemies followed him, trying to catch him. They almost did as Coyote was going over a small hill but Coyote changed himself into an old dead stick and they didn't see him. They looked around awhile and as they looked again, where Coyote was hiding, someone kicked the stick; Coyote jumped up and ran again.

The very same thing happened several times. The second time, Coyote turned into coyote dung and the third time into a bush. Finally the enemies gave up and Coyote got away. He then went back to the body of his older brother. His body was lying on an ant bed where his enemies had left him. Coyote put the clothes on his brother and then took him eastward some distance and left him there. In the morning Coyote heard a scream like that of a mountain lion as Toovuts came back alive. When Toovuts returned to life he didn't say anything; he just walked away. (Cedar city 14.)

Koosharem 7 adds the following elements to this story: "A long time ago when Coyote and Toovuts were having a war, Coyote hid himself behind Angels Landing in Zion National Park. The war covered all the land and caused many of the geographical changes and disruptions at Zion and other places that we see upon the earth today. Giant Eagle caused this by flapping his wings. That's what one old man from Cedar City told me."

HOW TOOVUTS CAME BACK ALIVE
Eagle Valley 1

I asked Eagle Valley informant 2 about the William R. Palmer's version "The Three Days of Darkness," (Palmer 1987) and about Alva Matheson's version: "Shinob Killed by Anupitts" (see "Reflections" by Alva Matheson in the public library at Cedar City, Utah, unpublished). The informant said, "Some of it is wrong! It was Toovuts that was killed and not Soonungwuv.[13] He was shot. The story of shooting the arrows up into the darkness was the same story of Toovuts getting killed when he and his younger brother, Soonungwuv, were at war with their enemies. The feathers of many birds were used in attempts to breach the darkness." I asked the informant specifically about these points.

[13] Palmer and Matheson erroneously pronounce the word Soonungwuv and Suhnuv as "Shinob. "

HOW TOOVUTS CAME BACK ALIVE
Kaibab 4

A long time ago Toovuts and his younger brother Soonungwuv were at war with their enemies. Toovuts told Coyote "Prepare! Enemies are coming!" He said this because he had seen lightning coming closer in the distance.

When the fighting started Toovuts would lie around just to see how good a fighter Coyote was. Coyote had a gray uniform made out of serviceberry bark and Toovuts also had one but his was green and prettier. Coyote was jealous of this and wished Toovuts would be killed in the fight. While Toovuts was fighting, he would kill many of his enemies with just one arrow, but he was soon killed when shot in the heel. When Coyote's brother was killed he cried until his eyes became swollen and he had to hold them open to see where he was going.

After Toovuts was killed, the enemies held a dance each night on their return home because they had killed a great chief. One of their old women, who lagged behind was caught by Coyote, and after questioning her he shook all her bones and meat out of her skin and put it over his own body. As they were dancing, he entered the circle, disguised as this woman, and acted out her part as it was her custom to do. After this he went to the camp where the children were, that this lady was supposed to tend, and he choked them. The enemies said that she had never done that before, and meanwhile, Coyote took his brother's clothes and ran.

THE SACK OF ALL TRIBES
Shivwits 8

One time, Coyote was supposed to take this sack to the middle of America someplace and <u>not</u> open it until he arrived there. He was told to do this by Kakaw´uhvoom ***Grandmother of Many.*** From way up north he came down along the coast then back up by way of a big river, probably the Colorado. On the way up, Coyote heard singing and drums inside the sack he was carrying. He wasn't told what was inside so when his curiosity got the best of him, he decided to open it just a little bit and peek in. When he did so, all the different Indian tribes came out, all the tribes that are now all over this land. They all came out so fast that he couldn't stop them. All that was left in the sack was some human dung. This was the Paiutes. It was there someplace south of the Shivwits country, where he opened the sack, where the Indians spread all over this country.

THE SACK OF ALL TRIBES
Shivwits 5

I think this story began at the hot springs near Hurricane, Utah, when there were no people in this land, but Toovuts (God) and his wife. They went down the

Virgin River in a boat or something. This river used to have a great deal of water in it. Someone told them where to get off. Toovuts pushed his hand forward and parted the ocean with his staff and they crossed over.

Way later, after they had many children, Toovuts told his younger brother Soonungwuv, the Coyote, to bring his children back to this land in a sack because there were no people here. He was also told not to dump the sack until he was in the middle of this land.

Toovuts parted the ocean again with his staff, where he had passed through before, so that Coyote could pass through with his sack full of Indians. Coyote then arrived in America on the East Coast and from there he went to the West Coast then up towards Las Vegas, Nevada. On the other side of Las Vegas he went up on a little hill and stopped there. He heard singing and all kinds of things going on in the sack, and wanted to look in it. He said, "I'm going to look in the sack." Toovuts had told him not to, but Coyote never listens to anyone so he looked in anyway. As he opened the sack to peek in, many people jumped out. Coyote then grabbed the top of the sack and closed it while there were still a few people left inside. He then brought them up this way and dumped the sack. That's where the Paiutes came from. As he dumped it he told some of the people, "You will be way up north and talk different," and to others, "You will go to a different place and talk different." That's how the tribes here originated.

During their journey up here they stopped at a cave at the base of the west side of Sunrise Mountain, just east of Las Vegas, Nevada. The Indians say that this cave has some long tracks in it. I heard this cave has now been destroyed by whiteman's construction.[14]

The Indians who got out of the sack below Las Vegas have the Bird Songs that tell of that part of the migration. The Moapa songs tell of crossing the ocean and coming up this way. Jim Chili used to explain parts of the Bird Song migration story when he sang them.[15]

Roadrunner was taken down south from Las Vegas, down towards Parker, Arizona, and that's where those Bird Songs started. A man came up from there, or California someplace, singing and bringing the bird songs up this way where it landed in that cave on Sunrise Mountain.[16] That's where the Bird Songs are and that's what it means: coming out and walking up this way. It also tells of crossing the ocean. A man from Moapa used to sing them and stop a few minutes and tell what each song meant. The Gosiutes and the Utes tell a similar story. (Compiled from notes made May 19,1986, June 27, 1989, and an earlier unrecorded date with Shivwits informant 5.)

---

[14] Archie was told by Dan Bullets of Kaibab, and a Meyers man from Moapa, Nevada, that they went to this cave and it was all ruined.

[15] Jim Chili was a Chemehuevi from the Banning, California area.

[16] Archie Rogers says, "This cave is where the Indians used to go when they wanted to learn the songs. They would go there and pray. You weren't supposed to be afraid when that man (spirit) came around to you during the night."

The Sack Of All Tribes
Kaibab 4, Shivwits 12, 17, & Kanosh 16

In the beginning, the Indians lived in another land and there was no one living here. Kakaw´huhvoom ***Grandmother of Many,***[17] told Soonungwuv to take a sack full of Indians across the water to this land and let them out in the center. The route was from island to island, which were stepping stones, and at one place she laid a feather across the water so he could come across. When Coyote arrived on this land he let the Indians out too soon. The Hopis remained towards the south while the other tribes scattered throughout the country. (As told by Kaibab informant 4.)

Annikie, an aged Paiute from the Richfield, Utah area, told Kanosh informant 16 that "Wolf was told to take the sack across the sea but he told the Coyote to do it for him. They crossed the water on dry land and Coyote opened the sack in Mexico." Shivwits informant 17 states that he heard that a feather was laid across the sea for Coyote to cross over on.

Shivwits informant 12 said he didn't remember where Coyote came from with the sack of Indians, but as he was coming down from the north he peeked in the sack and the richest tribes came out first. He thought this might have been in the Dakotas. Coyote kept peeking in as he went along and the other tribes also came out. The Paiutes came out last, down here in the south.

The Sack Of All Tribes
Indian Peak 1

Coyote (Soonungwuv) brought the Utes, Paiutes, Shoshonis, and Mookweetch up into this country from the south. He was carrying them in a sack. They got out of the sack at Pahranagat, Nevada. The Utes went northeast, The Shoshonis north, the Paiutes stayed in this country, and the Mookweetch went back south.

How Coyote Populated The Land
Kaibab 18

A long time ago, Coyote's brother Toovuts, would always tell Coyote what to do. Coyote, he'd always twist that around and make it the hard way for the people. One day Toovuts told Coyote to go over there someplace to a group of Indians. Toovuts said, "Those Indians are your children." Coyote replied, "How

[17] Morris Jake interprets this word in more modern terms than just ***Grandmother of Many.*** He likes to use the term "Mother Nature."

come they're my children?" His brother said, "Because you went with a woman and made all of them. Now you have a family over there that belongs to you and that woman."

Toovuts then told Coyote to go over there and see his children and talk to them and do many things for them. Instead of that, Coyote went over there and saw some pretty girls. That night he asked a girl to sleep with him. The girl said "No! You're my dad! I don't want to sleep with you, you're my dad!" Coyote then went to the other girls, wanting to marry them, but they always told him, "You're my dad so we don't want to marry you!"

Coyote then returned to his brother and his brother said, "How did you come out, feeding your children and all that? Go hunt! Go hunt someplace! Hunt deer, anything, so they can eat; feed your children!" They claim that's the way this land was populated. That was many years ago, I guess. My dad used to tell me about it. (Compiled from a tape made August 22, 1978 with Kaibab 18.)

Coyote And The Sage Hen
Shivwits 8

One morning, Soonungwuv, the Coyote, put on a brand new suit of buckskin clothes that he had just made, and went walking through the country to show them off. He purposely went alongside a lake so he could look into the calm blue water and admire himself in his new clothes. He really thought he was handsome with his new moccasins and beautifully fringed buckskin shirt and leggings.

While Coyote was walking along the lake admiring himself, Sechu´, the Sage Hen, saw him and thought he would play a prank on Coyote. Sechu´ hid in some tall bushes next to the trail that Coyote was coming down so that Coyote would pass between him and the water. When Coyote arrived at the hiding place of Sechu´, he was still admiring himself by watching his image in the water and paying attention to nothing else. As he was doing this Sechu´ jumped out from his hiding place and as he did so he yelled "Sechu!" This really caught Coyote by surprise and he was so frightened that he jumped into the lake and ruined his new suit of buckskin clothes.

Coyote came out of the water feeling the spirit of revenge. In order to get even with Sage Hen, he circled around the lake and tried to play the same prank, but it

didn't work to Coyote's dismay. When his prank didn't work, Coyote yelled to Sechu´ and said, "Hey! I didn't do that to you!"

Coyote And The Bear
Shivwits 8

One day Soonung´wuv had made himself a brand new rawhide rope and he really thought a great deal of it. He decided that he would go walking so he could show it off. While he was out walking along the top of a ridge, whistling along, Bear saw him and thought he would play a trick on Coyote. To do this, Bear lay down in the middle of the trail and changed his body so it would look as if it had been dead for some time.

When Coyote came up to Bear, he saw him and said, "Oh! here is my friend the Bear, and it looks like he has been dead for some time. I'll take him home to his family." So Coyote wrapped his new rawhide rope around Bear and threw him on his shoulders so he could pack him home. While Coyote was traveling down the trail, Bear thought that he would scare Coyote so he made his body come to life again. When Coyote saw that Bear was alive, he became so frightened that he dropped Bear and ran as fast as he could leaving his brand new rawhide rope behind.

Now this made Coyote mad to think that Bear had done this and got away with his brand new rope so he thought he would do the same thing to Bear and get his rope back. He did the same thing that Bear had done to him and lay down in the trail making his body look as if it had been dead for some time. When Bear came along he saw Coyote and said, "Oh! Here is my friend the Coyote. It looks like he's been dead for some time. I think I'll take him home to his family." He then put the rawhide rope around Coyote and placed him on his shoulders to take him home. Now all the time Bear knew that Coyote was trying to trick him so when Coyote came to life Bear wasn't frightened at all. This really made Coyote mad and he said to Bear, "Hey! I didn't do that to you!"

Coyote And The Bobcat
Kaibab 4

I can't remember who did the fooling first. It could have been Bobcat. Anyway, Bobcat sees Coyote coming up a wash one time so Bobcat lay down in the middle of the wash and made himself look as if he was dead. He looked as if he had died two or three days ago. When Coyote saw Bobcat lying there he was happy and said, "Now I've got some fur. I'll get some use out of that fur. I better bundle him up and take him home." He then threw Bobcat over his shoulders and started walking along. As he was going along, Bobcat let out a little puff of wind that sounded like a low whistle. Coyote said, "I wonder who said that? Someone

is sneaking around." He didn't think it was the Bobcat he was carrying because he was dead and all bundled up. He thought it must have been something else, maybe just some sound some place.

He then went on and a little while later Bobcat made that sound again. This time Coyote could feel the air from Bobcats whistling hitting his ear. When Coyote looked back Bobcat had his big yellow eyes wide open. Coyote got so frightened that he had to sit down. He just lowered himself to the ground very slow. Meanwhile, Bobcat made a big leap and took off.

Then Coyote tried to play the same trick on Bobcat. Coyote got ahead of Bobcat and lay down in the middle of the wash making himself look dead. Later on Bobcat came along and saw the dead Coyote all stretched out looking dead in the middle of the wash. Bobcat went up to him and caught hold of his nose. In those days Coyote had a shorter nose than he does now. Bobcat then stretched out Coyote's nose and made it very long and pointed as it is today. That's why the Coyote has a long nose.

Then Bobcat went on his way, leaving Coyote lying there. After while Coyote woke up. He could see his nose sticking way out further than it used to be. This made Coyote mad and he said, "I'll catch up with that guy." Coyote then went up the wash and there he found Bobcat lying there looking dead again. Coyote went up to Bobcat and started patting his nose and pushing it in making his head round. That's why Bobcat has a round head and a short nose today.

Coyote got the best of the deal in this trickery. In the past when he went to drink with his round head, his mouth would only reach down a short distance into those tiny water pockets in the rocks. Now that he had a long pointed nose he could stick it all the way down to the bottom and drink all the water. It was rather bad for Bobcat, however, who now had a round head and nose. He couldn't drink from those water pockets as easily.

Coyote And The Geese
Cedar City 14

One time Coyote was out hunting and he heard some singing. He looked around to see if he could tell where the singing was coming from but he couldn't tell. The singing had come from a flock of geese that were flying in formation overhead. The leader of the geese wished that Coyote would look up and find them. This wish came true as Coyote looked up and saw the flock of geese. Then he knew where the singing was coming from.

Coyote waved his arms at them and told them to come down to him. The geese flew down and landed beside him. Then Coyote asked them if he could go with them. They each gave him a feather so he could fly. Soon they took off and Coyote was flying alongside them. Coyote was doing everything wrong as they flew along. He spoiled the pretty "V-shaped" formation and he wasn't singing like the geese as they flew along. He seemed to be doing everything backwards.

After flying some distance the leader of the geese thought that Coyote hadn't better go any further with them because of all his mistakes so they took his feathers away from him and he fell to the ground. He landed head first on top of a rock, breaking his head open. He lay unconscious for some time and then he woke up. He looked around and he saw some white stuff lying next to him. It looked like mush that maybe someone had brought to him to eat. Thinking it was mush; he ate it. Soon the top of his head felt cold. He felt it and found that his head was busted and that the stuff he had eaten was his own brains.

Coyote And The Geese
Kaibab 4

One time Coyote was out hunting and he heard some singing. He looked around to see if he could tell where it was coming from but he couldn't. The singing came from a flock of geese that were flying in formation overhead. The leader of the geese wished that Coyote would look up and find them. Coyote looked up, spotted them, and then knew where the singing was coming from. Coyote waved his arms at them and told them to come down to him. The geese flew down to him and Coyote asked them if he could fly with them.

Each one of the geese gave him a feather so he could fly. They then took off and Coyote was flying along with them. Coyote was doing everything wrong as they flew along. He spoiled the pretty "V-shaped" formation and he wasn't singing like the geese. He seemed to be doing everything backwards. Soon the leader of the geese thought that Coyote hadn't better go any further with them because of all his mistakes, so they took his feathers away from him and he fell to the ground. He landed headfirst on top of a rock breaking his head open. He lay unconscious for some time.

When the geese returned, they woke Coyote up to tell him where he could find a pregnant woman so he could get her child and eat it as was the custom then. Coyote saw his brains lying on the ground, and thinking it was mush that someone had brought him, he ate it. Soon the top of his head felt cold. He felt it and found that his head was broken and that the stuff he had eaten was his own brains.

He then took off and ran and ran until he came to the place where the geese told him he could find the pregnant woman. He shook the woman and soon the child came out. It was a girl and he said that he was going to keep her for his own daughter. He fed and raised her and when she was getting quite big he took something and made breasts upon the girl. It was also about time for the girl to begin to menstruate. Meanwhile, Coyote and his daughter went south to Mount Charleston where his uncle lived. While they were there his uncle had killed a mountain sheep and he told Coyote and his daughter to go get it so they did.

Now Coyote was always keeping an eye on his daughter and told her that when she sat down, to sit facing towards him. She was doing this while Coyote was butchering the mountain sheep. Coyote, seeing the sheep's blood spilt upon

the ground, took a handful of it and threw it between his daughter's legs and thus she began to bleed. He also gave her rules and regulations regarding it and this is how it came to be that women menstruate.

Coyote And The Geese
Shivwits 19

(Translated from an old tape made by Shivwits informant 19. She didn't complete the story.)

Suhuhkwawhoyp oonguh Soonung´wuv oong uhduh. Aitawng ovaiuk suhuhkawhai,
Coyote was going along acting tough. Then while he was acting tough,

ovaiuk enee´nung uhd, "Huvantuh kwaik? Maaw´took sookopenee aik!"
While he was doing this, "Where is it said? Someplace something is said!"

Aipuhku. "Poowudoai ung, poowudoai ung" aipuhkuntuhm, oonineench.
He (the leader of the geese) said, "Medicine him, medicine him!" he said, while doing this.

Aipuhku "Hunin huneuk´uhunt oong, line up echuhvuhkunt owts´uhnee paiudook´ee toohoomp´ai?"
He (Coyote) said "I wonder what is his name, the one that lines up real good in the sky?"

"uhm" maipuhku, "oonee ´kawhunt toohoompaiudos."
"It was them" he said, "doing that in the sky."

"Soonungwuv ung mun oonin´ee suhuh´kakahais."
"There's Coyote, the one doing that, going along tough."

Punungk´wum puhnee´kawkai ungu´vawchuh. Aitawng, oongwus, Soonungwuv
They were looking down at him as they went along. At that time, he, Coyote

oong, uhm udook´waw tohok´w. "Mum udu aikuh´kunt 'poowudowunin,' ainun uhd," aipuhku.
was running under them. "It was them who said 'medicine me,' just as I said," he said.

Aitawng uhduh uhm uhvenunk uhm uhvuh´kwawhunt poa,
Then as he was following under their trail,

"Nuh mumeem´ whaimpai." Aitawng oonee oong wuhngwuhs oong,
"Let me go with you." Then did those same ones,

yuhsuhd´uhmuhnee, aitawng oovai, oomus aik
the kind that flies, right there, those same ones said.

This song is sung here:

"Nuhmee kwuneek´wu weev´uh awn tuhkaw neudum, uhmuh
"We're all going to eat grass real good," them.

"Nuhmee kwuneek´wu, uvuhn´ee, weev´uh awn tuhkaw neudum" uhmuh.
"We're all going, in a hurry, to eat grass real good" them.

Aikuh puhkuhm, uhmuhs oong, wetseech oong, wetseekadum oong.
That's what they were saying, them same ones, the birds, the ones that were flying.

The following song is sung here:

"Uhvuhchawng udum, aikooung, mamaw kawngwung, feathers emuntook."
"Lets all go, when he's saying that, and give him some feathers."

Toovai muhdoong ungwu´vachuhk (munee´kum puhvawk).
They went down to him; (went like this, right there).

Aitawng, feathers emunt´ook ootoo´vechuk. Oongwung´wuk oongwaius, Soonungwuv.
Thereupon, they pulled out some feathers and gave it to him, that same one, Coyote.

Ooneekai wuhmpuhku. "Uhvuhng´wuk try eng ook" aipuhku.
They kept doing this. "Go ahead, try it" they said.

Aitawng ooneeng´oomuhpuhku wetseek oomee´haieku try epuhkaik.
Then he kept trying to fly but only went a little way each time he tried.

Aitawng penunk, ovaiuk ooneehais, wetsee´kuhpuhku.
Then later, when he tried again, he flew.

This song is sung here:

"Kawtch uhvuh´nee nunum pawhun´ee uhvuh´nee num."
"Don't do it bad with us, any which way with us."

"Ooneeng´waisump poa vawn nuhmee´venunk wawhais."
"Don't do it again, on our trail, following along behind us."

"Wuhnuhm´ee poa vawn´ee nuhme oonee´num."
"Stand on our trail as we do."

ORIGIN OF MENSTRUATION
Koosharem 10

The reason a woman shouldn't eat meat during her period is that long ago Soonungwuv and some Indians were together. The Indians killed a deer and a woman was going to cut some of the meat up and fry it. While she was doing this, Soonungwuv threw some of the deer's blood on her dress causing her to have a period. Coyote then told her she wasn't supposed to eat meat anymore during her monthly. Maybe he said this because he wanted to eat all the meat himself.

ORIGIN OF MENSTRUATION
Shivwits 11

Coyote was told there was a pregnant lady lying down there someplace. Coyote pressed on her stomach and squeezed a baby girl out. The lady died when he did this and so Coyote was left alone with the baby. They then headed towards Mount Charleston, way up on top of that pointed mountain. The baby was crying all the way until they reached the home of Toovuts. That's where the girl grew up, at her uncle's place.

When she was big, Coyote and the girl went out hunting. Coyote killed a deer and while he was gutting it the girl was sitting towards him with her legs spread open. Coyote asked the girl to hold the deer for him. The deer's blood had begin to coagulate just like jello. Coyote then threw some of that coagulated blood between her spread legs. It got all over her pubic hairs. That's how come women have their period. Coyote said, "You are going to have a period." If he didn't do that women wouldn't have their period. See! That's what he did!

(Shivwits informant 11 gave the foregoing story fragment as part of the Mourning Dove Brothers legend. Many Paiute legends were extremely long, sometimes taking all night to tell and even days; therefore, there is no certainty whether these two legends are the same. The informant might have figured the stories were connected since Coyote went down near Mount Charleston to fight Iron Clothes. Since that is where Coyote was when he made the pregnant lady deliver, he might have thought the stories were connected. In reality, they could have been the same story.)

COYOTE AND THE DUCK
Kaibab 4

A long time ago Coyote's son was in love with a certain girl. Coyote was the jealous type. He wanted his son's girlfriend for himself but that girl didn't want Coyote; she wanted his son. Coyote tried many things to win her but failed at ev-

erything he tried. He eventually made the girl mad by telling all kinds of phony stories about himself.

Well, one evening, that girl went over there to see Coyote's son. Coyote showed up to cut his son out and so the girl said, "I'm getting tired of you; what you say all the time. I think I better go." When the girl got up she put her hand on the young man's head and stuck her finger down in his head, down through the skull. Then the young man went home. During that night he got very sick. Coyote didn't know what to do; it was all his fault. He started running around, scratching his head, not knowing what to do. Then he thought about that doctor who lived down by the lake, about twenty miles away.

The doctor was Chuhkaw Nawpuhts, ***Old Man Duck***. Coyote said, "I'm going down there to see my partner. He used to take care of any bad sickness." So Coyote took off down the country. As he was arriving, Duck was alongside the lake, close to the banks. He saw Coyote coming so he swam over towards the middle of the lake so Coyote couldn't get to him. Coyote was in a hurry, his son was awful sick. Therefore, he cussed Duck for going out in the middle and said, "Get back over here, I'm in a tough fix. If you don't get over here I'm going to lose my boy." Duck said, "What's it all about, what is it?" Coyote replied and said, "My boy, he's awful sick. Get over here and go doctor him! Get over here before I get after you!" Duck answered and said, "OK, get a big bundle of that peso´uv" (the grass that ducks eat that's on the water).

So Coyote got a great big load of it on his back and Duck climbed on top of it. Then Coyote took off as fast as his legs could carry him back towards his sick boy. As they were traveling, that old Duck began to chew on the top of Coyotes bundle of duck food, right from the top to the bottom. Coyote could hear him eating and eating. By the time they got about half way, that Duck had eaten all the food from off Coyotes back.

Then Duck took off and flew back towards the pond. Coyote turned his head to look back and nobody was back there; all that food he had on his back was all gone also. Coyote started back to the pond but before he got there he filled his pockets with stones. He was going to hit that Duck. As soon as Duck saw Coyote coming he did the same thing as before and started out for the middle of the pond. The same conversation occurred as before with Coyote ending up getting a very big load of duck food this time. They started back towards Coyote's home with Duck again riding way up on top of Coyotes load of duck food.

That old Duck, he did the same thing as soon as they started off. By the time they had gone half way he had all that stuff eaten up again and then he flew back to his pond and that really made Coyote mad. He picked up a stick this time. He was really going to beat up that Old Man Duck, that old medicine man. However, Coyote just had to stand on the bank bawling him out because Duck was again out in the middle of his pond. Finally Duck again came over and said, "This time really take a big load, don't just take those little jags."

This time Coyote really took a big load, he could hardly see where he was going. That duck food was all over his head and hanging down covering his eyes.

This time they made it to Coyote's home and sure enough that young man was really sick; he was ready to die any minute. Then Duck started singing a medicine song. He sang and danced, trying everything he could, and finally he figured out the cause of the young man's illness. Duck then told Coyote, "There was a girl after this boy and she got mad all because of you Coyote. You was trying to cut him out, so that girl stuck a fingernail right down in his head, down through his skull." The Duck sang and worked around the boy some more and then pulled the fingernail out with his long bill. Then he went back to his pond.

COYOTE AND THE PORCUPINE
Cedar City 14

One time Porcupine went hunting and killed a buffalo. After he had killed it he found that he didn't have a knife to skin it with. He then began looking around for something to skin his buffalo. As he was looking he said to himself "Empuhm´suhunt tuhun´ee?" ***"What could I use to skin it with?"*** He kept saying this over and over until it sounded like a song.

While Porcupine was doing this, Coyote was walking nearby and heard this peculiar song but couldn't tell where it was coming from. As he was looking to find where the sound originated, it suddenly stopped. Pretty soon it started up again and then he found that the sound was coming from Porcupine who was off to his right a ways. He started over towards Porcupine. When Porcupine saw that Coyote was coming, he knew that he would try to take his buffalo away if he found that he had one. Porcupine changed what he was saying to fool Coyote, and said, "Empuhm´suhunt wawwaws´evuts?" ***"What shall I use to wash it?"*** Coyote then said to Porcupine, "I heard what you said. What did you kill?" Porcupine said, "I didn't say that. I was just saying 'Empuhm´suhunt wawaws´evuts?'"

They kept on arguing until Porcupine finally gave up and told Coyote that he had killed a buffalo. He then took Coyote to the dead buffalo. When they got there Coyote said, "Let's play a game. Let's see which one of us can jump over the buffalo, and the one that does gets to keep it." Porcupine said, "I can't jump that high," but he agreed to play the game. Coyote backed up about ten steps and then jumped over the buffalo without even touching it. Then porcupine tried it but he couldn't even make it half way up. Coyote won the buffalo.

Coyote then cleaned the buffalo and cut it into different pieces. When he was done he hung it all up in a tree and went home to get his children to come and help him pack the buffalo home.

While he was gone, Porcupine came along and saw it hanging in the tree. Porcupine was sort of a medicine man so he made the tree grow tall putting the buffalo out of reach of Coyote. He then got up in the tree and waited for Coyote. When Coyote came along he began looking for the tree where he had hung the buffalo. He couldn't find it and said to himself, "That tree was right here someplace." While Coyote was looking, Porcupine used his medicine to make Coyote

look up and find him. Coyote then looked up and found his buffalo and the Porcupine. He knew that he couldn't get the buffalo so he asked Porcupine just to toss him down a little piece of meat. Porcupine said, "Yes," and tossed a little piece of meat down. It hit Coyote right on top of the head and knocked him out.

Coyote And The Porcupine
Kaibab 4

One time, long ago, Porcupine was fooling around on the other side of a river. It must have been a big river. There was a herd of buffalo on the other side. He hollered at them and told them to come over and get him; he had to be over there among them on the other side. Those buffalo they just laughed and said, "Where could we keep that guy if someone did want to take him across? We can't keep him on our backs when we swim. We go under water a little bit and that guy is liable to drop off and go down the river." Porcupine was fooling the buffalo. He had some tricks up his sleeve, that guy. So the buffalo crossed the river and asked Porcupine, "Where are you going to ride? If you're going across you have to ride someplace." That Porcupine said, "The best place to ride is way down inside of you, way down there alongside the heart."

Porcupine was wise. He knew what he was after and had his trick all figured out. Anyway he took a chance; he went way down inside and lay down close to one of the buffalo's heart. Occasionally, while they were going across the river, Porcupine would ask him how far they had come. Buffalo would answer, "We're just about half-way now, we're not over there yet, but we're getting close." Porcupine wanted to know exactly when they reached the shore because when they got out of the river a little ways he was going to hit that heart with that wicked tail of his; he was going to hit him right in the heart.

Porcupine kept on asking until they finally reached the opposite shore. He asked them again where they were and Buffalo said, "We're getting out of the river, we're going up on the bank now. We're not on top yet but we're getting out of the river." A few moments later Porcupine asked again, "About where are we now?" Buffalo said, "Well, we're getting up on the top now. We're clear out of the river." That's the time Porcupine hit Buffalo's heart with his tail. He tapped Buffalo's heart, really banging it, when it was pumping away. That old buffalo just went a little ways and keeled over and then the Porcupine came out from inside the dead carcass.

Then Porcupine wanted to start butchering that old boy. Now he didn't know what to butcher with. As he was looking around for something to butcher it with, he kept saying "Empuhm´suhunt tuhun´ee? Empuhm´suhunt tuhun´ee?" ***"What could I use to skin it?"*** He kept saying this over and over until it sounded like a song.

Now that old crazy Coyote was nearby and heard him. He had left home because his wife had sent him after some squawbush twigs. Coyote couldn't tell

where the song was coming from. As he was looking to find where the sound originated, it suddenly stopped. Soon it started up again and then he found that the sound was coming from Porcupine who was a little ways off to his right. He then went towards Porcupine.

When Porcupine saw that Coyote was coming, he knew that he would try to take his buffalo away if he found that he had one. Porcupine then changed what he was saying to fool Coyote. He began saying "Empuhm´suhunt wawaws´evuts. Empuhm´suhunt wawaws´evuts." ***"What am I going to wash it with?"*** When Coyote heard Porcupine saying this he ran up to him and said, "What are you talking about?" Porcupine then said, "I was only saying 'Empuhm´suhunt wawaws´evuts,' that's what I was saying." He was trying to fool that Coyote. "No! I heard it plain! I heard you! You said 'you wondered what you were going to butcher with!' I heard you! You're going to have to tell me where that buffalo is lying." Porcupine was trying to get out of his dilemma but Coyote got kind of rough and shook him around a little bit. Coyote said, "You better tell me where that Buffalo is lying, or whatever you killed! I heard you! You said, 'what am I going to butcher with.'" Porcupine answered "No! I didn't say that! I said 'I wonder what I'm going to wash with.'" Coyote said, "No, I don't believe you. Come on! You have to speak up or else I'm going to tap you on the head with a stick."

Porcupine kept on insisting that he hadn't killed anything and wouldn't tell Coyote what he had killed. Finally Coyote got himself a great big stick and tapped Porcupine over the head and stretched him out. He hit him two or three times and knocked him cold. Then he traced Porcupine's tracks and came to the dead buffalo, just laying there, a great big animal.

So he got his knife out and went to work. He quartered him and cut him all up good. While he was doing this he splashed blood all over himself so his old lady could see it. He put blood on his face and all over his body. Then he ran home to get his family and as soon as he came to his place he started talking to them while sticking his hands out so his kids and old lady could see all that blood on them. All of Coyotes kids then gathered around and licked on their daddy's fingers, licking all that blood off, just as Coyote pups would do. His wife thought that was the kind of a man to have, someone who would go out there and kill some meat.

I guess Coyote's wife threw her arms around Coyote right there and made love to him for a while. He had done a great thing. Really, however, Coyote had just taken another man's meat away. That's what he had done.

Then he started getting after his old lady and said, "How come you're always sending me after squawbush? You're the one that's always sending me after that bush. I shouldn't do that! It's better for me to go and kill something to eat." At the same time it wasn't Coyote who had killed the buffalo. He just took it away from the other guy. Then Coyote gathered up his ropes and sacks and wanted to move his family over to the dead buffalo to eat up all the insides that he had cut up and hung on a pine tree to cool off.

While Coyote was gone, Porcupine, the guy that he knocked cold, finally came to. Porcupine was sort of a medicine man so he climbed that tree where the buffalo

meat was hanging and he told that tree, "Grow, and keep growing until you get way up there and become a tall pine tree!"

Soon Coyote returned with his entire family stringing along behind to where he had left the buffalo meat. Coyote then began to look around where he had butchered the buffalo. He showed his kids and said, "What happened? There was a tree right here where that buffalo keeled over and where I hung the meat. It was around here someplace." Porcupine, meanwhile, was way up there using his medicine and saying to himself, "I hope Coyote looks up here." Coyote looked up and there it was, the butchered buffalo and Porcupine, way up there. That tree had grown. Coyote then felt rather ashamed. His wife and kids were there and had believed his big story and now they found out that all along Coyote was just fooling them. He wasn't the one that had done the killing; it was Porcupine that had done all the work.

Then Coyote said to Porcupine, "Why don't you throw me down some of that jelled blood. Why don't you throw that down, some for the boys too, if you don't mind." Porcupine had all the meat up there, including the hump, with all it's sharp bones sticking out; he had sharpened them. He then said to Coyote, and his pups, "All of you lie down alongside each other and then I'll let something down for you." When they were all lying down alongside each other Porcupine dropped the sharpened backbone down upon Coyote and his family. That backbone cut all of them up.

There was only one kid left out of the entire family. He was just a little boy. The backbone had just missed him. That kid started crying so Porcupine told him to come on up. So the little boy went on up and they dined for a while on that meat hanging in the tree. They had all the meat they wanted. After that kid had a heavy supper he said, "Where can I go to the bathroom? Where is it at?" Porcupine said, "It's way out there on the end of the furthermost branch. Get way out there! That stuff stinks!" Then the little boy went way out there on the tip of a limb. Just as he was taking his clothes off and setting down getting all ready to go to the bathroom, the Porcupine kicked the branch and shook that kid off. He fell off and hit the ground hard and was squashed flat.

Why Indians Don't Eat The Coyote
Kaibab 4

A long time ago, when the animals used to be human, each agreed to turn themselves into different kinds of animals so that the Indians would have some meat to eat. They all did this except Coyote. He didn't want to be eaten so he urinated all over himself so nobody would eat him. That's the reason Indians don't eat coyotes today.

EAGLE AND THE TURTLE
Kaibab 4

A long time ago Eagle and his mother used to live down by Needles, California, and would live off the mesquite trees there. Eagle wanted to come up north and see the country up here. He told his mother and she made him a lunch by pounding him something with a mortar and pestle. He then began his journey and while he was going along his way, he met Peekai the Turtle. Turtle said he wanted to go along. Eagle agreed and so they both went on their way.

While traveling along, Turtle made himself a pretty hat out of flowers to sort of show off when he got up north. Meanwhile the Shivwits were walking around down by Beaver Dam, Arizona, and saw Turtle. They made fun of him and took his hat away. This made Turtle mad and he turned around right there and said he wasn't going any further north. That's why you never see the turtle any further north than that.

In that area there was a couple that had a very pretty daughter that all the men wanted to marry. Her parents had a test that had to be passed before she would be allowed to marry. The test consisted of having to go back into a cave that the parents would fill with smoke. The person being tested had to endure this smoke without closing his eyes. Everyone who attempted this test failed. The Shivwits men tried also but they all failed and that's why they have squint eyes because they all tried to keep their eyes open in the thick smoke. Eagle tried this test and while he was in the thick of the smoke he closed his transparent inner eye lids that eagles have, and when the parents looked in they thought his eyes where still open. He passed the test and won the girl.

This made Coyote jealous and he tried to cause trouble between Eagle and the Shivwits. He challenged Eagle to some contests. One was a fist fight. Now the Shivwits used to be good fist fighters and the best was chosen for this fight. They fought and fought and soon became tired. Then Eagle used his long claws and scratched the other very bad and won the contest. They also had a foot race but here Eagle lost because an eagle can't run fast. He's even that way today.

They were next going to see who were the best hunters. They all went out hunting, but Eagle easily won and killed nothing but fat rabbits. His father-in-law was with him and Eagle told him to carry some of the rabbits home. When Eagle came home he wasn't carrying anything and the Shivwits made fun of him. Eagle felt sorry for them and Coyote, and told them that he had killed some rabbits out there, and that they could go and keep them if they would pick up all his arrows and return them.

When they went to get the rabbits Coyote decided he didn't want to return the arrows so he urinated on them and shot them away. When they returned they told Eagle they couldn't find his arrows. Eagle then went out and found where they had been shot and returned mad and said, "Maybe we should have a war and get it over with." Coyote said, "Not me!" The Shivwits also backed out.

Eagle then moved up north to the mountains to live and liked it. He returned and got his mother and said he had found a pretty place to live and so he took her with him and that's why the eagle lives in the mountains to the north and the turtle in the valleys to the south.

Chicken Hawk And The Fast Fly
Kaibab 4

One time a man beat up on his wife and left her out in the woods. He then told the people that she was lost and wanted someone to go find her. No one would go until he finally forced a little fly that can dart around quickly. As Fly could cover the country very fast he soon found her; she was sitting in the nest of Awsee´uvuhvuhts ***"Chicken Hawk."*** She was there with Chicken Hawk's mother, while he was away. Fly returned and told the man that he had found his wife. This man then said he would give his wife to anyone who would go and get her. No one wanted to until he finally persuaded a certain little bird that was the best fighter they had. A good fighter was needed to whip Chicken Hawk. Fly said, "I don't want to fight for her, but I'll lead the bird to Chicken Hawk's nest."

When they arrived there and Chicken Hawk found out what was going on he said, "What do you want to fight me for? I just found her all beaten up so I took her home to take care of her." This didn't change things so they got into a fight and fought and fought but couldn't kill each other. The mother of the bird that was fighting Chicken Hawk had told him that to kill Hawk you had to aim about two feet above his head as that was where his mind was. He remembered this and at last killed Hawk.

Now Chicken Hawk had told his mother that if he was killed she was not to feel bad but to take and boil him. She did this and he came back to life. He then went to continue the battle with Bird. Now it was said that when Chicken Hawk got mad it would become cloudy, and that when Bird got mad the land would turn gray. This happened while they were fighting and nobody could watch the fight except Fly; he could dart in and out of the fog and watch. They fought and fought and this time Hawk remembered that his mother had told him that Bird's mind was also about two feet above his head, as was his own mind, so there is where he aimed and he killed Bird.

When it was all over the Indians wised up and figured out that it was the husband who had beaten up his wife who was causing all the trouble. Now it was too late, because they had lost their best fighter.

ORION'S BELT
Kaibab 4

One time Coyote was building a shade house and he had his two daughters go up on top to place limbs over the holes. Coyote told them to stand over the holes so

he could see up between their legs. This led to sexual intercourse with them. Because of this, Coyote's daughters and one son left and went up into the sky. They are the three stars in Orion's Belt.[18] This constellation is called "Nawhung´" (plural for ***mountain sheep***).

Orion's Belt
Shivwits 5

A long time ago Soonungwuv (Coyote) had a wife, daughters, sons, and everything he needed. One day he went out hunting with his children. There was a big rock sitting there and he was trying to catch a squirrel in a crack in that rock. Coyote told his daughters to get the squirrel and then he tried to do everything to them (sexually) while they were doing as he told them.

---

[18] According to the Shivwits version, Coyotes daughters became the Constellation Pleiades, and his three sons became the three stars in Orion's Belt. This also conforms to the neighboring Hualapai legend wherein one of the three stars in Orion's belt is a mountain sheep.

His daughters couldn't catch the squirrel and got mad because of all the things Coyote was doing to them. They then started going up in the sky to get away from Coyote. They just kept going up and up. Later Coyote got mad at them and told them "You will become that one, Sonee´ung" (Pleiades), and so they became that constellation. Coyote's sons also went up and became Nawhung, the three stars in Orion's Belt.

How The Indians Acquired Salt
Kaibab 4

One time salt used to be human. That was when Indians didn't have any salt. Salt traveled all over the country and as he came to each little Indian camp he would ask them if he could stick his finger into their boiling meat. Some would let him and then when they tasted their meat they found that it tasted better. Salt then gave them instructions as to which way they should go. When the Indians followed his instructions and arrived at the designated place they found a salt deposit. They brought some home and ground it up on a rock and used it. This is how Indians got salt. There were some other Indian camps that wouldn't let him stick his finger into their boiling meat and unto this day there is no salt deposit around the vicinity of their land.

Why The Indians Have Lice
Kaibab 4

Coyote was the one who caused the Indians to have lice in their hair because he liked to lie in the lap of his two wives while they would pick the lice out. One time while he was doing this he fell asleep with his head on the lap of one of his wives. They raised his head up and put a log under it and then they both took off.

Owl And The Skunk
Kaibab 4

The Owl, his wife, and son, were living together. Owl didn't get along very good with his wife. One time, when Owl was away, his wife planned how to get to rid of him. She went and picked up all the flint flakes she could find and laid them at the place where Owl would always kick the snow off his feet when he arrived home. When he returned he did this, just as she figured, and got some flint chips in his feet that caused his death. Just before he died he told his wife to take their son and go to their uncle's place.

After his death they started off on their journey and on the way they came to Skunks home. Skunk was out, but his wife and little boy were there and so they

stayed awhile. While they were there Owl's little boy shot some arrows into a cactus. Before Skunk returned, Skunk's wife warned Owl and her son to leave because Skunk was real mean.

When Skunk returned home he looked around and noticed the little arrow marks in the cactus and asked his wife who had been staying here. She said, "No one." Skunk also noticed where someone had been sitting and had left a little depression. He asked again who had been there, but his wife replied, "No one." When Skunk saw the arrow holes in the cactus Mrs. Skunk said she made them while making a basket and accidentally stuck some of the twigs into the cactus. Skunk didn't believe her. She also said that she made the impression where someone had been sitting, but Skunk also didn't believe that and said, "Your seat makes a rough impression not a smooth one!" He then tested her by setting her down to see what kind of impression she made. It was rough and so he proved her wrong.

He then asked her which way they went but she wouldn't say so he circled the house until he found their tracks and then he began following them. When he came to a big valley he looked across it hoping to see them but he didn't. He then decided to go no further because he had not overtaken them. Before he turned around he let out a big scent that formed a cloud and traveled across the valley getting bigger and blacker. When Mrs. Owl and her son saw it they hurried to avoid the storm but it caught up with them and was so powerful that it overcame them and they passed out.

Somehow Badger heard what happened to them and traveled across the valley by burrowing his way under the ground. Every once in a while he would come to the surface and look around. Finally as he came to the surface he found that he had passed them so he left his hole and walked back to them. He then sang over them until he revived them. He sang again and in his song he was saying he wanted something that belonged to Mrs. Owl. Mrs. Owl tried to figure out what he wanted and said, "Is it this?" referring to a part of her clothes. He said, "No." Then she said "Is it this?" pointing at her pants.[19] He said "Yes" and she gave them to him. Then they went on their way. (More to this story; it is a long story.)

---

[19] This story probably has a sexual connotation here like the Shivwits version. Morris had a tendency to hold back a little in such cases.

OWL AND THE SKUNK
Shivwits 5

This story starts at Castle Cliffs, Utah, near Littlefield Arizona. There are two caves there; a big one and a small one. They are called Moo-oon´ Tuhngkawn ***Owl's Cave***. The big cave was mother Owl's and her son's cave; the other belonged to Father Owl. The sketch is an actual depiction of these two caves.

Owl used to go hunting rabbits down in the valley but brought only the poor ones to his wife and son. Owl's wife went and spied on Owl and got mad because he kept all the fat rabbits to himself. She collected a lot of rabbit bones and placed them so Owl would get poked by them when he stomped his feet to shake the snow off as it was winter time. That night Owl lay suffering and moaning saying, "oooo." Owl's son wanted to go see him but his mom said "No! Tell him to go, he's no good!" Before Owl died he told them to go to Eagle down on the other side of Las Vegas someplace and marry him. He also told them not to stop anyplace on the way down, like at Skunk's and Crow's houses.

Then they went down that way. First they stopped at the Skunk's mother's place on the Virgin River. Skunk was out hunting rabbits. Later on he came back and smelled around and said, "Someone has been here." His mother replied, "No! No one has been here." He didn't believe her and said, "I want to know!" He kept saying this to his mother. Way later she gave in and said, "Yes. I met that lady from up there at Owl's Cave."

Skunk then went and chased after Owl and her son. When they saw Skunk coming they covered a young Joshua tree cactus with a rabbit-skin blanket. Skunk

saw it and started to hold, kiss, and love it, thinking it was a woman hiding beneath the blanket. He got poked all over by the cactus so he lifted up the blanket and looked under it but no lady was there. They had gotten away. That's why the giant Joshua cactus has black (red) tips at the ends of its stickers. This cactus is called choowaw´ duhmp. The black tips are the skunks blood or something. After this, Skunk farted and made a great big black cloud float over Owl and her son and right there they passed out (died).

At that time Badger used to have a camp on that big hill this side of Glendale, Nevada, west of the road. He had lots of kids. Badger dreamed about what happened to Owl and her son He sent his children out to look for them but the only one that was successful was the youngest one. When they were found, Badger burrowed his way to them just under the ground because he can dig fast. He kept coming up on different sides of them, but finally he came up in the right place and restored them to life.

Badger wanted something as payment for his services so Owl said, "What do you want? Do you want my head? My arm? My shoulder?" She named nearly all of her body parts but Badger wanted none of them. Finally she pointed at her vagina and Badger said, "Toampok´weev" (his way of saying ***vagina***). "Yes! That's what I want!" He got his wish and that's why a Badger has a penis like a human.

After Owl and her son were revived they journeyed to the wash near Glendale, Nevada (by that old airport beacon). There's a cave and ledge there. Old man Owl also told them not to stop there on their way to Eagle's place beyond Las Vegas. When they arrived there they heard a lot of Indians there laughing and everything. (They had a name but I can't remember it.) Owl's son wanted to look in the cave but his mother said he shouldn't because his father told them not to stop there. The little boy didn't listen and stuck his head down in and saw all kinds of Indians. They were dancing, hollering, and everything. As soon as the Indians in the cave saw him sticking his head down in, they flipped their closed hands forward and opened up their fingers and Owl and her son passed out again.

Badger again dreamed about their deaths and knew where they were now because his youngest son had seen them. After Badger dug his way to her and revived her she already knew what he wanted. Badger again said "Toampok´weev" and he again received his payment for reviving them a second time. However, he didn't revive the boy until he was through with his mother. He was just left lying there.

Owl and her son then journeyed down past Las Vegas to a cave where Crow lived. They stopped there. That Crow, he just ate rotten meat and smelly old bones so they didn't get to eat well there. They then went on. (There are some songs here, when they got to that place, but I don't know them.) Then Eagle saw them, took them home, and they ate good. They got to eat rabbits, deer and everything. (As told by Shivwits informant 5, June 1984.)

THE COUNCIL OF BEARS
Koosharem 20

There is a cave up by Fish Lake, Utah, someplace where all the bears gathered one time. As they entered the doorway, there was one bear that asked each one their name and where they came from. When they all had passed this checkpoint they sat around in a council circle. A Paiute happened to be hiding nearby and heard what the bears had to say. The bears all talked Paiute and said they must kill all the Paiute Indians. One bear in the council circle had a very beautiful pipe.

The Indian then ran to tell his people that the bears had a council and were going to kill all the Paiutes. The Paiutes decided they must go and kill all the bears. The Indian who had overheard them said to the others "Don't kill that bear with the pretty pipe, I want that pipe for myself." The Paiutes then went to that cave and killed all the bears except the one with the pipe. He escaped. This is a true story. (As told to Koosharem 20 by Koosharem 10.)

THE BULLET HAWKS
Indian Peak 21

One time there were two bullet hawks, Kuhsawv and Sawkwaw´ Kuhsawv.[20] These two Hawks were diving down and killing all the animals and everyone complained about it. Soonungwuv then planned to kill these two Hawks and built himself a little house on the hill just east of Rush Lake, Utah. There he lay in wait for the two bullet hawks. They wouldn't come until all the water round about dried up. When they came to drink Soonungwuv shot them.[21] (Indian Peak 21.)

---

[20] The word sawkwaw can mean either blue or green. These colors are one and the same with many tribes.

[21] Carl Jake showed me Soonungwuv's (Coyote's) house at Rush Lake in 1956. He definitely called it Soonungwuv's house and not Toovuts' as claimed by William Palmer.

CHAPTER 2

WAR AND HISTORICAL STORIES

Nawduh´gwenup

They make a desolation and call it peace.
Jewish comment about the Romans.

The following stories fall into the bracket of Nawduh´gwenup. The Paiutes consider these stories as true. Some of them deal with battles between Paiutes and other tribes, particularly the Arapaho who were forever warring with them. Other stories deal with battles with the white man all of which can be documented in Peter Gottfredson's book *Indian Depredations in Utah.*[22]

After I heard the Paiute versions of their wars with the white man, I began to check dates and events against Gottfredson's. I began to think that maybe he should have entitled his book "Anglo Depredations in Utah." This will become apparent when some of the following evidence comes out. First of all, there is little discrepancy between the Indian and Anglo versions. This bears out the truthfulness of the Indian versions. The battles where the Indians were not caught off guard generally ended in a standoff with a couple wounded or killed on each side after which the combatants withdrew. The only complete victories the white man achieved were against peaceful Indians who tried to remain friends with the whites during the Black Hawk War. They didn't go into hiding as did the women, children, and aged of Black Hawk's fighting bands who went out into eastern Utah, probably in the remote Canyonlands area. This is evident in Gottfredson's book also.

The militia had little success in pitched battles with the Indians so they resorted to falsely accusing the peaceful bands and then massacring them. They would kill everyone including the women, children, and aged. One of the pur-

[22] Gottfredson, 1919.

poses in doing this was to intimidate the fighting bands. During the Black Hawk War this happened at the Circleville massacre of women and children, at the Grass Valley "Squaw Fight" as termed by Gottfredson, and on Kanab Creek where peaceful Paiutes were killed in retribution for a raid made by Navajos. Similar massacres occurred at other times. One happened in Spring Valley where peaceful Paiutes and Gosiutes were killed to intimidate warring Shoshonis, and another in Pahranagat Valley just for the acquisition of land.

BATTLE WITH NAVAJOS IN WAYNE COUNTY
Koosharem 3

Long ago in the fall, some Indians from the Escalante area in Utah came to hunt on Thousand Lake Mountain. They came by way of Rabbit Valley and over into a canyon east of Thousand Lake Mountain in Wayne County, Utah. This canyon runs all the way to the river and at the upper end it forms a box canyon with a little spring there.[23] There were only two ways into this canyon at the upper end consisting of two trails coming down each side of the canyon some distance below the spring. These Indians camped there for about two days. The men then went up on top of Thousand Lake Mountain to hunt.

On their way to this area they had unknowingly been tracked by a large Navajo war party. When the Navajos found that the Paiutes were trapped in this box canyon they descended and killed all but a few whom they took prisoners. Those killed were mostly old men, women, and children who had remained behind while the men had gone hunting.

One young boy ran through the Navajos who tried to shoot him but couldn't hit him. He got away from them and ran up out of the canyon and onto the mountain where he hollered, hoping the men of the hunting party would hear him. One of the hunters heard him and came to him. The boy said, "We've all been killed!"

They soon rounded up the rest of the hunters and started for the canyon. When they reached the head of the canyon the leader said, "Let's split in half and go along the top of both sides." They did this without looking down into the canyon. Soon the two halves reached the two trails but didn't see any tracks of the Navajos leaving the canyon. Therefore they knew they must still be in

[23] This canyon is probably Chimney Rock Canyon in Capitol Reef National Monument, Utah. I flew over this canyon with Jimmy Timmican after he told the story. The canyon he pointed out from the air appeared to be Chimney Rock Canyon.

the canyon and sent one man back along the top to see if he could spot the Navajos. He saw them and came back and said, "They are coming down the canyon leading four captive girls."

The Paiutes then laid an ambush within the canyon with men hidden on both sides and some downstream. The husband of one of the captive girls hid behind the topside of a rock. It was his wife who was in the lead with a Navajo right behind her. The Paiute behind the rock had told no one to fire until he fired the first shot. As his wife rounded the rock she spotted her husband and quickened her pace. A Navajo followed and as he came around the rock the Paiute shot him. The other Paiutes hidden close by also opened fire and the Navajos ran to the other side of the canyon into the hands of the opposite hidden group who then also commenced firing. The Navajos began running back and fourth until they were all killed except one who broke through and ran all the way to the Colorado River. The Paiutes pursued him but couldn't catch him. When he reached the other side they let him go. They hollered to him and said, "Send back some more Navajos." He clasped his hands behind his head and cried.[24] The four girls were recovered safely. (As told by Koosharem 3 who heard the story from his grandfather.)

THE ARAPAHO AT PARADISE VALLEY LAKE
Koosharem 3

A Paiute was out hunting on Thousand Lake Mountain and spotted an Arapaho in a pine tree. The Arapaho had made himself a protected cover in the tree so he would not be seen but he evidently went to sleep and was spotted. This Arapaho had probably come to steal a horse.

The Paiute ran down into the valley to the camp there where the Indians were playing the hand game. They were betting bows, buckskins, and other personal items. He told them that an Arapaho was up there in a tree looking down on them. The men then said let's pretend we're going out into the valley to hunt rabbits and then we will sneak up on him.

The Indians spread out into the valley as if they were hunting rabbits. When they came to a wash they went into it and up the mountain towards the Arapaho. They surrounded him and approached him slowly. He was still sleeping and one man got under him and shot him a good one in his belly with an arrow. The Arapaho jumped down and took off running. He then whirled around and came back where he had left his bow. From there he darted off in another direction, and then another, as he found he was surrounded.

---

[24] I once heard a Navajo story about a Navajo father waiting by a large butte east of Page, Arizona, for his son to return from a war party in Utah. He waited a long time and finally his son did return as the sole survivor of that disastrous war party. The Navajos gave a name to that butte that pertained to this event but I don't remember what it was. The Navajo story might pertain to the same event.

Among the Paiutes there were two men who were very good runners, being able to run down deer. The Arapaho darted past them and down the mountainside. These two good runners tried but couldn't catch him. As the Arapaho was approaching some Paiutes who were concealed down below, he keeled over dead.

The Paiutes turned his body over and when they looked at his eyes, they were glassy and staring. They then called the lake there "Moasuhm Paw Hawduhd," ***Glassy Eyed Lake***. This lake is by the road from Fremont to Emery. (This lake is probably Paradise Valley Lake. As told by Koosharem 3 who heard this story from Walker Ammon, son of Chief Walker.)

The Dead Arapaho On Mount Marvine
Koosharem 3

One time, a Paiute was walking along near the top of Pawguh Kwawseev[25] (Mount Marvine) just north of Fish Lake, Utah. This Indian spotted a pile of rocks with some feet sticking out from under them. He ran down to the Paiute camp just below, called "Yooveemp," ***Ponderosa***, and told them about it.

They all went up to investigate, approaching slowly from both sides. As they got closer one man said, "Maybe he's sleeping." They continued to approach cautiously and soon were upon him. One man took a stick and poked him in the feet but he didn't move. Then they took him by his feet and pulled him out and found that he was dead. He had probably died from some sickness or hunger. (As told by Koosharem 3 who heard this story from Walker Ammon, son of Chief Walker.)

Battle On Carter Peak
Koosharem

There was a battle one time between Paiutes and some other Indians. One group defended themselves from the top of Carter Peak situated between Sigurd and Salina, Utah.[26] (As told in 1957 by Shivwits informant 23 who heard the story from Koosharem 3.)

Horsetail Hair's Vengeance
Kaibab 4

One time two Paiutes were getting salt down in the Little Colorado River, near its junction with the Colorado. Some Apaches found them there and killed them.

When the Paiutes learned of this they wanted to get even. There was a Paiute from over around Bluff, Utah, somewhere who was bulletproof. His name was Kuvawkwusee Pauhk, ***Horsetail Hair.*** He led the Paiutes on a raid upon the

[25] This Paiute name means ***Fish Tail*** because the mountain resembles a fish's tail.
[26] There is now a booster antenna, of some type, on top of this peak.

Apaches who were then living around the San Francisco Peaks area in northern Arizona. They fought a battle in which the Paiutes won, driving the Apaches completely away from that area, down to where they stay now.

Horsetail Hair's Death
Koosharem 3

A long time ago some Arapahos came down from the north and attacked some Paiutes encamped near the Strawberry Reservoir in northern Utah. When the Paiutes saw the Arapahos charging on horseback down off the hill north of the present reservoir, they fled for cover. Among those fleeing was a young married couple. The man had on leggings with long fringe that became entangled in the brush and he couldn't go on. His wife stayed behind with him to help him get untangled, but by then the Arapahos were upon them and they were both killed.

The Paiutes then wanted to be avenged and sought help from the Utes. Twelve of the strongest Utes were organized to retaliate. Horsetail Hair (Kuvaw´kwusee Pauhk) was their leader as he was considered the greatest of them all. The twelve traveled far north past the mountainous land to some rolling grassy plains spotted with pine-covered buttes. There they found the Arapaho camp, stretched out for several miles along a river. They managed to round up all the loose Arapaho horses at night and seven of the Ute warriors started south with them. Horsetail Hair, his brother, and three others stayed behind to hold off the Arapahos.

When the fighting started, one of the Utes became separated from the others and hid under a little grassy bank along a gully. From there he spotted an Arapaho tipi where he figured menstruating Arapaho women isolated themselves. He sneaked into the tipi and spent the night with an Arapaho woman staying there by herself.

Two of the other Utes were surrounded by Arapahos and fought side by side. The horse of one of the Utes had been shot. The Ute who still had his horse asked the other, "How did you dream?" The other said, "I dreamed we made it safely." The two then rode double upon one horse and broke through the Arapaho lines to the safety of a pine-covered butte.

Meanwhile, Horsetail Hair and his brother had destroyed about a mile of tipis and their inhabitants. They made a great slaughter upon the Arapaho because he and his brother were bulletproof and couldn't be killed. However, they eventually became tired and were captured. Even then they couldn't be killed easily because of their bulletproof power. It took a long time before they eventually died.

The two Utes who had escaped on the single horse watched from the seclusion of a pine-covered butte to see what happened to Horsetail Hair and his brother. When all was quiet they sneaked over to where he and his brother had been left and saw that they were dead. After studying the signs it became evident to them that it had been extremely difficult for the Arapahos to kill the two brothers because of their lingering power. Marks on their flesh revealed that bullets from the Arapaho rifles were not able to penetrate their flesh.[27] The only weapon that appeared effective was a hot knife stuck in the rectum. They had been scalped but from the evidence it appeared that the Arapahos had to use a hot metal knife to burn their hair off.

The two surviving Utes started back south and on the way they spotted someone drinking water from a creek. They thought that it might be an enemy Arapaho but it turned out to be the Ute who had spent the night with the menstruating woman. All ten eventually reached home safely in Utah. (As told by Koosharem 3 who heard this story from Utes from the Fort Duchesne, Utah area.)

Medicine Power Destroys An Indian Band
Koosharem 10

A long time ago there used to be many Paiute Indians living in Wayne County along the Colorado river. They were the Suhuh´ Vawduhuts Band, ***Squawbush Water People***.[28] One time they were having a big dance there and the wife of a medicine man got into a quarrel with the wife of another medicine man. Soon the two medicine men also began quarreling with each other due to their quarreling wives. They started fighting each other with medicine. Their medicine wasn't very strong and it killed all the Indians there one by one. The man who called the dance together was the first one to die. All this happened because of the two women.

---

[27] Since rifles are mentioned in this story this event must have happened in historic times.
[28] Jimmy Timmican, a brother to Florence, says that this is the name of the band that lived near the confluence of the Colorado and Green rivers. These words mean "Squaw Bush Water People." This name was Anglicized by the white man to Sheberetch.

Apaches Kill Paiutes On Kaibab Moutain
Kaibab 4

One night, long ago, the Apaches[29] raided a camp of sleeping Kaibab Paiutes who were camped at a spring on the south side of Kaibab Mountain. The Apaches killed them all with stone clubs.

John Kinley And His 12 Paiute Recruits
Koosharem 3

One time there was a man named John Kinley who came up from Mexico to recruit some Paiutes. He was a Paiute who had been taken south by the Spaniards and sold as a slave or possibly a half-breed son of a Paiute slave. When he arrived in this area he went to St. George, Cedar City, Kanosh, and over to Koosharem, Utah, to recruit warriors to help him fight the Mexicans or someone in Coahuilla, Mexico. He recruited 12 warriors, including two from Koosharem. These 12 warriors were all bulletproof and nothing could kill them. John Kinley told them that if they would go with him they would see many things. One of these things would be a glass house where all the Spirits lived.

So John and the 12 Paiutes went south, camping as they traveled along. They came to the glass house out in the valley some distance from the mountains. This glass house was where the spirits of all the dead went; they would enter the house as butterflies. In this glass house there was a Mexican who would catch these butterflies. He was a big man and would sway back and forth as he caught them. After he caught them he would bury them in rows on the sandy floor. Afterwhile these buried butterflies would turn into little dolls. These dolls would look just like Indians. Some were Paiutes dressed in their rabbit blankets and yucca sandals. You could also see some Arapaho and Navajo dolls, and all kinds of tribes.

Then this Mexican would take these dolls and stand them in rows along the walls of the house. These dolls could only move their heads from side to side.[30] They couldn't talk or do any thing else. As they stood along the walls they grew bigger. The house itself also grew wider and taller until it reached up to heaven and it then punched a hole in the sky.

This story mentioned a white horse, some dust, the moon marrying a frog, and how dead Indians would come back to life. The story continued about how these 13 men met someone and were fed and told not to fight. In this story there was also

---

[29] These "Apaches" were probably Yavapais or Tonto Apaches from north central Arizona who often raided the Havasupais within the Grand Canyon who were nearby neighbors to the Kaibab Band. This might have happened in the Nankoweap area as this word means ***Indians Killed Off*** (Nengwoo' Koahoyp).

[30] Both Navajos and Chippewas have been reported to be able to manipulate dolls from a distance.

a wagon or something dragging some branded cowhides. These hides were thrown in the water. After about a half-hour the water started moving and up out of the water came a line of living cows.

These 13 men eventually reached the ocean by Mexico or someplace. They also met "Suhnuv" (God) and shook hands.[31] When these men returned to Utah they all testified about all the things they had seen.[32] (As told by Koosharem 3 about 1961).

Vera Charles got a similar story from Florence Kanosh, a sister of Jimmy Timmican (Koosharem informant 3). She says the story is true. Florence was 95 at the time she told this story and according to the informant she would jump from one story to another. Florence said, "There were some Indians from Kanosh who went down to California. On the way many things happened and they had to fight enemy tribes as they went. When they arrived at the ocean they saw a greatgrand–mother there pounding buffalo jerky. She would put something with it and then toss it into the water and live buffalo would come out."

"The old lady mentioned something about some white dolls. These were fore-telling the coming of the white man. They would have bad breath and an underarm odor that would make all the Indians die off."

White Men Massacre Indians On Utah Lake
Koosharem 22

A long time ago the soldiers attacked some peaceful Indians at Utah Lake during the winter when the lake was frozen over. Many of the women, children, and aged sought to flee to safety across the ice, but were overrun by soldiers on horseback who cut their heads off with swords.

Battle With The White Man In Wayne County
Koosharem 3

Some of the white men of Wayne County, Utah, and the nearby area, got together to fight the Indians. Among these men were Hatch and Jack Ourite (not sure of spelling) or "Sawngkuhts," as the Indians called him, because he limped. He was from Fremont, Utah, and would trade whiskey to the Indians for hides.

[31] Supernatural descriptions as in this story do not make it a mythical legend. It was all considered true by the Paiutes. Compare the similar supernatural events that took place when some of the Plains Indians went to Nevada to visit Wovoka during the Ghost Dance days.

[32] This is the only story I didn't write down immediately after I heard it in about 1960. I actually wrote it down several years later after I had forgotten some of it. It was a very long story.

These white soldiers were discovered accidentally while an Indian was out hunting. He spotted a man in a white blanket and being curious, he sneaked closer to get a better look. When he saw that he had a white face the Indian ran back to his camp on Pine Creek south of Bicknell. He told his people of what he saw and they decided to evacuate the women. The women all left their camp that night and started up O-aw´ Kaiv,[33] a nearby mountain while the men waited behind to fight the soldiers.

Early that morning the soldiers spotted the women through their telescope going up the last of the trail near the top of the mountain. They also saw the men down in the valley sitting around at the camp.

The Indians meanwhile had concealed some men in the brush where the soldiers would approach so they might ambush them. As the soldiers approached and were starting into the ambush, the lead man spotted one of the Indians who was probably wearing a red blanket. The lead man whirled around dashing past one other concealed Indian and out into the clear. The soldiers then ran up onto the point of the hill the Paiutes called Pachu Tuhngkun´evuhts[34] and commenced firing down on the Indians. The Indians and soldiers were not too close to each other so they were firing from long range. The Indians at this time had good rifles.

There were two Indians concealed behind a rock, somewhat closer to the hill, that almost got hit. One of these Indians spotted a man on the hill who was firing these shots. He told the other that he saw where the shots were coming from and that he was going to aim and wait for him to stick up again. When he stuck up, the Indian shot him between the eyes.

Jack Ourite hollered down from the hill in Paiute, as he spoke good Indian, and he said "Tuhnunk´wu evun´ee, kwou tuhkaw kwaivadum. Kaw yavawhaisump!" ***Come up here; let's smoke. Don't be afraid!*** In the battle two white men were killed and no Indians. (As told by Koosharem 3 who heard this story from Walker Ammon, son of Chief Walker. Gottfredson gives the date of this battle as September 21, 1865. He tells of it on Page 167 of his book.)

WHITE MEN MASSACRE INDIANS IN GRASS VALLEY
Koosharem 3, 10, & 20

One time soldiers were sent down into Sevier Valley from the Mount Pleasant area. Some Paiutes were encamped at Glenwood at the time. The Bishop of Glenwood warned the Indians and told them to leave. They then broke camp and

[33] This Paiute name means ***Yellow Mountain***. It is a small mountain situated on the north end of Boulder Mountain, Utah. On the USGS map this hill is called Black Ridge although it is only the trees on top that make it appear black. It is locally known as "The Petrified Forest." The lower west side of the hill is yellow and red.

[34] This Paiute word means ***Bat Cave***. It is at Rock Point on Pine Creek near Loa, Utah.

followed the horse trail over the mountain and down into Grass Valley where they stopped.

The next day or so, one of the Indians was out hunting and spotted someone in a white blanket standing on a point. He sneaked up close and saw that he had a white face. He went back to the camp and told his people. The Chief said, "Don't worry, I have a paper from the Bishop; they won't bother us." Feeling safe, they remained there that night.

Early in the morning, before the sun came up and while they were all sleeping, the soldiers attacked them and killed them all. Some were still sleeping in their blankets. One Indian ran up the side of the hill and was shot between the eyes from a long way off as he looked back down.

One very small boy who had on a sheepskin cloak was lying beside his dead mother and when the white men spotted him they picked him up and took him with them, as they started back north. They hadn't gone far when the boy got loose and ran away. The soldiers didn't bother to chase him figuring he would die of starvation.

The little boy walked all the way up to the top of Mount Marvine which overlooks a Paiute camp he must have seen at one time while traveling with his folks. The Indians at this camp (Yooveemp) had just broke camp and were traveling towards Fish Lake. One old man however, had forgotten his water jug and returned to get it. He retrieved it and as he started off he faintly heard someone hollering. He rode up closer to where the hollering was coming from and saw the little boy in the sheepskin. He called to the boy and told him to come on down and that he would wait for him. When the boy arrived the old man asked him where his folks were. He lied and said, "They were on their way."

The old man then put the little boy on the horse behind him and they started after the rest of the band. While they were on their way the boy told the truth, that his people had all been killed. When they reached the others they told them what had happened. They then formed a war party and asked the little boy to show them where it had happened. They followed the horse trail down off Fish Lake Mountain to Cedar Grove, near Burrville, and there they saw the massacred Indians.

They said, "Let's go chase the soldiers." The old man took the boy back and the others followed the trail for two days but couldn't catch up to them so they returned. The bones lay there for a long time until the white men took them. (As told by Koosharem 3 who heard this story from Walker Ammon, son of Chief Walker.)

Vera Charles, a daughter of Jimmy Timmican (Koosharem 3) said that Florence Kanosh, a full sister of Jimmy, told her that the Indian name for the massacre site is Tawhoo´kwechun or Toohoo´wutsekai meaning something like a "***Wail***" or "***War Cry from a Ridge.***" The informant said she couldn't translate it well. Gottfredson (page 159) gives the date of this massacre as July 18, 1865, and calls it "The Squaw Fight."

(The following version was told to Vera by Florence Kanosh): The Indians killed at the Burrville, Utah, massacre were from the Koosharem Band. When the soldiers attacked the Indians, a little old Indian man went out with a piece of paper

in his hand and showed it to the soldiers. He said, "We are not at war with you! We are at peace and have a treaty!" He was the first one killed. The soldiers cut his head off with a sword. There were no men in the camp, only old people, women, and children. My grandfather was a young boy and escaped and went and told the Indians at Fish Lake. They came and found the bodies of the Indians scattered around in the cedar trees.

Battle With White Men At Rocky Ford
Koosharem 3

Soldiers from up north came down to Sevier Valley to fight the Indians. The Indians laid an ambush for them at Rocky Ford near Sigurd, Utah. As the soldiers approached, the lead man spotted one of the Indians sleeping in a red blanket. This alerted the soldiers who then retreated. After this retreat they returned and attacked and the Indians retreated to the hillside. One Indian was shot through the leg just above the knee, not hitting the bone. The bullet went on through his leg killing his horse. Another Indian came back after him and pulled the wounded warrior up behind him on his horse and took him to safety.

These two, or two others, took refuge in a wash below the hill and were the closest to the soldiers. One white man who had no shirt on and who had painted his body would charge at them on his horse and tempt them by coming very close before retreating. One of the Indians had an old muzzle loader and the other had a bow. None of the Indians were well armed, some having bows and the others muzzle loaders.

These two men tried to hit the white man on horseback but couldn't. They both tried several times. One time he came close and almost hit them. The Indian with the muzzle loader then loaded it very careful with a quartz crystal. He painted his rifle with war paint and prayed. When the white man came close again, he fired and killed him. In this fight the Indians lost two horses and suffered one wounded man. They killed two white men.

The white men claim that they killed White Horse Chief[35] in this battle by shooting him in the belly from a great distance as he was standing on top of the hill. This is not true. All during the fight, they never got very close to each other, always firing from a distance. (As told by Koosharem 3 who heard this story from Walker Ammon, son of Chief Walker. Gottfredson, page 279, gives the date of this battle as the spring of 1868.)

Slaughter Of Indians At Circleville
Koosharem 3

There used to be a big old log house in Circleville, Utah, beside the road where it curves near where the potato cellars are. Years ago the white men at Circleville locked up in that house all the Indians who were living nearby and told them they were going to cut their throats. They began doing this by taking them outside one at a time and cutting their throats.

There were two young men inside who decided they were going to escape. One said to the other "We will have to dash through them and run just as they

[35] The Paiute name for White Horse Chief was Tosaw´ Kuvaw Neahv. It was Anglicized to Shenavegan.

open the door." They did this and ran through the white men who were gathered all around, some on horseback. They opened fire on these two Indians but couldn't hit them. They ran towards the cemetery on the hill to the north and as they were going over it, one of the pursuing white men on horseback shot one of the Indians in his side by his ribs but it was only a flesh wound. From there they ran up into the mountains and then the wounded Indian put some Indian medicine on his wound and wrapped it in part of his shirt. The white men didn't follow them far so from there they went on over to Parowan or Beaver. (As told by Koosharem 3 who heard this story from Walker Ammon, son of Chief Walker. Gottfredson, page 144, gives the date of this massacre as April 22, 1866.)

POISONING OF INDIANS AT MANTI
Koosharem 3

One time a man who lived over near Price and Emery, Utah, came down into the valley near Manti. He could see the Indian camp there with the tipis all around. He noticed that there was no smoke coming out of them. He also noticed that no one was around. The horses were out in the meadows grazing and were not fenced in. When he arrived at the camp no one was there, just blankets and belongings. There were not even any dogs to be found.

He went on up toward Nephi and told the Indians about it. They told him that the white men had given the Indians poisoned meat and flour and it had killed them all. The white men had come and got the bodies.[36] (As told by Koosharem 3 who heard this story from Walker Ammon, son of Chief Walker.)

MASSACRE AT SPRING VALLEY[37]
Indian Peak 24

One time some Indians from Parowan, Utah, and some Gosiutes were camping together in Spring Valley, near the present town of Baker, Nevada. The white man had killed some horses belonging to the ranchers and the Indians were

---

[36] This is probably the incident that started the Black Hawk War of 1865-67. Gottfredson states that "During the winter of 1864-65, a small band of Indians were camped near Gunnison, San Pete Co. It is said that they had contracted small-pox, and that many of them died. The Indians seemed to think that the white people were to blame in some way for this and were threatening to kill the whites and steal their horses and cattle. Arrangements were consequently made for a meeting between the Indians and the whites at Manti on the 9th of April, 1865, to talk over the matter." This meeting broke up in disharmony and the Black Hawk War followed. (Gottfredson 1919, p.128.)

[37] E. N. Wilson who wrote the book *The White Indian Boy* and who participated in this massacre says it happened just before the Civil War (Wilson 1919). A Nevada book gives the date as May 6, 1863, when 23 Indians were killed.

blamed. Soldiers then crept upon the encampment hoping to surprise it when an Indian spotted them and shouted the alarm. There wasn't enough time to prepare or flee. One Indian mother threw her blanket over her daughter and covered it with dirt hoping the soldiers wouldn't find her. The soldiers massacred everyone including women and children. Later on the girl lifted up the blanket and saw that everyone had been killed. She was old enough to know what happened and later tell other Indians about it.

Massacre At Spring Valley And Elsewhere
Eagle Valley 2

Juicy (Josey) Point (Poench?), wife of George Point, from Ibapah, Utah, was my uncle's wife. One time when she was just a little girl, soldiers dressed in blue uniforms, caps, and stripes, attacked her people in Spring Valley, Nevada (between Baker and Ely). They were camped by a tree and a ditch. The soldiers killed everyone, even ladies and little kids. They wanted the land. Juicy's mother told Juicy to run and hide. She ran down the ditch and up the hill to the top of the mountain. The mountain has a point on it where she ran. She always used to tell me this story when I visited her.

Soldiers also killed Indians near Milford, Utah, and some Shivwits also. Down south at Pahranagat Valley, Nevada, they killed lot of Indians camped in a circle with the Chief's house or tipi in the center. (For more information on this massacre see Paw Doogoo´nuntseng in Chapter 10, Homelands of the Old Ones.)

Indians Die Of Infected Clothing
Indian Peak 24

One time there used to be some Indians living in the cedar trees north of Lund, Utah. A wagon train of white people passed by, and dropped off some rags near the Indians that were infected with typhoid fever. They knew that they would pick them up. They did and died of this fever.

Indians Diminish At Eagle Valley
Indian Peak 24

The Indian population of Eagle Valley, Nevada, Pahranagat Band diminished because the government sent all the Indians off to school. Some went to school and returned but others were fed to pigs and some were given to cannibal-like Chinamen who ate them.[38]

---

[38] Such stories probably originated because of the numerous Indian children who died when they were sent off to school. In 1901 a measles epidemic at the Uintah School killed 17 of 65 pupils. Utes were complaining then that, "Their children always died when they went to school." (Conetah 1982, p. 131.)

PETE, THE MEDICINE MAN
Eagle Valley 2

I was raised by my grandfather Pete. He was a Shoshoni but spoke both Paiute and Shoshoni. We lived in Eagle Valley, Nevada, where I was born. I was raised in a tipi when I was young. It was the custom of Pete's people to live in tipis. The tipi was canvas but earlier he had one made of elk hides. When it rained nothing happened to the elk hides because they were stretched tight on the tipi poles (the hides didn't get stiff).

One time, Pete fought with the soldiers and the soldier's bullets were just like mud when they hit him and he couldn't be killed. (The sketch is from an old photograph of Pete.)

In those days many of the Indians were killed by the white man all over Indian country all because of a child that had become lost. The white man blamed the In-

dians and that's why they killed them. Later they found the child but it was too late.[39]

When Pete was about to die he and many others were at Indian Peak. Before he died there appeared lights in the sky and everyone saw them. I saw them also. The lights seemed to be caused by a mirror that kept coming closer, wobbling some way. As the lights approached, Pete died. When they buried Pete it began to rain but there was no clouds in the sky. He was buried at Indian peak. Pete died when I was an adult.

MOUNTAIN MEADOWS MASSACRE
Eagle Valley 2

Two Indians saw the Mormons kill the white people at Mountain Meadows. The Mormons killed everyone, even women and children. The Mormons asked these two Indians to help them pack up all the booty. The Mormons kept the horses and milk cows, and they told the two Indians that if they saw any round gold pieces (coins) lying on the ground the Indians were not to pick them up because they were poison and would kill them. However, the Mormons picked up all the coins and put them in a sack and kept them. They hid everything else in a tunnel in a round red place down there someplace. The two Indians didn't help the Mormons in the killings.

MOUNTAIN MEADOWS MASSACRE
Indian Peak 24

The Paiutes fought with soldiers near Iron Springs, Utah, before the Mountain Meadows massacre occurred. Isaac Hunkup was involved in that massacre. The Mormons told him and some other Indians that they could have all the loot except the round yellow stuff (gold). They said, "It was no good for the Indians."

INDIANS MASSACRED IN KANAB CREEK
Kaibab 25

The following two stories refer to a massacre mentioned by Gottfredson on page 255 of his book as happening in early January 1867. He says that Col. Pierce, James Andrus, and others were pursuing some Navajos who had made a raid on a horse herd in Washington County. According to the Paiutes, the white men never caught the Navajos but instead killed an innocent band of Paiutes. The

[39] Compare the similar versions of "The Sleeping Dairy Herder." This is probably the same story.

Paiute versions are as follows: My father and grandfather were killed by the white man at a place called "Bullrush" in Kanab Creek below Pipe Springs, Arizona. Among the dead were five brothers, one of them my grandfather. The trouble started when the Navajos killed a sheepherder named Whitmore. Tony's band lived in Zion and was on its way to the Colorado River to eat yunt (agave). A group of white men from St. George and other places found them in Kanab Creek and massacred all the unsuspecting innocent men. (Kaibab 25.)

A daughter of Kaibab informant 25 said that Tony Tillahash and his grandmother were the only survivors left by the white man. Both of Tony's parents were killed there. Tony's grandmother, being left an orphan, received the name Tuhduh´heets ***Orphan.*** This is how Tony got his anglicized last name of Tillahash. Evidently this name was given to her after the massacre. The general meaning the Tillahash family give this name is "The Beginning and the End of a Family." The name Tuhduh´heets comes from the root word tuh´du, meaning ***desolate, barren,*** or ***naked.*** The Tillahash family use this name in referring to the desolation of this family caused by the massacre. (From the genealogical records of LaVan Martineau.) (See Plate 2, page 104.)

INDIANS MASSACRED IN KANAB CREEK
Kaibab 4

After the Navajos had killed Whitmore they gave some of his clothes to one of the members of a band of Paiutes. When the white men found these clothes among the Paiutes they killed them all including men, women, and children. The only survivors were Georgey George's father and his brother who ran away northward and stayed with another band of Paiutes. These two escaped because they were young men and could run fast, while those who were killed were mostly old people.

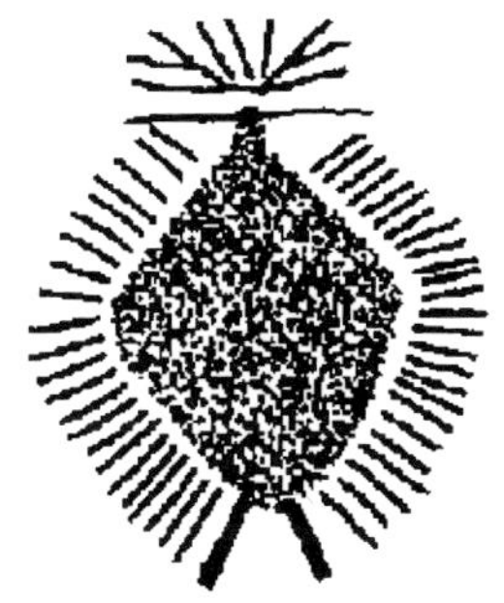

One of the white men in the killing party recognized one old lady who used to do his washing for him in St. George and he didn't want her killed. James Andrus, however, wanted to kill her. In order for this man to save her, he had to grab her and lift her up to the side of his horse and hold her weight by having her stand on his foot in the stirrup. James Andrus, meanwhile, was trying to grab her but this white man kept spinning his horse around to keep her out of the reach of Andrus. Andrus finally decided to let her live. The friendly white man gave her some money to try to make her feel better. She threw the money on the ground feeling that it was not worth the lives of her loved ones they had just killed. The money is still there. (From the genealogical records of LaVan Martineau.)

The Sleeping Dairy Herder
Shivwits 9

In St. George, Utah, there were two white boys who used to watch the milk cows down below town. One day they lay down and went to sleep. A white man saw them and thought they had been killed by the Indians because they were lying on the ground. This white man killed an Indian over this and was still fighting with others when the boys awoke. When they came to him he stopped fighting.

The Sleeping Dairy Herder
Kaibab 4

One time a white boy was taking a milk cow out to pasture south of St. George, Utah. On the way back he went to sleep in a haystack. When the white men missed the boy they thought the Indians had killed him so they rounded up all the Indians camped near the temple, where they used to camp, and locked them up in the Tithing House. They planned on killing them if the boy was found dead.

First they sent a man on horseback to look for the boy by the pasture and he found him sleeping in the haystack. They then turned the Indians loose. Kwetoos was one of those who were locked up. Erastus Snow said to him in Paiute, "Kwetoos, kawtch yaw´vawgai," ***Kwetoos, don't be afraid.***

The Sleeping Dairy Herder
Indian Peak 24

A white boy was playing by the river down at St. George and didn't return. The Mormons then blamed the Indians for stealing him and killed some. When the boy returned, the Mormons could say nothing.

James Andrus Shoots At Indians
Shivwits 5

Two Shivwits, were coming up to the Santa Clara River from Seveen´ Tooweep[40] to the south. James Andrus saw them and chased them over the two little hills near Bloomington, Utah. The two Indians hid behind a rock and shot his hat off with an arrow and he fled. They did this to scare him from killing any more

---

[40] Seveen Tooweep is the Shivwits name for a whitish area of land out on the Shivwits Plateau on the Arizona Strip. The word Sevee´ has to do with a white type of unidentified earth that is to be found in that area. It is from this word that the Shivwits take their name (See´veets). The word tooweep means ***earth*** or ***land***.

Indians. James Andrus used to kill Indians and was a very mean man towards them, while others were good. (Compiled from notes made on May 19, 1986, and another unrecorded date.)

Cessation Of Slave Trade Among The Shivwits
Shivwits 26

One time three Yootaw[41] Indians, two from Cedar City and one from Gunlock, seized two married women to sell as slaves. These women ran away down to the Grand Wash to their relatives and asked for protection. This was in Moapa Indian land and those Indians there had a meeting to decide what to do about the three men pursuing the women. They decided to kill them. They killed the two from Cedar and the other one from Gunlock ran away as fast as he could. He was chased and shot in the back with an arrow. He kept running and when he reached the Indians at Bunkerville he asked them to pull the arrow out. They refused saying, "This is what you wanted." This Indian couldn't pull the arrow out himself. The Indians used to say that an arrow in the back would keep working itself in. He went the rest of the way to Gunlock and died there from the wound.

The meeting the Indians held was at Fort Thomas on the Virgin River. The Shivwits, St. George, Moapa, and Kaibab Indians never got along with the Cedar Indians and others north of the St. George area. It was from the Cedar Indians that the Shivwits first got their guns in trade for children. (From the Martineau Paiute genealogical records.)

Toab
Shivwits 28

A long time back, the Shivwits and Cedar Indians had a disagreement over the Cedar Indians coming down and taking children to sell to the Mexicans. Toab and John Rice went to Silver Reef where they had a big meeting over this disagreement. They were almost to the point of war when Toab went and stood in the midst of the big fire they had built. He was not hurt and as he stood there in the fire his hair stood straight up caused by the wind of the ascending flames. This had the desired effect upon the Cedar Indians as it frightened them, and so trouble was averted. As this was going on John Rice was standing by ready to back up Toab.

[41] It is evident from this statement that the Shivwits considered the Indians north of them as Yootaw or Ute Indians.

Toab had the power to heal and would heal people but sometimes he would lose it when somebody was using witchcraft. Toab was also bulletproof and one time while he was healing someone he allowed himself to be shot in the chest with a muzzle loader to show his power. He just spit the bullet out.

Toab
Shivwits 26

When Toab killed George (Brig George's father) Toab ran over to Kaibab for protection from the Indians around St. George, Utah. He stayed there awhile but soon was turned in to the white man by someone and was sent to Fillmore, Utah, for trial.[42] He didn't kill Kwetoos as claimed by the whites. It was George he killed.

Powell's Men Killed
Shivwits 26

When the Indians around Parashont saw Powell's three men coming up Whitmore Wash they had a meeting with the surrounding groups to decide whether to kill them or not. Some of the young men wanted to kill white men and they were in favor of it. The young men said, "The white men come and kill our people so why can't we kill their people?" Chief Kweetoos replied, "If they did this then the white men would come and kill all the Indians." The young men decided to kill them anyway. They killed them near the head of Whitmore Wash.

My mother was a little girl when Powell came down the Colorado. When he first approached the Indians my grandfather told the children to run and hide as maybe he was going to come and take the girls. My grandfather said he had seen the rock that Powell's men wrote upon when the party split up and the three men were killed. Maybe no white man has seen this rock. (From Martineau genealogical records.)

[42] Utah prison records state that Toab served five days of his sentence of one year for stealing a horse (Grand Larceny). He entered the prison on Sept. 14, 1907, and was released Sept. 19, 1907. The horse belonged to a Mr. Ashby. The horse was old and turned loose to die. When Toab was going to take it he was told by another Indian that it wasn't Toab's horse but he said it was and took it. Washington County Pioneer stories tell of Toab killing Kwetoos. Bessie said it was George that he killed. If he went to prison for this then Utah State Prison records do not show it.

PAIUTES MASSACRED IN PAHRANAGAT VALLEY
Anglo

In the late 1800s sometime, before I was born, the Indians were camped at Ash Springs, Nevada. As they were eating breakfast the Mormons attacked them killing men, women, and children. Those who managed to escape fled south to Hells Half Acre where they were followed and finally all wiped out by the Mormons. One Indian lady stuffed her little boy down a crack and he was the only survivor. His name was Bill China. He was raised by an old white man who died a couple of years later and the Sharps finished raising the boy.

The Mormons attacked the Indians for no reason at all as they had all the land they wanted and weren't bothered at all by the Indians. The Mormons responsible came out of Utah heading for Mexico. The Mexican government didn't allow them across the border so they moved to Pahranagat Valley where they perpetrated this massacre.

The stories of who were responsible for all the murders in Pahranagat Valley are written down in Josh Butler's diary. The Mormons were always blaming the Indians for any murder of a white man but it was always a white man behind the killings. (As told by Blanche Davis,[43] Hiko, Nevada, to LaVan Martineau October 19,1976.)

THE GIANT SNAKE
Moapa

One time an Indian from Moapa went up into the mountains west of Moapa Valley, and later on returned by the same way. As he was coming down the trail he noticed a brown spot that was lying next to a little knoll beside the trail. He knew that he hadn't seen it on his way up so he was quite curious as to what it was. He circled around it and sneaked upon it until he was just above it. When he looked down off a point at it he saw that it was a giant snake all coiled up with its head lying across its tail. He decided to try to kill it so he aimed his arrow at the back of its neck and shot. The arrow hit true and the snake began to flop all over the place making a great deal of dust. The Indian got scared and ran. When he got home he told the other Indians about it. They didn't believe him, so he told them to go and see for themselves. They went and found the dead snake. You could see the bones there for a long time. (As told by Kaibab 4 who heard this story from Charley Steve, Moapa.)

---

[43] Blanch Davis was a Fergeson and married into the George Davis family. She was born in about 1900 and is an Anglo.

WILLY BOY
Chemehuevi 41

I was related to Willy Boy. The stories that the white man tell about his death are wrong. He was not killed by the Sheriff's posse. The posse couldn't catch him so to save face they burnt some animal bones in a thicket and said it was Willy Boy. Willy Boy stayed in the Reno area for a long time and died an old man in a hospital in Las Vegas, Nevada.

PLATE 1

Photograph and identifications given to me by Edrick Bushhead. Merricats standing in back, Captain Pete sitting on left, and brother to Tom Parashont on the right. Palmer lists them from left to right as: Y-puts, William's brother, and Joe.

CHAPTER 3

THE WAYS OF THE OLD ONES

The envious assume the position of curator and censor.

The following quotations are copied from hand-written pencil notes I made beginning in the mid-1940s. These notes were made for my own use to help me remember the material with no thought of publication in mind at the time. In many cases I wrote the informant's name down, but often I didn't think to do this. I was in my teens when many of these notes were made and had no training whatsoever on how to record ethnographic material. I just wrote it down as I heard it without adding, taking from, or analyzing the material. I wanted to keep it as pure as possible as it came from the Indians.

Personally, I feel fortunate that I lacked formal training. Consequently I recorded all that I heard and didn't omit certain points that are avoided by some who ignore the areas of Indian culture that are sensitive to them. My notes compiled from the mid-'40s until about the mid-'60s were not obtained, in most cases, from asking questions. They were just comments I heard in passing and noted so as not to forget them. In later years as I began to see the gaps left in many modern records, I sought answers to some of the points avoided by modern scholars.

When I did question informants I never put words into their mouths as is so often done. I also didn't change any essential wording. If the informant used the word "heaven" then I quote it. That doesn't mean that I, nor the informant, equated that heaven with the white man's heaven. If the informant spoke English I used his English words. If he spoke Paiute then I used the nearest English equivalents. As I spent most of my life from childhood on living with and married to Paiutes, all the material came to me naturally over many years.

In the following notes I do include informant's names, if I recorded them, so that the material can be assigned to the band that I obtained it from. However, it should never be thought that that belief belonged solely to that Paiute band. Most of the following beliefs were held in common by most or *all* Southern Paiute bands.

The majority of the following information I heard repeated dozens of times among different bands. It is common to all bands to know if another band believes a little different. Such differences were a common topic of interest and sometimes a form of joking. Therefore, when differences did occur they were common knowledge. These differences will be noted in this work. If I do not note that the information is peculiar to one band then it should be assumed that the beliefs were common to all, at least in more recent times. However, I do allow for exceptions to this with some of the information that isn't that well known. For this reason I try to list the band name for most of my notes so that it will be available for future evaluation.

The number listed at the end of each note is the number assigned to each original hand-written note as I wrote them down in numerical order from the late 1940s until the time of this computerized writing (1990). In this compilation the notes have been sorted into alphabetical order with a few lumped together out of order, if by the same informant, or sometimes, if on the same subject. My original numbers are retained for future comparison with my original hand-written notes and to show the sequence in which much of the information was written down. If no number occurs at the end of a note that means they were compiled from some of my other hand-written files, or that they were recorded after my material was computerized in alphabetical order rather than numerical.

The following notes cover a large range of Paiute lore not covered in the other sections of this book:

Notes

ABSENTEE MESSAGES The Indians used to hang a bundle of sage from their wickiups or tipis so that visitors could tell how long they had been gone by looking at how dry the sage was. If it hung there until it fell it meant the owners were not coming back. Shivwits 9, note 130.

ACUPUNCTURE One Gosiute, who said he was not an Indian doctor, used a needle to make two punctures on each side of a little boy's head near the temple. He also made three punctures on the bridge of the nose squarely between the eyes. He let these punctures bleed. The blood was black when he first did this. This procedure was to help make the little boy well who had a bad cold. I believe the punctures bled until the blood became red. This boy might have had a headache too. Eagle Valley 2, note 41.

ARROWHEAD COLLECTING Indians didn't like to pick up arrowheads they found on the ground because some had been poisoned in the past and if cut by them they could die. Indian Peak 24, note 169.

ARROWHEAD POISON The blue thing on a rabbit's liver combined with something else was used for arrowhead poison. Arrowheads were also baked in something, maybe a plant, to poison it. Kaibab 4, note 139.

BABIES AND CAVES It isn't good to take a baby near a cave where ancient people (Tookoov?) might have lived. Helen Lehi's brother was taken near such a place and he became sick and died. Koosharem 10, note 109.

BABIES AND MIRRORS It isn't considered right to let a young baby look into a mirror. Note 104.

BABIES AND PHOTOGRAPHS It isn't considered right to take a picture of a young baby. Note 105.

BABIES CRYING AT NIGHT If you let a baby cry at home during the night, or at a strange place, a spirit of a dead person (unoopeets) will have intercourse with the baby. You can tell this has happened because foam will come out of the eyes, ears, nose, and mouth of the baby. Koosharem 10, note 106.

BABIES WITH CLOGGED THROATS When a baby or child is weak, not hungry, not playful, cries a lot, sleeps too much, coughs a lot, has a red face, vomits, or any of the above combined, the baby is choking. There is a lump of mucus deep inside of the baby's throat that causes this. To make the baby well, wash your hands and leave your index finger wet. Then stick your index finger down the baby's throat as for as it will go depressing this lump. This sometimes has to be done a couple of times depending on how hard the lump is. Be temperate at doing this. This practice is called Munuh´kee. Eagle Valley 2, note 61.

BABY GUM RUBBING When a baby is first born you should rub its gums so it will have good teeth when it gets older. If you don't, its teeth will be bad. Shivwits 30, note 83.

BABY HAIR CUTTING Shortly after a baby is born you should cut its hair short leaving it about a quarter to a half inch long. This will help the baby to have longer hair when it gets older. Indian Peak 31, note 70.

BABY TOSSING It isn't considered right to toss a young baby up into the air when you are playing with it at night. Eagle Valley 2, note 78.

BABY'S SKULL CRACK When a baby is sick, the crack or soft spot on the top front of its skull will be depressed. When the baby is well the crack will be flush with the rest of the head. Eagle Valley 2, note 60.

BAKER MOUNTAIN Baker Mountain is a medicine mountain that can't be ascended. Indian Peak 1, note 42.

BEDROCK MORTARS The water found in bedrock mortar holes was used by medicine men. Kaibab 33, note 209b.

BIRD COLORS The beautiful colors of the birds are the beadwork that the birds had on their buckskin clothes when they were human. The Indians get their colors for their beadwork from the colors of the birds. Koosharem 10, notes 23-24.

BIRDS AND ANIMALS AS HUMANS Before the Indians were here, the birds and animals were human and could talk. Koosharem 10, note 39.

BIRTH The manner that a Paiute woman in Utah would deliver a child was to place two upright forked poles in the ground three or four feet apart and then to lay a strong pole across the forks. Each time the woman had a labor pain she would grasp the horizontal pole with both hands and place some of her weight on it.

The Moapa Band had a different way of delivering a child. An assistant would stand behind the woman who was about to deliver. Each time the pregnant woman had a labor pain she would raise both of her arms and clasp her hands around the back of the neck of the assistant standing behind her suspending some of her weight on that person. The helper would then reach around her waist and press down on her stomach. The Paiutes living around Willow Springs and Navajo Mountain, Arizona, have a special house called Toowu Kawnee ***Birth House***. A rope is suspended from the ceiling for the woman to pull on. Shivwits 8.

BIRTH AND MENSTRUATION RULES Don't touch your face or hair when you are on your period. Drink hot water after giving birth. Shivwits 9, note 102.

BIRTH SPACING The Paiutes used to have their children spaced a few years apart. Indian Peak 1, and Shivwits 34, note 90.

BIRTHING PRACTICE (Toomu´kunt) Paiutes dug out a shallow pit the length of a woman's body and then lined the length and width of it with hot rocks. Then they covered the rocks with a layer of sand and then a blanket. The woman would lie on this for six days if she had given birth to a girl, and five days for a boy. The purpose was to stimulate good blood circulation thus cleaning out the body and making the woman healthy. The Paiute word for this is Toomu´kunt. That's where the name Timmican comes from. (Koosharem 3 note 100. Mable Yellowjacket, born at Minersville, Utah, and a daughter of Coal Creek John, said her band did the same thing.)

BIRTHING RULES After you have a baby, don't touch your face or hair. Drink warm water for one month. Northern Ute and Shivwits 35, note 101.

BIRTHING RULES A woman is not supposed to eat meat for one month after giving birth, and the husband for two weeks. Cedar City 37, note 110.

BIRTHING RULES A woman shouldn't eat meat and should only drink warm liquids after childbirth. After the birth she should wrap her belly tight to keep it from remaining large. The Indian Peak people also practiced toomukunt as

did the Koosharem Band (the woman lying on sand-covered heated rocks after birth). Eagle Valley 2, note 151.

BIRTHING RULES Comb your hair with a stick when your wife has a baby. Use greasewood (tonov) for scratching your head. Note 4.

BIRTHING RULES From the time a baby is born until the navel cord falls off the father should do the following: He should not eat meat or his teeth will decay. He should not touch his face with his hands or it will become wrinkled earlier in life. He should scratch his head with a stick, and not his hands, or his hair will become gray sooner. Eagle Valley 2, note 55.

BIRTHING RULES When a baby is born the father and mother should not wash their faces with their hands until the navel cord comes off. If they do their face will become wrinkled and they will get old quick. Note 72. When the navel cord falls off the father should then eat meat with some sage leaves (sawngwuv) and chew them very fine. Koosharem 10, note 56.

BIRTHING RULES When your first baby is born you should walk a long ways. You should shoot a deer, and make sure you don't miss or you won't be able to kill any the rest of your life. When you shoot the deer, just jump over it, leave it lying there, and send someone back to get it. Don't touch the deer! The reason for doing this is so that you will not look old soon. Indian Peak 1, note 89.

BIRTHING RULES When your wife has a baby do not be lazy. A husband should never ask anybody to do anything for him; he should do it himself! He shouldn't eat anything that has grease in it. He should get up early and take a cold swim for one month. Indian Peak 21, note 6.

BLOOD LETTING Sometimes, when a person's arm ached, the Gosiutes would cut the blood vein lengthwise in the armpit of both arms and then let a lot of blood run out. This made the arms feel better. I'm not sure if this was practiced by all the tribe or just by some. A tourniquet was used when they did this. Eagle Valley 2, note 40.

BLOOD LETTING When a person has a headache, cut a place in the forehead near the hairline and let the dark blood drain out until the blood becomes lighter. This is for curing headaches. Use an obsidian flake and make the cut small. Note 74.

BODY HAIR GROWTH When a baby is about one week old, dampen some Indian paint (ochre) and then rub it on the baby's arms, chest, and legs. Rub it in such a manner that it will roll. This will roll all the fine hair off the baby. If you do this the baby will not be hairy when it is full grown. My mother, Florence, Kanosh, did this to me and now I have no body hair. Koosharem 22, note 97.

BONE MEDICINE Indians used to take one to three of the finger bones of a dead person and use them as "Bone Medicine." They used these bones for four purposes: women, cards, hand game, and to kill. The bones would sometimes talk to the one that took them and require the life of his children. The more of his children he lost the more power he would gain. When the bones wanted a child and the child got sick, the bones owner was helpless to cure the child unless he threw the bones away. Indian Peak 24, note 164.

BREATH QUIVERING When a person breathes once in a while in a quivering manner, as though he had just finished crying, it means that someone is going to die. Koosharem 32, note 84.

BULLETPROOF POWER Kenneth Charles' grandfather used to be bulletproof. You could shoot a bullet at him and he would just cough it up. Shivwits 5, note 216.

BURIALS AND THE POSSESSIONS OF THE DEAD In the old days when an Indian died, the family would leave the house that he died in and move someplace else and make a new house. They would bury him anyplace in the rocks. There was not any one particular place of burial (graveyard). All the belongings of the deceased would be destroyed, grinding stones broken, belongings burnt, and animals killed. Shivwits 38, note 20.

BURIALS The Shivwits would bury their dead in a cave, under a rock, or in a crack with the head to the west but looking east. They did this so that when Toovuts returns to resurrect the dead they can rise up and meet him. If they are buried with the head looking west they will just stay there when he comes. Shivwits 5, note 237.

BURIALS A place would be found in the rocks and cleaned out such as a cave, crevice, or hole. The body with possessions would be placed in and covered with rocks. The body was not brought there until the place was found and cleaned out. Kaibab 4, note 125.

BURIALS ON SCAFFOLDS The Paiutes used to bury their dead off the ground on a scaffold. The reason for this is because they believe the dead will come alive again. Koosharem 32, note 17.

CAMP LOCATIONS NEAR CEDAR CITY The Cedar City Indians used to live in Cedar Valley about a mile west of the old steam electric plant west of Cedar City, Utah. The railroad later came through the middle of their land so then they moved to where the ball parks are now on the east side of Cedar City. From there they moved to their present location just on the north side of town. Indian Peak 24.

CATARACT CURE Lizard tails were used to sand off the blue-grey film from some blind people's eyes to restore their sight. Kaibab, note 119.

CAVE IN THE MORMON MOUNTAINS There is a cave in the Mormon Mountains in Nevada that the Moapa Indians tell about. This cave is like Lehman's Cave in Nevada. It goes way down under the ground. Shivwits 5, note 190.

CAVE OF THE CRY SONGS There is a sacred cave in the mountain east of Las Vegas, Nevada. Coyote stopped there as he passed through carrying the sack containing all the Indian tribes (see the legend of the "Sack of all Tribes"). The Indians say this cave has some long tracks in it. This is where the Indians used

to go when they wanted to learn some kind of songs. They would pray there, and you weren't supposed to get scared when that man (Spirit) would come around at night. Dan Bullets and a Meyers guy went there and said that cave is all ruined now. Shivwits 5, note 181.

CAVES Johnny Domingo from Las Vegas used to tell me many stories about different caves in that area. In one cave a person could learn the cry songs. There was also a cave that two brothers approached in the rain. One brother had been warned by his father not to go in such caves so he didn't want to enter even to get out of the rain. His brother, however, talked him into it and they spent the night there. In the morning they emerged as two mountain sheep. Johnny Domingo also said that the hill they now live on in Las Vegas used to be a lookout station or a place to pray towards Sunrise Mountain; I don't remember that well. Indian Peak 24, note 233.

CHERT SOURCE (A chert quarry site north of Cedar City was pointed out to me from the highway by Carl Jake. This site is on the vertical white outcrop on the west face of the mountain just north of Fiddlers Canyon. Chert may be found for a considerable distance along this outcrop and also on the alluvial fan at the foot of this mountain.) Note 242.

COUSINS A cousin is considered as a brother or sister. Note 2.

COYOTE AS GOD Toovuts tried to make everything good but Coyote took everything away from him and made it as it is today, so therefore he is our God. When the world ends, Toovuts will be our God. Toovuts wanted to make children come out of the finger by pricking it and then flipping it, but coyote ruined that because he wanted to lie between a woman's legs, so that's how it is today. Coyote only had daughters, that's why he is called Yohovuhts because he was nasty. Kanosh.

COYOTE HIDES Red coyote hides are worshiped. I know why, but I won't tell. Ask a Navajo, he knows. Eagle Valley 2, note 171.

COYOTE ONCE HUMAN Coyote used to be human, but he would howl and scratch like a coyote so that's how he turned into a coyote. Shivwits 5, note 225.

COYOTE To me, the word Soonungwuv (Coyote) sounds as if it means a person that everyone laughs at; a kind of a joker. The word soonuv just refers to a regular coyote. Koosharem 20, note 251.

COYOTE'S HOUSE AT RUSH LAKE The stone circle on top of the highest section of the hill just east of Rush Lake is Soonungwuv's house.[44] Indian Peak 1.

COYOTE'S RACE NEAR LUND One time Coyote had a race through the Escalante Desert near Lund, Utah, up to where Salt Lake is. Indian Peak 1, note 85.

---

[44] This house was not Toovuts' house as stated by William R. Palmer. Carl Jake used both words, God and Soonungwuv but not Toovuts.

CRADLEBOARD CARE Turn a baby cradle over so a ghost will not sleep in it. Shivwits 9, note 90b.

CRADLEBOARD CARE When a baby's cradleboard is not in use it should be covered or turned over to keep bad ghosts out of it. Eagle Valley 2, note 108.

CRADLEBOARD CARE When a baby cries in its cradle and doesn't like to stay there, it means a ghost has been lying in it. Koosharem 10, note 82.

DEATH AND A RIVER CROSSING When a person dies, his spirit leaves his body and goes up into the sky. There's a hole in the sky that his spirit then passes through. He then goes some distance and comes to a wide river like the Colorado River. He has to jump over it. If he has pierced ears it will help him to jump over and get to heaven. Cedar City 14, note 96.

DEATH I've heard some of the old Indians say that death is like stepping over a line. There is really no difference between life and death. Indian Peak 24, note 168.

DEER MIGRATION In the old days there never used to be any deer on the Kaibab Mountains in the winter. In the spring they would migrate down from the north. Kaibab 4.

DESTROYER The Paiutes say that the reason that so many Indians died off when the white man came was that the Destroyer was traveling all over this land killing all the Indians. Some say that as he traveled across the land some of the people could hear him screaming. Others say that some of their grandparents saw this ghost and were nearly killed by him. Maggie Dick, Kaibab, note 95.

DR. FARROW Dr. Farrow used to be the Shivwits Indian Agent. His Indian name was Moyyoontch ***Skinny Legs***. He was responsible for giving Will Rogers his name. Shivwits 5, note 222.

EAR RINGING When you hear a ringing in your ear it is a dead relative talking to you. You should answer him by saying in substance, "I'm fine and still here, but sometime I'll come where you are." Shivwits 9, note 126.

ECHOS Unoo´peets (***Ghost***) was locked in a cave. That's why we have the echo; Ghost is answering back. Note 247.

FIRST KILL The first deer that a young man kills should be left where it fell to insure better hunting in the future. Note 3.

FIRST KILL You are not supposed to give any meat (from your first kill?) to the dogs or cats or you will not be able to kill any more. Koosharem 32, note 98.

FIRST-BORN When you have your first baby you should give away one of the

best things you own. This will help you get into the habit so you will be generous and not selfish. Koosharem 10, note 99.

FIRST-BORN When you have your first boy you should give away something that you value. Shivwits 35, note 152.

FISH LAKE'S ROCK BANK There is a rock and dirt bank heaped up against the west side of Fish Lake for much of its length. This was made by Soonungwuv. Koosharem 3, note 54.

FLYING SERPENT A big snake landed on Mount Nebo. It was a very big snake! The snake just rested there then flew away again. A person will go crazy when he goes on this mountain. This snake was flying north. It first landed on a mountain northeast of Paragoonah and then it landed on Mount Nebo. Indian Peak 1, note 43.

FLYING SERPENT AND PIKE'S PEAK Bert Craig of Kaibab said that a flying serpent landed on top of "Pike's Peak"[45] and left his poison there. If anyone climbs to the top he will become dizzy because of the poison and maybe die. Kaibab 4, note 137.

FLYING SERPENTS Flying snakes used to fly overhead and you could hear them rattle for a long way. They would land on the highest mountains. Kaibab 4.

FLYING SERPENTS Isaac Hunkup told me that there used to be many flying serpents somewhere out past the Enterprise, Utah area. They would fly through the air and bite you. Cedar City 37.

FOOT RACE TO INDIAN PEAK Two Indians once made a wager that they could run from Cedar City, Utah, to Indian Peak and reach there before the sun came up. They told those who didn't believe this to send someone to Indian Peak to check on the runners when they arrived. The runners won the bet. Indian Peak 1, note 142.

FROZEN FEET When you get your feet frozen they won't heal until the last snow on the mountain tops melt. Kaibab 4, note 122.

---

[45] Pike's Peak is in Colorado and Bert either heard this story from a Ute or might have been referring to Mount Nebo near Nephi, Utah, where there is a similar story. This story is probably an Indian attempt at explaining the dizziness experienced on high mountain tops where the oxygen becomes thinner, and would probably apply to all high mountain peaks.

GHOST DETECTING If a ghost is in the house a baby will be scared of it and won't go to sleep but will cry and cry. Koosharem 32, note 88.

GIANT ANTS My mother, Minnie Jake, used to tell me about some ants about as big as a dog near Mesquite, Nevada, that used to eat large animals. You could see a pile of large bones they left behind. Indian Peak 24, note 232.

GOD OF THE WHITE MAN The white man's God is very smart; that's why the white men are smart. The Indians' God is not so smart and that's why the Indians are the same way. Koosharem 10, note 38.

GOLD IN PINE VALLEY MOUNTAINS There is gold in Pine Valley Mountains someplace. I know about where it is. Cedar City 39, note 176.

GOLD ON MONROE MOUNTAIN There is gold and some mountain sheep horns in a cave about half-way up the face of Monroe Mountain just southeast of Annabella, Utah. Koosharem 3, note 175.

GOLD ON SAWTOOTH PEAK There used to be gold on Sawtooth Peak (a peak about 60 miles north of Wah Wah Springs). Years ago a Mexican found an Indian with a gold necklace who led him to the gold there. Indian Peak 1, note 50.

GUN MEDICINE MAN Toompeoo Poowu´hunt. A Gun Medicine Man could draw a bullet out of a wound with his mouth. Kaibab 4, note 133.

HEAT TREATING ROCKS FOR ARROWHEADS I used to watch the old Indians down at Five-Mile on the Shivwits Reservation make arrowheads. I was a little boy then. They were burning some type of black rock. I don't know how they did it. They hit the rock with some kind of pointed stone. Some of the heated stones changed to the color red. Shivwits 5, note 202.

HEAVEN When you die you go up to heaven. There is a man sitting there asking, "Where are you going?" and "Are you dead or not?" You have to say "Yes!" If you say "No" then he sends your spirit back to your body lying there. If you say "Yes" then that man lets you pass through some kind of door. That's where all the Paiutes, grandmothers, grandfathers, and all the old-timers go, up there. Shivwits 5, note 182.

HOPIS MOVE SOUTH A long time ago the Hopis used to live in this country but they couldn't get things to grow well so they moved south to where they now live. Kaibab 4 and 18.

HORNED INDIANS Maggie Dick says that her grandmother told her that some Indians had short horns. Kaibab 4, note 134.

HORSE CARE A horse will get poor when he gets cockleburs in his mane and tail. To prevent this cut the mane and tail short. Indian Peak, note 5.

HORSE CARE There is a little white thing in the corner of a horse's eye that causes some horses to jump at the slightest movement at his side. If you cut that white thing out the horse will no longer be jumpy. Indian Peak 1.

HORSE RESTRICTIONS A woman is not supposed to ride a man's horse as she will ruin it. Indian Peak 1, note 111.

HUNTING ON SUNDAY It's considered bad luck to go hunting on Sunday; you might get hurt. Note 11.

HUNTING RULE Do not comb your hair when you go hunting. Note 4.

HUNTING TRIPS While hunting overnight put on red paint (oampee) and burn green cedar leaves slowly. This will ward off evil spirits. Note 10.

INDIAN FREEZING ON PARKER MOUNTAIN The old Indian trail from Loa, Utah, to the Koosharem Reservation descended off Parker Mountain just south of Highway 24 near the Windy Ridge Reservoir. One time, long ago during the winter some Indians were descending off this mountain. One of the Indians had not been wearing a blanket during the entire trip and was making fun of the other Indians who were wearing blankets. He said, "I'm a Ute, not a Paiute and don't need to wear blankets like you."[46] On the way down off Parker Mountain he froze to death and his bones could be seen along the trail for many years. Koosharem 7.

INDIAN KILLING An Indian once killed another Indian, or white man, at the old stage stop just north of Lund, Utah. He then ran over the hills to the west and was never caught. He lived a long time after that. Indian Peak 31, note 161.

INDIAN TEMPLE Jimmy Timmican of Koosharem once told Cedar City informant 37 that the big mountain that looks like a temple southeast of the visitor's center at Capitol Reef was once a real temple. God turned the temple to stone when the Indians started doing bad. At the base of this stone temple there was a medicine rock used for healing. A long time ago there used to be many bows, arrows, pottery, and other things lying around this rock as offerings made by people once healed by it. Jimmy looked for this rock once but could never find it. Cedar City 37, note 157.

INDIAN TRAIL AT GLENWOOD The old Indian trail from Glenwood, Utah, to Koosharem cut through the pass just east of Glenwood. This trail goes through the lowest pass southeast of mile post 7 on highway 119. Koosharem 3, note 199.

JIMMY TIMMICAN'S VISION When I was a young man, I was riding horseback with some older Indians and we camped on the east rim of the Koosharem Valley near where the road to Fish Lake, Utah, reaches the top. While I was sleeping something woke me up. I jumped up quickly and could see the south end of the Koosharem Valley burning. The fire was coming towards me and getting closer and closer. As it got close I could see a white man leading a large group of Indians. They swerved from their course up the valley and they came over to where I was standing on the mountain rim. The leader was carrying a book in his hand and he told me I would have to learn to read it someday if I was to be saved from the burning that was to follow him. He then left and continued north with the Indians that were following him. This was a real event. I wasn't dreaming. I actually saw this like the real thing.

---

[46] In those days it is questionable as to whether the Indians of Wayne County considered themselves Paiutes so this term might have been the informant's wording. Today the Koosharem Band is termed Paiute due to their isolation from the Utes on the U & O Reservation, and also due to their being lumped within the Paiute Indian Tribe of Utah.

JOSEPHINE MINE My father, Jimmy Timmican, told me that long ago the Spaniards came to Fish Lake and found a gold mine there (now called the Josephine Mine). They enslaved the Indians and made them work the mine. When they were through they killed all the Indians so they wouldn't tell others where the mine was. They also sealed up the mine by caving in the entrance so no one else could find it and then they left. My father knew where the mine was. Koosharem 20, note 208.

KIMBERLY PEAK'S LARGE CAVE One time a man was hunting deer on Mount Kimberly and followed one into this little opening on the mountain. When he got inside a long distance, it opened up and was huge inside, just like the world outside. Koosharem 7.

KNIFE PRECAUTIONS You should not stick the point of a knife into any meat or food, or stir your food with it. If you do this some evil Indian doctor can some way cause you to be sick. Note 71.

KOOSHAREM INDIANS THAT MOVED TO THE UINTAH AND OURAY RESERVATION Jimmy Timmican gave me the following list of names of Indians from his band that moved to the Uintah and Ouray Reservation. He didn't say when. From what I can find out some of them left about 1900.

Dick and John Kwib, two brothers (related to Lester Kurrip a Ute).

Nick. He died at Bridgeland, Utah.

Andrew Greyhead.

Old Man Greyhead and his first wife. One wife was called Peuv'.

Shawkom (***White Rabbit***) and Charlie. They married two sisters of Duchesne. Shawkom died at Duchesne, and Charlie died near Gusher, Utah.

LAME MAN OF KOOSHAREM A long time ago there was a short man who lived at Koosharem. His name was Sawngkuhd´ (***Lame***). He was acquired by trade when he was a child and, because of disobedience, his leg was broken when he was hit on the leg with a stick. He limped afterward and that's how he got his name. Koosharem 7, note 195.

LEAD MINE NEAR WASHINGTON The Indians used to get lead for their old rifles just below the old Washington City dump. There used to be a horse trail down there. Foster Charles or someone went looking for it one time but couldn't find it. Shivwits 5, note 218.

LEGEND ENDINGS All legends are ended with the phrase "Yoom´pukoam kweyoon." It means ***something back behind the head***.[47] At Kanosh they end it with a different phrase and say "Kawngkwus´evait." signifying ***some kind of tale,*** I guess. Shivwits 5, note 188.

LEGEND OF KWETOOS The story that Stewart Snow used to tell about the giant Kwetoos sounded like a joke to me that isn't true. There are many stories like that. They have no meaning. One is about the lizard. Indians had jokes like that a long time ago. Shivwits 5, note 183.

---

[47] The word "kweyoon" is the back of your head where the hair swirls to the center on the scalp.

LEGEND SIMILARITY Southern Paiute and Shoshoni legends from Idaho are the same. Shoshoni.

LEGEND TELLING Do not tell legends in the summertime or a snake will bite you and do not tell more than one legend a night or there will be a long winter. Note 7.

LEGEND TELLING If you tell legends in the summertime it will snow. Koosharem 32, note 81.

LEGEND TELLING Paiutes didn't start telling legends until the fall during the pinenut harvest. Shivwits 29, note 250.

LEGEND TELLING TO THE WHITES The Old People told me that you were not supposed to tell legends to the white people because it cost lots to tell them. Shivwits 5, note 187.

LEHMAN'S CAVE The Gosiutes say that there is a little hole inside Lehman's Cave, Nevada. A man is not supposed to go in it or a woman will get him. Also a woman isn't supposed to go in it or a man will get her. Shivwits 5, note 230.

LIGHTNING AND CRYSTALS Lightning strikes the ground and then goes through the ground and back out to the surface. Sometimes it leaves a crystal. If someone takes the crystal for medicine he must be brave because lightning will strike all around the crystal. Kaibab 4, note 132.

LIGHTNING AND CRYSTALS There is a hill on the Shivwits Reservation where lightning always strikes. It is the long hill that runs north and south directly east of Highway 91 on the south boundary of the Shivwits Reservation. Everyone used to be warned not to go up there. When lightning hits, it leaves a long glassy thing (crystal) about the size of a 30-30 bullet. It only stays a little while after a lightning strike and then disappears. Brig George (Shivwits) once had one of these. James Yellowjacket told him to get rid of it as lightning was always hitting around Five-Mile where they stayed. Brig George hid it someplace in Five-Mile and now that's why lightning and thunder hangs around there. Shivwits 5, note 226.

LIGHTNING AND MIRRORS During a storm, when there is any lightning, you should cover any knives and mirrors that are laying around so the lightning won't strike them. Koosharem 10, note 91.

LIGHTNING AND MIRRORS In a lightning storm you should cover mirrors as they attract lightning. Lightning rod sticks are made out of mountain mahogany and painted with war paint. They are then placed on or near a house to protect it. Cedar City 36, note 86b.

LITTLE CREEK CANYON When I was a kid my father used to take me up Little Creek Canyon just north of Paragoonah, Utah; this is the way we went to Richfield. At the mouth of this canyon there is a big rock with vagina symbols pecked on it and one natural-looking depression resembling one. This canyon is called Wuhump´ee Ooweng´wu ***Vagina Canyon*** because of the symbols on this rock.

My father, Carl Jake, said that there are many big snakes living up this canyon. They were as big around as you could wrap your arms around. You

could also see their tracks on each side of the canyon. These tracks resembled a groove made when a big rock slides down a hill. These snakes were very dangerous so whenever any men went up this canyon they had to go very early in the morning when the snakes were still drowsy and weak from the coolness. The only way you could travel safely up this canyon during the day was to have a woman along with you who was on her period. This made the snakes weak and you could pass through them safely. That is why this canyon is called Vagina Canyon. There are no more snakes there now.

There were also many big snakes out by New Castle and it was dangerous to pass through there. They would stick their heads up over the trees and you could see their bodies glistening in the sun from a long way off. These snakes could inhale air and blow themselves up like a balloon and then fly as a blimp does. Even a rattlesnake can do this because they have been found up high on a cliff where they couldn't possibly have crawled; they had to fly there. Indian Peak 24, note 184.

LYCANTROPHY It is said that some Navajos turn into coyotes and that they rob the graves. One Navajo said he was with a group of them at one time in a hogan. The others were eating a dead body. He got away from them and told others about this. One little Navajo/Paiute baby buried in Richfield was stolen by one of these Navajos. One or two of the Richfield Indians saw a little hole on top of the baby's grave and dog tracks around it. Koosharem 10, note 62.

MEDICINE MEN Some medicine men witch the wrong person. If he is discovered he can recall his curse. If he doesn't he may die by retaliation from another medicine man. Kaibab Indians are noted for their powerful medicine men. Utes seldom journeyed among them because of this. Kaibab 4, notes 116-118.

MEDICINE ROCK AT MOUNTAIN SPRINGS There is a medicine rock near Mountain Springs west of Lund, Utah. If you're sick and lay on the rock it will make you better. Indian Peak 21.

MEDICINE ROCK IN STEPHENS CANYON There is a big rock on the right side of the trail, near the top of the big cedar-covered mountain, directly up the canyon behind the Cedar City Indian Village. This rock has a hole in it big enough to stick your head in. When someone had a headache and wanted it to go away he stuck his head in the hole in this rock. This is what my father, Carl Jake, told me. Indian Peak 24, note 165.

MEDICINE ROCK NEAR GUNLOCK, UTAH There used to be a little red rock where the gravel pit is now just west of the second bridge north of Gunlock, Utah. The Indians used to stop there long ago and leave a penny or some money by this rock and pray to it and tell it what was wrong with them. The rock would then heal them. This rock was destroyed when the gravel pit was put there. Girls were not supposed to go near this rock. Shivwits 5, note 223.

MEDICINE ROCK ON COAL CREEK There used to be a medicine rock by Coal Creek just south of the present Indian village. It is now covered. Indian Peak 21.

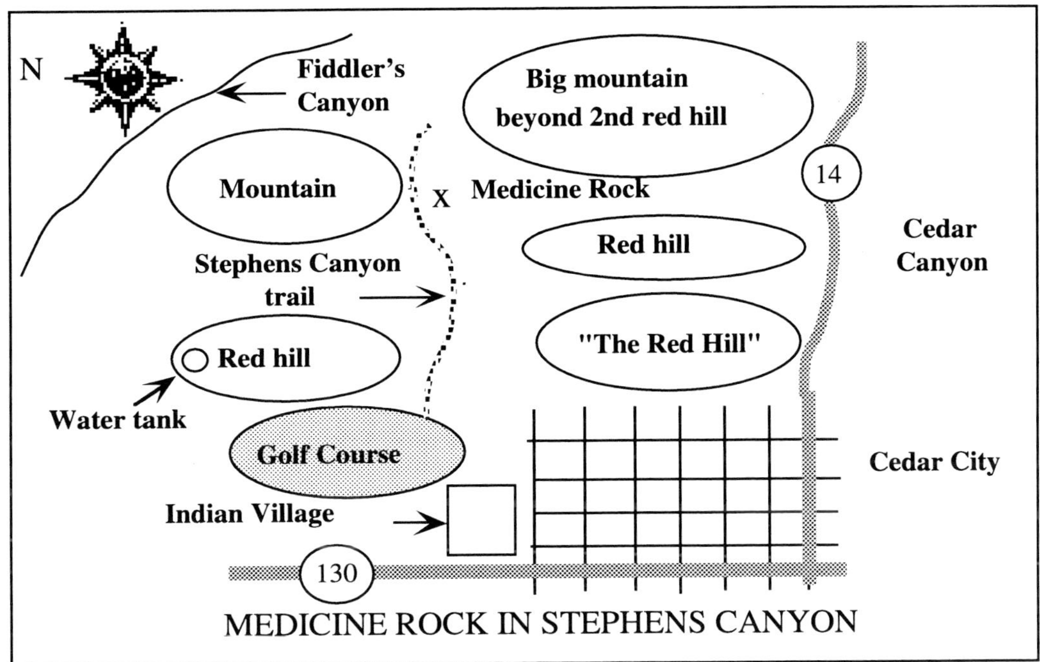

MEDICINE ROCK IN STEPHENS CANYON

MENSTRUATION AND MEAT A woman should not eat meat during her menstruation. Cedar City 14, note 18.

MENSTRUATION AND RIFLES If a woman on her period handles a man's rifle it will make it no good so the man can't kill a deer. This can be remedied by having a little boy urinate in the barrel and putting ochre in the urine on the gun. Cedar City 37.

MENSTRUATION AND THE MOON The Old People say that when a girl bleeds a lot on her period, that it happens at a time when the new moon comes out. This is because the moon is married to her and has raped her. Shivwits 35.

MENSTRUATION HUTS In the old days when a woman had her period she would not camp with the tribe. She would camp in a separate tent off to the side of the camp a ways until her period was over. Cedar City 14, note 19.

MOOKWEECH Florence Kanosh told me that the Paiutes remember the Fremont people. They were here recently and were a small people. Koosharem 20, note 204.

MOOKWEECH The Mookweech used to live in the cliff dwellings so when an enemy came along they could run and hide there. They only planted corn. They would store the corn in the cliffs or in the ground. They came up from the south. Shivwits 12, note 239.

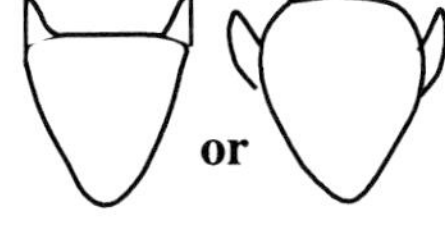

MOOKWEECH The Mookweech lived here before the Indians and the Tookoov. They were the builders of the ancient ruins discovered in Utah. They knew all this land around here very well but they left their land here and moved somewhere south of the Hopi people. They moved because they knew that white people would come to this land, and that if they stayed here they

would be treated just like the Indians that live here today are treated. Koosharem 10, note 32.

MOOKWEECH AMONG THE KAIBAB The Mookweech used to live among the Kaibab Indians but soon left because they couldn't get anything to grow good. Kaibab 4, note 127.

MOOKWEECH AND TOOKOOV The Mookweech and Tookoov people are not considered good. The Tookoov had no bodies and could not be seen. Koosharem 10, note 35.

MOOKWEECH DESCRIPTION The Mookweech were short people with pointed ears and a face like in the sketch. The Mookweech lived here at the same time the Paiutes did. Indian Peak 1, note 49.

MOOKWEECH PIT HOUSES The Mookweech built their houses under ground. Indian Peak 1, note 52.

MOTHER'S MILK CONTROL When you want to increase the milk in a mother's breast have her squirt some on a hot mano. When you want to decrease it have her squirt some in some ice water. Use both breasts. Shivwits 35.

MOUNT NEBO There is supposed to be a wild Indian and some white men on Mount Nebo. Indian Peak 1, note 66.

MOUNT NEBO'S "DRAGON" One time two brothers were living at Utah Lake and wanted to go hunting mountain sheep on top of Mount Nebo. When they got on the top they saw two horns sticking out and wiggling. One of the brothers then went over there to shoot it but it was a big dragon with horns on its forehead.[48] It killed this fellow and breathed on the other making him sick. He escaped however, and went home to a medicine man who healed him. Koosharem 7.

NAME OF THE DEAD It is not right to speak the name of the deceased. They might hear their name called and come to you. Note 15.

NAMING A BABY It is a custom that the person who gives a baby an Indian name should also give him or her some money. Shivwits 34, note 73.

NICK OF KOOSHAREM Nick, the short Indian who used to live on the Koosharem Reservation, moved to the Uintah Basin. When he died, Nick's son

---

[48] I use the actual word "dragon" as told to me by the informant. "Dragon" was probably his own interpretation. This story was most likely referring to the flying serpent on Mount Nebo mentioned under "Flying Serpents." He said horns (plural) on the forehead. Most tribes across North America have stories about serpents with a horn, or horns, on the forehead.

sold his body to a white man who put it in a glass case and made him look as if he was still alive. They had him on display in Salt Lake City. Koosharem 10, note 207.

NICK, THE MOQUI CAPTIVE Malan R. Jackson's grandfather told him that Nick, from the Koosharem Reservation in Utah, was not a Paiute but a cliff-dweller Indian who lived on the Colorado River with his parents. The Paiutes raided this village and the mother and father of Nick jumped over a cliff. They left two kids in the cave, a boy and girl, the boy being Nick. The girl died later. Nick grew up being a Paiute. (This is the same Nick whose body was put in a glass case.) Malan R. Jackson, Anglo, Fremont, Utah, note 146.

NORTH WIND A north wind during a winter storm means it will clear up tomorrow. Shivwits 40, note 113.

NURSING BABIES When you're pregnant and you're nursing or feeding a baby milk, your baby won't be born until the one you're nursing walks. Koosharem 10, note 75.

OBSIDIAN USE Obsidian was chosen for knives, more than it was for making arrowheads, because it was better for cutting. Koosharem 10, note 27.

OFFERINGS TO THE MOUNTAINS Whenever an expedition is taken into the mountains and canyons it is always wise to give an offering of bread or food to them. Doing this will insure that you will be safe while traveling through such places. Shivwits 8, note 12.

PAHRANAGAT LAKE'S GRASSHOPPER ROCK There is a lake on the other side of Caliente, Nevada, someplace. Maybe it is Pahranagat Lake, I don't know. According to the Moapa Indians there is a big rock in this lake that used to be a grasshopper. A long time ago a man kicked it into this lake. It's still there. Shivwits 5, note 189.

PAINT LOCATION IN NEVADA There is a barren pointed hill between Glendale Junction and Overton, Nevada, that has Indian paints of all colors in it including red, green, and black. This paint is called Toodoov. You can't get this paint free. You have to stick a coin or a dollar bill into the ground. You first push the money in with your finger then you can have the paint. Red ocher is also found along the railroad track on the way from Glendale to Overton. Eagle Valley 2, note 171.

PAINT PREPARATION Ochre should be fried in grease before being used.[49] Cedar City 14, note 28.

PAINT SOURCE IN HUALAPAI COUNTRY The Shivwits obtained their red paint across the Colorado River south of Mount Trumbull. It was found in a small cave high up on a cliff. One Indian drowned one time when crossing the Colorado River below Lava Falls while going after this paint.[50] James

---

[49] The grease makes the paint easier to wipe off the skin. It also brings out the red in the iron, if it is of a yellowish or orange hue.

[50] This source of red paint (iron ochre) is undoubtedly the one the Hualapais still use today. It is located in a cave high up on a cliff in Diamond Creek on the Hualapai Reservation. Its location is Township 27 N, Range 10 W, Section ll. Hualapai informants say it is very difficult to climb to this cave and one must pray and use poles to climb to it.

Yellowjacket, Shivwits note 143.

PAINT SOURCE ON THE SHIVWITS RESERVATION The Indians had one source of red ochre on the Shivwits Reservation. This location was on Utah Hill on the west border of the Reservation and north of Highway 91. When the white man came the Indians covered it with dirt and now the location is lost. Shivwits 28, note 144.

PAINT SOURCES The Shivwits used to get their red paint on Shivwits Mountain (Shivwits Plateau) someplace. They got their white paint on the Santa Clara River just below Gunlock. The water behind the Gunlock Dam now covers this white paint source. The white paint is called awveemp. Shivwits 5, note 229.

PAINT SOURCES IN SEVIER AND WAYNE COUNTIES Red ocher and a white paint were obtained by Paiutes at "Paint Cave" up a canyon just west of Greenwich, Utah. A blue paint was obtained a few miles east of Torrey, Utah, in a little canyon just before you come to the cafe. The paint is on the south side of the road. As told to Vera Charles by her father Jimmy Timmican, note 185.

PAINTING CHILDREN Red ochre is put on little children at night to keep ghosts from bothering them. Koosharem 22, note 14.

PALMER'S BOOK OF LEGENDS I don't believe some of William Palmer's legends that he put in his book. He tells them a different way. His book is wrong. Shivwits 5, note 201.

PALMER'S INDIAN NAME William R. Palmer of Cedar City, Utah, was called Onchok′ ***One Eye***.

PETROGLYPH ORIGIN Some rock writings were written by eastern Indians who came here to war against the Paiutes. These eastern Indians were numerous and the Paiutes few, but the Paiutes won. These writings pertain to their warring. These eastern Indians had Mohawk-style haircuts. They came from across the ocean. Koosharem 10, note 37.

PETROGLYPHS AT PAROWAN GAP The rock writings around Parowan Gap were written by God. Eagle Valley 2, note 36.

PETROGLYPHS IN INACCESSIBLE PLACES The inaccessible rock writings in southern Utah were written by a little man around a foot tall. He lives somewhere in the rocks in the mountains east of Cove Fort, Utah. He cannot talk. He gives medicine power to those people he likes. He gave this power to one of my grandparents who was walking in the mountains. He did not see this little man at first because of his smallness, but when he looked down lower he found him. This little man has no name and he is the one who goes around inscribing the writings on the rocks. Koosharem 10, note 34.

PEYOTE DEITIES In the Peyote religion God is the Father, Jesus the Brother and Mary is Mother Earth. The first baptism is the baptism at birth. The second baptism is the babies first washing. Indian Peak 21.

POTATOES AND GOPHERS You shouldn't eat potatoes that a gopher has been eating. If you do, sometimes your heart will be cut off, or in other words you will be cut short of breath when climbing a hill. Shivwits 34, note 93.

POTTERY COLLECTING The Paiutes believe that they shouldn't keep any

Mookweech pottery that they find. This is a part of their religion. Much of the pottery found was not made by the Paiutes, but by the Hopi Indians who lived in the Paiute land before the Paiutes came. Cedar City 37, note 16.

POTTERY KILNS Paiute pottery was cooked by digging a hole in the ground and placing the pot in the hole. Hot ashes were then put all around the pot and inside of it. It was then covered and a fire made on top of it. That's why you see them black on both sides. Kaibab 4, note 138.

PRAYING TO SOONUNGWUV When I pray, I pray to Soonungwuv, and not to Toovuts.

PREGNANCY TABOOS When a girl is pregnant, she should not eat as she usually does or she will get fat. She should also get plenty of exercise. Koosharem, note 149.

PROPHETS A Pawdoo´koots is a person, either man or woman, who would fall down on the ground unconscious for a half hour, or hour, and the people would leave them alone. When he or she woke up they would tell all the visions they saw. There used to be a Pawdookoots lady at the Shivwits Reservation. She would ride horseback all by herself out to the Shivwits Mountain (Shivwits Plateau). Several would go out there. One time a Pawdookoots foretold the coming of telephone poles, the radio, and a machine you could see people in (television). It was also foretold by someone that the white man would come and take all this land away from the Indians. When this old man used to tell this story all the people would gather around him, but I was just a kid and didn't pay much attention. I only remember a little bit. Shivwits 5, note 214.

RABBIT EARS Rabbit ears are the feathers of the Indians. Eagle Valley 2, note 22.

RACETRACK AT PANGUITCH LAKE There is an old Paiute racetrack next to the road at Panguitch Lake where the Indians raced their horses. Mable Yellowjacket, Cedar City, note 192.

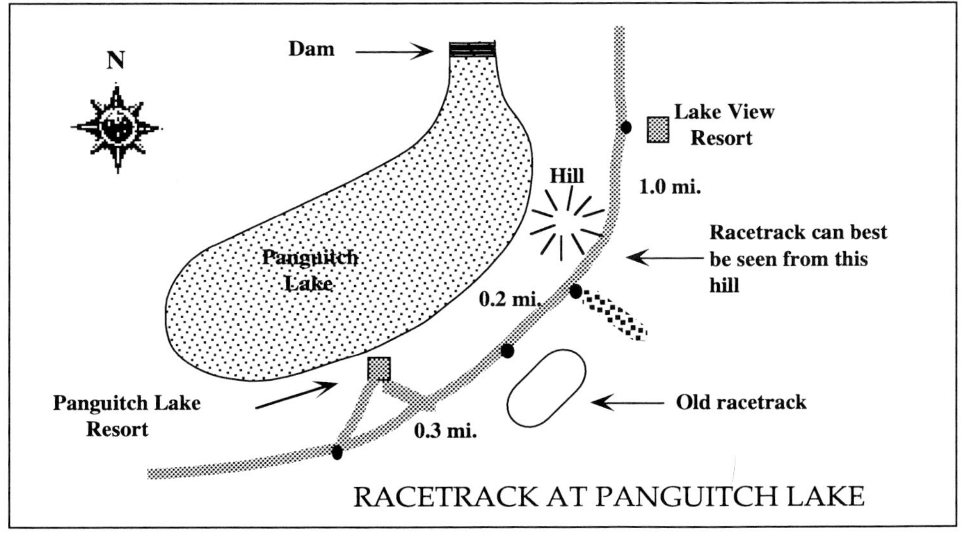

RACETRACK AT PANGUITCH LAKE

RACETRACK NEAR MODENA There is an old Indian racetrack west of Modena, Utah, by the road. Eagle Valley 2, note 190.

RAINBOW VIEWING If your father is living you are not supposed to look at the rainbow. If he is dead you may. Koosharem 10, note 65.

SALT MINE The Indians used to get salt up a little side canyon on Brine Creek just west of Highway 24 about three miles south-southeast of Sigurd, Utah. Shivwits 23.

SEVIER LAKE There used to be some people with a light on their foreheads who lived in the Sevier Lake near Delta, Utah. One time an Indian there was chased by a buffalo and one of these people came out of the lake and rescued him. That's what my father, Jimmy Timmican, told me. Koosharem 20, note 206.

SEX DETERMINATION OF THE UNBORN When a woman's young male son cries a lot during the woman's pregnancy this means she will have a girl. If he does not cry it will be a boy. Note 107.

SHARING The Old People at Shivwits used to all work together in the fields there. In the winter they would boil big tubs of corn. That's all they had to eat then was corn and deer meat. When an old man killed a deer he would give a piece to everyone. Today the Indians don't do that. Shivwits 5, note 215.

SHIVWITS BAPTISM My father told me that many of the Shivwits that were baptized in St. George in the last century died shortly after their baptism as a result of being baptized. Kaibab. Martineau Paiute Genealogical Records. (The event being discussed at the time was the baptism of March 19, 1875.)

SHIVWITS CAMPING PRACTICES The Shivwits used to live up on the Shivwits Plateau in the summer where they would hunt. In the winter they would go down on the Colorado River where some would live in caves. They would carry wood down. They would go on the top to hunt in the spring. Shivwits 5, note 235.

SHIVWITS FLAG The Shivwits used to have a flag. It was a long stick with seven eagle feathers tied in a row on it. I think it was seven. Shivwits 5, note 236.

SLIVERS When you get a sliver in yourself, pull it out and eat it. This will decrease the chances of getting more. Note 13.

SNAKE BITES For snake bites on humans and horses a medicine man would sing and suck on the bite and suck a little snake out that the big snake had put in when it bit the victim. Any herb or poison that would kill a rattlesnake could also be applied to the bite and this would kill the little snake inside the bite. To determine if the snakebite victim would die, two Indians would hold the rattlesnake by the jaws and split it by pulling both ways. If the snake split all the way to the tail the person would live, but if the split diverged before reaching the tip, the person would die. Kaibab 4, note 135.

SNAKE BURNING Do not burn a snake or the land will become dry. Kaibab 4, note 120.

SNAKES AND ASHES Indians used to sprinkle ashes around their house to keep the snakes away. Shivwits 5, note 221.

SPIRIT HELPERS An Indian medicine man got his power in his dreams. When-

ever he went someplace and needed help a spirit like an eagle, mountain sheep, or other things would come to him to be his helper. Some helpers would come from back East. Some helpers would also require the death of one or two of your close relatives before they would give you power. This offer was made to Seth Bushhead and George McFee from Shivwits but they wanted nothing to do with it because they would lose close relatives. Shivwits 5, note 217.

SPIRIT HELPERS Medicine men dream of certain animals that become their helpers in healing and discerning witches. These helpers are unseen but they can tell you what is causing a sickness or whatever you are seeking to know. Kaibab 4, note 115.

SPRING Paiute spring begins in February. Note 1.

STONE BOOK NEAR ANTELOPE SPRINGS, UTAH Near Antelope Springs, west of Delta, Utah, there is an Indian book in the rocks. One can pull out layers of slate tablets and see animals and plants drawn on them. There is also a cave, or hole, nearby in which some legendary event happened.[51] Koosharem 3, note 140.

SWEAT LODGES The Paiutes would go into a sweat lodge occasionally; however, it wasn't a religious ceremony like among the Sioux and other tribes. They just went into the sweat to purify the body. My grandfather died in a sweat. Shivwits 34, note 211.

TOOKOOV Kainuhseev owns the deer and the mountains around here. He's very short and sometimes you can hear him yelling in the mountains. When you see him you won't see any deer around. Sometimes when you can't hit a big buck, maybe the buck is Tookoov.[52] He lives in a cave. Indian Peak 1, note 48.

TOOKOOV The Tookoov people are the people who built the cliff dwellings. There weren't very many of these people. I don't know, but maybe they lived here after the Mookweech, and maybe alongside the Paiutes. Koosharem 10, note 33.

TOOKOOV AND CHILDREN My father, Jimmy Timmican, used to scare me when I was a child and wouldn't mind. He told me that the Tookoov would come down out of the canyon and get after me if I wasn't good. Koosharem 20, note 209.

---

[51] I searched for this stone book in the 1950s but didn't find the cave or the book. I also came to the conclusion that the drawings on the slate were probably natural marks. I saw a few loose slates with different blackish designs on them. I didn't find any slates that I could pull out and replace as Jimmy said. The area is quite extensive and I could have missed the ones he was referring to. This is a very poplar area among the whites for finding trilobites.

[52] It is my understanding that Kainuhseev and Tookoov are two different names for the same spirits. I'm not absolutely sure of this.

TRAIL SIGNS I learned the following from Carl Jake. He said these trail signs can be found in the Cedar Breaks area.

TRAIL SIGNS

Top view of three rocks. This sign means the trail goes straight ahead.

Side view of four rocks. This sign indicates the trail turns to the left or right. Look for another pile of rocks to determine direction to turn.

Side view of three rocks. This means the trail goes down hill.

Side view of two rocks. This sign indicates the foot of a hill.

TWO KWEYOON A person who has two kweyoon (hair swirls in the center of the scalp) should not work in the rain or he might be struck by lighting. If he wears a hat it is all right. Koosharem 10, note 64.

WAH WAH VALLEY'S EARTHEN DAM There is an old dirt dam across Wah Wah Valley just north of Wah Wah Springs. Eddie Wiggits knows where it is. Indian Peak 1, note 46.

WAR TACTICS One war tactic of the Paiutes was to attack an enemy when the sun was directly behind you. When doing this the enemy couldn't see you well because the sun was staring them in the eyes. When the Paiutes were about to attack they would also take big mirrors and use them to reflect the sun's rays into the enemy's eyes. These are the ways they would fight the white man. Shivwits 8, note 76.

WATER BABIES NEAR GLENWOOD There used to be Water Babies near Glenwood, Utah, where the fish hatchery is. Koosharem 7, note 205.

WEST WIND AND SNOW It is a tradition that the west wind means that it will snow. Kaibab 4, note 112.

WHIRLWIND When you see a whirlwind, it is a ghost. Koosharem 10.

WHISTLING AT NIGHT Do not whistle in the night because it is said that the devil will twist your mouth if you do. Note 9.

WHITE-TAILED DEER EXTINCTION There used to be a different kind of deer in the Sevier Valley before the white man came. It was called Chigoos´. Its rump was whiter and it's tail bushier than a mule deer. Koosharem 3.

WIKIUPS AT FIVE-MILE When I was young I used to see some brush wickiups at Five-Mile on the Shivwits Reservation. Shivwits 5, note 228.

WIND HOLE ON THE SHIVWITS RESERVATION There is a wind hole on the Shivwits Reservation on Utah Hill. It is in the hills west of Highway 91 before you leave the south boundary of the reservation. There is grass growing in a little hole and wind blows out of it. Sometimes it blows hard. Shivwits 5, note 200.

WITCHCRAFT PRECAUTIONS The Utes will witch you by using your urine, and the Navajos by using your hair, if you leave them where they can be found. Kaibab 4, note 114.

CHAPTER 4

CEREMONIES AND DANCES

The most attractive feature of the Utes is their religion. It is a more devout, trusting, childlike devotion than the white man has ever known.

Thomas M. Mckee

The only ceremonies and dances that are still being performed today by the Paiutes are the Bird Dance, Salt Songs, Bear Dance, and an occasional Circle Dance. Some Paiutes still dance the Sun Dance but they go to the Ute Reservations to do this. The Paiutes never had many dances in the old days. They basically had the Bear Dance, Circle Dance, War Dance, and Scalp Dance. The Shivwits had a few more. They had the Mountain Sheep Dance, Quail Dance, and Coyote Dance The Coyote Dance was acquired from the Mojaves. The Paiutes acquired the Sun Dance from the Utes who in turn acquired it from the Shoshonis in about 1890. The Paiutes acquired the Bird Dance from the Mojaves and the Salt Songs from the Cahuilla.

Circle Dance

The Circle Dance (Kwenok Ooweékai) is a dance common to many tribes throughout North America. Many tribes call it a Round Dance. In the Paiute version the dancers all hold hands and dance in a clockwise circle to the beat of a drum and a song. The Paiutes had only one person beating the drum who danced in the circle with the rest of the dancers. Everyone sang. The Circle Dance was strictly a social dance in recent times where either male or female could cut into the line and dance with anyone they wanted. (See Plate 2, pg 104.)

During the 1940s and '50s when the Paiutes would migrate and follow field work, they would hold a Circle Dance almost every weekend that would often last all night. Cedar City was a favorite place for this. The younger generation didn't drink much in those days so the dances were orderly. It was drinking and the cessation of migratory Paiute camps that caused the demise of the Circle Dance as a social gathering.

Florence Kanosh gives the following information about the Circle Dance as it was practiced long ago, as she heard it from Woots Parashont (Waok) of Cedar City, Utah:

> *Years ago the Paiutes used to dance the Circle Dance for rain. When they danced, a lot of dust would ascend to God. God would then send them rain and snow which would cause all the plants to grow that they used for food. The Circle Dance is a prayer to God for food and the dust carries their request to him.*

The Paiutes have their own Circle Dance songs and have learned many from the Shoshonis, Gosiutes, Hualapais, and Havasupais. Likewise these tribes have learned many Paiute songs as they have visited each other's dances over the years and shared songs. There are virtually hundreds of songs.

Most Circle Dance songs consist of short phrases that are repeated over and over. The origins of some of these songs have been lost. Some probably came from songs sung in the ancient legends. Many Circle Dance songs are contemporary songs composed with either English or Indian words. Edrick Bushhead tells of a Circle Dance song contest held in Moapa in the 1940s. He recorded the song for me that won first place.

Following are some of the phrases to be found in a few Paiute Circle dance songs:

Big Eagle's son is going to cry at the edge of the earth (coast)

The mirage is playing

Brown Eagle, snow in Arizona

Pocatello, Idaho

Tony, what are you doing?

Pinyon Jays making noise over the earth

American bouncing along by Snow Mountain

Green rock sitting

The mountain is shaking

Snow is in the sky

North wind blowing

Bear Dance

The Paiute origin story of the Bear Dance (Mawkon) goes something like this:

> *One time two Indian youths were out in the woods and came to a bear's den. One of the youths told the other "I am going in and won't come back out until spring, so go home and don't be worried about me or tell any one what happened to me. I will return in the spring." The youth went in the cave and the other one returned home. During the winter hibernation the bear taught the youth the Bear Dance Songs and how to do the Bear Dance. When winter ended and the bears came out of hibernation, after the first spring thunder, the youth who spent the winter in the bear's den returned home. He then taught the dance and songs to the Indians and this is how the Bear Dance originated.*

No one knows for sure who started the Bear Dance or how old it is. There are some ancient rock writings depicting the Bear Dance that gives it some antiquity. The Colorado Utes claim that they learned it from the Uintah Utes. The Paiutes have been doing it for a long time. During the early part of this century Bear Dances were being held at Kaibab, Shivwits, Elsinore, and other places. Bear Dances were strong annual events at Shivwits until the early 1950s. Since then they have only been put on when someone has had the inclination. Bear Dances have been held recently at Richfield, Cedar City, and Kaibab.

Bear Dances are always held in the spring except at Blanding, Utah, where they put one on in September. A Bear Dance corral is built out of upright juniper trees with an opening towards the east. It is made big enough to hold the anticipated crowd. The musical instrument for the Bear Dance today is a notched axe handle and a bone or another stick used to rub up and down the notches to make a rasping sound in rhythm to the songs. The end of the axe handle is placed on top of a large piece of tin that is situated on top of a long rectangular wooden box. The sound that the rasp makes sounds much like a growling bear. In the old days a piece of wood was used in place of the axe handle, and rawhide was used in place of the tin.

A Bear Dance is put on by a Bear Dance Chief. It is always a woman's choice in choosing a dancing partner at a Bear Dance. When the singers start a song the women go and choose their male partners by flicking their shawl at the man of their choice. Two women may choose the same man and he must dance with them both. The women then go and stand in a line and wait for the song to end. When the song ends the men go and line up facing the women. When the singing starts again they start dancing. The men will place their right arms at the women's waist and the women their right arms on the men's left shoulder or waist. They dance towards the entrance in sort of a running step in rhythm with the music. When they get close to the corral fence they reverse the direction they are dancing without either person turning around. The couples do not have to dance in a line. Everyone dances at their own pace and the dancers have to watch out to avoid colliding with dancers coming at them in a head-on direction. They continue to dance back and forth until the song has ended and then they return to the place they were sitting.

The Utes start their dances off a little different. After the women have chosen their partners they go and stand in a line and wait for the song to end. When the song ends the men go and line up facing the women. The line of men all hold hands with each other and so do the women. When the singing starts, the line of women first approach the men for about three steps. Then as they retreat about three steps the line of men dances towards them the same distance the women retreated. The two facing lines continue dancing back and forth, approximately the same amount of steps, facing each other for the duration of the song.

The Utes have a "Cat Man" called Moosuts in Ute, who carries a long willow to whip the dancers into keeping the line straight and to separate the dancers into partners when he chooses to. When he separates them they separate from the line and dance in couples, or trios, as described above for the Paiutes. The Cat Man also uses his whip to get after the male dancers who don't want to dance because they don't care for the women who chose them.

I'm not sure how long the Paiutes have been separating into partners at the beginning of the dance, but I saw them doing it as early as 1950. This could have come about because the younger generation wants to be able to hold their partners whereas the older generation was always a little more reserved. Both the Utes and Paiutes used to only dance during the day, but now the Paiutes have both day and night dances.

The Bear Dance generally lasts for three days. The last song on the last day is a very long song that is aimed at tiring out the dancing couples until someone falls from exhaustion or trips. Those not dancing may cut in to relieve a friend. When a couple falls they must remain on the ground until the Bear Dance Chief comes and prays over them. Then they arise and the dance is over. A feast is always held during a bear dance.

WAR DANCE

There is very little information remaining about the Paiute War Dance. Florence Timmican knew one of the old War Dance songs which I recorded, and Minnie Jake gave me the following information:

I saw a War Dance when I was young. The men killed an enemy and cut his head off. The head was stuck on top of a long pole which was held

in the air by a dancer. Others also danced around it. This was the War Dance. We had a Scalp Dance too but I never saw one.

Scalp Dance

Jim Chili, a Chemehuevi from around Banning, California, gives the only information I've been able to obtain on the Scalp Dance. Remember that the Chemehuevis are basically Paiutes with the same culture and language with only minor variations.

One time there was a scalp dance held near Las Vegas, Nevada. There was a pole in the middle of the dancers. Sometimes a dancer would take the enemy scalp and do all kinds of vulgar things with it like pulling it through the crotch of his legs to mock the dead enemy.

Sun Dance

The following information about a Sun Dance (Tawhoo Wuhnee, lit. ***Thirsty Standing***) held at Fish Lake, Utah, comes from Koosharem informant 7.

The Paiutes used to have a Sun Dance at Fish Lake, Utah, in the Bowery Creek Campground just northwest of the old sawmill that used to be there. Tom Amnisky (Tom Mix) put it on and invited a Ute medicine man down to run it. It was in the 1930s. There were about 7 dancers: Walter George, and Georgey George of Shivwits, Toby John and Joe Pikyavit of Kanosh, Toohood´ a Gosiute, a Ute, and one other dancer. Dan and Fred Bullets were there from Kaibab and many others. Fred Bullets lost a member of his family and they had to bury her at Koosharem. Deer Kanosh helped sing, and a few white people were there to watch the dance.

Indian Peak informant 24 tells the following about the last Sun Dance held at Panguitch Lake, Utah:

The last Sun Dance held by the Paiutes was at Panguitch Lake, Utah. The walls of the Sun Dance lodge were only of sagebrush. At this last dance the singers ran out of songs (or claimed to). This is what my father Carl Jake told me. The photographs of a Paiute Sun Dance at Cedar City were of a dance only put on for tourists and it was not the real thing like at Panguitch Lake.

BIRD DANCE

The Bird Dance is danced all night long at funeral ceremonies. The male singers sing with a gourd. They sit on chairs in a row facing the women who sit opposite them about ten feet away. When the lead singer starts a song, both sides arise and dance back and forth in a walking step in rhythm with the song. As the men dance forward the women dance backward, and then the men dance backward while the women dance forward and so on until the song is finished. After each song they sit down for a few minutes before they start the next song. All the dancers participate in the singing. The songs are to be sung in order since each song tells a portion of a long migration story. It takes all night until sunrise to sing all the songs. Wendell John, a Shivwits singer of Bird Songs told me that there are 167 Bird Songs.

Coffee and cake are served at midnight. The family and relatives of the deceased cook and provide meals for all the visitors. The Bird Dance is generally danced two to three nights in a row for an important person and only one night for a child. Salt Songs are generally sung at the same time by a different group of singers in the same room, or outside in the same area. Although there are two different types of singing going on at the same time the wake is essentially just one ceremony. The Gosiutes occasionly have these ceremonies also.

James Marble, a Mojave Bird Song singer married to a Shivwits lady and living at Shivwits at least half of his life, gives the following information about the origin of the Bird Dance:

> *These Bird Songs and dance came from the Cahuilla Indians near Palm Springs, California. The Mojave Indians learned them from the Cahuilla and changed the songs some. They all fall in order and tell a story. The old-timers used to tell the meaning of each song between songs. The Salt Songs came from the Chemehuevi tribe and the Coyote Songs come from the Mojave tribe. These songs are similar to the Salt Songs; they are also sung in order and tell a story. There are also some Mountain Sheep Songs similar to the above two but I don't know where they came from.*
>
> *The Paiutes are the northernmost tribe that hold these ceremonies. The Paiutes have combined and modified the above songs and hold them to the best of their understanding. Several other Southwest Indian tribes hold the above ceremonies with some variations.*
>
> *The Bird Songs used to be sung only at good times and not funerals. Sometime in the 1920s, when a famous Mojave singer died, the Bird Songs were sung at his funeral and have been sung at funerals ever since. They used to be sung just to help people stay awake. The Mojave songs tell of a migration of people crossing the Colorado River and going south. Their chief was old and was carried along. Down near Needles, California, someplace he died. The people told him to "Get up! Get up!" but he*

wouldn't. He died and turned to stone there someplace. Those are the words of the last Bird Song.

Paiutes haven't been singing Bird Songs very long, they have sung Salt Songs much longer. Frank Mustache, a Paiute, was captured by the Hualapais or Supais when he was a young boy. He grew up with them and learned their Bird Songs. He later married Minnie from Kaibab and lived there and was the one who brought the Bird Songs to the Paiutes.

The following legend about the origin of the Bird Dance was given to me about 1950, either by James Yellowjacket of Shivwits, or James Marble:

Many years before the Indians came to be, the chief of the birds died. All the birds of every kind then came together to mourn for him. As they mourned, each bird sang his own song one after another, until they had all sung their songs. Along about morning the sub-chief pulled out all his feathers and cast them into the fire just as the sun came up. Then this sub-chief also went into the fire.

Archie Rogers of Shivwits gives the Paiute version about the Bird Songs as they tie into the Paiute Legend "The Sack of all Tribes":

The Indians who got out of the sack below Las Vegas have the Bird Songs that tell about that part of the migration. The Moapa Bird Songs tell of coming across the ocean and coming up this way. Jim Chili used to explain parts of the Bird Song migration story when he sang them.

Roadrunner was taken down south from Las Vegas, down towards Parker, Arizona, and that's where those Bird Songs started. A man came up from there, or California someplace, singing and bringing the Bird Songs up this way where they landed in that cave on Sunrise Mountain just east of Las Vegas, Nevada. That's where the Bird Songs are and that's what they mean, coming out and walking up this way. They also tell of crossing the ocean.

This cave is where the Indians used to go when they wanted to learn the songs. They would go there and pray. You weren't supposed to be afraid when that man (spirit) came around to you during the night. I heard that that cave has now been destroyed by the white man. A man from Moapa used to sing all the songs and stop a few minutes and tell what each song meant.

Salt Songs

Salt Songs are sung all night at the same time the Bird Dance is going on. Both groups are often singing at the same time. The lead Salt Song singer uses a gourd and sits in a row of chairs along with other men. The women sit facing them and sing with the men. Sometimes the rows of chairs are several deep and the seating is mixed. There is no dancing with the Salt Songs.

At these wakes the casket of the deceased is present and left open for visitors to view. At different times during the night the Salt Singers and Bird Dancers will dance around the casket and then at the end of the song they will all cry. The older women have traditional wailing songs that are sung at this time. A wailing song is a crying melody. Occasionally during the night someone will give a speech about the dead person.

The songs are sung in a row which last until sunrise and tell of a migration. Wendell John, a Shivwits Indian, said there are 140 Salt Songs. The singing lasts two to three nights for an important person and one night for a child. A song is also sung at the grave site and a last viewing held before the casket is lowered.

One year after a person has died a "Cry" (Yahup) or memorial is held wherein both Bird and Salt Songs are sung all night long just as in the ceremony held when the person died. Many gifts are brought to give to the deceased. These gifts consist of cloth, blankets, and other things of value. They are displayed on ropes in an arbor and when the ceremony is over at sunrise on the last day they are all burned so they can be sent to the dead.

Stewart Snow, a proficient singer of the Salt Songs, says, "The Paiutes got their Salt Songs from the Cahuilla Indians of California." James Marble, a Mojave Bird Singer, said, "The Mojaves got their Salt Songs from the Chemehuevi." The Hualapais say they also got their Salt Songs from the Chemehuevi when they were in confinement at Halapasa across the river from Parker. "Serum and Walapai Charlie got the songs." (McKennan 1964, p. 195). From Stewart Snow's information it appears that the Chemehuevis got them from the Cahuilla and then in turn shared them with the Mojave and Hualapai. The Salt Songs are not in the Paiute language but in the Cahuilla language which should confirm this. The Cahuilla no longer sing these songs but remember having them.

James Marble gives the following information about the Salt Songs:

> *Frank Snow, Stewart Snow's father from Shivwits, was the first one to learn the Salt Songs which he started among the Paiutes. Sam Mike from Banning, California, was also a good Salt Song singer. They used to explain the Salt Song meanings at funerals.*

Seth Bushhead of Shivwits has the following to say about the origin of the Salt Songs:

> *The Cry was not originally held among the Paiutes. It came from the south among the Mojaves and from southern California. The Moapa Indians first learned this ceremony from their southern neighbors and one of the Moapa Indians brought this ceremony up to the Shivwits Reservation.*

Celebrations

Spring and summer were always a favorite time for celebrations or "Big Times" as the Paiutes called them. Some of the favorite places to hold these Big Times were near Indian Peak, Panguitch Lake, Fish Lake, Rush Lake, and several other places. At Panguitch and Fish lakes, Paiutes would come by wagon and spend the entire summer camping, hunting, fishing, gambling, horse racing, foot racing, dancing, archery contests, and numerous other things. Since there was an abundance of food in the mountains these gatherings were like a Fourth of July that lasted all summer.

When an unscheduled celebration was planned horsemen would be sent out four or five months ahead of time to tell the people the time and place. As the time approached many deer would be killed and food products harvested in preparation to feed the coming visitors. Many would come by wagon or horseback. As each family arrived they would be made welcome and shown where to camp. They would also be given help in setting up camp and making sagebrush or cedar windbreaks.

When the celebration started the chief would stand up and update everyone on all that had happened since they last met. Each of the visiting chiefs would do the same thing. Many would shed tears as they talked and told of what had happened in their own areas and to themselves. Then the events would take place, horse racing, gambling, and dancing.

Dances Of The Shivwits

The Shivwits had several dances that other Paiute bands lacked. They had the Mountain Sheep Dance, Quail Dance, and Coyote Dance. The Smithsonian Institute recorded the songs to these dances. I did also in the early 1960s. These Shivwits dances are described below:

Mountain Sheep Dance

Many members of the Shivwits band used to go to Gallup, New Mexico, in the 1940s to perform their dances at the commercial ceremonies held there each summer. They won quite a reputation at these places with their Mountain Sheep Dance which placed first in the competition for several years. The Shivwits called this dance the "Joe Lewis Dance" because it never lost. Pictures of the dancers even appeared on post cards. At Gallup the Shivwits were advertised as one of America's least known tribes.

I learned this dance from Charley Greyman, Kenneth Charles, and Bessie Tillahash of Shivwits who taught our Richfield dance group how to do this dance in about 1960. In the Mountain Sheep Dance one dancer represents the sheep and wears a headdress of sheep horns, a sheep robe, and a long stick in each hand to act as the front legs of the sheep. He dances around in a stooped over position, in sort of a walking step, moving his head about looking for the hunters. The hunters all wear skirts made out of the bark of cliffrose, carry quivers on their backs, and a bow in their hands. There could be any number of hunters dancing. They dance along with bows at their sides in step with each other as they follow their leader looking for the sheep.

When the sheep is spotted they all look happy and each hunter pulls an arrow from their quivers and places the nocks on their bow strings. Then they all point their arrows at the sheep and draw them back and forth, drawing and easing them many times, in rhythm to the music. The hunters dance side by side in one place facing the sheep as they do this. Meanwhile the sheep continues to dance around while the hunters keep their arrows pointing in its direction as they draw the stings back and forth. Finally the hunters act as though they have released their arrows and the sheep then staggers, as if mortally wounded, and falls to the ground. The hunters all whoop in glee and circle the fallen sheep. This ends the dance. Following are the phrases from one of the Mountain Sheep songs:

Maveng wavenggaip
Chuhkee kai kom pum
Ooweepaw odoyovun

Aiming at the animals
As they come bouncing down the mountain
Gathering around the water

In many Paiute songs some words are shortened to where they are often difficult to recognize. The following translation helps identify some of these words: Maveng wavenggaip (from waw vuhnekai, ***aiming***). Chuhkee kai kom pum (from yuhnchuh´kawhai, ***bouncing along*** and kaiv, ***mountain***). Ooweepaw odoyovun (from ooweep ***canyon***, and soo´pawdoai ***gathering***).

The following is a phrase from another song: Totsee avaw´dunai ***favorite place sitting in the shade*** (plural). Little Jim Smokes Mountain Sheep Song has the following words in it; I didn't get a translation: Tuhmputsee cho onumay'.

THE QUAIL DANCE

In the Shivwits Quail Dance, each dancer wears a decorated skull cap with small feathers attached to a curved stick, or wire, and placed in front of the cap to resemble the feather top knot of a quail. In this dance all the men imitate the mating struts of a quail. A tail bustle of feathers may also be worn. Archie Rogers says that the Quail Dance tells of how a man turned into a quail.

Following are some phrases in the Quail Dance song:

Awkawduh nuntsee ukaip oouv,
Tuhmpee oatchu yahvai oong,

Quail who used to be
Went to get a rock water jug

Coyote Dance

The following information about the Coyote Dance comes from Charley Greyman, Edrick Bushhead, Wendell John, and Bessie Tillahash:

> *This dance was performed by women who stood in a line as in the Bear Dance. They bent forward a little and let their arms hang down limp, full length, swaying them back and forth to the left and right in rhythm to the music. They would also dance back and fourth as in the Bird Dance. Burden baskets might be placed on their backs or on the ground. This dance was a prayer for an abundance of food.*

The following is the explanation Archie Rogers gives about the origin of the Coyote Dance:

> *One time, long ago, all the animals were human. One man used to go around pawing at the ground and acting like a Coyote now acts. As a result of this he turned into a Coyote. The Coyote dance is put on to tell how this happened. The dancers go forward and then turn around. We got this dance from down south.*

James Marble (Mojave) gives the following information about the Coyote Dance:

> *The Paiutes got the Coyote Dance from the Mojaves where it was sung at funerals. The dancers would go back and forth as in the Bird Dance and sometimes stoop over and hang their arms down full length and then raise and lower them by lifting the shoulders (arms still hanging) in rhythm to the music. The Paiutes turned this dance into a social dance when they got it. Their song for it is one of our songs telling of "Looking for water on the other side of a mountain." A long time ago James Yellowjacket used to sing and the Shivwits women would dance the Coyote Dance very well.*

PLATE 2
Paiutes near Kanab, Utah, circa 1872, wearing rabbit-skin blankets and dancing the Circle Dance. Courtesy of the Utah State Historical Society.

CHAPTER 5

GAMES

A true Indian has a song in his heart for all things.

Shinny (Kwepu´kok)

The equipment needed for this game is a buckskin ball about the size of a baseball and a stick of the proper size to strike this ball comfortably. This stick resembles a hockey stick and should be shaped similar to the stick in the sketch. The base of the stick should be flattened some on the striking end to hit the ball squarely.

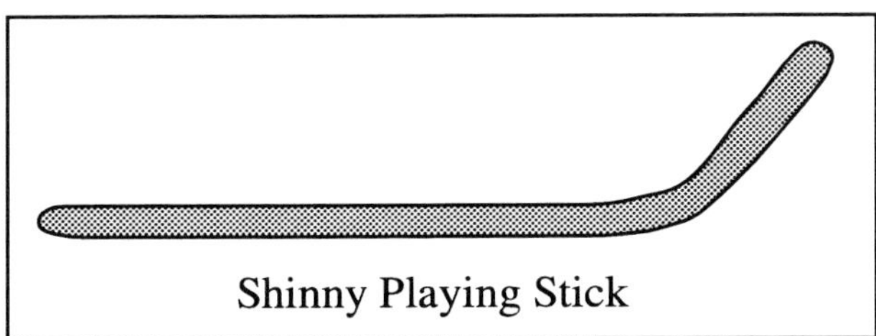

Shinny Playing Stick

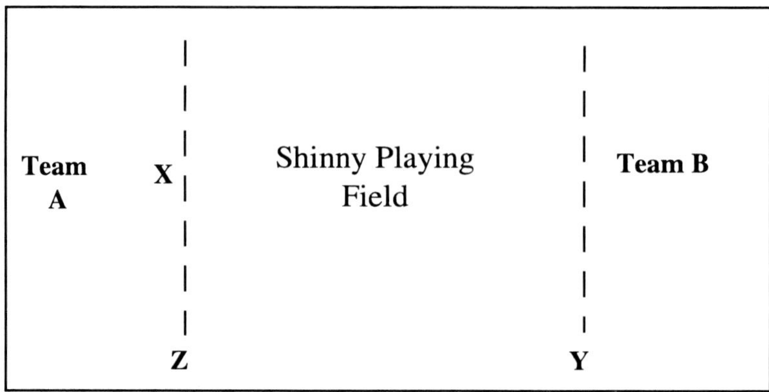

Choose a field approximately 50 to 75 yards long. Two teams are formed with an equal amount of players on each side. If team A was to start the game off it would hit the ball from the X mark knocking it towards the other end of the field as shown in the accompanying sketch. Team A's purpose would be to get the ball across the goal line marked Y. Team B's purpose would be to prevent them and get the ball across the goal line marked Z. Players and bystanders would bet any of their personal possessions on the side they thought would win. I was told that when one side got the ball across their opponents line they won the game. However, they may have also used some kind of point system.

After one team won they would rest a little while and then play again. The teams would change goals between each game and the winning team would start the game off by hitting the ball towards their goal.

Stick Dice (Too´dookweep)

I observed this game being played during the late 1940s and early '50s by the Paiutes from Navajo Mountain and Willow Springs, Arizona. They were migrant workers camping in the fields near Richfield, Utah, and would play with other Paiute bands from Utah also working there. To play this game make a layout on the ground with small stones as shown in the following sketch.

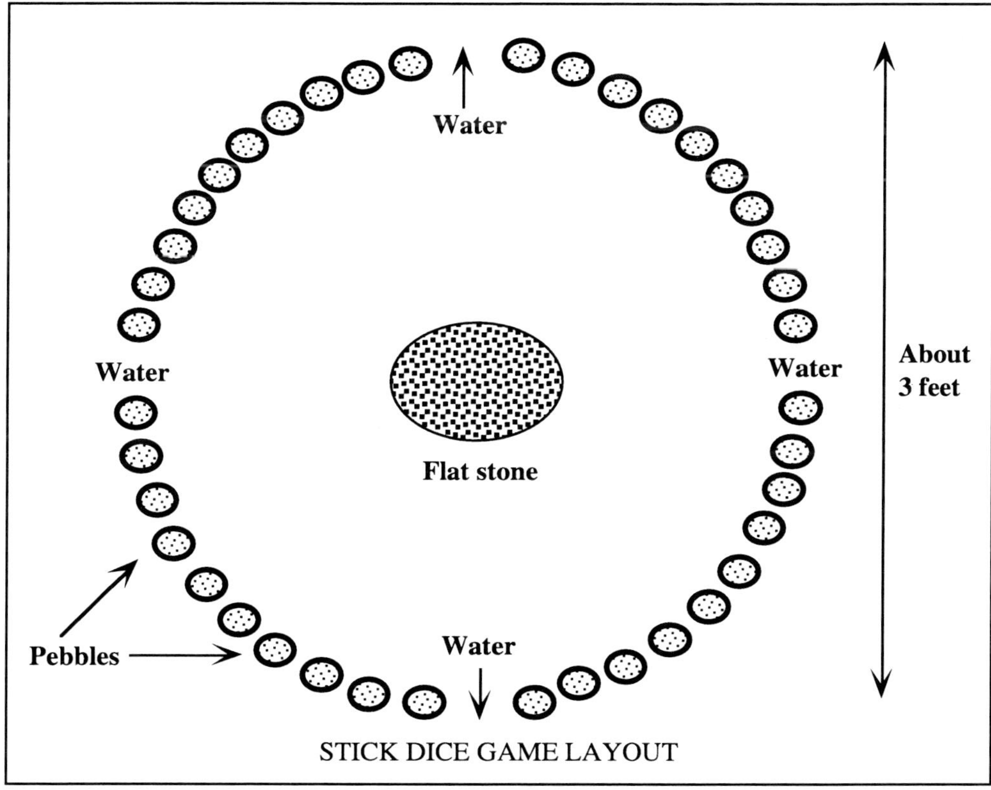

STICK DICE GAME LAYOUT

Make three flat sticks about 6 to 8 inches long and about one-half to 1 inch wide. One side of each stick should be colored a dark color while the other side should be left plain. Whoever starts the game off would take the three sticks in one hand and strike the ends of all three at once on the flat rock in the center of the playing area in a manner that they will bounce and land which ever way they will on the ground. They can land any of the four ways shown in the sketch which shows the values of the stick combinations at each toss.

If the sticks land with one plain and two colored sides up, the player will move over three pebbles clockwise from the starting point. The player would then place a little twig at the spot marked X on the circle. Each person playing has a twig representing himself. Everyone takes turns and moves over whatever amount of pebbles the sticks allow him depending on the way they fall. If a player lands in the water (shown in the sketch) he loses a turn or starts over (I'm not sure which.) The first player to go all the way around wins. Matching bets are made of articles or money which goes to the winner. If a player who tosses the sticks gets 10 points he gets another turn. Four 10s win.

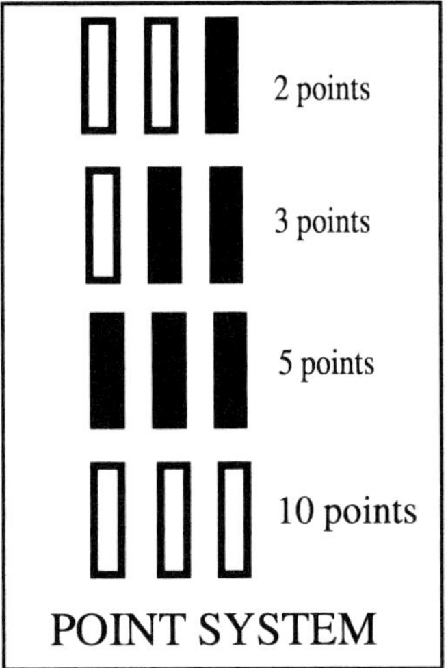

RABBIT HEAD GAME (TAWSUHNG´UHMP)

Tuhsuhng´uhmp is the Paiute word for the Rabbit Head Game. A rabbit skull tied to a pointed bone with a cord approximately 8 to 12 inches long is the instrument used in this game. This instrument is called tawsuhng´ unump. The rabbit head is tossed into the air while maintaining hold of the bone pin which is pointed upward and moved about so as to cause one of the holes in the skull to land on the pin. Each skull hole has a different value in points as follows: Nose, ear, and eye holes counted for 2 points; tooth sockets 5 points; the small hole below the ear 10 points. The tiny hole on each side of the nose hole won the game.

This game is a gambling game with the winners taking a matched bet. Several people may play on opposite teams, or one individual against another. One side kept playing as long as it could cause one of the skull holes to land on the pointed bone to a designated number, or until it hit the winning hole. When a player failed to catch a hole the opposite team took over. Hamblin John, Kaibab.

HAND GAME (NAIUNG´WEE)

Naiung´wee is the Paiute word for the widespread Hand Game, or Stick Game, that is played in Utah, northern Arizona, Washington, Oregon, Nevada, California, Colorado, Oklahoma, Alberta, Saskatchewan, British Columbia, and other places with only minor variations. It is a very old game and can be played by tribes who do not understand each other's languages since hand signs are used. This game was very popular in the past for intertribal or local competition and is still popular today. The Paiutes had a reputation among surrounding tribes for their skill in playing the Hand Game. It is basically a gambling game. In the old days the bets would consist of valuable personal belongings, such as saddles,

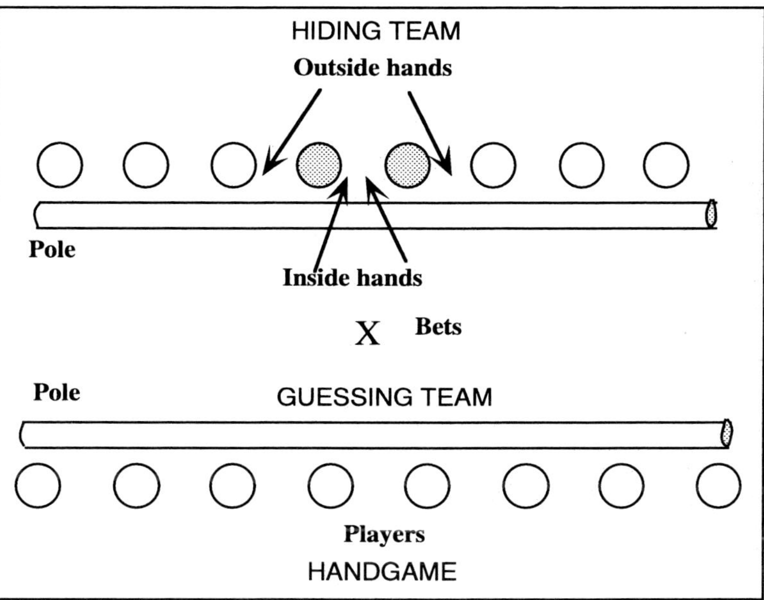

bows, rifles, and other things; today these bets consist of money with stakes sometimes ranging up to several thousand dollars.

Players choose who they want to play with and try to pick someone who is well known for their skill in hiding or guessing the bones. Two opposing teams are formed which do not have to consist of an equal number of players; they then make their bets. A person on each side collects all the bets on his side until the bets on both sides are matched. Players and spectators can bet on whichever side they think will win. If a player wins then his bet is doubled. If he loses then he gets nothing.

The players of each side all sit in a row on the ground facing the opposite side sitting about five feet in front of them as shown in the sketch on the right. Two long poles are used in this game. One is placed on the ground at the feet of the players on each side to be hit with a stick by each player as they keep rhythm to a song when their side is singing. The money that has been wagered normally sits on the ground between the opposing teams near the point marked X.

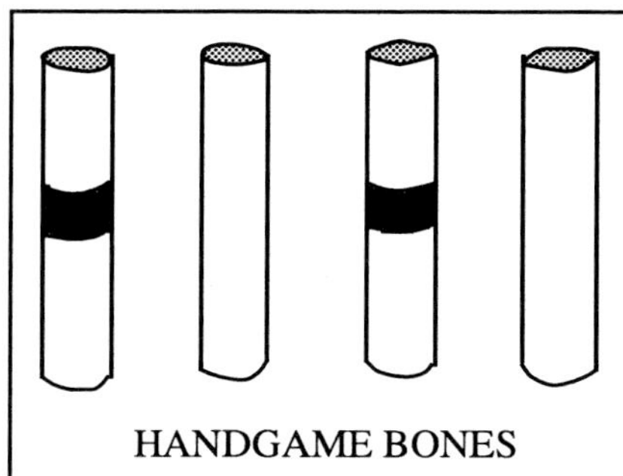

HANDGAME BONES

The object of this game is to guess in which hand the opposing team has concealed a white bone. Four bones are used in this game, two solid white ones and two white ones with a black strip circling the center (see sketch of handgame bones). Each bone is about three inches long so it can be hidden in the palm of the hand. When the game starts the side hiding the bones starts singing and two people on that side are chosen to hide the bones. Each person takes one white bone and one stripped bone. He may either place his hands behind his back or under a blanket or coat so the opposing team can't see which hand the white bone is hidden in. After the bones have been hidden the two hiding them in their fists fold their arms in front of their chests for all to see so they can't switch the bones into the other hand.

The opposing team must then guess which hands contain the two white bones. The ideal thing to do is to guess both white bones in one guess. If the person on the opposite side doing the guessing wants to guess the inside hands of both opposite players he will point his flat hand (palm facing left) in the middle of the players hiding the bones and say sekaw´vee (***in the crack***). If the person guessing wants to guess the outside hands of both players he will spread his thumb and index (other fingers closed with palm down), point them at the opposite team and say wuhkaw´vee (***summit***). The handgame sketch shows the inside and outside hands of the side hiding the bones. The two shaded circles represent the two players hiding the bones. The guesser has to say sekaw´vee, wuhkaw´vee, or make any vocal sound when he guesses or the guess is invalid. He may point and make all the hand and face signs he wants but until a vocal sound is made while pointing, the side hiding the bones is not required to show the hidden bones. The guesser may also pick up one of the counting sticks and point, which also confirms that he has made his guess and requires the hiding side to show the bones. The guesser may also want to guess both left hands of the hiding team. To do this, the guesser points his index to his own right, which is the hiding team's left side, and makes a sound. If guessing their right hands he points to his left.

If the guessing side guesses both white bones then it becomes their turn to sing and hide the bones. If it only guesses one of the white bones then the opposite side forfeits those two bones and continues singing and playing with the two remaining bones. However, the guessing side has to forfeit one of the counting sticks and then guess again. When the hiding side has only one set of bones left then the guesser just points at the left or right hand while making some sound. He does not use the two phrases given above which are used to guess two players at once. Whenever the guessing side misses its guess it forfeits a stick. If it misses two white bones in one guess then it forfeits two sticks. When it guesses the last white bone then the guessing side takes the bones, starts singing, and hides the bones in the same manner.

The guessing side is never pressured to guess. They may take as long as they wish while making as many fake gestures as they want while the hiding side sings and beats on the long pole. The game is over when one side wins all twelve counting sticks. Sometimes ten are used. These sticks are about the thickness of a pencil and approximately one foot long. They are decorated with paint and pointed on one end so they may be stuck in the ground. In the beginning of the game the counting sticks are called "live" sticks and are stuck into the ground in a row pointing upward at an angle. A neutral person can hold them or six can be given to each side. When a team wins a stick it is then called a "dead" stick and is given to the side that won it where it must be laid down. They keep playing until all the live sticks are dead and one side has won all the dead sticks of the opposing team if it has any.

If the hiding side wins all the counting sticks in one song it is called a "home run" in modern terms. Sometimes a game can be over in a few minutes with six consecutive inaccurate guesses, and at other times it may take a day or two to win as the counting sticks go back and forth from one side to the other.

CHAPTER 6

CRAFTS

Nature takes care of her own. He that fears it cannot claim to be her child.

ARROW POISON Boil rabbit blood with Indian salt for arrow poison. Chemehuevi 41.

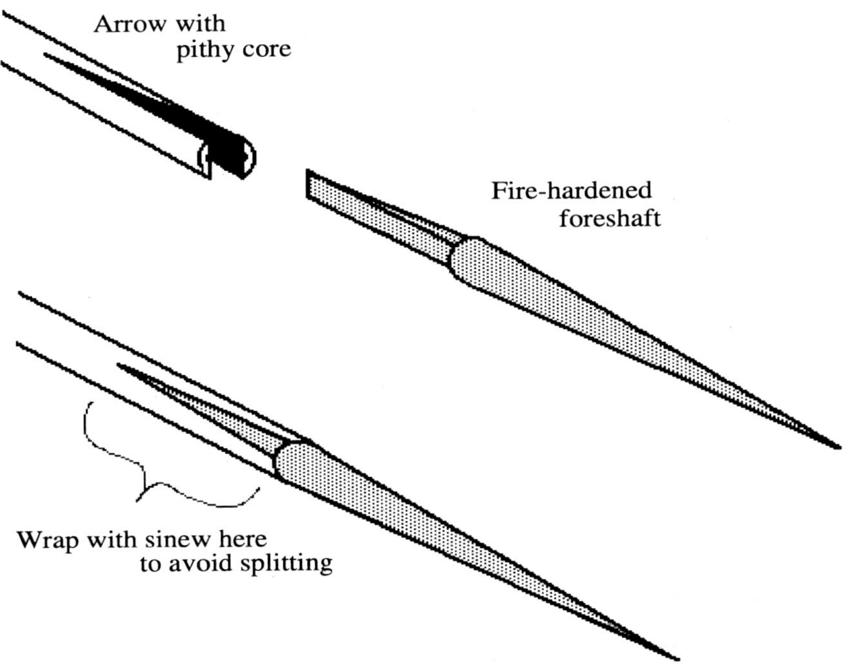

FORESHAFTS FOR NATIVE CURRENT ARROWS

ARROWS Arrows are made out of black native current *Ribes hudsonianum*, and golden current *Ribes aureum*. The green shafts are heated on a bed of coals until the bark pops which helps remove the outer bark. The above sketch shows a method of applying fire-hardened points to this type of arrow: (Koosharem 3.)

ARROWS Arrows made out of green Greasewood are straightened by heat. To straighten arrows from the common reed *Phragmites* first dampen the shafts and then press between two hot flat stones. Green arrows made out of certain other woods are cut and then the same day the outer bark is scraped off leaving the inner bark on. If the entire bark is scraped off the shaft will dry too fast and split. The shafts are straightened by hand a few times each day and wrapped up in a bundle after each straightening until dry and perfectly straight. The following sketch shows how arrows are made out of the common reed: (Koosharem 3.)

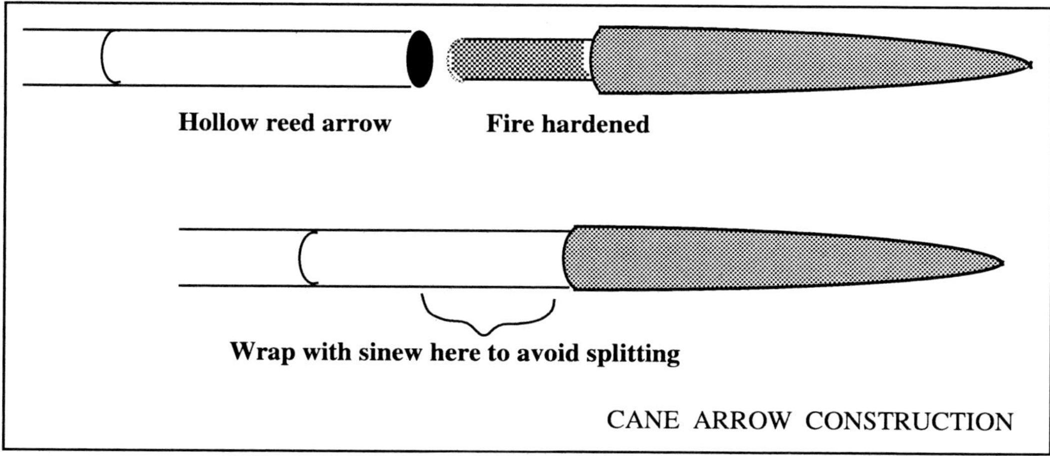

CANE ARROW CONSTRUCTION

ARROWS Dried arrow shafts can be straightened by poking them under hot coals to heat them (not on top as they will burn); then straighten them with arrow wrench since they're too hot to hold. Sand off marks made by wrench with a rock (Kaibab 4).

ARROW FLETCHING In fletching arrows any feathers of the right size are used except the great horned owl (moo-oom´puhts). Pine hen (kaom´puhts) and sage hen feathers (sechu´) are very good. Koosharem 3.

BARK USES The Old People wove leggings out of bark from ankle to below the knee for wearing in the snow to keep their feet dry. They also made bark sandals in the winter to wear with the leggings. Bark blankets and skirts were also made. The best bark is cliffrose *Cowania stansburiana* (peow´oonup) because it doesn't scratch when next to the skin; however, juniper bark would suffice for snow protection if cliffrose wasn't available. Shivwits 26.

BASKET MAKING October and November are the best times to cut squawbush *Rhus trilobata* that is to be used in making baskets. Shivwits 26.

BASKET MAKING Willow *Salix exigua* (kawnuv) was used for the coil in a basket.

Squawbush *Rhus trilobata* was split and used in the weaving (Eagle Valley 2).

BASKETS You should give away the first basket you make then you will make many more. Eagle Valley 2, note 173.

BOW AND ARROW WOOD The Kaibab Band made bows out of narrow leaf cottonwood *Populus angustifolia* and arrows from serviceberry *Amelanchier*. Arrowweed was used for arrows in the St. George area; it doesn't grow at Kaibab. Kaibab 4.

BOW PRESERVATION Oil bows with deer fat to prevent splitting.

BOW WOOD Old man Levi from Las Vegas told me that Paiutes made their bows out of screw bean mesquite and arrows out of arrowweed and cane *Phragmites*. Moapa.

BOWS AND ARROWS OF THE SHIVWITS The Shivwits had a longer bow, than most tribes, that was easy to bend. It was made out of narrowleaf cottonwood *Populus angustifolia* (sawhawv´). Long arrows were used with this bow. The Shivwits never used poisoned arrows. They glued arrowheads on with heated lac from creasote *Larrea tridentata* (yutump). Shivwits 26.

BOWS OF HORN Mountain sheep horn will soften when it is boiled. It is then easy to bend and shape into a horn bow. Wes Levi, Lonnie Kouchomp, Kanosh, Utah, and Roy Tom, Indian Peak.

BOWS WITH HORN BELLIES To put a horn belly on a bow, find an old decayed white deer horn that can be pounded and ground to fine powder. This powder is then boiled to a paste, put on the belly of the bow, and allowed to dry. Roy Tom, Indian Peak.

BUCKSKIN CLEANING White flour is used to clean white buckskin dresses. Rub the flour in with a toothbrush and then shake the flour and dirt out. This brings out some of the dirt.

BUCKSKIN CLOTHING In the old days, Paiutes in southern Utah made beaded necklaces, buckskin shirts, and leggings similar to the Utes (Eagle Valley.2).

BUCKSKIN DRESSES In the old days buckskin dresses were made with the flesh side of the tanned hide out. Koosharem 10.

CRADLEBOARDS The Paiutes had their own styles of cradleboards. They are called koanonts´. They came in very handy in the old days when the bands were migrating and at many other times. They are still popular today among the Paiutes and have not outlived their usefulness. The cradleboard allowed a woman to carry her baby on her back while traveling so her hands would be free to carry other things. When a woman was out harvesting seeds and berries she could take her baby with her in the cradle to lean up against a tree so the baby could watch what was going on. If the cradle fell forward the hood or visor protected the baby from falling on its face. The hood also kept the sun out of the baby's eyes and could be covered with a light blanket to keep flies off a sleeping baby's face. The cradle could also be hung from a limb to let the wind rock it. The cradleboard serves as an excellent bed on cold winter nights so the arms can remain covered and the baby cannot kick off the blankets. On warm nights the arms can be left out. The snugness of being wrapped in a cradle gives the baby a sense of being held, loved, and helps them grow up with a straight posture. They are never left tied in the cradle all the time, but only at night and at other times when the baby wants it or it becomes handy to do so. Babies do become accustomed to them and often won't go to sleep until they are put in one.

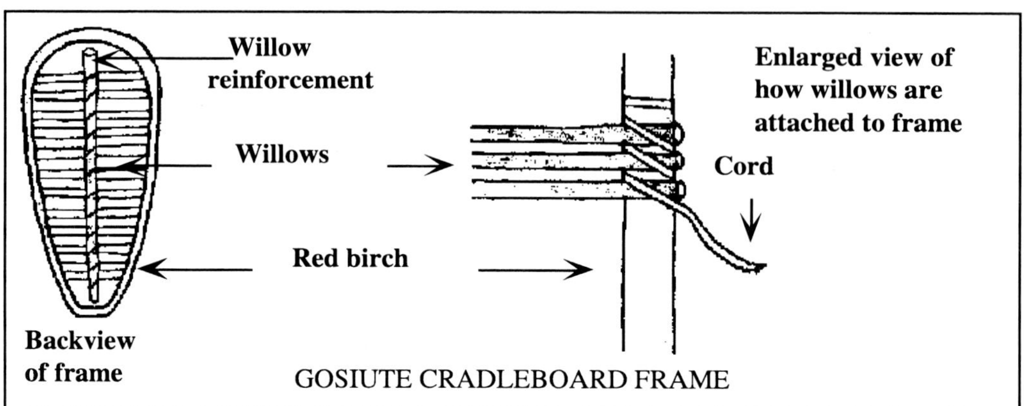

GOSIUTE CRADLEBOARD FRAME

In recent times the Gosiute cradleboard has been very popular among the Southern Paiutes who either purchase them from the Gosiutes or make them. This cradle is about 36 to 38 inches long and at least 15 inches wide at the widest place. The above sketch shows the framework construction of a Gosiute cradleboard. The wood that is used to go around the outside of the large frame is a single piece of red birch beveled at both ends so they can be fit together snugly with the same diameter as the rest of the birch. This splice is placed at the side of the frame and wrapped to hold it together. Willows are laid horizontally side by side across the width of the cradle from just above the top of the baby's head down to about three or four inches from the bottom. The willows are wrapped individually on the frame by wrapping a cord or buckskin string around the end of each willow as shown in the sketch. A long vertical willow is placed on the back of the frame to reinforce it and keep the horizontal willows spaced even. The sketch on the next page depicts a finished Gosiute cradleboard covered with canvas or buckskin on both sides and the two pieces sewn together with a needle and thread. Then the canvas or buckskin is laced to the frame on both sides. The lacing is placed on the inside of the red birch stick that forms the frame. Use an awl and poke a buckskin strap between about every four or five willows as the covering is laced down. A small thick piece of buckskin is sewn over the base of the cradle to reinforce it as it wears quickly here when it is stood up. Buckskin loops are laced on each side of the covering at the center so that another strap can be run through the loops to tie the baby into the cradle. The baby is generally tied beginning at the top. Some people use two strings and start in the middle.

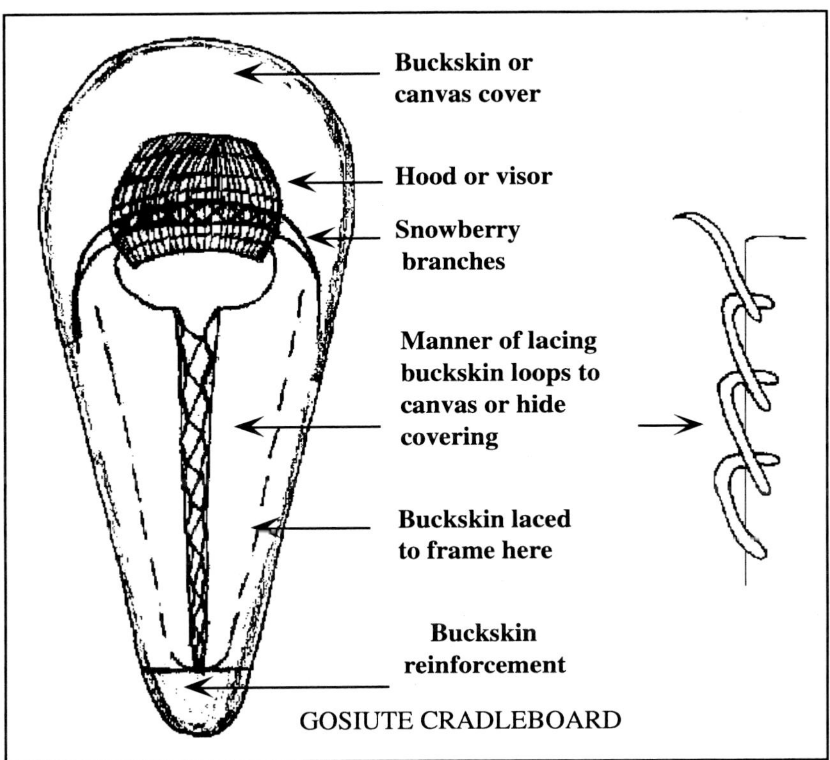

GOSIUTE CRADLEBOARD

The following sketch shows a close-up of a Gosiute hood and the manner of weaving the long narrow shoestring bush twigs together with split squawbush.

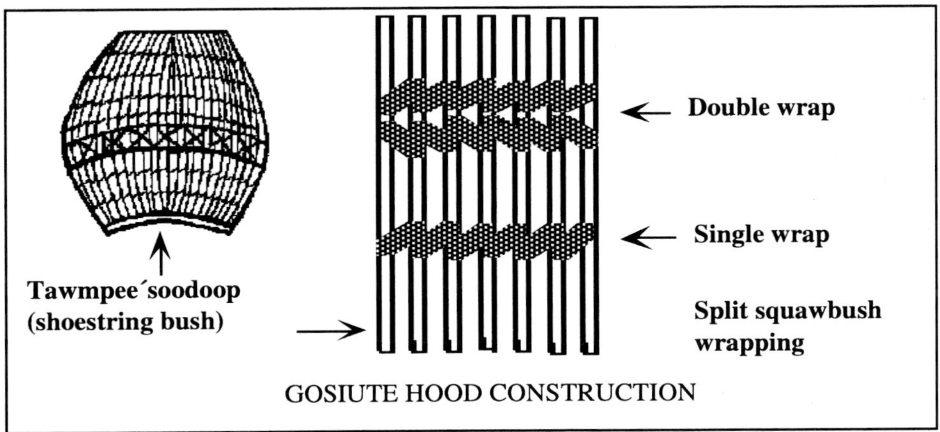

GOSIUTE HOOD CONSTRUCTION

The squawbush is split three ways and thinned as in common basketry. Either double or single wraps may be used.

The following sketch depicts a Shivwits cradleboard made for me by Bessie Tillahash.

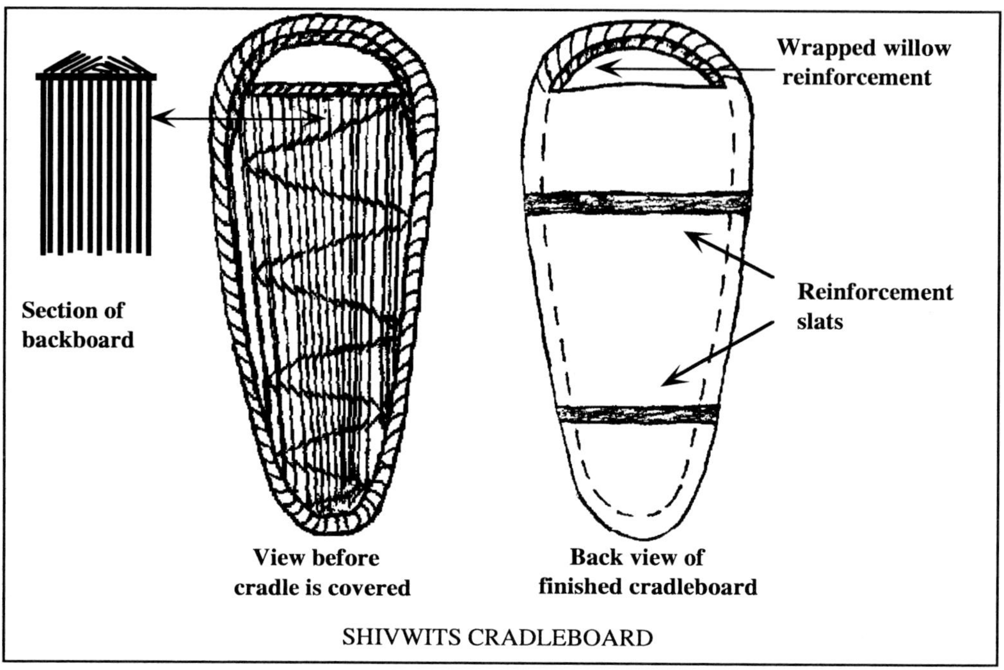

SHIVWITS CRADLEBOARD

The cradleboard is about three feet long. Since the Shivwits didn't always have access to better materials they often made their cradles out of whatever was available. Mesquite root was ideal to go around the outside of the frame but if none was available willows or other woods would have to do. This outer piece was reinforced at the top to make it strong enough here to hold the weight of the baby when picked up at the top only. This reinforcement consists of several small willows wrapped together with split squawbush to hold them together. Then the wrapped willows are placed up beneath the mesquite root and bent to conform to the inner top curve of the cradle. The mesquite root is wound with split squawbush catching one or two of the smaller willows with each wrap to hold the root and wrapped willows together as one.

The backboard consists of vertical willows woven together in a zigzag fashion with split squawbush. Another willow is laid horizontally across the top and then all the vertical willows are bent down and laid against the horizontal willow so they can be wrapped to hold them together as shown in the section of the above sketch entitled "Section of backboard." Nothing is done to the bottom end of the backboard. The vertical backboard has a tendency to sag in the middle so two horizontal flat slats are placed on the back after it is covered to keep the backboard from sagging. The cradle is covered and laced in the same manner as the Gosiute cradle except that the covering does not go all the way to the top. This opening is to facilitate holding the cradle at its top with the hand which the Gosiute cradle lacks.

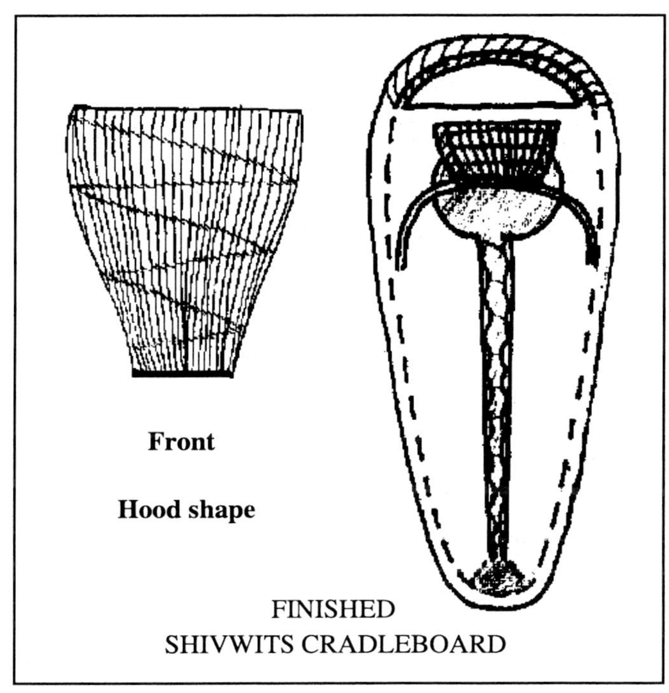

FINISHED
SHIVWITS CRADLEBOARD

The sketch on the left shows the finished cradleboard and the shape of the hood or visor. The bark on the long thin vertical willows is peeled off. They are bent on both ends and wrapped to a horizontal willow as shown under "Section of backboard" in the sketch of the Shivwits cradleboard. A little strip of buckskin or cloth is folded over both ends and sewn on to reinforce them. The visor is made flat and then soaked and bent to shape in a slight downward arc. It isn't cupped beneath as with the Gosiute hood. The narrow end goes to the front whereas on the Gosiute cradle the narrow end goes to the back against the baseboard. The two ends of the arched stick that holds the front of the visor to each side of the frame are notched at the ends to allow a string to be tied around them so they can be tied to the backboard. Carrying straps about two inches wide are attached at the back of both the Gosiute and Shivwits cradleboards. They are tied on each side to the strong outer stick about one third of the way down from the top of the cradle.

Designs are woven into the hood with colored yarn. Different colors and designs are used on them for female and male babies. The colors blue and green were for boys and red for girls. Sometimes beadwork is added to the buckskin covering. Florence Kanosh said, "It isn't considered right to make a cradleboard for a baby until after the baby is born." Note 77.

DIGGING STICKS Digging sticks were made from toonump (curl-leaf mahogany) and kweyu´soov (unidentified). Koosharem 3.

FIRE BY FRICTION Juniper wood is used in fire by friction.

FLINT BAKING Before arrowheads are made out of agate, chert and similar rocks they are baked in "tus" (a fishhook type barrel cactus). Kaibab 25.

FLUTES Flutes were made from tonup´eev because of its pithy center. Elderberry was also used. Koosharem 3.

FLUTES Old Tom made a flute out of juniper. He split it, hollowed it out, and glued it back with pitch. Flutes were used as love calls. Kaibab 4.

GLUE Glue was made from boiling deer antlers.

HORSETAILS Horsetails were hung in Indian tipis to hold combs (Eagle Valley 2).

LIGHTNING RODS A short stick of toonump´ (curl-leaf mahogany) was used as

a lightning rod. It was painted with ocher and stuck in the hat band when traveling around. It was supposed to keep lightning from striking the person wearing it. Mable Yellowjacket, Cedar City.

MOCCASINS After moccasins soles have been sewn on with sinew, tie a knot in the end of the sinew and burn the frayed ends that protrude beyond the knot with a piece of charcoal. The sinew will curl up and keep the knot from coming loose. Eagle Valley 2.

MOCCASINS Badger hide, with the fur on, was sometimes used as the top piece over moccasin toes. Badger hide was also used for moccasin soles since it is fairly thick. Eagle Valley 2.

MOCCASIN PATTERN The moccasin pattern shown in the sketch is the typical pattern presently used by Southern Paiutes. The soles are soft and are sewn on inside out using a welt. The tongue in the sketch is typical but different shapes may be used. An Indian man once showed me an old pair of Shivwits moccasins dating from the early 1900s. They were high tops reaching just above the ankle. The soles were rawhide and were sewn on with a hidden stitch and curled up some just like Hopi and Navajo moccasins. The main difference was that a welt was used between the soles and uppers. Also, the uppers were not buttoned but wrapped around the ankle and then held in place with a wrap around string. The uppers were smoked or dyed brown.

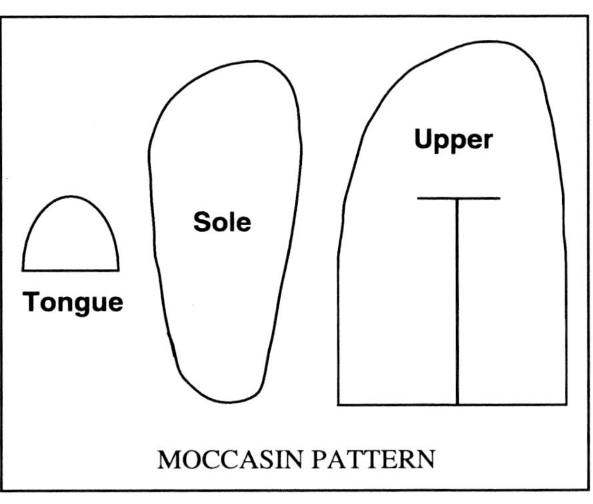

MOCCASIN PATTERN

MOCCASIN SOLES Moccasin soles, moccasin tops, and gloves were cut lengthwise of a hide as shown in the sketch on the right so they won't stretch out of shape when worn. Kanosh 15.

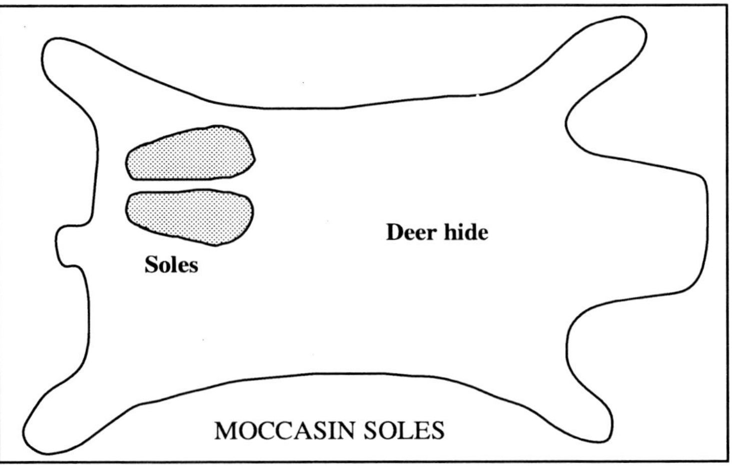

MOCCASIN SOLES

PAINT Ochre came in yellow, orange, and red colors. Yellow or orange ochre can be made red by frying it in grease. The grease makes it easy to apply to the face and then wipe off.

PIPE STEMS Pipe stems were made from elderberry wood (Eagle Valley 2).

PIPE STONE The pipe stone used by the Paiutes was a light-colored stone but I don't know where it came from. Eagle Valley 2

PITCH Paiutes mixed fine horse manure with pitch and then applied it hot to basketry type water jars to waterproof them. The manure consists of fine grasses that help keep the pitch from cracking when dry. Eagle valley 2.

QUILLWORK Paiutes did porcupine quillwork on buckskin. They used roots for dyes, and had lots of colors. Eagle Valley 2.

RABBIT-SKIN BLANKET Rabbits are skinned in the winter when the hair won't slip. If hides are dirty they are first washed and the holes sewn up before cutting. Hides are cut into long strips one-half to one inch wide. They are cut in a spiral manner, starting at a hind leg; the ears are not left on. Wrap the strip over a cloth string while hide is still green (a yucca string was used long ago). Wrap the rabbit hide around the string so the fur side is out and twist. This string reinforces the hide and keeps it from breaking. Each strip of hide can be sewn to the string at the splice, or ends wrapped over each other. After a very long strip is once twisted it is then doubled over and twisted again for a thicker, stronger blanket. Tie the twisted hide from tree to tree to dry.

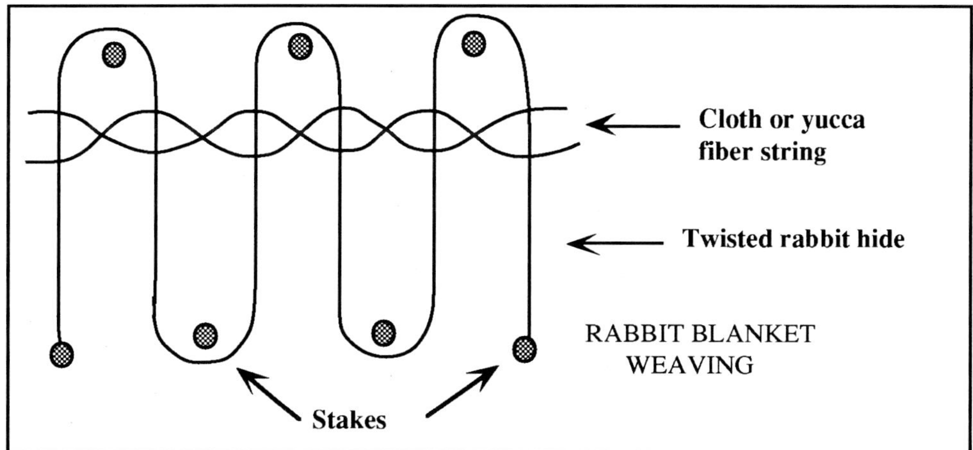

RABBIT BLANKET WEAVING

When you are ready to weave the blanket, stakes are placed in the ground and the twisted rabbit hides placed on them as in the sketch. They are then laced together with cloth or yucca fiber. Each lace is about three inches apart and stakes are placed at approximately the size of a desired blanket. It takes over one hundred rabbit hides to make a blanket. The blanket is hung up to keep bugs out of it. (I witnessed Minnie Jake make a blanket for me using the above process, LaVan Martineau.)

She also stated that white rabbit-skin blankets can be made out of winter snowshoe rabbit hides. Black designs can be put into the blanket from pieces

of dark hides. In making black and white blankets the hides are not cut into strips, but tanned and then cut into rectangles and sewn together. Snowshoe rabbit hides are thicker than jackrabbits and will not rip.

SANDALS FOR WINTER USE In the winter when the snow was slushy, the Indians made sandals out of yucca. They were woven and had a strap across the toe. Rabbit hides were wrapped around the feet, fur inward, to keep the feet warm while wearing the sandals. Eagle Valley 2, note 246.

SHIELDS Shields are made by heating a green buffalo hide over hot coals. The heat causes the hide to shrink and thicken. Koosharem 3.

SINEW Sinew from the lower leg of an animal is stronger than back sinew and is preferred for bowstrings.

SMOKING HIDES Cedar bark was used for smoking deer hides. You must be careful so as not to allow the bark to burst into an open flame or it will burn the hide. Eagle Valley 2.

SMOKING HIDES My mother said that hides are only smoked when it is cloudy because its not windy then. Shivwits, note 212.

SNOWSHOES Paiutes used to make snowshoes. They were shaped like an egg. Juniper bark was ruffled up and put around the feet to keep them warm. Buckskin was used to hold the bark onto the feet. Rabbit hides were also used with the fur against the feet. Eagle Valley 2.

TANNING A Koosharem informant boils deer brains, instead of frying them. She doesn't use grease in tanning; she says it stains.

TANNING Buffalo, horse, and bear hides are tanned by first staking one out on the ground with the hair side down. After it is fleshed, brains or salt is applied to the flesh side. Then each day thereafter the hide is dampened with warm water or a wet gunny sack placed on it. As the hide begins to dry, and while it is still damp, rub the hide with a pumice stone or pound it with a club. Do this each day until it remains soft. The hair is left on when using this process. It is difficult to take the hair off the above hides as can be done with a deer hide by using a pole and draw knife. The tails were generally left on horse hides. Horse hides are hard to tan below the knees. Eagle Valley 2.

TIPI MAKING One time when some other Indian dancers and I were making a canvas tipi in Richfield, Florence Kanosh watched silently from her nearby window. We followed the basic Boy Scout pattern of a full half circle that overlaps in the middle above the door where wooden pins hold it together. When we came to the point of cutting the holes for the pins, Florence came out and instructed us to add a canvas extension for these pins so that the half circle would remain a half circle and the tipi would set squarely on the ground and be a little wider at the base. I didn't know until then that she had lived in a tipi and had helped make them. Her instructions gave us a much better looking tipi than than we would have had following some of the published patterns. Later when a whirlwind carried our tipi over a nearby fence she came out and told us we should have something to tie it down to in the center near the fire pit. (LaVan Martineau.)

TIPI POLES The Indians in my area used to use 12 tipi poles from the red birch. When camp was moved these poles were taken to the next camp. This was done by drilling a hole in the end of each pole and then tying 6 on each side of a horse with one end of each pole dragging on the ground. Koosharem 3.

TIPIS Elk-hide tipis didn't get hard when rained upon because they were stretched tight over the tipi poles. I was raised in one of these. Eagle Valley 2.

TIPIS Tipis were made out of elk hides. Kaibab 4.

CHAPTER 7

THE FOUR-LEGGED ONES

Justice to the white man is to take the land from the Indians and then call them poachers and trespassers.

The following list gives the names of the wildlife that I obtained from elderly Paiutes over the years. This list is in no way complete as the Paiutes had names for all visible creatures, great and small. Additional information given to me by the Paiutes, pertaining to the wildlife in this list, is also included. I do not give what I have learned from other tribes and sources in order to keep this information strictly Paiute. The information given here is meager and in no way represents the vast knowledge and beliefs the Paiutes had concerning the abundant wildlife of their diversified homeland.

ANTELOPE wunts, wuntsee´puhts. This animal was a favorite game animal. Jimmy Timmican showed me an antelope run southeast of Loa, Utah, that his ancestors used. The run consisted of low rows of rocks running for a considerable distance and ending in a narrow funnel shape. Occasional piles of rocks for people to hide behind were scattered at intervals along the run. The rocks were permanent landscape features so the antelope would become accustomed to them. The rocks were situated so that hidden Indians could rise up with a blanket to scare the fleeing antelope if they sought to break through the sides of the run. The antelope were being spooked in the direction of the narrow funnel-like section of rocks where the antelope would have to crowd together and slow down. Armed men would hide behind the rocks in this narrow place and rise up and shoot the antelope as they crowed through the funnel.

ARMADILLO punu´ tuhmpee nahdo (lit. ***iron rock clothes***). The name is derived from the hard body cover of the armadillo.

BADGER oon´, oonum´puhts. Badger fur was used for moccasin tops (on the toe)

and its hide used as moccasin soles when thicker hides couldn't be obtained. Badgers were also favored as pets and when raised from youth "They would follow you around like a dog."

BEAR kweyu´hunt, kweuts´ (kweuts is the word for rattlesnake at Moapa). The bear is also referred to as kawgoon´, or kawgoots´ (maternal grandmother). "The bear doesn't like to be called kweyu´hunt. She likes to be called kawgoots´[53]. Call her kawgoots when you are near her and kweyu´hunt when she can't hear you. Maybe she likes to be called kawgoots because she likes to go about her own business unmolested." Eagle Valley 2.

BEAR (Black) too´kwawdum kweyu´hunt, too´kweyu´hunt (lit. ***black bear***).

BEAR (Brown) undo´kwawdum kweyu´hunt (lit. ***brown bear***).

BEAR (Grizzly) tosaw´ kweuts (lit. ***white bear***).

BEAVER paoons´.

BILLY GOAT savaw´toots. Sawvaw´toots was Frank Beckwith's Indian name. He was the well-known writer from Delta, Utah who wrote a lot about the Kanosh Band of Paiutes.

BOBCAT tookoo´puhts, took´. Bobcats were eaten; "They tasted like pork." Eagle Valley 2.

BUFFALO

1. moahoy´ kootch (lit. ***blanket cow***) Kaibab.
2. tuhdu´ kootch (lit. ***desert cow***) Kanosh.

"At one time there used to be buffalo around the ledges on the north side of the Colorado River near the Kaibab Mountains. Overanxious Hopi or Hualapai ate them before they could increase and they became extinct. Soonungwuv placed them there. Old timers say you could dig down a little ways and still find their manure." Kaibab 4.

CHIPMUNK The following chipmunks or ground squirrels were not fully identified.

1. tawvawts´ (two stripes).
2. oy'oychuts´ (two stripes).
3. onchop´.

CHISELER

1. kuhmp´pawts (Kanosh).
2. spees, sepees´.
3. chuhpeesh´ (Koosharem).

"Chiseler" is a local name. This animal was eaten and was common in both the Koosharem and Kanosh area. It could be a ground squirrel, prairie dog, or something similar. Jimmy Timmican calls it chuhpeesh and says it's like a gopher and good to eat, and he says the white man calls it kweemp as pronounced by the Paiutes. I'm unsure of spelling and haven't been able to find chiseler or kweemp in any animal books.

---

[53] Minnie Jake used the Indian word kawgoots. Jimmy Timmican used the word kawgoon.

CHUCKWALLA *Sauomalus obesus* chukwawd´. The modern word "chuckwalla" comes from the Paiute name. This lizard has a lot of meat on its tail and was eaten by the Shivwits. When pursued it would seek safety in a crack of a rock and inflate itself so that it couldn't be pulled out. It would often have to be punctured in order to extract it. Paiutes carried a special pointed stick for this purpose. Chuckwallas were roasted in ashes and then eaten.

COLLARD LIZARD (Black) *Crotaphphytus insularis* chungunts´.

COTTONTAIL *Sylvilagus* tawvoot´s. A popular meat among Paiutes. The cottontail often runs into holes when chased and in such cases a stick was pushed into the rabbit's fur and twisted causing it to cling to the rabbit so it could be pulled out.

COUGAR, MOUNTAIN LION peu´ dook, peu´ tookoop´ (lit. ***big cat***).

COYOTE

1. soonuv, suhnuv.
2. yoho´vuhts (Lit. ***one who always has intercourse***. Another name for the deity Soonung´wuv.)
3. Soonung´wuv (a legendary deity who was once human).

"Coyote and owl are messengers telling you about something that's going to happen someplace else. For this reason they are not killed." Kaibab 4. "If a coyote cries three times in a row during the day it's a bad sign." Indian Peak 21.

DEER (Mule) tuh´euts, tuh´ee. A popular meat among all Paiutes. The biggest of the two point bucks has a special name. It is called soowees´. Koosharem 3. The marrow in the lower front leg of a deer was used as a lotion and hair tonic. Marrow in rear lower leg wasn't eaten as it made runners weak. Paiutes also did not eat the bone meat where ribs connect at chest or the thin layer of meat hanging over the belly area. Koosharem 20.

DEER (White-tailed) chigoos´, chegoop´, chegoots´. "There used to be a deer in the Sevier valley before the white man came. It was called chigoos´. Its rump was whiter and it's tail bushier than the mule deer." Koosharem 3.

ELK pawtuh´ee (lit. ***water deer***). The animal was eaten and the hides used for clothing and tipi covers (Indian Peak and Kaibab).

GILA MONSTER *Heloderma suspectum* hawtsee´mo. The Shivwits say that this gila monster "turns over in order to bite a person." Both types were eaten as a food believing that it made a person light complexioned and helped you live longer." Shivwits.

GILA MONSTER (Banded) *Heloderma cinctum* etseev´. Eaten by the Shivwits.

GOPHER *Thomomys* muheyuhm´puhts.

HORNED TOAD, SHORT-HORNED LIZARD *Phrynosoma* mukaw´chuts. It is believed that if you kill a horned toad it will rain and the wind will blow hard. For this reason a Paiute will not kill a horned toad unless he wants it to rain. "If you are out in the desert and become thirsty, put a horned toad in your shirt pocket and your thirst will be eased and you will not be thirsty." Indian Peak 1.

HORSE kuvawts´ (Spanish caballo). "The horse was eaten; it tastes salty. Its hide was used for mats and its tail used in tipis in recent times to hang combs in." Eagle Valley 2.

JACKRABBIT kumoonts´. The jackrabbit was a very common food, even the meat on the head was eaten. Jackrabbits with blisters under the hide were not eaten. Jackrabbits were commonly hunted in rabbit drives where they were driven into nets and clubbed. They were also hunted with rabbit sticks made of oak and shaped similar to a boomerang.

A recent favorite way of hunting them at Kaibab was on horseback when the snow was just deep enough to hinder the rabbit from outrunning a horse. Each rider had two rabbit sticks and when a rabbit was routed the horsemen gave chase trying to kill it by throwing their rabbit sticks at the running rabbit.

The blue thing on a rabbit's liver, combined with something else, was used for arrowhead poison. Kaibab 4, and Indian Peak 1).

Rabbit hides were worn with yucca sandals to keep the feet warm during the winter when the snow was slushy.

JUMPING MOUSE *Zapus princeps* paiyuhm´puhts.

KANGAROO RAT *Dipodomys* tawwee´uts.

LIZARD sekoo´peets (the name for most lizards in general).

MAMMOTH, MASTODON mooyai sevee´u. Jimmy Timmican told me a story of a large animal once seen in the Sevier River near Joseph, Utah. This animal was large with his head hanging down and had never been seen before. The animal was called "mooyai sevee´u." Mooyai means ***to hang down the head*** and sevee´u was the name of the animal. The Paiutes named the Sevier River "Sevee´u" after this animal. The whites Anglicized it to Sevier.

It is doubtful that this name referred to the buffalo as the Paiutes were acquainted with this animal and called it moahoy´ kootch and tuhdu´ kootch. Anglo informants claim there were buffalo wallows and bones in the area in the 1870s. It is questionable that they had seen a wandering buffalo and named the river after it. Place names are often very old, therefore an animal other than the buffalo would be the most likely candidate for this name. There is a nearby petroglyph depicting a mammoth or mastodon that could account for this tentative identification.

MOOSE paiyoo´kwutch.

MOUNTAIN GOAT kai´tos (Moapa and Las Vegas).

MOUNTAIN SHEEP nawk´, nawgaw´. Mountain sheep were hunted from blinds in the Moapa area. They were also attracted within archery range by the imitated sounds of bunting horns made by two men hitting clubs together near the mountain tops.

Mountain sheep horns were used for bows, spoons, dippers, and arrow wrenches. The Shivwits had a Mountain Sheep Dance (see Paiute Dances).

MOUSE pooee´chuts.

MUSKRAT pawdung´wunt.

PACK RAT kawts. Used as a meat product particularly in the Grand Canyon area where other foods were lacking. Kaibab 4.

PORCUPINE yoongoom´puhts, yuhuhm´puhts. The quills were used for quillwork. The porcupine is the one who owns and hides the wild game. When you

shoot a porcupine say to him, "I wouldn't have killed you if you would have given me some animals." Indian Peak 24.

PRAIRIE DOG aiah´vuhts. This was a favorite food among Paiutes. The hide would be left on and a slit made along the stomach so that the intestines could be removed. The stomach would then be laced back together with a green stick. The fur was burned off and then the prairie dog would be placed on hot coals and roasted. The burnt skin would be peeled off and not eaten. Kaibab.

RACCOON yumus´uts.

RINGTAIL CAT *Bassariscus astutus* moosoon´ tookoopuhts.

ROCKCHUCK, YELLOWBELLY MARMOT yu'uhm´puhts, yu'um´puhts. A popular food among the Paiutes. It was cooked the same way as prairie dogs. "When your wife is pregnant you shouldn't hunt woodchucks. The reason is that when you shoot a woodchuck and he falls down into his hole he is sometimes hard to pull out. This means your baby will not come out easy." Indian Peak 21.

SKUNK poanee´.

SNOWSHOE RABBIT tosaw´kawm (lit. ***white rabbit***). The snowshoe rabbit was eaten and the hide used for white rabbit-skin blankets or white blankets spotted with black. The hides were tanned and sewn together since they were stronger than jackrabbit hides and didn't rip (see crafts).

SQUIRREL (Flying) *Glaucomys sabrinus* oahon´ tawvawts (lit. ***pine squirrel***). This squirrel has the same name as the white-tailed squirrel on the Kaibab Mountains.

SQUIRREL (Gray) *Sciurus griseus* ung´kuchawn.

SQUIRREL (Red) *Tamiasciurus hudsonicus* ungkaw´ sekoots´ (lit. ***red squirrel***).

SQUIRREL (White-tailed) ***Sciurus kaibabensis*** oahon´ tawvawts (lit. ***pine squirrel***). This is the white-tailed squirrel found on the Kaibab Mountains. Kaibab 4.

SQUIRREL (Rock) *Spermophilus variegatus* sekoots´.

TORTOISE (Desert) *Gopherus agassizii* aiyu´, pee´kai. The desert tortoise was a favorite food among the Shivwits, Moapa, and Las Vegas bands.

WEASEL pawvee´tseets.

WOLF

1. kwetoo´unuv (lit. ***master wolf***)
2. peah´ suhnuv (lit. ***big coyote***)
3. Toovuts (This word refers to wolf in the sense of God)

UNIDENTIFIED ANIMAL pawkai´okos.

UNIDENTIFIED LIZARD chuai´ muuv. A big lizard found at Bull Springs in Western Iron County, Utah.

UNIDENTIFIED LIZARD moogwee´uts "a brown lizard with a long tail."

UNIDENTIFIED LIZARD aitawk´ oovuhts (lit. ***one who disappears***).

UNIDENTIFIED LIZARD yookwee'vuhts.

CHAPTER 8

THE FEATHERED ONES

If an eagle seeks the praise of a swine,
it will never receive it until it wallows in the mire.

BIRD wetseetch´ (the general name for most small birds).
BLACKBIRD (Red-winged) *Agelaius phoeniceus* pawhaw´chukup, pawhawn´tsukup (Koosharem).
BLUEBIRD *Sialia* nawnchoots´.
BLUE GROUSE, PINE HEN *Dendragapus obscurus* kaohm´puhts. This is the grouse that is found living on Cedar Mountain in southern Utah that often lands on pine branches when pursued. This grouse is locally called "pine hen." A different informant gave the name of grouse as sawwhaw kaompuhts (lit. ***blue grouse***) which is probably the same bird.
BUZZARD, TURKEY VULTURE *Cathartes aura* wekoomp´uts, week´w. The feathers of this bird were not used because it was a scavenger. Indian Peak 1.
CANARY o-aw´ wetseetch´ (lit. ***yellow bird***).
CHICKADEE wetsee´geets.
CROW *Corvus.* There should be a distinction between the raven and crow but I didn't get this settled while the older people were still alive.

1. yutaw´puhts, awtaw´puhts.
2. yataw´kots.
3. hataw´konts (Kanosh).

DUCK (in general) tsuhg' singular, chukuts, tsuhguts plural. Duck eggs were a favorite food. The Paiutes used to camp just off the northeast corner of Rock Point, Utah, near Bicknell, to gather these eggs. Koosharem 7.
EAGLE (Bald) pawngwu´. The feathers of this bird were not used by the average Paiute because this bird was a scavenger. Indian Peak 1.
EAGLE (Golden) kwununts´. The feathers of this bird were used for ornamenta-

tion, arrow fletching, and for religious purposes. The feathers from a live bird were preferred and therefore they were trapped or taken from the nest when young and raised. The feathers were pulled when they were one year old and then again when they were two years of age. After the feathers grew back the eagle was turned loose. They were favored pets while in captivity. The two center plumes on an eagle's tail are the "Medicine plumes". Indian Peak 1.

FLICKER (Red-shafted) *Calaples cafer* kwunu´wunts.

GEESE *Branta* ka'ov´.

HAWK (Red-tailed) *Buteo jumaicensis* sunu´ kwununts (lit. ***pitch eagle***).

HAWK (Swainson's) *Buteo swainsonii.*

1. kwununt´seets (lit. ***little eagle***).
2. undo´kwununts (lit. ***brown eagle***).

HERMIT THRUSH *Hylocichla guttata* sawngwuv´ooet (lit. ***sage sparrow***).

HORNED LARK *Eremophila alpestris* sechoo´nunts.

HUMMING BIRD moo´toonchuts, moo´toontuts.

JAY (Arizona) *Cyanocitta woodhousei* choeng´kee.

JAY (Blue) *Cyanocitta cristata* oahon´ chaiuk´utch (lit. ***pine Jay***).

JAY (Pinyon) *Gymnorhinus cyanocephala* ungunts´.

JAY (Steller's) *Cyanocitta stelleri* chaiu´kutch.

JUNCO (Slate-colored) *junco hyemalis* noovu´ toampoa´koytch (lit. ***snow toampoa´koytch***).

KILLDEER *Charadrius vociferus* pawntuh´keets.

MAGPIE maw´kwaiuv, maw´kwaiuts (kwaiuv´and kwaiuts´ are shortened forms of this name).

MALLARD achuh´.

MARSH HAWK *Circus cyaneus* ma'aw´vu chukuts.

MEADOW LARK *Sturnella neglecta* ee´toowuts.

MOCKING BIRD yump.

MOURNING DOVE aiyov´.

NIGHTHAWK (Common)*Chordeiles minor* peum´oanoaupuhts.

NIGHTHAWK (Lesser) *Chordeiles acutipennis* pee´yoots.

OWL (Burrowing) *Speotyto cunicularia* mookoo´hoots. "The ground owl makes a good pet. He will stay around your house. Feed him meat. This owl is a good bird. His Indian name is mookoo´hoots." Indian Peak 1.

OWL (Great horned) moo-oom´puhts. "The feathers of the owl were not used because this bird was an

omen of death or bad luck if heard crying near the camp at night." (Indian Peak 1.) "A medicine man might use the feathers for some purpose." George McFee, Shivwits. "Coyote and owl are messengers telling you about something that's going to happen someplace else; for this reason they are not killed." (Kaibab 4.) "An owl is not a good bird; he is not liked." (Koosharem 10.) "When a bird, especially an owl, sings at night near you it is telling of something bad that is going to happen. That's why owl feathers are not to be used." Eagle valley 2. "An owl hooting is only a bad sign when it does something unusual like landing on your house or maybe talks like a human." Kanosh 15.

OWL (Screech) waw´nawkweetch.

PHEASANT

1. unkawd (lit. ***red one***).
2. chupun´ee wetseech´ (lit. ***Japanese bird***).

QUAIL ungkaw´duhmpuhts. Used as food. The Shivwits had a Quail Dance (see Ceremonies and Dances).

ROADRUNNER

1. Soonung´wuvee toowuv´ukaip (lit. ***Coyote's son who once was***).
2. Soonungwuvee toowung (lit. ***Coyote's son***).
3. oachuv´ookaip.

ROBIN senk´o kwunuv, tse´konung, tsek´wunkwunuv.

SAGE HEN *Centrocerus urophasianus* sechu´. This bird was used as food. Jimmy Timmican showed me a sage hen hunting blind southeast of Loa, Utah, that was used by his band. It consisted of a shallow hole about 18 inches deep and about 5 to 6 feet in diameter with a circle of low rocks around it. It was big enough for the hunter to hide in in this low brush-covered flat where there was little concealment. Jimmy Timmican says the feathers of the sage hen are the best for arrows. They are strong, last a long time, and help the arrow shoot straight. Cedar City 37.

SCAUP (Lesser) *Aythya affinis* too´ koochoomputs (lit. ***black koochoomputs***).

SEA GULL noovu´dos.

SPARROW o´euts (a general term for sparrow-like birds).

SPARROW (English) *Passer domesticus* yuh'uhng´kawhunt (lit. ***stealer***).

SPARROW HAWK, AMERICAN KESTREL *Falco sparverius* kuhdee´nungkuts (lit. ***cut neck***).

SWALLOW (Barn) *Hirundo rustica* paw´sutoakoytch.

TEAL (Green-winged) *Anas carolinensis* oampee´ koonu´vuhts (lit. ***ochre sack***?).

TURKEY (Domesticated) tuh´keets, too´kee (Eng. turkey). I didn't get the Paiute word for the native wild turkey but the Northern Utes call it kweyoot´.

WARBLER (Myrtle) *Dendroica coronata* toanchoa´noych.

WHIPPOORWILL or COMMON POORWILL *Phalaenoptilus nuttallii* or Caprimulgus *ridgwayi* pawn´uhoytch.

WILSON SNIPE *Capella gallinago* koeet´.

WOODPECKER oavee´ toapoaneench (lit. ***wood pecker?***) a general name for all woodpeckers.

UNIDENTIFIED BIRD chi´deveens. A small bird that lives in the sage near Lund, Utah.

UNIDENTIFIED BIRD puhntuh´keets. A small bird that lives by ponds near Enterprise, Utah, and makes a sound like "tweet."

UNIDENTIFIED BIRD we´ukuv. A small bird that makes a hanging nest in trees and sings a lot. It is common on Highway 89 south of Richfield, Utah.

UNIDENTIFIED BIRD tawpeyoots. It makes a certain sound. It's a day bird and lives by the water. It's bigger than a robin. (Compare the last part of this name with the lesser nighthawk peyoots. It is probably a similar or related bird.)

UNIDENTIFIED BIRD noovu´ toampokweets (lit. ***snow ?***) a snow bird with a black head.

UNIDENTIFIED BIRD wai´voosuts.

UNIDENTIFIED FALCON sawkhwah kawsuv (lit. ***blue or green falcon***).

UNIDENTIFIED HAWK awsee´u vuhvuhts. Kaibab 4 called this bird a "chicken hawk." The name sounds as if it has ***gray*** in it and ***scary***.

UNIDENTIFIED SWALLOW paw´sadokupets.

OTHER CREATURES

ANTLION LARVAE, DOODLEBUG *myrmeleontidae* kuh'uh´toanoyntch.

ANTS tawsee´uv (the general name for most ants).

ANTS (Red) ungkaw´ tawsee´uv (lit. ***red ant***).

BAT pawchuts´, pawtsuts´ (Kanosh).

BLACK WIDOW SPIDER too´ hookwump (lit. ***black spider***).

BLOODSUCKER (A beetle found in southern Utah)

1. suhum´ohots "It has a big head and stripes and is called wild horse by some southern Utah whites."
2. chuhum´uhoyts "It looks like suhuhm´ohots but is red with black stripes."

BUTTERFLY aw´sevuhts, awsee´voadonts (Kanosh).

CENTIPEDE

1. tuhmpee´ tohouv (lit. ***rock snake***).
2. suhng´ump (Shivwits and Koosharem).

"When a centipede (suhng´ump) bites you it counts its feet. The person it bit will die the same number of either days, months, or years, that the centipede has feet." Koosharem 10.

CRICKET

1. chuh´duhts.
2. tsuh´duhts (Kanosh).
3. skedeets´ (Shivwits).

This is the common cricket heard in the evenings throughout southern Utah.

DRAGONFLY saw´duhveengkuhts (Shivwits).

FROG

1. pawkwun´, pawkwun´nuv.
2. wawhots´.
3. sawwhaw´hawduhm wawhots (lit. ***green frog***) Kaibab.
4. pawkots´ (Willow Springs, Arizona.)

The above names prob
ably indicate different types of frogs. Wawhots was described as a "green spotted frog." Pawkots was said to be the name for frog among the Willow Springs, Arizona Paiutes.

GNATS

1. ungeev´.
2. moapuhmp´ (Koosharem). Moapuhmp´ is a different type of gnat than ungeev´.

GRASSHOPPER awdung´kupeets, awdung´kawts. Grasshoppers were roasted, ground into a meal, and then made into cakes or a mush.

HELLGRAMMITES *Corydalidae* pawsuh´kawmeents (Sapir called pawsuh´kawmeents a water lizard *Phyllodactylus tuberculosis.*)

INSECT, BUG pa'awts´ (this word refers to any insect or bug).

JERUSALEM CRICKET, COPPERHEAD *Stenopelmatus fuscus* tuhgoo´tuh neahv (lit. ***burying chief, grave chief***). "Copperhead" is the popular name of this bug in Sevier County, Utah.

LOCUST kuhv, kuhoov´. "Locust" is the popular name in southern Utah. This particular locust makes a loud pulsating buzz.

LOUSE pouv´.

MOSQUITO moouv´.

MOTH

1. moo´sevuhkots (Koosharem).
2. wuhsee´uvuhkuhts (Shivwits). Wuhsee´uv (wawseev´) is the Paiute word for the soft scales that comes off the moth's wing. This word also represents the very fine hair-like stickers found on prickly-pear fruit.

PRAYING MANTIS

1. tuheuts´.
2. nuhmu´hawpeev (Shivwits).

SCORPION

1. kwawsee´ kwepump (lit. ***hits with the tail***).
2. podo´tsekunt (lit. ***has a cane***).

SPIDER kookwump´.

STINKBUG hookoo´vechuts. This is the common southern Utah black hard-shelled bug that raises its rear end up and emits a foul odor when approached.

TARANTULA kawngeng´chohots.

TICK

1.mutuv´.
2. touv´ (the word used at Shivwits for a rabbit tick).

TROUT pawguh´uts is the general name for all fish. Ungkaw´ pawguh´u (lit. ***red***

fish) is the name of the trout. This trout was the one once so common at Fish Lake, Utah, with red meat. It was a favorite food among many Paiutes. Until the 1930s Paiutes from many areas would congregate at Fish and Panguitch lakes to spend much of the summer living off fish and deer. This fish was speared and trapped. Jimmy Timmican said that this fish was once so plentiful at Fish Lake that the wagons would run over many just crossing the creeks on the west side of Fish Lake. He said they could even be scooped out by the handfuls at certain times.

WORM toowee´ toho´uv (lit. ***earth snake***).

YELLOW JACKET whechun´u kawmoont.

UNIDENTIFIED BUG pawntus´. A black beetle that looks like the following sketch:

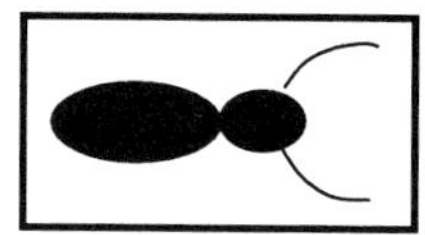

UNIDENTIFIED BUG kawkoo´puhts, kawhoo´peets. This name sounded like "kawgoon" (your grandmother) to the informant who said it was a "red furry bug with red and black legs."

Snakes

BULL SNAKE, GOPHER SNAKE, BLOW SNAKE *Pituophis melanoleucus* koahom´puhts. "A man would wrap a bull snake around his arms and body to help make him strong and have muscles like the snake." Kanosh 16. One informant gave the same name (koahom´puhts) for a yellow and black ringed non-poisonous snake.

KING SNAKE suhng, suhng´uv, suhng´ump (recent informants also gave suhng as the poisonous coral snake and the whip snake).

RATTLE SNAKE

1. toho´uv.
2. kweuts (the word for rattlesnake at Moapa and the word for bear in Utah).
3. wauhts´ (the word for any snake at Moapa).

RED RACER nuntuh´nuv. The skin of this snake was used as a decoration on bows. Indian Peak 1.

SIDEWINDER tawnu´keets, tawnu´kuhts.

WATER SNAKE paw´ toho´uv (lit. ***water snake***).

UNIDENTIFIED SNAKE tuhngchuhng´kots.

UNIDENTIFIED SNAKE moonchuv. Jim Chili, Chemehuevi.

CHAPTER 9

EARTH'S ADORNMENT

The dead want to kill everything around them.

I acquired most of the Paiute plant names in this chapter in the late 1940s and through the '50s. My main informants for the majority of the plants listed here were Jimmy Timmican and Florence Kanosh of Koosharem, and Carl Jake of Indian Peak. At the time, I was not aware of the value of using scientific names, and when I couldn't find a plant name in a book I would often ask Anglos to identify them for me with popular names. Years later as I began to see the confusion in popular names I started to seek the scientific names.

As I began to compile my early hand-written notes for this publication I found that some of the plants I had identified earlier needed better identification. I found that there are few Paiutes left alive today that remember many plant names. Such names in modern conversations among younger Paiutes are almost entirely lacking, except for the more common names like cedar, cottonwood, yucca and a few others. Since they no longer live off the land they have little reason to discuss plants in a language that is fast dying.

A similar situation exists with the average Anglos of today when they are asked the English name for many plants. Their knowledge is quite meager even considering the availability of this information. They will know some of the more common plants, but as soon as you start asking them for the names of the rare ones they are at a loss. To get the English names of the majority of plants today one has to ask a botanist or read a book on the subject.

Most of the Paiutes in the old days were botanists because they used all the plants, and therefore knew all their names. I could never stump the above informants on any name. It is my regret that I didn't take full advantage of what they had to teach me and learn them all with proper scientific identification. I always jotted down any name or information they told me, and when they had time, I had them show me the plant. However, several names I acquired were only accompa-

nied with descriptions. The informants died before I could take them to where the plants grew to get them identified.

The names of the plants in this list are all native to the Paiute homeland area. Some plants, however, are only found among the Shivwits and Moapa bands who lived in the desert areas while other plants are only found among the bands living in the higher elevations of Utah and Nevada. The Paiute names for the plants common to both areas were identical in most cases with some exceptions. In this century all the Paiute bands have intermixed and some plant names that might have been peculiar to one area have taken a back seat to the more commonly used names. However, a few still survive which I note in the plant list that follows.

In some cases, I've purposely avoided giving the second scientific name of a plant because of the variety of similar plants. If there was a noticeable distinction then they would have had different Paiute names to distinguish them. However, if the distinction was so fine that it would take a scientist to distinguish them then they probably had the same Paiute name.

I'm not giving all the uses of each plant that I have learned from other tribes or that I could dig out of books. I've confined the material under each plant to what I was told by Paiutes. Information on some plant uses is lacking because I didn't think to ask at the time. However, as I was more curious than average, I did obtain an abundance of information that is now lost.

I'm also not including all the plant names I could get from Kelly and others. That information is already published and available. I did check them and in most cases they agree. In some cases their pronunciation isn't completely accurate making it difficult to identify the plant. Basically, this compilation is a list of the plants and their uses that I personally jotted down years ago so as not to forget them. Some of the statements were told to me in Paiute, or poor English, so I have worded them in a manner that they will be best understood. If I add any of my own comments it will be obvious in the text or will be in the footnotes. I avoid adding material from other tribes even though it is most likely applicable. My basic purpose in this list is to **keep it Paiute**.

Indian medicine has been underrated and often ridiculed; therefore a statement by Virgil J. Vogel, a scholar who has perhaps studied Indian medicine deeper than anyone else, becomes appropriate here:

> *The most important evidence of Indian influence on American medicine is seen in the fact that more than two hundred indigenous drugs which were used by one or more Indian tribes have been official in "The Pharmacopeia of the United States of America" for varying periods since the first edition appeared in 1820, or in the "National Formulary" since it began in 1888. So complete, in fact, was the aboriginal knowledge of their native flora that Indian usage can be demonstrated for all but a bare half dozen, at most, of our indigenous vegetable drugs. In a surprising number of instances, moreover, the aboriginal uses of these drugs correspond with those approved in the "Dispensatory of the United States." There is in*

addition a list of several aboriginal remedies which have been used in domestic medicine as well as by physicians, although they have not won official acceptance.[54]

In the next quotation Vogel lists some of the more important contributions made by the Indians of the Americas to world medicine:

> *Yet the Aztecs, whose herbal knowledge is revealed in the Badianus Manuscript, knew and used cochineal, liquidambar, cotton, tobacco, passion flowers, datura and other drugs which have been adopted into European and American pharmacopeias. South American Indians contributed such well-known drugs as coca, cinchona, curare and ipecac to world medicine. The Mayas used capsicum, chenopodium, guaiacum and vanilla, along with many other drugs which were later adopted by Europeans.*[55]

Most Indian medicines had medicinal ingredients. However, the Indians considered some of them faith medicines, only effective through faith and prayer. They were therefore often the exclusive possession of certain medicine men who knew the right prayers or songs.

PLANT NAMES AND USES

APACHE PLUME *Fallugia paradoxa* meah´puh oonup (lit. ***small oonup***). Oonup´ is the common name for both cliffrose and apache-plume. The plant was boiled and drank for an undetermined sickness.

ASH *Fraxinus* wawmpeep´.

BLACK SAGE *Artemisia nova* ungkaw´po sawngwuv. This sage is a very good tea for colds and influenza. It is more powerful than big sage.

BLAZINGSTAR *Mentzelia albicaulis* koo'-oo´. Pick the flowers and dry them. Seeds can be beaten or tapped out onto a blanket; they are parched and ground into flour. The flour makes good dumplings or mush.

BOXELDER *Acer negundo* pawhoy´uv, pawkoy´uv. A different informant identified this name as the singleleaf ash *Fraxinus anomala.*

BRIGHAM TEA, INDIAN TEA *Ephedra* ootoop´. Simmer the leaves for a tea.

BROOMRAPE *Orobanche fasciculata* too'-oo´. Peel and eat raw.

BUD SAGE *Artemisia spinescens* koochup´o sawngwuv (lit. ***ash sage***), mawkaw´chuh sawngwuv´vuhts (lit. ***horned toad sage***). Simmer the leaves and then drink the tea for colds.

BUFFALO-GOURD *Cucurbita* onook´weemp. This gourd is too thin to use for a rattle so it wasn't used for that purpose. The seeds were eaten.

BUFFALO BERRY *Shepherdia argentea* opeev´. The berries from some of the trees are sweet and from other trees bitter. Pick the ripe berries (ungkawp´) and float

[54] Vogel 1970, p. 6.
[55] Ibid, p. 7.

them in water; the good ones will sink to the bottom while the bad ones will float to the top. Dry them and then boil when needed.

BUNCH GRASS *Muhlenbergia* noou´veev. The seeds are picked in the fall and ground into a flour.

BURDOCK *Arctium* awvaw´tuh kawmenuv (lit. ***big kawmenuv***).

CANAIGRE, DOCK, WILD RHUBARB *Rumex hymenosepalus* kwevuv´. Roast the young stalks and when done eat the paste in the center. In recent times the stalks were boiled and eaten with sugar.

CATCLAW ACACIA *Acacia greggii* sechuh´uhdump (lit. ***scratcher?***). The seeds were used as food. My notes list this plant as "screwbean" but because the name refers to claws the plant must be the catclaw. These trees look similar from a distance.

CATTAIL *Typha latifolia* toa'oyv´. The Paiutes used to burn off areas of cattail early in the spring and then they would cut off the young tender shoots when they grew to about 6 or 8 inches tall. They would roast and eat these. They would also boil (or roast?) the young tender green tops that resemble a cat's tail and eat them.

CHOKECHERRY *Prunis Virginiana* toanup´. The berries are edible and were used in the past but they are not cared for much in recent times Kaibab 4.

CLIFFROSE *Cowania stansburiana* peow´oonup. The bark is called suhnup´. Blankets and skirts are made out of the bark of this plant since it didn't scratch like juniper bark. The bark was also used for diapers since it was absorbent. The leaves were boiled for a tea and drunk as a medicine.

CLOVER *Trifolium* koosawd´.

CLOVER *Trifolium* paw koosawd´uhmp. Koosawd´ is the general name for clover. Paw koosawd´ means ***water clover*** and is the name of a clover that grows in or near the water. The name of the Reservation and town of Koosharem, Utah, comes from the words koosawduhmp (***clover***). This plant was said to be abundant near water in the Koosharem Valley. The roots of this plant were eaten.

COCKLEBUR *Anthium strumarium* kawmee´nuv. The burrs on this plant were used as "women medicine" to help a man catch a woman. A cocklebur placed in the track of a desired woman would help you catch her, just as the bur attaches itself to someone and clings on.

COLORADO COLUMBINE *Aquilegia coerulea* whechee´ ungkopenump.

COMMON REED *Phragmites* pawhump´. Arrows are made out of this wood with attached fire-hardened foreshafts or with stone points (see "Arrows" in Chapter 6 on Crafts). These arrows are light, fly fast and far, and were often used in competitive long-distance shooting.

The leaves of this plant have a sweet brown sugar-like substance on them. It is the excrement left by aphids as they drew out the sap. A blanket is placed beneath the plant and it is beaten with a stick to obtain this sugar-like product.

CORKY-SEED PINCUSHION *Mammillaria tetrancistra* taws. Tony Tillahash said that this cactus was used to line roasting pits designed for heat treating chert, agate, and similar rocks. The rocks were baked before the arrowheads were

chipped. One informant said it was the inedible ovu´gawv (white spined claret cup *Echinocereus melanacanthus*). Tony Tillahash said it was taws, a fishhook-type barrel cactus. This cactus was also roasted and eaten.

CREOSOTE BUSH Larrea tridentata yutump´, yutuv. Boil the leaves and small stems and drink the water for an upset stomach; the taste is very bitter. This bush is also used as a medicine for syphilis. Also considered good for paralysis. The leaves are also boiled and rubbed on skin that has been sun burnt. The tea is drunk for arthritis. The lac found on this plant is used for glue. Creasote leaves are also boiled to wash chicken pox sores so no scars will be left. It is also drunk for colds and rheumatism.

CURLEYGRASS *Pleuraphis jamesi* wuhkuh´moasoa (lit. ***vagina hair***).

DANDELION *Taraxacum officinale* o-aw sawent (lit. ***yellow flower***). The leaves are boiled, fried in grease, and eaten.

DEATHCAMAS *Zigadenus.* I was shown this white-flowered plant on the Kaibab Reservation by Morris Jake who said that he was told by his father that it was poison and that they didn't eat it.

DESERT VELVET, TURTLEBACK *Psathyrotes ramosissima* wuh´pawwhawts. A very small white flower that grows in low mounds.

DOG MINT toowee´seev. This plant is a Utah weed with a sage smell. I once had it identified in the '50s by an Anglo who called it "dog mint." Today, I cannot re-identify the plant nor even find the name "dog mint" in any Utah flora book. The plant was boiled and the water used to wash the head and cure headaches.

DOUGLAS FIR *Pseudotsuga* sumu´ oahomp (lit ***blanket pine***). The boughs of fir trees are used to make pine-bough beds because the needles are not sharp.

DROP-SEED *Sporobolus cryptandrus* moanomp´eev. The seeds make gravy after they are ground into a flour. This plant is a red-colored grass with long protruding branches near the top. The seeds are on the branches. I could be mistaken on the identity of this plant as my written description now sounds more like *Amaranthus palmeri* (careless weed).

DWARF JUNIPER *Juniperus depressa* sumu oahomp´ (lit. ***blanket pine***). A Koosharem informant mentioned this plant under the same name as used for fir trees because it is spread out low on the ground like a blanket.

ELDERBERRY *Sambucus* koanoak´weev, koonook´w. The fresh berries are pounded into cakes, dried, and then put into stews, or roasted over coals and eaten.

FERNBUSH *Chamaebatiaria millifolium* moo-oon´ tuhuv. This plant is boiled and drunk for an undetermined sickness.

FOUR-WING SALTBUSH, WHITE GREASEWOOD *Atriplex canescens* moodoo´nuv. This plant is commonly known as white greasewood by southern Utah ranchers. The wood makes good cooking coals.

FREMONT COTTONWOOD *Populus fremontii* soa´veep. This wood makes a good fire within a tipi because it does not spark and burn holes in nearby blankets.

GAMBLE OAK *Quercus gambelii* kweyuv´. Bows are made out of this wood but they are slow and need sinew backing. Acorns were also eaten but they are not particularly sought after in more recent times.

GENTIAN *Fresera* kaiv´u okoonump (lit. ***mountain okoonump***). This plant generally grows in the mountains. It has leaves with a purple base. It is good for cleaning out the stomach when you've been vomiting. Soak the roots overnight and then drink the water; the roots may also be boiled.

GLOBEMALLOW *Sphaeralcea* kuh´eyokomp.

GOLDEN CURRENT *Ribes aureum* poahomp´eev. Arrows are made out of this wood. An unidentified plant called pawdo´umpeev is probably a variety of current, or a name used by a different Paiute band. The informant gave the name and stated, "Arrows are made out of this bush and it has berries." I didn't record the informant's name. Another type of current is called kwechuv´.

GREASEWOOD, BLACK GREASEWOOD *Sarcobatus vermiculatus* tonov´. This wood makes good cooking coals. Fishing arrows, without feathers, are also made out of this wood. The sharpened points are straightened and hardened by heating "when green." These arrows are made extra long for fishing, probably from 3 to 4 feet long, and are quite heavy. This type of wood is especially good for fishing because the fish do not slip off easily due to all the little holes in the greasewood shaft. This wood also makes good arrow foreshafts. Koosharem 3.

GUMWEED *Grindelia squarrosa*. This plant was boiled and drunk for stomach troubles. Koosharem 10.

HOREHOUND *Marrubium vulgare*. The plant is boiled and the tea drunk for diarrhea.

HORSETAILS, SCOURING RUSHES *Equisetales variegatum* pawhaw´ wuhchuh´ choogwenump. This name has the word ***sweep*** (ochoon´awk) in it. This reed is boiled and the water drunk for a stomach sickness. The rushes were also used as a fine sandpaper to sand bows.

INDIAN CABBAGE, PRINCE'S PLUME *Stanleya pinnata* tuhmu´duh. The seeds were edible and the plant used as a potherb.

INDIAN PAINT BRUSH *Castilleja*

1. moo´tuntu sueep (lit. ***hummingbird's flower***) Koosharem.
2. toho´ oaho´ suent (lit. ***snake tongue blossom***).

Recently the roots have been boiled and used as a medicine for a venereal disease. Paiutes believe that this flower belongs to the snake and that it's petals resemble the tongue of a snake. Eagle Valley 2, note 53.

INDIAN POTATO *Orogenia linearifolia* whechuhn´. This plant has a white flower and comes out in early spring. Dig the tubers out of the ground and boil.

INDIAN RICEGRASS *Oryzopsis hymenoides* and related species wai. The husks are burnt off the seeds; the seeds are then rolled under a mano, winnowed, and dried. Then they can be roasted, ground into a flour, and water added to make a mush.

INDIAN TOBACCO *Nicotiana trigonophylla* tawmo´nump, sawwhaw´ kwoup (lit. ***green smoke***).

JIMSONWEED, SACRED DATURA *Datura meteloides* moamop´. The slightly

smashed green leaves are good for applying on sores and swellings. Shivwits 34. A small portion of this plant (roots or seeds?) was boiled and drunk by a few individuals for it's hallucinogenic value. Cedar City 14. One informant made the following statement about this plant: "If you eat moamop it will cause you to see many different things, something like visions but not of God." Some Indians smoked this weed and others put it in their food. Indian Peak 1, note 68.

When you go deer hunting, grind up the roots and sprinkle some of the powder into the tracks of the deer and then pray. The deer who made the tracks will then get tired and sit down and you will be able to shoot it. Koosharem 3, and Indian Peak 1.

JOSHUA TREE *Yucca brevifolia* osaw´dumpeev, choowaw´duhmp (probably two different varieties).

JUNIPER *Juniperus utahensis* and *osteosperma* wawup´. When you bruise a muscle you should chew up some needles from a cedar tree and then rub the chewed needles on the sore spot.

Bows made out of this wood maintain their shape and have more snap than other woods. They do not really need sinew backing, but if not backed, they tend to break within a couple of years. When making a bow out of cedar, choose a limb or section of a trunk without knots.

The berries of certain trees are not bitter and are eaten for food. The trees are tested to determine which are sweet. The berries are brown inside when ripe. Old dried bark was used to smoke deer hides.

LAMBSQUARTERS, PIGWEED *Chenopodium album* and *fremontii.*

1. koav´.
2. pegee´ nungkaw´vawm (lit. ***pig's ears***) Cedar City.

LOCOWEED *Astragalus purshii.*

1. pataw´kai nump (lit. ***pops***).
2. sawdu´ganump (lit. ***rattles***).
3. chuhkwe´kaivu (Koosharem).

LOCUST *Robinia neomexicana* peu´sechump´eev (lit. ***sweet claws or scratcher***). The blossoms of this tree are boiled and eaten.

MAHOGANY (CURL-LEAF) *Cercocarpus ledifolius* toonump´, toonup´. This wood makes excellent arrow foreshafts and digging sticks because of its hardness.

MANZANITA *Arctostaphylos* awdu´dumpeev at Kaibab. The berries are edible. The leaves were also ground up and used as a tobacco. Indian Peak 1.

MATCHBRUSH, BROOM SNAKEWEED yoowaw´dump, yoowu´unump. A brush was made out of the twigs to brush off the fine hairs on prickly pear fruits.

MESQUITE, HONEY MESQUITE *Prosodis* opeemp´. The seed pods are yellow when ripe. They are dried, pounded in a mortar, mixed with water, dried into a big ball and stored for winter use. The ball becomes hard and breaks like candy when dry. The pounded meal, or ground-up balls, can be mixed with cold water for a drink. Mesquite wood is an excellent firewood. It makes coals that last a long time.

MILKWEED *Asclepias* pe-e´ whawvoo´kwunump (lit. ***milk squirter***). The milk from this plant is used for a chewing gum. Pluck all the leaves off several plants leaving the stem standing. At each place where a leaf has been plucked off, milk will seep out. Wait until all the milk that has seeped out becomes of the right texture that it can be waded into a ball. Then collect all the semi-dried milk from all the plants that have been prepared and wad it up and chew like chewing gum. If the wind is blowing very hard it will blow all the milk away that has seeped out. Therefore choose a calm day for collecting this gum.

MULBERRY *Moraceae* moakov´.

NARROWLEAF COTTONWOOD *Populus angustifolia* sawhawv´, sawhup´. The Shivwits made long bows out of this wood.

OREGON GRAPE *Mahonia repens* weump´eev. The bright yellow roots make a good yellow dye and are used for dyeing buckskin. This was done by boiling the roots and then soaking the article in the cooled solution. The fresh berries were also used as a purple paint to paint designs on the toes of moccasins. To do this, burst and rub the ripe berries in the desired design on the moccasins. (The design soon fades so a mordant of some kind might have been mixed with the berry juice.)

PALMER PENTSEMON *Penstemon palmeri* toho´u sawdu´gawnump (lit. ***rattle-snake rattler***). The green leaves are stuck into a hole in a tooth to help alleviate a toothache. The leaves dipped in water and then applied to a horse's back are good for sore backs.

PINE Probably limber pine, *Pinus flexilisis,* or bristlecone pine, *Pinus aristata,* pawnaw´ oahomp. Oahomp is the general name for several pines. The word pawnaw could mean ***forked***; therefore the above two pines, which are sometimes forked, are candidates for this name. Not identified in the field.

PINYON *Pinus edulis* and *monophylla*. The larger pinyon nuts are called toov´ or toovuts´. They are edible raw but have a much better flavor when roasted. They were roasted in a winnowing tray mixed with hot coals. The coals and nuts were constantly tossed in the air together to keep from burning the winnowing tray. An experienced woman could roast many pinyon nuts without ever burning her tray. They can be ground into flour and then mixed with water and made into a gravy or mush.

The pitch from these trees is called sunup. Hardened pieces of pitch were eaten as a chewing gum. It becomes just like chewing gum after it is chewed for a while. The pitch was boiled and mixed with other things to waterproof water jugs. It was also used as a waterproof glue on arrows and in hafting stone knives. The pitch was good for earaches. Eagle Valley 2. Pitch also acted as a disinfectant when applied to cuts and wounds. Koosharem 3. Sap from pine trees is good to straighten out a twisted mouth that comes from a stroke. Rub it on the cheeks and around the mouth. It helps put the mouth back in place. Shivwits 35.

PONDEROSA *Pinus ponderosa* yooveemp´.

PRICKLY PEAR *Opuntia engelmannii* yoowuv´. The ripe tunas (yoomuv) are eaten uncooked in the fall when they become purple. A drink is also made from the

fruit. Too much of this fresh fruit could cause a stomach ache.

QUAKING ASPEN *Populus tremuloides* suhuv´. Boil the bark and drink for rheumatism. A wet concoction of bark is also good for pimples and face rashes. The sap is consumed as a sweet because of its sugar content. It is gathered in the early spring when the sap is running; the bigger trees are better. Peel the bark off an area about 2 feet long by 8 inches wide and then use a flat front leg bone of deer, or a knife, and scrape upward on the tree pressing out the sap onto the scraper. The sap is then put into a container and drunk without cooking, or bread dipped into it and eaten. If any fragments of bark become mixed with the sap it makes it bitter. The scraping bone is called muntseev´, and the sap is called suhngu´ veuv (lit. ***aspen sugar***). Koosharem 3.

RABBIT BRUSH *Chaysothamnus nauseosus* skoomp, spoomp. Peel the outer bark off the roots and chew the inner bark; it soon becomes a gum. Among the Shivwits, dolls were made out of the branches of the plant and were called "Skoomer Dolls" in English. The stems on half of a short branch would be removed. Those remaining would resemble a skirt when the bare end of the branch pointed upward.

RAGWEED *Ambrosia*? pawwhu´munump. This plant cannot be presently identified with accuracy. It is a Utah plant I once only identified with the popular name of "ragweed." This plant is used as a medicine. Smash the roots, when they are fresh, put them into some warm water, and apply to swollen parts of the body. A rag or something can be tied over these roots when they are applied to the swelling to hold them in place. This treatment is good for any swelling. A poultice was also made from this plant and applied to swollen cheeks for mumps.

RATTLESNAKE WEED *Euphorbia albomarginata* tooveep´uh kawhaiv (lit. ***earth's necklace***).

RED BIRCH, WATER BIRCH *Betula occidentalis* kai´soov, kai´shuhduhts. The slender branches of this tree were used in the construction of cradleboards (see "Cradleboards" in Chapter 6 on Crafts). September is the best month to gather this wood.

Fishing spears are made out of this wood. These spears are made very long and are straightened by heating. They aren't used until they are dry.

Arrows are also made out of this wood in the same manner as with poahom´peev (black native current) except that flint or steel points were normally used. This wood doesn't have a pithy center like the current, and therefore points can be attached solidly. The outer bark is peeled away from these shafts before they are dried. The longer poles were used as tipi poles. Koosharem 3.

RED CEDAR *Juniperus virginiana* spawngwup´.

RED OSIER DOGWOOD *Cornus sericea* ungkaw´ kawnuv (lit. ***red willow***). The slender branches are used in making baskets. This wood is very strong.

ROCKY MOUNTAIN BEEPLANT *Cleome serrulata* soa´kwunuv (lit. ***armpit odor smeller***).

SAGEBRUSH (BIG) *Artemisia Tridentata* kawhup´. The general name for all sage plants is sawngwuv´. *Artemisia tridentata* may be called sawngwuv but its specific name is kawhup´.

To prevent coughing, rub sage leaves in palms of closed hands so that the fragrance of the sage will not escape and then bring hands up to the nose and inhale deeply. Also boil the leaves and small stems into a tea and drink for colds. The dead leaves are also used for diaper padding.

The fresh leaves are used in the practice of munuh´kee (see "Babies with Clogged Throats" in Chapter 3, The Ways of the Old Ones). The leaves are smashed and rubbed on the index finger before it is inserted into the throat. The sage acts as a disinfectant. A more recent practice is to smear the index finger with Vaseline.

SAGUARO or ORGANPIPE CACTUS *Cereus* ha'awv´ (Jim Chile, Chemehuevi).

SALTGRASS *Distichlis spicata* awsoamp´ (from awsoap´ ***salt***).

SCARLET BUGLER PENSTEMON *Eatonii* moo´tuntutsee pechuh´meen (lit. ***what the humming bird sucks***). This plant is boiled and drunk for an undetermined sickness.

SCOULER WILLOW *Salix scouleriana* kwetchum´paw kawnuv (lit. ***ugly willow***). A tree like willow that grows around the shores of Fish Lake, Utah.

SEGO LILY, MARIPOSA LILY *Calochortus nuttallii, C. nuttallii* seko´, segoo´. The bulbs were dug out with a digging stick. They could be cooked at the time and eaten or preserved and eaten later. The modern word for this plant "sego" comes from the Paiute and Ute word segoo´.

SERVICEBERRY *Amelanchier* tuh'uv´. This wood is an excellent hardwood for making bows and arrows. These arrows are strong and are good for killing deer. Flint arrowheads were normally used on these arrows for hunting deer. Fire hardened wood, or steel points, were used for small game.

The berries are called toowump´eev and are edible while fresh or they can be dried and used later. The berries can also be made into a juice like the squawbush berries (Kaibab 4). The leaves may be simmered green for a tea, or dried, ground up, and stored for future use. Cedar City 14.

SHADSCALE *Atriplex confertifolia* kawnguhmp´.

SMALL SNAKEWEED *Gutierrezia microcephala* kuh´kwunump. This is a Kaibab term.

SNOWBERRY *Symphoricarpos* awvaw´koonump (lit. ***thing that goes over***). This plant grows in the mountains and has long narrow arching branches, one to two feet long, that have fairly uniform thicknesses. The shape and uniformity makes this plant ideal to use on cradleboard hoods (visors). The plant takes its name from this usage. (See Crafts.)

SPRUCE *Picea engelmannii* and *pungens* munu ohomp (lit. ***sticker pine***) a name given to spruce trees due to their sharp needles.

SQUAWBUSH *Rhus trilobata* suhv, suh'uhv´. The long shoots are split three ways and used in making baskets and cradleboards. September is the best month to gather this wood. When squawbush is being cut for baskets the women would

also collect the very small hard pieces of gum from this plant and chew it like gum. It tastes good.

The berries are called e-ees´ and ee´-see. Some bushes are sweet and others have a kerosene taste. Only the sweet bushes were picked with each bush generally being owned by a particular family. Other people would not pick from them without permission. The berries can be eaten fresh or pounded in a mortar to a course pulp; then mixed with a little water and the pulp squeezed until all the red juice comes out of it. The pulp is then discarded. Water can be added to the mixture until it is the desired strength. The berries can also be dried, pounded to a pulp, stored, and then water added to it later. The drink is somewhat strong so occasionally the sweet aphid excrement from the common reed would be added. This drink is often called "Indian lemonade" and the Old People liked to eat bread with it.

STINGING NETTLE *Urtica dioica* kwawsoo´ kwepump (lit. ***sting hitter***).

SUNFLOWER *Helianthus annuus* huhkuhmp´, kawngoomp. Collect and dry the seeds, roast them, grind them and then boil them into a mush.

SWEETCLOVER *Melilotus officinalis* peu´ whawnunump.

TAMARISK, SALTCEDAR *Tamarix pentandra* spawngwup. This plant was imported from the Mediterranean area and has spread itself over a vast area of the West. The Indian name spawngwup is the name of the red cedar *Juniperus virginiana* which is native to Utah. This Cedar is noticeably lacking in the Moapa and Las Vegas areas. Therefore the name for the red cedar was borrowed from the Utah Paiutes for this new desert plant.

TANSY MUSTARD *Descurainia* awk. The seeds were processed and eaten.

THIN-LEAFED ALDER *Alnus Tenuifolia* pawwhay´uv. The bark is used for a brownish red dye. Boil bark and then soak the article in the cooled solution.

THISTLE *Cirsium* tsengu´peev. This thistle has thorny-looking dandelion type leaves. The outer skin of the young tender stems is peeled off as you would a banana. They are then cut into pieces, about two to three inches long, boiled and eaten. They taste better when cooked with deer meat. The informant mentioned that one type of thistle is poisonous.

THISTLE *Cirsium* paw´tsengu´peev. One informant identified this thistle as having pinkish-red flowers. Jimmy Timmican pointed out a thistle with a purple flower that I identified as the wheeler thistle. The stems were peeled and eaten raw. The first word (paw) in the Indian name could mean ***blood,*** in reference to the color of the flower, or it could mean ***water***.

TOMATILLO, WOLFBERRY *Lycium* suhnu´ oop (lit. ***coyote-berry***). I'm not entirely sure which *Lycium* this is but it would be the one the coyotes like and therefore probably the most bitter of the tomatillos. The Paiutes mashed the berries, boiled them, and then drank the solution.

TULE, BULRUSH *Scirpus* sawmpeev. This plant was used to line pits for roasting toa'oyv (cattail). The roots of tule were also edible plus the white base of the stems.

TUMBLEWEED *Salsola iberica* mawntee´nu munuv, noopu´nump (lit. ***rolling thing***).

UTAH AGAVE *Agave utahensis* nunt. This plant was dug out of the ground just as the stalk starts to rise. A sprouting stalk was a sign that it was ripe and full of sugar. If a person waited until the stalks were full grown then the sweetness would all go to the stalk. All the spines were cut off many agave plants and then the hearts were placed in a heated rock-lined pit. They were then covered with other plants and dirt to seal in the heat and left to bake overnight.

WATER CRESS *Nasturtium officinale* pawmuhmp´. This plant is eaten when young and tender and is good for your stomach.

WESTERN YARROW *Achillea millefolium* oychu´ kwawseev. The Paiute name means ***squirrel's tail*** from the shape of the leaves that resemble the upright tail of a squirrel. The leaves, when smashed into a wet mash, are used as a dressing for bullet and arrow wounds. The leaves can also be steeped in water and drunk for whooping cough.

WHITE-SPINED CLARET CUP HEDGEHOG *Echinocereus melanacanthus* ovu´gawv. See the discussion under corky-seed pincushion. Another informant gave the name of a cactus that he called awvaw´koav "a red flowered cactus." He said that this cactus was recently used as a medicine for kochuv (venereal disease). Both names are probably the same cactus. I received these names long ago and never heard them repeated. I could have easily misheard one of the names.

WILD ONION *Allium*

1. koongkuv´ (Koosharem).
2. kwechus´eev (Cedar City).

Boil the flowers and leaves. They have an onion smell, especially before boiling. Bulbs are also eaten.

WILD PARSLEY *Ligusticum porteri* pawkoov´, pawgoov´. The smell of this plant will keep rattlesnakes from biting you. Dry and grind the roots into a powder and tie this powder into a little ball in a piece of cloth or buckskin. Tie this ball onto your shoe when near rattlesnakes. It is believed that this plant is poison to a rattlesnake if chewed and spit into its mouth. This was done one time at Kaibab and the snake died. The dried root is also good to put into your mouth when you have a cold. A very similar plant with yellow flowers is called toanchawv´. This plant was mixed with oats for sick horses.

WILD PEPPERMINT *Mentha piperita* and *canadensis* pawkoa´nunump, pawwhaw´ nunump. The leaves and stems are boiled for a tea. It is also used fresh as an incense in the Sun Dance.

WILD RASPBERRY *Rubus idaeus* nuhaw´ wunawtump (lit. ***mountain-sheep-penis***). The berries were eaten.

WILD ROSE *Rosa woodsii* seump´eev, cheump´eev. Arrows are made out of this wood, however they sometimes split when they strike an object. The same method of inserting points is used with this type of arrow as with golden current.

Rose hips are eaten raw without the seeds. The hips may also be dried, ground up, and boiled for a mush; they need sweetening. They can be stored for winter use.

WILD RYE *Elymus triticoides*, or wheatgrass *Agripyron* wawv´.

WILLOW *Salix exigua* kawnuv´. Young straight willows are used in making cradleboards (see "Cradleboards" in Chapter 6). September is the best month to gather this wood. Arrows can also be made out of this wood; however they are not strong.

WINTER-FAT, WHITE SAGE *Eurotia lanata* pawvee´cheev.

WOLFBERRY *Lycium andersonii* or *Lycium torreyi* oo-oop´. These berries are somewhat sweet when ripe and were eaten raw or mashed and boiled for a drink. Juice can be made out of these berries just like described under squawberries. They can also be dried whole after the green stems have been pulled off.

YAMPA, WILD CARAWAY *Perideridia gairdneri* yump. The modern name "yampa" comes from the Paiute and Ute word for this plant. The tuberous roots can be dried and ground into flour, or boiled and eaten when first dug up.

YUCCA (Narrow-leaf) *Yucca utahensis* and probably *baileyi* chumuv´eep. This plant had the same uses as *Yucca baccata*.

YUCCA, BANANA *Yucca baccata* oos´eev. The older roots are used for a shampoo. Scrape off the bark from the root and pound the root on top of a rock until it is soft and stringy. Then take the pounded root and rinse it in a pan of water until the water is filled with suds. After filtering out all the loose fibers from the water the hair is then washed in this sudsy water. This Indian shampoo makes the hair shine. The unused roots can be stored for future use.

The ripened fruit was split to extract the seeds and eaten raw, or roasted over coals, turning them often, so as not to burn them. They were eaten after roasting or dried and made into balls and stored for future use. They were also boiled after splitting, or after drying.

The young shoots or fresh stalks (ovweep) were placed in coals and covered for about three hours and then eaten; they were also boiled. They look a lot like asparagus and taste very similar.

UNIDENTIFIED PLANTS

KAW´KOP A bush that looks like Brigham tea. Dry and grind this plant and mix it with ochre. When this mixture is put in the tracks of a horse, or when the horse is caused to smell it, it will tire quickly. This medicine was used in horse racing. It's a way to win a race by doing this to the opponent's horse. Koosharem 3, and Indian Peak 1.

KOOCHU´ KAWNUV (lit. ***gray willow***). The name of this willow comes from its gray-colored bark. This willow grows at Fish Lake, Utah.

KWECHUH´UV A bush that grows in Cedar Canyon east of Cedar City, Utah. It might be *Peraphyllum ramosissimum*?

KWEYU´SOOV This plant wasn't positively identified at the time but the description, and what I remember, suggests one of the mahoganies other than curl-leaf. Digging sticks are made out of this wood because of its hardness.

MOOHOO´DOOMP Boiled and put on chicken-pox sores. Chemehuevi 41.

ONTOMPEES An unidentified bush.
PAWNGWUV´ This grass grows in the valley at Cedar City, Utah.
PESO´UV This grass like plant grows in the water and is eaten by ducks.
SAWKWAY´UM MOOSOO´TOOKWEEV (lit. ***stomach medicine***). This plant grows along the road to Green Lake above Cedar City, Utah.
SAWWHAW´ KAWNUV (lit. ***green willow***). A willow similar to the sketch.

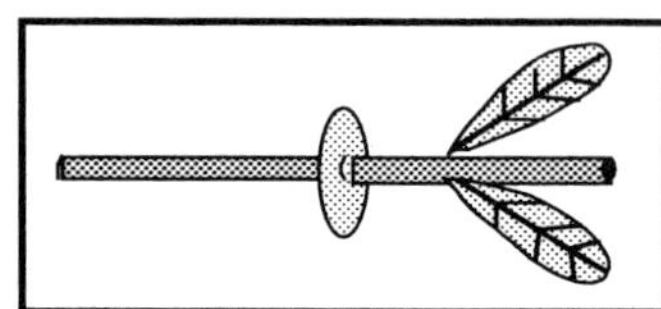

SECHUKANUMP (lit. ***sage hen thing?***). The seeds are ground into a flour and used for gravy. The flower looks like a sunflower and has a yellow center. My notes say this plant is the "mountain sunflower" but it could also be arrowleaf balsamroot *balsamorrhiza sagitata.*
SECHU´ (lit. ***sage hen***) A seed-bearing plant that grows abundantly on Cedar Mountain near Green Lake just southeast of Cedar City, Utah. This plant might be similar to sechukanump.
TAWMPEE´SOODOOP (lit. ***shoestring bush***). This plant is used in making cradleboard visors (see "Cradleboards" in Chapter 6). This wood is good to use all year round.
TOAHO´U MUUV (lit. ***rattlesnake bush***). This plant is a bush about 18 inches high. The leaves are mashed and put on acne and pimples; it burns but cures them quickly. Kaibab 42.
TOANCHAWV´ This yellow flowered plant is very similar to wild parsley *Ligusticum porteri*. The plant was mixed with oats and given to sick horses.
TOOP A bush with black berries that grows near St. George, Utah. It is used as a black dye.
UNIDENTIFIED PLANT Ashes made from an unidentified plant are put in a bag over a horse's nose for a time while it runs. If the horse has a cough, this will clean him out.
UNIDENTIFIED PLANT There is a plant that grows in Zion National Park, the root of which when boiled, makes a good red dye.

CHAPTER 10

HOMELANDS OF THE OLD ONES

The Southern Utes and other Utes used to all live together.
Trouble caused them to leave.

It is difficult to draw a boundary between Southern Paiute and Ute homelands since both groups speak the same language, have a very similar culture and religion, and call themselves by the same name. A controversy often develops on this subject which I'm going to avoid since my basic intent is to record and preserve information given to me by both Paiute and Ute informants.

The Kanosh and Koosharem bands were considered Utes in the last century. Some families of the Koosharem band were moved to the Uintah basin as was the entire group that was gathered on the reservation at Spanish Fork, Utah. The remaining Kanosh and Koosharem bands affiliated more with the Cedar City, Kaibab, and Shivwits bands and consequently were called Paiutes by the whites. According to a Shivwits informant the Utes, or Yoo´taw as they were called by the Shivwits, included the Indians at Cedar City and Gunlock.

In the old days the Paiutes and Utes only referred to themselves as Nengwoonts or Noonts signifying ***People*** and in more recent times ***Indians***. They also distinguished each other by band names. The Utes and Paiutes had no clan system nor priest class as found among many tribes.

To help understand the difference between Paiute and Ute let us study the derivation of both of these names. William Palmer says that Paiute, "Pahute" as he spells it, means "Water Ute." Not only did he err in his translation, but because he was hard of hearing, he even pronounced it wrong. He pronounced the "a" in paw ***water*** as the "a" in hat. The correct pronunciation of the "a" is as in saw. I once brought this to his attention and told him it should be pronounced as explained above. He replied "Yeah, that's right, pah," pronouncing it exactly as he did before, as in hat.

A quick perusal of his English interpretation of his Paiute words shows that he didn't put much effort towards accuracy in his meager Paiute dictionary in back of his book "Why the North Star Stands Still." When it comes to pronunciation, many of his Paiute words are in a much worse shape.

He claims that the word Pah means "water" so the Paiutes are "Water Utes." This seems a little out of character since the bands he was best acquainted with were desert people during much of the year when the mountains were snow covered. The Old People that I have questioned have never accepted this interpretation and have always said that they really didn't know what it meant. When I ask the Utes I get a couple of plausible explanations, that if true, would account for the Paiute silence on this word. Following are six quotations from Utes all of which agree with the two possible linguistic explanations of the word Paiyuh, one of which is ***to call back*** and the other ***poor***.

> *Paiute means* ***to call after*** *from the word Paiyoo because the Paiutes did not like to fight and always had to be called to help.*
>
> *Paiute means* ***poor, having nothing, or with worn-out shoes.*** *Paiutes were named this after they left the Blanding, Utah area because of too much fighting there. They migrated to central Utah and when they arrived their shoes and clothes were all worn out and so they received the name Paiyuhch.*[56]
>
> *The Paiutes never quite did things right or complete. They were always a little lazy, therefore the Utes called them Paiutes.*[57]
>
> *Paiute (Paiyoots) means simple people who often have to be told how to do things.*[58]
>
> *The word Paiute comes from the Ute and Paiute word Paiyuh,* ***to return*** *or* ***go back****, because the Paiutes always did everything backwards from the way the Utes told them. They were mischievous so the Utes told them to leave.*
>
> *Paiyuhch means* ***poor****.*

It seems plausible that the Anglos could have picked up the word Paiute from the Utes and applied it to all the Southern Paiutes which then spread even to the Northern Paiutes. This Northern group doesn't even speak the same language, however they do dress similarly, look similar, live in a similar type of environment,

[56] Harriet Taveapont, White River Ute.
[57] Dick McKuen, Northern Ute.
[58] Vincent Sireech, White River Ute.

and consequently fit the Ute category of being poor and simple. This would explain why the Southern Paiutes don't want to admit what Paiute means even though it's one of their words.

A similar comparison of a tribe not understanding what their tribal name means, or not wanting to admit the meaning, may be made with the linguistically related Commanche People. Ask a Commanche what Commanche means and most of them won't be able to tell you. The reason is that Commanche is a Ute and Paiute word meaning ***strange*** or ***different*** that is applied to them by the Utes. Somewhere along the line, either the whites or Spaniards, picked up this word and it soon became the household name for the Commanche. It was not their name for themselves.

In 1776, Father Escalante called the Paiutes in southern Utah "Payuche" with the distinct Southern Ute ending of "ch" as opposed to the Paiute dialect of "ts." Also, in the following quotation the Paiutes are mentioned as being in New Mexico in the 1700s: "Four nations in New Mexico: Utes, Chaguaguas, Payuches, and Moaches."[59] This would lend evidence that the word Paiute originated there with the Utes living in northern New Mexico and spread westward with civilization.

The linguistically related Hopis shed a little more light on this subject. The Hopis call the Paiutes Paiyoot´see (singular) and Paiyoot´seem (plural). To the Hopis these words refer to anyone "Not initiated into any of the Hopi societies," a meaning similar to the Ute description calling the Paiutes "poor" and "simple." The Paiutes were certainly very simple in religious structure, compared to the Hopis, thus representing a good example of being uninitiated from the viewpoint of the Hopi. I'm not sure if the Hopi example is a pure Hopi word or a Ute word that they used for the Paiutes and then extended it to refer to the uninitiated. If it is a Hopi word then it is similar enough in meaning to cause no conflict since both tribes are linguistically related although their languages are not mutually intelligible.

The Navajos call the Paiutes Bayoh´tseen which is probably a takeoff from the Ute or Hopi word. The linguistically related Shoshonis from Idaho call the Paiutes "Paiyooch." The above collaborations from surrounding tribes plus the early New Mexico quote indicate the word Paiute is a long-standing Indian word for certain bands of Southern Paiutes.

It is common for different tribes and bands to use derogatory names for each other. The Wee´mee Noonts band at Towoac, Colorado, is a good example. This word means Humping Indians, a name given to them by the Capote Band at Ignacio.

The Hualapais have a word that might also describe the Paiutes. This word is pawyoot which refers to "a man sneaking up to spy on someone" such as a scout would do. They also have a dance by this name where the men dance with staffs. The Hualapais normally call the Paiutes "Suveech" after the Shivwits band which was basically the main Paiute band they had contact with other than the

[59] Thomas 1940, p. 131.

Chemehuevis. Their word Pawyoot being applied to the name Paiute is only speculation on the part of some Hualapais.

The term Ute has several possible derivations. One might be an Anglo corruption of their own word for themselves "Noonts" signifying ***People*** and could easily be mispronounced by whites to "Utes." The Hopis call the Utes "Utaw" (singular) and "Utawm" (plural); another possible explanation. The Navajos call the Utes "Notaw" which is similar. The Shoshonis call the Utes "Yoo´tawtch."

The band territory lines drawn on the following map are drawn arbitrarily as in most cases the exact boundary lines are not known. The list of bands are far from complete and come only from information given to me long ago. William Palmer gives a good list of band names, some of which I didn't get, that extends from Kanosh to Parowan. I find no reason to disagree with him on his list since I didn't get conflicting comments. The weakness of his band names is his mispronunciation and failure to explain what the Paiute names mean. Some are even difficult for me to recognize and interpret so I won't confuse the issue by attempting. However, when discussing certain bands I will make comments to clarify some of his mistakes.

The material that I give in my list all comes from the mouths of my informants unless noted otherwise. My main informant on bands in central, northern, and eastern Utah came from Jimmy Timmican of the Koosharem band. Southern information came from Archie Rogers, Shivwits, Jim Chili, Chemehuevi, and a couple of others.

In the following list it will become apparent that some bands had several names and that band names changed when the band moved to a different area. Band names originated from such things as the type of country they lived in, what they ate, a peculiar physical characteristic, derision, and other things that will become evident when the following band list is studied. Some band names were often just nicknames for a small group who actually belonged to a larger group.

I'm not including all that is written by others about the boundaries of these bands since that information is available in other publications. My intent is to keep to statements of Indians and thus preserve their information in this compilation as *their record* rather than one compiled from books.

I do record a few other names and information of interest, or for the sake of clarification. I also correct known mistakes, particularly in the mispronunciation of Indian names, made by Anglos in recording band territories. I'm also including the Ute Bands from Colorado since I have received information from them that deserves to be preserved and that often has a bearing on clearing up misconceptions.

Band territories were not exclusive of other bands. At certain times of the year several bands would camp together, share the natural animal or plant harvest, and participate in sports, gambling, dancing, foot races and horse races. Indian horse-racing tracks can still be seen at Panguitch Lake and west of Modena, Utah. Places where this occurred, that were brought to my attention, were Panguitch, Fish, and Rush Lakes, Utah, the Kaibab Mountains for hunting deer, and Indian Peak and Frisco Mountain for harvesting pinyon nuts.

These encampments lasted until within this century and at Fish and Panguitch lakes they had Fish Chiefs who gave permission to fish and supervised the visitors. At Kaibab and Shivwits they also had Hunting Chiefs. There were other areas also but the above were all that I noted. These visits to other band territories were on an exchange basis where the granting band would also be allowed to harvest within the territorial limits of the bands they allowed within their lands.

From this information it becomes evident that the Paiutes weren't strictly desert people, always digging for roots, as portrayed by early pioneers and present-day readers who seem to think the early Paiutes never had enough sense to avail themselves of the beautiful and rich mountains. The Paiutes did take advantage of the nearby mountains and spent the summers there where food was abundant. In this respect most Paiute bands were really Mountain Indians as noted by early observers about the Utes. Even the Shivwits, Kaibab, and Las Vegas bands had their pine-covered mountains.

The suffixes -eev´w and eng at the end of a band name are plural and represent a group of people. Eng is sometimes slurred to een. An example of singular and plural concerning a band's name is as follows: Suhuh´ Vawn Tuhnts is one person from the Squawbush Water Band and Suhuh' Vawn Tuhtseev is several from that band.

BAND NAMES

The number in front of each band name corresponds to the numbers on the map of Band Territories on page 155 to give an approximate location of each homeland:

1 UNGKAW´ PAWGUH´U VUTSENG ***Red Fish People***
2 UNTAW´DUHEUTSENG
3 SUHUH´VAWDUTSENG ***Squawbush Water People***
4 PAW GOOSAWD UHMPUHTSENG ***Water Clover people***
5 UNGKAW KAWNUH´GUTSENG ***Red Foot of the Hills people***
6 TOSAW KAWDUHD NENGWOONTS´ENG ***White Sitting People***
7 TOOGOO´VUHTSENG ***Sand People***
8 YUHNGUH´ KAWDUHTS´ENG ***Porcupine Sitting People***
9 TUH´DUVAW DUHTS´ENG ***Barren Valley***
10 AWVO´UTSENG ***Semi-circular Cliffs People***
11 O-AW´TUHUTS´ENG ***Yellow Mouth of Canyon People***
12 KAWNAW´ DUHTS´ENG ***Willow Mouth of Canyon People***
13 KAI´VAHV EETSENG (Kaibab) ***Mountain Lying Down People***
14 YOOVEEN´KAWDUHTS´ENG ***Ponderosa Sitting People***
15 SEE´VEETS ENG (Shivwits) ***Whitish Earth People***
16 YOOVEEN´TUH (Uintah) ***Ponderosa People***
17 KOOMU´ UMPAW´HAW (Cumumba) ***Talks Different***
18 OU´VAW´ TUHTSEEV ***Salt Water People***
19 PAWGOO´U NOONTS ***Lake Shore People***
20 SAWMPEE´TUTSENG, SAWMPEETSENG ***Tule people***
21 TOOWEE´ NAWAIP´UHTSEEN ***Earth Burnt People***
22 TOAOYV´UHTSENG ***Cattail people***
23 PAWAWVAWN´TUHTSEEVW (Pahvant) ***By the Water People***
24 PAWDOO´ GOONUNTSENG ***Water Up People***
25 PAWDOOS´UTS ***White Water People***
26 TOO´ NOOKWEENTSENG (Tonoquint) ***Black Flowing People***
27 TUHNDUH´ESU
28 PADUN´UGUTS (Pahrangat) ***Sticking Feet in the Water People***
29 MOU´ PAW (Moapa) ***Mosquito Water***
30 LAS VEGAS
31 NAVAJO MOUNTAIN
32 WILLOW SPRINGS
33 BLANDING

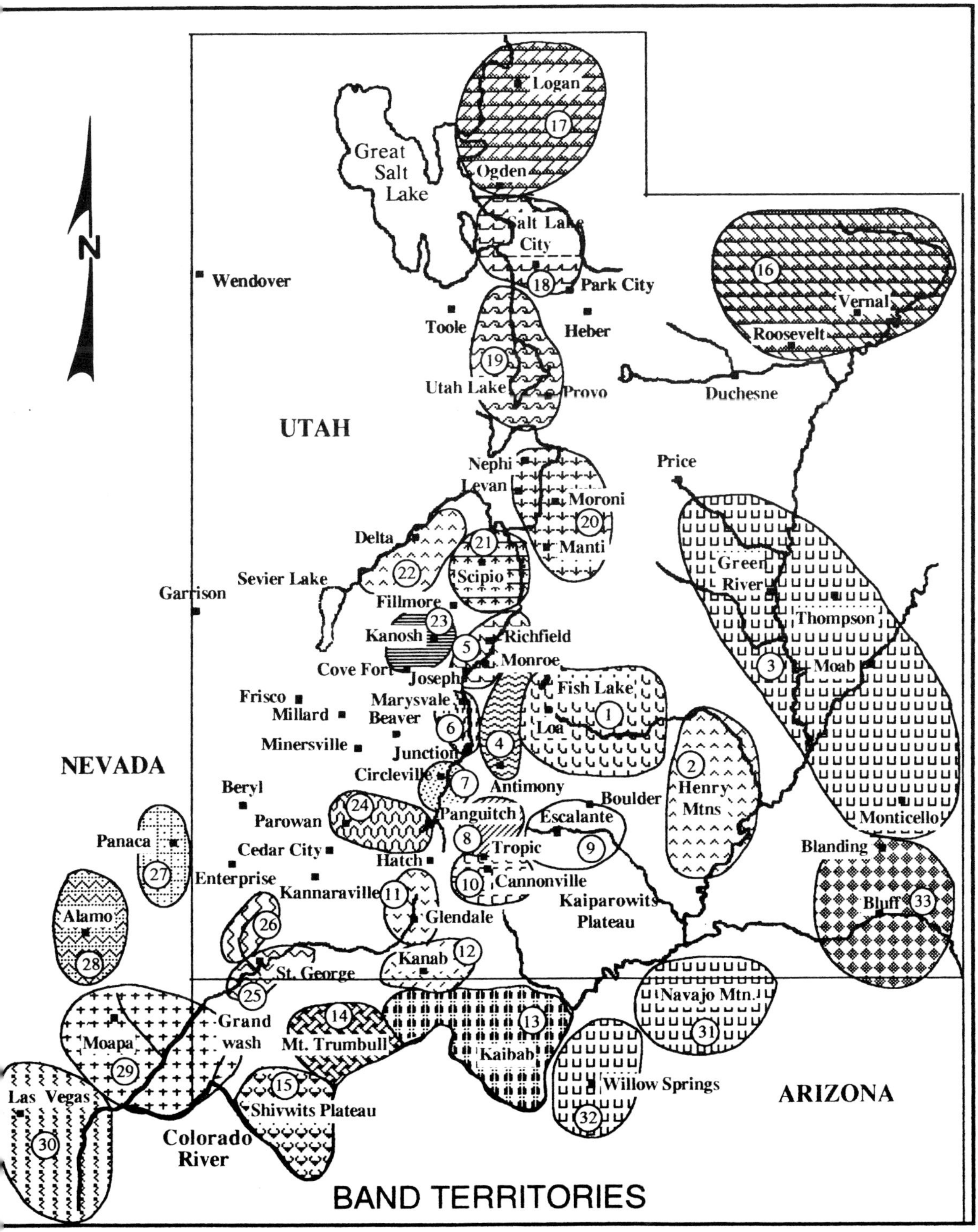

N

UTAH

NEVADA

ARIZONA

Great Salt Lake

Logan
17
Ogden
Salt Lake City
18
Park City
Wendover
16
Vernal
Roosevelt
Toole
Heber
19
Utah Lake
Provo
Duchesne
Price
Nephi
Levan
Moroni
20
Manti
Delta
21
22
Scipio
Sevier Lake
Garrison
Fillmore
23
Kanosh
5
Richfield
Monroe
Cove Fort
Joseph
Fish Lake
1
Loa
Frisco
Millard
Marysvale
Beaver
6
4
Minersville
Junction
Circleville
7
Antimony
Green River
Thompson
3
Moab
2
Henry Mtns
Monticello
Blanding
Beryl
24
Parowan
Panguitch
8
Tropic
Escalante
Boulder
9
Panaca
27
Cedar City
Hatch
Enterprise
10
Cannonville
Kannaraville
11
Glendale
Kaiparowits Plateau
33
Bluff
Alamo
28
26
St. George
25
Kanab
12
13
Kaibab
14
Mt. Trumbull
Navajo Mtn.
31
Grand wash
Moapa
29
Willow Springs
32
Las Vegas
30
15
Shivwits Plateau
Colorado River

BAND TERRITORIES

BAND NAMES

The following band names represent both Ute and Paiute bands. Most of the information in this chapter was given to me by Paiute informants. The names of Ute bands originating in Colorado are listed in a later section in this chapter. The number in front of each band name corresponds to the numbers on the foregoing map of Band Territories to give an approximate location of each homeland.

1. UNGKAW´ PAWGUH´U VUTSENG ***Red Fish People***. This is the band that lived at Fish Lake, Utah, during the summer. According to Timmican other bands would come here and camp during the summer and share in the abundant fish and wildlife. In the late 1800s they had a Fish Chief here who took charge of this large summer encampment. His name was Pawguh´u Neahv meaning ***Fish Chief***.

   Timmican says his band would make a yearly migration from Fish Lake, that would include the Henry Mountains and the Escalante area, as they followed the seasons for harvesting certain food products. This route was through the territories of other bands.
2. UNTAW´DUHEUTSENG Untaw´duhee is the name of the Henry Mountains but I couldn't obtain a translation of this word.
3. SUHUH´ VAW DUHUTS, SUHUH´VAWDUTSENG (Sheberitch) ***Squawbush Water People***. This band's name has been Anglicized to Sheberitch. This band was described by Florence Kanosh as the largest in the state of Utah covering the area from Wellington through Moab, to Montecello, Utah, including Canyonlands and the area of the confluence of the Green and Colorado rivers. Writers state that most of this band died out from a smallpox epidemic in about 1873. Florence Kanosh relates an interesting story about the demise of this band due to the quarreling of two women. See the story "Medicine Power Destroys an Indian Band" in Chapter 2 on War and Historical Stories.

   A Paiute informant from Willow Springs, Arizona, says some of the Paiutes there are remnants of this band. See band number 32 for more information.
4. PAW GOOSAWD´UHMPUHTSENG (Koosharem) ***Water Clover People***. This is the name from which the word Koosharem is derived. This is also the name of the band once living in the Koosharem Valley. According to Jimmy Timmican "This entire band is now dead." Most were killed by the white men in the Grass Valley massacre of 1865. Later, when the Wayne County Band from Fish Lake was moved to the Koosharem Valley, and given a reservation there, they took the Reservation name of the valley and became known as the Koosharem Band. None of them came from the original Koosharem Band living there at the coming of the whites. (see Plate 2, page 171)
5. UNGKAW´ KAWNUH´GUTSENG ***Red, Foot of the Hills People***. Sapir says that a band of this name formerly lived in Long Valley near Orderville, Utah. (Sapir 1930, P. 549.) This band name doesn't fit the description of Long Valley as well as it does the Richfield area where most of the west mountains consist

of red sandstone. Long Valley lacks much of this red. Jimmy Timmican was more familiar with this area than Sapir's informant Tony Tillahash (see Oaw´ Tuhuts´eng in this chapter). The aged Minnie Kanosh gives the following information about the Richfield Band:

> *The Indians in Sevier Valley near Richfield used to live along the foot of the hills from Monroe to Annabella and on the big hill between. They also lived in the foothills just west of Richfield.*

6. TOSAW´ KAWDUHD NENGWOONTS´ENG ***White Sitting People***. Tosaw Kawduhd is the name of the snow-capped peaks of the Tushar Mountains. Tushar is the Anglicized form of the Paiute word Tosaw Kawduhd. Timmican said this band lived around Marysvale.
7. TOOGOO´VUHTSENG ***Sand People***. This is the band that lived around the Circleville, Utah, area including the surrounding mountains. Jimmy Timmican said the word means ***Sand Indians,*** however this isn't the common name for sand as used by other bands nor do younger Paiutes any longer recognize this word. This is true of many words that died out with the older Paiutes who spoke poor English. Timmican was of this older group. The Paiutes had several words for sand depending on its coarseness and other mixtures. The word toogoo, therefore, most likely represents a peculiar type of sand in the Circleville valley. This area isn't known for the type of sand most people are familiar with. Years later his daughter Vera, not knowing the actual name, said the word sounded like it meant "swampy" to her, referring to the wetlands along the Sevier river.

   This band was massacred, without just cause, by the settlers of Circleville, Utah (Gottfredson, 1969, p. 144). For the Paiute version of this massacre see "Slaughter of Indians at Circleville" in Chapter 2 on War and Historical Stories.
8. YUHNGUH´ KAWDUHTS´ENG ***Porcupine Sitting People***. This band lived near the Widtso area in Garfield County, Utah. Their band name comes from a nearby mountain called Porcupine Sitting. No known survivors of this band remain.
9. TUH´DUVAW DUHTSENG ***Barren Valley People***. This band lived around the Escalante, Utah area. Tom Amnisky better known as "Tom Mix" was from the Escalante area. Two of his sisters never left the area and were buried there in a white cemetery. They and Tom were the last of this band.
10. AWVO´UTSENG ***Semi-circular Cliffs People***. Awvo´uv is the name for Bryce Canyon, Utah, and refers to the semicircular type cliffs found there. This band inhabited this area including Tropic and Cannonville.
11. O-AW´ TUHUTS´ENG ***Yellow Mouth of Canyon People***. This band lived around the Mount Carmel area near a canyon with a yellow mouth. Perhaps it was from this name that Tony Tillahash confused this band's name with the Red Foot of Hills People near the Richfield area.
12. KANAW´DUHTSENG ***Willow Mouth of Canyon People***. Kanaw´tuh is the

correct pronunciation for ***Willow Canyon Mouth***. The town of Kanab takes its name from this locality and band name. This is the band that lived in Kanab Creek and the Kanab area. This area is attributed to the Kaibab Band by Kelly, but according to Timmican a different but related group lived at Kanab.

13. KAI´VAHV EETSENG (Kaibab) ***Mountain Lying Down People***. This band lived on the Kaibab Mountains, in House Rock Valley, and on the Paria Plateau. (see Plate 4, page 172)
14. YOOVEEN´KAWDUHTS ENG (Uint-karets) ***Ponderosa Sitting People***. This band lived around Mount Trumbull and on the Colorado River on the Arizona Strip. Morris Jake of Kaibab includes Kanab Creek in their area. This band took their name from the Indian name of Mount Trumbull, Yooveen Kawduh, ***Ponderosa Sitting***. The word ***sitting*** is used to signify ***mountain***. Palmer calls them Uint-karets.
15. SEE´VEETS ENG (Shivwits). Archie Rogers, a member of the Shivwits Band, gives the following explanation of this band name:

> *The word Shivwits comes from Seeveen´ Tooweep which is a name for a soft whitish area of earth someplace down in Shivwits country on the Arizona Strip.*

The word Shivwits is correctly pronounced See´veets. This band ranged on the Shivwits Plateau and in the Grand Canyon with the Colorado River being a loose boundary between them and the Hualapais. The Shivwits often crossed the river to get red ochre from Diamond Creek and even visit the Hualapais. The Hualapais themselves state that the Shivwits came to visit them, often staying for some time. They also fled there for safety when they had troubles in Utah with the whites [60]

The Shivwits were called Haawp´ukunt **To Have Horns** by the Moapa band. Shivwits 5.

16. YOOVEEN´TUHTS (Uintah) ***Ponderosa Pine People.*** This was a band of Utes living in the Uintah Mountains before the coming of the white man. When the U.S. Government moved many of the Indians from the Spanish Fork Reservation and other places to the Uintah Basin they then became known by the same name as the band once inhabiting this area.
17. KOOMU´ UMPAW´HAW This band lived north of Salt Lake City, Utah. This name appears in books as "Cumumba." In Paiute it would be pronounced Koomu´ umpaw´haw ***Talks different***. They were probably Shoshonis with a Ute mixture to account for this name.
18. OU´VAW´ TUHTSEEV ***Salt Water People***. This was a band living along the shores of the Great Salt Lake. No specific locations were given by the informant.
19. PAWGOO´U NOONTS ***Lake Shore People***. This name comes from the words

[60] "Walapai Papers." Published by the United States Senate 1936.

paw ***water*** and koong-wawv´ or koo-waw´ ***edge.*** Paw Koo´wu Nuhwuhnt´see is the pronunciation at Kanosh. This was the band that lived at Utah Lake. Some writers refer to this band as Tumpanawach an Anglicized name that probably comes from the name of the Timpanogas River correctly pronounced Tuhmpaw Nookweent ***Rock Water Running***. Rock Water People could well have been another name for this band.

20. SAWMPEE´TUTSENG, SAWMPEETS´ENG (San Pitch) ***Tule People***. This band lived in the valley and mountains between Mayfield and Nephi, Utah. The Indian words have been changed by the whites to San Pitch and San Pete. This valley had plenty of water and an abundance of tules (*Scirpus*) therefore the name ***Tule People***. The Paiutes tell a story of how this band was annihilated through poison by the early settlers. See "Poisoning of Indians at Manti" in Chapter 2 on War and Historical Stories. The whites say this band died of smallpox.
21. TOOWEE´ NAWAIP´UHTSEEN ***Earth Burnt People***. This band lived near Scipio, Utah.
22. TOAOYV´UHTSENG ***Cattail People***. This band is named after the abundance of cattails growing in the lakes near the Delta, Utah area. Palmer has them living further south. Timmican only mentioned that this band lived around the Delta area.
23. PAW AWVAWN´TUHTSEEVW (Pahvant) ***By the Water People***. Paw´ awvawnt means ***by the water***. Kanosh pronounces it paw uvawntuhsee´wu. (see Plate 5, page 173) This name has been changed by the whites to Pahvant. The following Indian quotes pertain to this band:

> *The Sevier River, west of Kanosh, used to be the boundary between the Utes in the area and the Gosiutes to the west. The Pahvant Band would go out to the desert area and gather duck eggs during the season then return and camp at Corn Creek. There used to be many Gosiutes out west of Delta but the soldiers killed many of them off. When the government wanted them all to come in to sign a treaty the Gosiutes at Ibapah wouldn't come in out of fear of being killed.*[61]

> *The Pahvant Indians have all died out. The Levi and the Pikyavit families were not originally from there. The original Indians near Delta weren't Paiutes, they were Gosiutes. In the Gosiute language they were called Paw´ugunt. They lived near the Delta area by a lake. The Gosiutes also lived near Baker, Nevada, Garrison and all over that way. The Gosiutes used to plant gardens on a piece of land near Baker that was given to them; maybe they sold it.*[62]

---

[61] Kanosh 15 and Koosharem 7.
[62] Shivwits 5.

24. PAW DOOGOO´NUNTSENG (Pah-ra goons) ***Water Up People***. This name has been Anglicized to Paragoonah. This band is also referred to as the "Parowan Band." An Indian Peak informant added this statement, "Paiyoo´koots is another name for the general locality and also this band; they had great power." Indian Peak 24.

Isaac Hunkup, who died in Cedar City in the 1950s, claims that he saw the first white man arrive in the Parowan Valley on a white horse. Hunkup also claims to have sold Parowan Valley to a white man for half a pig. Cedar City 37.

Most of the members of this band were massacred by soldiers from Camp Floyd, Utah, while the Paiutes were encamped with some Gosiutes near the Utah-Nevada border. E.N. Wilson tells of the soldiers from Camp Douglas and their planned sneak attack on the Gosiutes and Parowan Band. He witnessed the massacre and gives this account:

> *I could see little children not over five or six years old with sticks fighting like wildcats....This was the worst battle and the last one I ever saw. It lasted about two hours, and during that short period of time, every Indian, squaw, and papoose, and every dog was killed.* [63]

A different Anglo version of this massacre seeks to take the heat off the citizens of Utah, as a planned attack as stated by Wilson, by stating that the soldiers:

> *...were members of the California Volunteers forces commanded by Gen. Patrick Edward Conner stationed at Camp Douglas. Perhaps it was the nasty water they had to drink, or the invariable bilious diet of bacon and sour-dough bread which made them evil-dispositioned. At any rate they wanted to kill somebody.*[64]

This is the same massacre referred to by Juicy, the lone Gosiute child survivor of this battle. See "Massacre at Spring Valley" in Chapter 2 on War and Historical Stories for the Indian versions of this battle which was an unprovoked attack on peaceful Indians. If the Parowan Band was on the warpath it is doubtful they would have taken their women and children with them thus giving credence to the truthfulness of the Indian versions. It was often the policy of the army to kill innocent Indians to intimidate the warlike ones. The massacre of most of the members of this band would account for Isaac Hunkup's ability to sell Parowan Valley for "half a pig" as mentioned above. He was one of the few that stayed behind.

---

[63] Wilson 1919, p. 165.
[64] Sharp & Bennion 1936.

This band ranged from Parowan Valley to the Panguitch Lake area. They were friendly to the Gosiutes and one Southern Paiute informant, who is one-fourth Gosiute and has a grandfather from Panguitch, states that the name of Panguitch is Gosiute rather than Paiute:

> *The word Panguitch is a Gosiute word Pawngweets meaning **fish**. Some Gosiutes used to come down here and catch fish and dry them to take back with them.*[65]

The Paiute word for fish (pawguh´uts) is similar to the word Panguitch, but the Gosiute word Pawngweets is even closer. Once an Indian word has been Anglicized it sometimes becomes difficult to determine it's true derivation. Since it is on record that the Parowan Band was massacred while visiting the Gosiutes there is no reason to doubt that the Gosiutes would also visit the Paiutes in the Panguitch Lake area.

The Congressional Record of the Fifty-ninth Congress states that twelve thousand five hundred and twenty-five dollars was appropriated for the support and education of seventy-five pupils at the Panguitch Indian School in 1906. Today it would take two or three bands to total 75 children. At this time the Panguitch Lake area was still a favored summer encampment for many of the surrounding Paiute Bands which made up this number, even though the Parowan Band had been annihilated. These large encampments died out sometime in the 1930s due to alcohol and the killing of one Indian by another at Panguitch Lake.

I never got any information on a distinct Panguitch Band as listed by others. There might have been one, as Kelly indicates, but the Panguitch area is very cold in the winter suggesting that it was best utilized during the summer months. Many bands gathered each summer at Panguitch Lake and there was much intermarriage between all the bands. Jimmy Timmican extended the Parowan Band to Panguitch Lake. Palmer states that, "In time they became so intermixed that the Pah-ra-goons virtually absorbed the Pa-gu-its and they became as one." There are only one or two families living at Cedar City today who are descended from the Parowan Band and from the Panguitch Lake area.

Father Escalante in his 1776 journey through Cedar Valley mentions the "Huascaris" living there. I have attempted to find out what this means: The valley around Rush Lake, just north of Cedar City, was called Wuhsuh´goont or Wuhsuh´goom. Informants weren't sure of the meaning of this word. One suggested wawseev´ signifying the fine stickers found on certain types of cactus. Escalante's name of Huascaris would then mean ***Fine Stickers Sitting*** referring to a hill of this name. Another suggestion is wesee´vee, an unidentified plant.

---

[65] Indian Peak 24.

Rush Lake was a favorite gathering place for several bands, at certain times of the year, just like Panguitch and Fish lakes. Informants state that the Indians didn't live at the present site of Cedar City until the white man settled there:

> *There never was a Cedar City, Utah, band of Indians, but after Cedar was settled some moved there on the northwest outskirts of town. Later one Paiute traded this land off for a wagon and team plus other items, without the consent or knowledge of the other Paiutes. From there they moved up near Squaw Cave just south of Cedar and from there to the east side of Cedar where the baseball parks are now. From there the Mormons moved them down to the present Indian Village at the northeast corner of Cedar City. During one of these moves the Mormons told all the Indians to burn all their possessions and shacks before moving to their new locations.*[66]

25. PAWDOOS´UTS (Pa-roos-its). This was the band that lived along the Virgin River in Washington County, Utah, referred to by Escalante as Pahrusis, and by Palmer as Pa-roos-its. The name is pronounced "Pawdoos´uts" by both the Kaibab and Shivwits bands. The word pawdoos´ can have two meanings: One is ***water going under*** from the words paw and udook (Kaibab 4) and the other is ***white water*** from the words paw and tosaw´kawd. The word ***white*** is often slurred to "doos" within a sentence structure. ***White Water*** would then refer to the white foaming water as caused by the many small rapids as this river traverses Zion Canyon.

    The Pawdoos´uts were farmers to a certain extent and were also known as Uhu´ Nuhwunts´eng ***Farm People***. This name was also applied to their neighbors the Too´nookweent Band living along the Santa Clara River. I once read that an early pioneer estimated that one thousand Indians lived along the Virgin River when the white man first arrived. Today there are no survivors or known descendents of this band. They were among the ill-fated early bands to have first contact with the white man causing their extinction through disease and other causes. The only Paiute Bands surviving today, like the Kaibab, Wayne County, Shivwits, and Indian Peak bands, were the last to live side by side with the white man. This makes a statement that most whites would rather not hear especially when many claim that they seek to save the Indian.
26. TOO´ NOOKWEENTSENG (Tonoquint). This band of Paiutes lived along the Santa Clara River from Santa Clara to some distance above Magotsu. They took their name after the Santa Clara River which is called Too Nookweent ***Black Running*** and spelled Tonoquint by the whites. They were also known by one of the same names as the Virgin River Band, Uhu´ Nuhwunts´eng, because they were also ***farming Indians***. A Shivwits informant gives the following statement about this band and it's last survivor:

---

[66] Ibid

Peter Harrison, recently living at the Shivwits Reservation, was the last survivor of this band. They talked like the Indians at Kaibab and not like the Shivwits. Some of this band used to live and have orchards above the Shem dam and at Magotsu.[67]

Like the Pawdoosuts Band, this band has now become extinct. Jacob Hamblin estimated that in his time "800 Indians were living in Santa Clara Valley" (Palmer 1951-54). Another writer states that "When the Mormons in 1855 helped the Indians dam the Santa Clara near its juncture with the Virgin, five hundred Indians gathered to watch the work."[68]

27. TUHNDUH´ESU Jim Chili, a Chemehuevi who has one parent from Furnace Creek in Death Valley, and the other from the Banning, California area, gave the above name of a Southern Paiute Band living near Panaca, Nevada. He didn't give a translation of this name.

28. PADUN´UGUTS (Pahranagat) ***Sticking Feet in the Water People***. This name comes from the word pahdun´uh meaning ***to stick your feet in the water.*** The name has been Anglicized to Pahranagat. There are several springs and lakes in the area that would account for this name.

This band lived in the Pahranagat Valley near Alamo and Ash Springs. Johnny Jake, a son of Minnie Jake from Eagle Valley, Nevada, states that the Pahranagat Band extended to Eagle Valley and that his mother was of this band. There is a good chance that Eagle Valley had a strong mixture of Shoshoni as indicated by Minnie Jake. She spoke both languages and said her grandfather Pete was Shoshoni. She also mentioned that "Many of the old timers in the Indian Peak and Eagle Valley area died of smallpox."

An Anglo informant presently living in the Pahranagat Valley claims this band was massacred by the whites with Bill China being the only survivor. See the story "Paiutes Massacred in Pahranagat Valley" in Chapter 2 on War and Historical Stories. A Shivwits informant also mentions the lack of descendents from this band and a move of some of them to Moapa although he didn't state whether this was before or after the Massacre:

Some were moved to the Moapa Reservation and there are only two Indians left from this band, one in Las Vegas and one at Moapa.[69]

29. MOOU´PUHTS (Moapa). This band takes its name from the words Moou´ Paw ***Mosquito Water.*** The Paiutes pronounce this name Moou´puhts. The Shivwits called the Moapa Band "Pawuhn´kao" ***Smooth Forehead***. This name comes from the word pawung´kuhee ***to be smooth***. Archie Rogers states that "The

[67] Shivwits 12.

[68] Wilkerson, Cragun, and Barker 1963, p. 55.

[69] Ibid

Moapa People used to be called Pawuhn´kao by the Shivwits because they had big flat bare foreheads."

30. LAS VEGAS The Las Vegas Band presently call themselves Tuh´du Ningwoo and also Tuhdu Noo ***Desert Indians***. They ranged from Cottonwood Island on the Colorado to Mount Charleston. Johnny Domingo of Las Vegas said, "The Indians on Cottonwood Island killed their agent and were moved to Las Vegas so they could be more closely watched." Powell calls the Cottonwood Island Band "Mo-vwi´-ats" (Powell and Ingalls, 1874 p. 10-11). The word Mo-vwi´ats probably comes from the Paiute word moogwee´uts "a brown lizard with a long tail." Lizards are identified with the desert by most Indians so the name is be appropriate. I didn't get a Paiute name for the band living at Pahrump, Nevada. The name Pahrump could come from the Paiute word pawhump´ ***common reed***, *Phragmites,* or from the words paw and tuhmp ***rock*** and ***water***. Many members of this band have moved to Las Vegas.

31. NAVAJO MOUNTAIN Today these Paiutes are called Awdu´so Nengwoonts´eng. Awdu´so is the Ute way of saying ***Arizona*** so these Paiutes are called "***Arizona Indians***." One informant includes some of the Paiutes at Bluff, Utah, in this category.

    Molly Deer, a Ute Mountain Ute, mentions a band of Paiutes called "Tuhyuh´wepuhtseng who lived somewhere in Arizona in the Navajo Mountain area, all of whom died." Koosharem Paiutes pronounce this name "Toyo´wepuhts´eng." Today all the Southern Paiutes from Koosharem, Kanosh, Cedar City, Shivwits, and Kaibab refer to all Arizona Paiutes as Nengwoo´ Pawhawng´weets meaning ***Indian Navajos,*** or ***Paiute Navajos.*** This is because so many of them have intermarried with the Navajos and are trilingual speaking Paiute, Navajo, and English.

32. WILLOW SPRINGS Mark Owl, a Paiute from the Navajo Mountain area, gives information that suggests that some of the Paiutes at Navajo Mountain and Willow Springs, Arizona, are remnants of the Sheberitch Band. He gives the name of Shuhuh´ Vaw Duhuts for his people there and says it means ***Squawbush Water People.***

    A member of the Kanosh Band gives the following information that would seem to substantiate the above statement since the Henry Mountains are adjacent to the homelands of the Squawbush Water People: "My father told me that some of the Paiutes near Willow Springs, Arizona, once came from somewhere near the Henry Mountains." Kanosh 15.

33. BLANDING A Ute informant states that "The Blanding Utes are a break-off from the Moowhuch Band from Ignacio." Some Utes call them Weum´pee Nengwuht ***Wiggling Lizard People***. There is a mixture of Paiutes among them from Posey's Band and some Arizona Paiutes. Posey and his band along with some Utes fought the last official Indian War in the United States in 1915. (see Plate 6, page 174)

    A Southern Ute informant from Ignacio makes the following statement concerning the Blanding or White Mesa Band:

The White Mesa Band was originally Southern Utes (especially the White family). They once lived near the Cimarron River with Southern Utes as part of the Moache Band (Pronounced Moowhutch´yu by her). However they had to flee to avoid retaliations for something one of the family did to a tribal member. They moved because their chief advised he could not be responsible for what anyone did in retaliation.

Many words in the White Mesa and Southern Ute language have changed since this split. One is the phrase maawtudu ***going up a hill.*** *Some Paiutes from the south later joined the White Mesa Southern Ute group. They have mixed with the Paiutes there and now are all called Utes. Old man White from there once asked me about many Old People he once knew before they left Ignacio.*

Harriet Taveapont, a White River Ute from Whiterocks, Utah, gives the following statement:

Paguh´ ***(Fish)*** *was a short man with long hair. He was a fighting Indian from Blanding who made his last stand at Crescent Junction, Utah, by the red rock east of the highway and windmill. He died a natural death. Paiutes left Blanding to get away from him. They went to the Teas Valley, Utah area.*

INDIAN PEAK I never got a name for this band. Mable Yellowjacket who was born at Minersville, Utah, and who was a daughter of Coal Creek John says that "Some of the Indians living in Cedar Valley near Cedar City moved to Indian Peak." Indian Peak could also have been within the boundaries of the Panaca or Pahranagat bands.

CHEMEHUEVI Tawntuh´vaits is the Southern Paiute name for the Chemehuevi. It means ***Tawn Below*** or ***Southern Tawn***. The word tawn is probably an old name for both the Southern Paiutes and Chemehuevi before they split up. The Chemehuevis call the Southern Paiutes Tawntuhts or ***Upper Tawn***. James Marble, a Mojave, gives the following information concerning Chemehuevi territory:

The Black Mountains in northwestern Arizona were inhabited by the Chemehuevis. The Chemehuevis and Mojaves used to fight at the sand dunes west? of Fort Mojave. The mountain due west of the dry lake (7 miles south of the junction of U.S. 95 and 93) southeast of Las Vegas is a sacred Spirit Mountain. Old People used to leave offerings to it when passing through there. It's also sacred to the Chemehuevi. Their songs turn around there.

PAWNO´MEENTS (Panamint). This is a Southern Paiute Band mentioned by Jim Chili as living in the Tahatchapi Pass area. No details given.

WEE´SEGEE YOOTAWTS ***Large Two Point Deer People***. This band was mentioned to me by Richard Mckuen a Northern Ute from Fort Duchesne, Utah. He states, "My mom's dad came from the other side of Las Vegas, Nevada, someplace. His band was called Wee´segee Yootawts which comes from the word Wee´segeets ***a two point deer with large horns***."

PAIUTE NAMES FOR OTHER TRIBES

APACHE The Chemehuevis called both the Tonto Apache and the Yavapai "Yawveep´ai," and also "Moowhee Nungkuuhng" ***Nose Earring***. The lack of distinction arose because the Yavapais in north central Arizona lived adjacent to the Apache, dressed like them, intermarried with them, raided with them, and even looked like them to the point that General Crook said they were "all Apache." Pioneers, writers, and even Mojave, Hualapai, and Havasupai Indians have referred to the Yavapai as Apache. They have also been designated as Mojave-Apache and Yavapai-Apache. This tribal confusion carried over to the Chemehuevis.

The Yavapai-Apache reservation at Camp Verde consists of about half Apaches and half Yavapai. Their languages are not mutually intelligible. Kaibab 4 calls the Apaches Too-oo´kunt meaning ***Wanting to fight*** or ***Mean***. This term again probably refers to both Apache and Yavapai.

ARAPAHO The Arapahos were called Sawdeets´ Eekuts ***Dog Eaters*** by the Northern Utes and the Koosharem Band.

BANNOCK This name is correctly pronounced Punai´teh and Punai´kee. I did not get a translation.

COCOPAH They were called Wekuhup´aw by the Chemehuevis.

DIEGUEÑO They were called Kawmai´u by the Chemehuevis.

GOSIUTES They are called this name by the Paiutes. The name is spelled Gosiute and Goshute. A Koosharem informant claims that:

> *The Gosiutes derive their name from the fact that they live in an area where there is a lot of gray clay. When the wind blows they become covered with this gray dust and so they are called Gosiutes referring to their gray color when covered with this gray dust.*[70]

HOPI The Hopi were called Moo´kweech or Mookeech by all Ute and Southern Paiute bands. It is from this Paiute word that the word Moqui is derived.

HUALAPAI They were called Oaw´duhpaiuts which sounds like a Paiute attempt at pronouncing this foreign word.

---

[70] Koosharem 7.

MARICOPA The Chemehuevi, Jim Chili, says they were called Awt´awpaw and Aiut´uduhm.

MISSION The Mission Indians of California were called Koomu´ Nengwuh ***Different Indians.***

MOJAVE The Mojaves living along the Colorado River were called Aiut´, meaning unknown, and also Mawuhkaw´ Uhveetch. Jim Chili says there was a Mountain Mojave Band that the Chemehuevis exterminated. They were called Tuh´du Aiut which literally means ***Desert Aiut.*** The desert area they inhabited consists of both mountains and desert. The informant translated the term as ***"Mountain Mojave."*** The Paiute word tuhdu can refer to anything ***barren, desolate,*** or even ***outside***. This word certainly describes the type of mountains found in the area being discussed as opposed to the Colorado River banks farmed by the other Mojaves living there.

NAVAJO Pu-hawng´ Weets. Jimmy Timmican says this term means ***Cane Knife People***. Kaibab 4 said that the Kaibab band called the Navajos Wee´ Kwuseets, ***Knife Tail***.

NORTHERN PAIUTE Mawtuh´suts. This is the Paiute name for Northern Paiutes and also the Nevada Shoshoni. Palmer gives a similar name Ma-tis-ab-its for a band living at Panaca and Meadow Valley, Nevada. This was an area where Southern Paiutes and Shoshonis came together and because of intermarriage, boundary distinctions often become difficult. Jim Chili Gives a name for the Southern Paiute Band at Panaca as Tuhnduh´esu. Palmer's informant was probably referring to the Shoshonis who ranged close to this area.

SHOSHONI Some Utes and Paiutes call the Shoshonis of Idaho and northern Nevada Koomunt´see. This name means ***Different*** or ***Strange*** and is the same name that is applied to the Commanches. The Wyoming Shoshonis and other bands are generally called Soahots´. The Las Vegas Band calls the Nevada Shoshonis Koahoyts.

UTE The Paiute name for the Utes is Yoo´taw. A Shivwits informant also referred to the Indians at Cedar City and Gunlock as "Yootaw Indians."

YAVAPAI They are called Yawvee´pai after the Yavapai word Nyahv´kopai ***East People***.

YUMA They were called Kweechun after their own name for themselves.

UTE BANDS

KAWPOO´TAW This name appears in books as Kapota and Capota. They are now on the Southern Ute Reservation at Ignacio, Colorado. An Ignacio informant hinted that this name had a derisive meaning given by the Ute Mountain Band. It might come from the Spanish word puta meaning whore. This name

could also come from the Spanish word capote, a kind of cape, cloak, or coat. Many tribes were noted for wearing this type of garment. This band was the southernmost of the Ute bands.[71]

KUMOO´TUHKUTS ***Rabbit Eaters***. A recent name given to Utes living at Randlett, Utah, in Reservation days. Johnny Ioupe, Northern Ute.

MOOWHUCH´ This name appears in publications as Moguache and Moache. Moowhup´ means ***cedar bark***. Moowhuch´ is ***Cedar Bark People*** because they spent a lot of time living in the cedars and utilizing the bark. Some now reside at the Southern Ute Reservation at Ignacio, Colorado, and the rest in northern Utah.

MOOWHU´ TAWVEE´WAWCH ***Cedar Bark Sunny Slope People***. The Moguache and Tabeguache bands once lived on the eastern and southern slopes of the Rockies in Colorado. The name Moowhu' Tawvee´wawch came when the two Ute bands, Moowhuch and Tahvee´wawch, came together in Utah. This includes some of the Uncompahgre. Annebelle Eagle of Ignacio said, "When I was young we referred to the Moowhu Tawveewach as some of the Utes who moved to Utah." According to Ouray McCook, this name is a combination that means ***Cedar Bark Sunny Slope People***. This seems to be the most accurate translation since these two bands were once separate bands having the two separate names.

Other less reasonable translations of this combined name have arisen such as "***Walking Moguache***" and "***Those Who Walk in a Silly Manner***" or "***Copy-cats***" from the words moa-hup ***silly*** and tavee´wai which can mean ***to walk***.

PARIANUCHE This name is correctly pronounced Pawduh´ee Noonch ***Elk People***. They lived south of the White River Utes in Colorado with their area extending into eastern Utah.

PAWGOO´AWVEETCH This is a recent name given to the Utes living at White-Rocks, Utah, in Reservation days. Pawgoo´ Awveetch (Pawgoo´u Nengwoonts) means ***People Living by Water***. Johnny Ioupe, Northern Ute.

PAWGUH´UTUHKUTS ***Fish Eaters***. A recent name applied to Utes living at Ouray, Utah, in Reservation days. Johnny Ioupe, Northern Ute.

SEE´VEDO NOONTS The following statement comes from Ouray McCook: "I once heard of a band called See´vedo Noonts. I know nothing about them." Francis McKinley mentions hearing of a band south of the Uintah Basin someplace with a name similar to this, He said it meant "Silver People because their arms were chaffed and silvery looking." The word silver is of English extraction.

I personally wonder if this name might refer to the Sheberitch or Suhuh´vawduhuts eng ***Squawbush Water People*** who lived to the south. The Indian names are similar and I doubt that the word "silver" would be an ancient name. Utes do have a different word for chaffed arms.

TAVEEWAWCH This name appears in publications as Tabeguache. Francis McKinley and Ouray McCook said this name means "***Sunny Slope People.***"

[71] Annabelle Eagle, Southern Ute.

This name comes from the word tawvee´ meaning ***to hit*** or ***alight*** and refers to the sun's rays that strike the eastern slope of the Rockies. Annabelle Eagle of Ignacio says the Taveewach band was the northernmost Ute band living in Colorado.

UNCOMPAHGRE This name is correctly pronounced Ungkaw´ Paw Kawdee ***Red Water Sitting*** or ***Red Lake***. They received this name from the reddish-colored waters found in the mountains south of Ouray, Colorado. Ed Wyasket, a Uncompahgre, makes the following statement about this band:

> *The Southern Utes and other Utes used to all live together. Trouble caused them to leave. They moved to Red Lake and became the Uncompahgres. From there they moved to Pueblo, Denver, and eventually to Utah.*

Ouray McCook said, "The Uncomphgre Band once lived in the Alamosa Valley with other Southern Utes. When they left there they moved west and became the Uncompahgre. The Moowhuch who stayed became Southern Utes. Those coming to Utah later became Moowhu Tawvee´wawch."

WEEMINUCHE Pronounced Wee´me Noonts by Utah Indians. This name means ***Humping Indians*** from the word wayno´mee meaning ***to wiggle in sex.*** This is the band now living at Towoac, Colorado, on the Ute Mountain Reservation. This name was applied to them in derision by other Utes. They are also called Segoo´ Nengwoontch and Seguh´ Noahoytch meaning Lizard People. A Ute from Towoac, Colorado, makes the following statement:

> *The band term Kawpoo´taw and Wee´me Noonts are more recent band names arising over enmity and fighting between the two bands. Both names are derogatory. Wee´me Noonts means Humping Indians and my band, which is now stuck with this name, claims it really belongs to the Kawpoo´taw Band. The Ute Mountain Band is really called Segoon Nengwoonts* ***Lizard Indians*** *because of the lack of water where they live.*

YAMPARIKA, WHITE RIVER This name is pronounced Yumpaw´ Tuhkuts ***Wild Caraway Eaters***. A Northern Ute informant, Russell Root states that they lived around Craig and north of Meeker, Colorado. He further states that, "In Utah Reservation days the White River Utes were called Koohoo´uts ***Conical People***

from the Reservation type white men's conical hats they got in Pine Ridge, South Dakota."

UTE NAMES FOR OTHER TRIBES

Tribes that the Utes are not very familiar with are generally called Guhmuch or Kuhmuch ***Different*** or **Strange.**

ALASKA INDIANS They were called Pawdus´u Nengwoonch ***Ice Indians***.
APACHE Awvach ***Shadow***.
BANNOCK Punai´kee.
BLACKFEET Koochoo´ Tuhku ***Buffalo Eaters***.
CHEYENNE They were called Saiu´nu and Shaiah´nu after the word Cheyenne.
COMMANCHE They were called Kuhmuch´ee meaning ***Different*** or ***Strange***.
DELAWARE Yooaw Guhmuch ***Plains Different***.
HOPI Moo´keech.
KIOWA They were called Kaiowu after the word Kiowa.
OTO Paw´ Guhmuch ***Water Different***.
PAIUTE Paiuhch ***Poor, Simple.***
POTAWATOMI Yooaw Guhmuch ***Plains Different***.
PUEBLO One Ute informant called them Poo-oo´vuh Duch ***Hairy Arm People***. Francis McKinley thought this name referred to either the Taos or Jicarilla Apache. A Northern Ute informant gives the following name for the Pueblos:

> *One lady who was half Ute and half Arapaho told me that the Pueblos were called Pinyon Jays by the Utes because each morning they would sit on top of their Pueblos calling out to people what to do every day.*

SHOSHONI Soahoach´.
SIOUX The North Dakota Sioux were further removed from the Utes than the Sioux in South Dakota and so they were just called Guhmuch or Koomuch´ ***Different***.
SIOUX The South Dakota Sioux are called Mukoo´taw, which is often shortened to Koo´taw. The Ute word is probably derived from the Sioux word for themselves Dakota and Lakota.

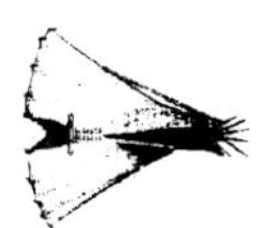

PLATE 3

This is a 1905 R. D. Adams photograph of Wayne County Indians after they moved to the Koosharem Reservation at Greenwich, Utah. Back row, left to right: Mr. Hatch (white), Joe Bob, Nick (Moqui), Mustache, Joe Bishop, Mrs. Bishop, Crockett Kanosh, George, Tom, John Timmican, his wife Rosy Quakanab. Next row: Alice, (little girl), Peaweeds (wife of Chief Walker), Henry (the small boy), Dora (holding cradle with baby in it), Walker Ammon, his wife Dora (Walker Ammon is a son of Chief Walker), Alma (Walker's boy), Mokwonusik, Charlie Arrowgarp, and his wife Millie Arrowpane, Minnie and Jesse Jim (and their child standing in front of them). Sitting on the ground: Minnie Kanosh, Nancy Timmican, Florence Timmican, and Jimmy Timmican. Identifications made by Florence Timmican Kanosh.

PLATE 4

Kaibab Paiutes at Pipe Springs, Arizona, 1904. Photograph by Charles Heaton. The Paiutes in this photograph were identified left to right by Morris Jake as follows: 1. Charley Bullets 2. Toby John 3. Minnie Tom 5. Moroni (Maimie's child) 6. Frank Mustache 7. Young William. 8. Dave Cannon 9. Tommy Tom 10. Tom 11. Tappio Dick 12. Annie Frank? 13. Pikyavit (**Peku´ Kwetoots**) or **Wawuhunt** (Monkey Frank's grandfather) 14. Adam Cumador or Rainjacket 15. Fannie Cumador 16. Fannie's grandchild 17. Fannie's grandchild 18. Dick.

PLATE 5

Kanosh, Utah, about 1880. Left to right: 1. Dick 2. Bill Mustache (sequence might be reversed) 3. unidentified 4. Hunkup 5. Hunkup's son (at his feet) 6. unidentified 7. Jack 8. unidentified 9. Joe Levi 10. Sobquint 11. Old Blind Jim 12. Jim (son of Old Blind Jim). Identification made by Lonnie Kouchomp and Wes Levi son of Joe Levi (9). Photograph courtesy of the Utah State Historical Society.

Plate 6

Leaders of the last American Indian War ratified by the United States Congress. This war was fought in 1915 by Paiutes and Utes near Bluff, Utah. This photograph was taken in 1915 at Moab, Utah. Courtesy of the Utah State Historical Society. Left to right: interpreter, Posey, Posey's son, Tse-ne-gat, Polk.

CHAPTER 11

PAIUTE PLACE-NAMES

When mankind devastates the land, nature gets revenge by devastating mankind.

The following list of place-names was accumulated over many years. Many of the Paiute names for the Indian Peak and Cedar City area were given to me by Carl Jake. Most of the names for Wayne, Sevier, and other central Utah counties were given to me by Jimmy Timmican from Wayne County, Utah. Both of these informants were born in the last century and were well informed on such names.

In reading the following Paiute names it should be remembered that Indian languages have many idioms not found in English. If you remember the meaning of the following words it will be easier to understand some of the place names. The word kawduhd means ***sitting*** and can refer to anything stationary like a ***mountain, hill*** or ***lake***. The word awveech means ***lying*** and refers to a ***ridge, long hill*** or ***long mountain***. The words suhpeech, tsuhpeech and chuhpeech mean ***coming out*** and are used to denote a ***spring***. Rivers and creeks are often denoted by the word nookweech, or nookweent, meaning ***flowing*** or ***running***.

UTAH

BEAVER COUNTY

FRISCO PEAK This peak is located in the San Francisco Mountains west of Milford, Utah. The name is Toovu´ Kawduhd signifying ***Pinenuts Sitting*** or ***Pinenuts Mountain***.

GARFIELD COUNTY

BRYCE CANYON Awvo´uv ***Cliffs in a Semi-Circular Amphitheater Shape***. This name also applies to the area where the town of Tropic, Utah is.

ESCALANTE The Indian name is Tuhduvai ***Desert.***

MOUNT DUTTON AND THE SEVIER PLATEAU Wunu Kaiv ***Arrowhead Mountain?***

PANGUITCH From the Paiute word pawguh´uts or the Gosiute word pawngweets, both meaning ***fish***.

GRAND COUNTY

MOAB From the word moouv meaning ***mosquito***.

IRON COUNTY

ANTELOPE PEAK This is the peak jutting out of the Antelope Range west of Cedar City, Utah It is about five miles south of Table Butte. This hill is called puhyuh kawduhtseech ***Heart Sitting***.

ANTELOPE RANGE This mountain was identified as the one south of Table Mountain (***kawduhd***). This mountain is called Yoonu Kaiv ***Lava Mountain*** also Yoonu Kawduhd ***Lava Sitting***.

BLACK MOUNTAIN This is the mountain south of Wood's Ranch in Cedar Canyon east of Cedar City, Utah. The Paiute name is Seu Kweechoount ***Aspen Peak***.

BLUE KNOLLS SPRING The Paiute name is Tookoo Vaw ***Tookoov's Water***. Tookoov is a supernatural being or spirit. This spring is in the Blue Knolls about ten miles northeast of Lund, Utah. Carl Jake of Indian Peak gives the following information: "Tookoov used to drink water at the warm springs by the blue knoll northeast of Lund, Utah, as he was traveling across the valley from east to west and vice versa. This place is called Tookoo´ Vaw."

Carl Jake said that "The Paiutes used to camp at the west foot of a butte west of Iron Springs on their way to Indian Peak to get pinenuts. There is a spring here. It was one days journey from Cedar to this butte." I assume that this campsite was at Blue Knolls Spring. Carl didn't name the butte. He also said that the Paiutes would camp at Sulphur Springs. This is the spring with the lone lombardi popular by it about a mile northwest of Lund.

BLUE MOUNTAIN This is the mountain range about eleven miles north of Lund, Utah. The name is Tawgoo´ Kawduhd ***Thirsty Sitting***. This is an appropriate name; the maps show no springs on this mountain.

BRIAN HEAD The Indian name is Too´ Kweechoovunt ***Black Peak***.

CEDAR BREAKS The name of Cedar Breaks is Ungkaw Pekonump ***Red Cove***. The name comes from the words ungkaw ***red*** and peko´uv ***circular corner*** or ***cove***.
CEDAR CANYON The Paiute name for the canyon east of Cedar City is Awvaw´u Weep ***Shady Canyon***.
CEDAR CITY The area where Cedar City is now situated was called Wawai´ Yoowawv ***Cedar Flat***. The Paiutes pronounced the word Cedar as Suhdu´ (English, Cedar).
CEDAR MOUNTAIN The mountain east of Cedar City with the "C" on it was referred to as Peow Kaiv ***Big Mountain***. However, the entire mountain range east of Cedar City is often locally referred to by the whites as "Cedar Mountain."
COAL CREEK The Paiute name is Too´yoo Weep. ***Black Canyon***.
CROSS HOLLOW HILLS The hill on the southwest side of Cedar City is locally known as Leigh Hill. The Paiute name is Wawu´ Kawduhd ***Cedar Tree Sitting***.
EIGHT MILE SPRINGS This is the water just north of Quichapa Lake. The only water shown on the map is Eight Mile Springs. I assume this is the location of this name. This water could be located by tasting it as it is supposed to taste rotten. This water is called Pawmpee´ke Paw signifying ***Rotten Water***.
ENOCH The spring at Enoch is called Pavuhts ***Spring***. Carl Jake said there is an old Paiute campsite at Enoch that has now been plowed up.
ESCALANTE DESERT This large expanse of desert north of Beryl, Utah, is called Ungwawno Yoowawv ***Wide Plain***.
FIDDLER'S CANYON The Paiute Indian name is Tuhmpee´ Awvoouv ***Rocky Amphitheater***.
GRANITE MOUNTAIN The mountain south of Iron Springs is called Mawko Awveech ***Rough Lying***.
GREEN LAKE This little lake on the west side of the mountain southeast of Cedar City is called Paingup´ee Kawneev ***Water Babies House***.
INDIAN PEAK The Indian name is Moohoo´uv Kwee´choovunt meaning ***Spirit*** or ***Heart Peak***. Sometimes it is just referred to as Kwee´choovunt. The old Paiute campsite is about one-quarter of a mile east southeast of the twentieth century village site that was torn down by the Utah Fish and Game when they took over Indian Peak.
IRON SPRINGS The Paiute name is Pawnaw´oogeep ***Water Passage Between Hills***.
KANNARAVILLE From the word kanaw´duh or kanaw´duhts ***willow***.
LITTLE CREEK PEAK This peak northeast of Parowan, Utah, is called Kwee´choovunt ***Peak***.
LITTLE CREEK This is the canyon northeast of Paragoonah, Utah. The Paiute name is Wuhhuhm´pee Ooweeng´w ***Vagina Canyon***. This canyon received its name from a rock at the mouth of the canyon that has many vagina symbols pecked in it (see the story, "Little Creek Canyon," in Chapter 3, The Ways of the Old Ones).
MEADOW SPRING This spring is located northwest of Polliwog Spring and is called Pawkum´ Paw ***Reed Water***.
MEADOW SPRING WASH The Paiute name is Tono Weep ***Greasewood Wash***.

This wash is between Lund and Indian Peak, Utah.

MOUNTAIN HOME This is the mountain north of Indian Peak. The Paiute name is Chongkwaw Kawduhd ***Rough Sitting***.

MOUNTAIN SPRING PEAK This peak is called Wuntsee´ Kawduhd ***Antelope Sitting***. This very noticeable peak is located on the north side of the Pine Valley road going west from Lund, Utah.

MOUNTAIN SPRING This spring is located west of Lund and about one-half mile north of Mountain Spring Peak. It is called Pontsee´ Paw ***Quartzite Water***. Paiutes from Cedar City used to camp here on their second day from Cedar as they were going to Indian Peak to gather pine nuts.

PARAGOONAH This location was called Pesu Vawduhgoon ***Small? Water Up*** and Paw Doo´kooee meaning ***Water Coming Up***. This name has been Anglicized to Paragoonah.

PAROWAN Correctly pronounced Paw doo´gwuntuh meaning ***Water Fighter***. This name comes from the words paw ***water*** and too-ookunt ***fighter***. The word for ***fight*** is the same word as used for Apache (Too-oo´kunt) which can be extended to mean ***ill tempered***. Tillahash explained to Sapir that this water was "So named because its water rises on the approach of a person to fight him, drag him in, and drown him," (Sapir 1930, p. 597).

PINE VALLEY This valley east of Indian Peak is called Wawu´ Muhuv ***Cedar Tree Pass***.

POLLIWOG SPRING This spring is the first spring northwest of Mountain Spring. It is called Pawdo´kwaw Vawts ***Rainbow Water***.

POTSUMPAH SPRING The spring south of Mountain Home is called Pontsee´ Paw ***Quartzite Water***. It is named after the quartzite outcrop located there.

QUICHAPA Kwee´chu Paw is the Paiute name for this lake. The name comes from the words kweechup ***dung*** and paw ***water***. This large muddy, and often dry lake, is situated in the valley just west of Hamilton's Fort, Utah.

RED HILL This hill just east of Cedar City is called Ungkaw´ Kaiv ***Red Hill***, also Ungkaw Awveech ***Red lying***. On the USGS map it is shown as The Red Hill.

RUSH LAKE The Indian name is Pawdoo´puts meaning ***Sinking Water***. There is an old Paiute camp in the cove east of the Rush Lake farm. Fremont pot shards were seen there.

RUSH LAKE FLAT AND CEDAR VALLEY The valley west of Cedar City and around Rush Lake, Utah, was called Wuhsuh´goont or Wuhsuh´goom. The tentative meaning is either an unidentified plant or the ***fine stickers*** found on a cactus.

SHEEP SPRINGS This spring is located south of Indian Peak and is called Awvoo´uv ***Circular Cliffs*** or ***Amphitheater***.

SHIRK'S CANYON The Indian name for the slope of the mountain just east of Hamilton Fort was called Kai´shuhduhts´ ***Red Birch***. The nearby town of Hamilton Fort was also referred to by this name. An area in the mountains near Shirk's Canyon is called Kweyuhuntu Kawn ***Bear's House***.

SQUARE MOUNTAIN This is the mountain that juts out from Cedar Mountain

just southeast of Cedar City. The name is Sechu´hunt (a plant with edible seeds).

STEAMBOAT MOUNTAIN This is the big square mountain south of Indian Peak in the same range. This mountain is called Awsee´ Kawduhd ***Gray Sitting***.

SUMMIT, UTAH The area, where this town now resides, was called Sawngwud´uh ***Sagebrush***.

TABLE BUTTE This is the butte north of Antelope Springs west of Cedar City. This butte is called Kawduhd ***sitting***.

THE KNOLL This is the hill directly north of Cedar City, within the city limits, and shown on the Cedar City Quad map as "The Knoll." It is just south of mile post 4. There is a historical marker on the west side of this hill telling of the first settlement of pioneers camping in the cove here November 11, 1851. The name is O-aw Kawduhtseech ***Little Yellow Sitting***.

THE THREE PEAKS The three peaks north of Iron Springs are called Waw´ugunt ***Range of Peaks***. This is not Three Peaks that lies to the west with a similar name.

UNNAMED CANYON This is a canyon leading north from the old Indian village at Indian Peak. It is probably a side canyon to Indian Creek. I was shown this canyon in the 1950s but now I can't identify it accurately. I only include what I wrote in my notes at the time. This canyon is called Eyawkon Ooweeng´w ***Afraid Canyon***.

UNNAMED CREEK This is the first creek south of Indian Creek at Indian Peak, Utah. This creek is called Sawgaw´ Ooweep ***Narrowleaf Cottonwood Canyon***.

UNNAMED HILL This hill is the white hill just northeast of The Red Hill east of Cedar City. There is a small ridge behind the larger red hill and a larger gray one further northeast. This name could almost apply to any of them. The Indian name is Awsee´ Awveech ***Gray Lying***.

UNNAMED SPRING This spring on the west side of Indian Peak is called O-aw´ Vaw ***Salt Water***. I didn't have time to locate the spring. There are two springs west of Indian Peak that are unnamed on current maps plus a spring by the name of Willow Spring. It would be easy to identify this spring by finding the one with the salty taste.

JUAB COUNTY

IBAPAH From the Gosiute words awveem ***gray*** and paw ***water***. The Paiute word would be similar, Oaveem´ Paw ***Whitish Earth Paint Water***.

MOUNT NEBO The Indian name is Paaw´ Kawduhd ***Tall Sitting***.

KANE COUNTY

DUCK CREEK The Indian name is Chuhgunt´u Kweent ***Duck Flowing***. This is probably a modern name after the name the whites have given it.

KAIPAROWITS This name comes from the Paiute words for ***mountain*** and ***son***.

KANAB From the word kanuv, or kanaw´duhts ***willow***.

MAMMOTH CREEK The Paiute name is Pa-whay´oomp.
NAVAJO LAKE The present Paiute name is Pu-hawng´way Evu Kawduhd ***Navajo-There-Water***.
PARIA This name comes from the Paiute word pawtuh´ee ***elk***.
SKUTUMPAH Skutumpah Canyon is a tributary to Johnson Canyon east of Kanab, Utah. The name means ***Rabbit Brush Water*** from the words skoomp ***rabbit brush*** and paw ***water***.
WAHWEEP O-aw Ooweep ***Yellow Canyon***.

MILLARD COUNTY

COVE FORT The Indian name is Nawhoo´kwee Kawn ***War House***.
KANOSH The word Kanosh comes from kawnaw´os ***willow jug***. This is a basket-type water jar made from split willows and covered with pitch.
SAND RIDGE This large sandy area is about 14 miles straight west of Meadow, Utah, and about two miles northwest of the Hole in the Rock Reservoir. It is a favorite habitat for jackrabbits. It is shown as Sand Ridge on the 1968 USGS Sand Ridge Quad Map. This location is called Sewung´ Kawm ***Jackrabbit Sand***.
SEVIER LAKE The name is Uhvuh´ Paw ***Bad Water***.
UNNAMED HILL This hill is the southernmost small volcanic outcrop south of Black Rock Volcano, 3.7 miles west-southwest of Kanosh, Utah. This site consists of three small connected knobs within three-quarters of a mile from old highway 91. The Indian name is Unoo´peets Kawn ***Ghost's House***. The name comes from the fact that many Indians who go to this area have strange feelings that suggest the presence of ghosts. (see Plate 7, page 193)
UNNAMED SPRINGS These springs probably have an English name but they don't show on the 1973 Cruz, Utah, USGS Quad. These springs are located on the south line of Section 4 which straddles Townships 24 and 23 S, Range 9 W, of the above named map. These springs are about one mile east of the Cudahy Mine. The springs are called Wuntsee´ Vawts ***Antelope Water***.
WAH WAH From the word wawv´w a tall wild seed bearing grass that grew there. This grass is either wild rye or wheatgrass.

PIUTE COUNTY

ANGLE Sakhwaw Hawduhd ***Green sitting***.
CEDAR GROVE This is the grove of trees on Parker Mountain shown on the USGS map as Cedar Grove. The Indian name is Pa-waw Topuhneench. The meaning seems to be ***Red Cedar Grove***.
CIRCLEVILLE VALLEY This valley was called Toogoov´. Jimmy Timmican gave me this name saying it meant, "Some kind of sand." He wasn't too good at

English. Years later, his daughter, not knowing the actual name, said the word sounded as if it meant "swampy" to her, referring to the wetlands along the Sevier river.

GREENWICH CREEK This creek is called Toanko´muneench and refers to the chokecherries that grew along the creek.

MOUNT DELANO The Indian name is Tuh´du Kawduhd ***Barren Sitting*** referring to the lack of growth on its top.

MOUNTAINOUS AREA BETWEEN MARYSVALE PEAK AND LANGDON MOUNTAIN This is the area drained by Box Creek and its south fork west of Greenwich, Utah. This mountain is called Kwawsuhmp´oa Nouv ***Dress Carried Up***. This name refers to a time when a woman's dress flew up as she was riding horseback up over this mountain on the trail to the Marysvale area.

PARKER MOUNTAIN The Indian name for the general area is Wuntsee´ Kaiv ***Antelope Mountain***.

PINE PEAKS ON PARKER MOUNTAIN The crests of Pine Peaks, that are covered with trees, are called Pawhon´ Tuhkawv.

SPRING IN GREENWICH CREEK This spring is located on the old Koosharem Indian Reservation south of Koosharem, Utah. The spring is called Kweu´ Suhpeetch ***Gamble Oak Spring***.

SPRING ON PINE PEAKS This spring isn't shown on USGS maps. The Paiute name is Wuntsee´ Vaw ***Antelope Water***.

TUSHAR MOUNTAINS The word Tushar comes from the Paiute name Tosaw' Kawduhd ***White Sitting***. This name is derived from the fact that its top is covered with snow for a long time during the year.

UNNAMED HILL This is a small hill at the base of the mountain between the old Koosharem Indian Reservation and Greenwich, Utah. It stands out in color from the rest of the mountain slope. It is called Ungkawseu Kawduh´tseech. Kawduh´tseech means ***small hill***; ungkaw means ***red***, and I was unable to determine the meaning of seu´. This word might mean aspen but from the distance I observed this hill, and from it's elevation near the base of the mountain, it did not appear that aspens grew there.

SAN PETE COUNTY

MUSINIA PEAK This is the highest peak east of Gunnison, Utah, Township 20 S, Range 3 E, Section 28, Woods Lake USGS Map. It is bald with no trees on top of it. This peak is called Moo-oon´ Totseets ***Owl's Head***. Tom Amnisky (Tom Mix), a Paiute from the Escalante Band, said that this peak once had an owl's head on it that broke off and rolled down the mountain.

SAN PETE This name isn't of English or Spanish derivation. It comes from the word Sawmpeets´ ***Tule***. This is the name of the Indian band that lived in this area.

SEVIER COUNTY

BOOBE HOLE MOUNTAIN The Indian name for this mountain is Whechuhn´u Moouv´ee Kaiv ***Wild Potato Pass Mountain***.

BOWERY CREEK The Indian name of this creek at Fish Lake is Kawnun´ Nungkots ***Willow Leaves***. Paiutes used to hold their Sun Dances here in the Bowery Creek Campground just northwest of the old sawmill.

BRIMHALL SPRING This is the spring on Peterson Creek a little over a mile off Highway 24 that leads from Sigurd to Fish Lake, Utah. This spring is on the west side of the graveled road that leads through Bear Valley to Burrville, Utah. It is called Neyoho Pawts ***Intercourse Water***. Indians camped on the mesa above the spring.

BULL CLAIM HILL This is the big volcanic hill northeast of Annabella, Utah. It is called Too´ Awweech ***Black Lying***.

CLEAR CREEK CANYON The Indian name of this canyon is Pawhum´ Paw ***Reed Water*** (*Phragmites*).

CRATER LAKES These are the dry lakes south of Fish Lake. The Indian name is Ungko´kwaw Kawduhd. This name refers to a certain type of grass that grew there.

DANIEL'S PASS Daniel's pass north of Fish Lake was referred to by the Indians as Whechuhn´u Moouv ***Wild Potato Pass***.

DOCTOR CREEK This is the first creek encountered as one approaches Fish Lake from the south. The Indian name is Nahmuh Nengwoo Kawtsoo´uts ***First-Indian-Edge***. In English the name sounds better worded as the ***Edge of the First Indians***, or ***Boundary of the First Indians***. This name comes from the fact that this camp was the first one encountered and somewhat marked the southern boundary, or edge of the camps at Fish Lake. See map under Fish Lake.

FISH LAKE HIGHTOP PLATEAU The Paiute name for this mountain is Yungum Paw Kaivu Awveen ***Woodchuck Water Mountain Lying***.

FISH LAKE The Paiute name is Pawkuh´u Vaw ***Fish Water***. There are several old Paiute campgrounds around Fish Lake. One campsite is on the east side of the valley north-northeast of Fish Lake; Paiute pottery was seen there. Jimmy Timmican showed me another old campsite in about 1958. It is in a clearing below the tree line about 1.0 miles north of Jorgenson Creek.

There is a deed in the courthouse at Loa, Utah, dated March 1, 1889, showing that the Paiutes sold all their rights to Fish Lake for "Nine horses, 500 lbs. of flour, 1 good beef stear, and 1 suit of clothes."

FORD NEAR ANNABELLA BRIDGE This crossing was called Ungkaw´ Pawdov ***Buffalo berry Ford***. There are many red buffalo berries all along the river in this area. These abundant red berries are called ungkawp and are the source of this name. I didn't determine which of the two Annabella bridges the ford was near. Florence Kanosh says that "A long time ago the entire valley near Richfield was very swampy and difficult to cross. The ford near Annabella was

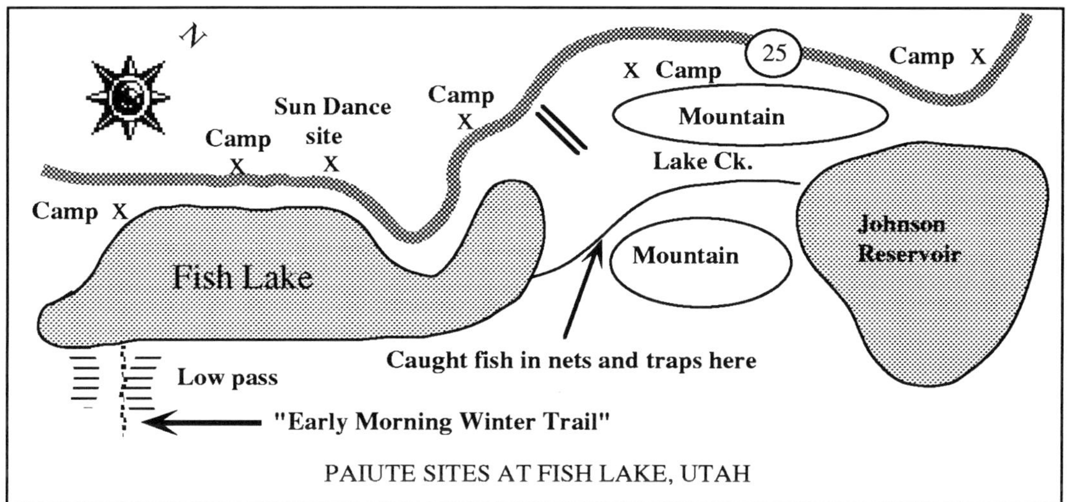

PAIUTE SITES AT FISH LAKE, UTAH

one of the only ways across."

FRYING PAN CREEK This creek shows no name on the Fish Lake USGS Quad but it is locally called Frying Pan Creek. It is the creek that flows down off the mountain immediately south of the Frying Pan Campground and flows a short distance into Lake Creek that drains Fish Lake. The Indian name is Kawnu Suhpeech ***Willow Spring***. There is an abundance of willows along the short course of this creek.

GLENWOOD MOUNTAIN This is the large mountain southeast of Richfield. It was called Mo-oo Goovaiu ***Owl's Face***. This name comes from the fact that when there is the right amount of snow on the face of this mountain you can make out the outline of an owl's face on the slope facing Richfield.

JORGENSON CREEK This creek at Fish Lake is called O´tokots ***Black Bed***. The bed of this creek looks very black due to the soil and rocks the water runs over, thus suggesting its name. The name is a Paiute idiom and I use the word bed as the nearest way I can think of, in English, to interpret this name. The Paiutes camped by this creek. Fremont pot shards were seen here. See map under Fish Lake.

KOOSHAREM From the word Koosaw´duhmp which is the name of a wild clover growing in that area.

MOUNT MARVINE The Indian name of this mountain just north of Fish Lake is Pawguh´u Kwawseev. This name means ***Fish Tail*** because the mountain is in the shape of a fish's tail.

PARADISE VALLEY LAKE This lake is on the road from Fremont to Emery, Utah. The name of this lake is Moasuhm´ Paw Hawduhd. These words mean ***Glassy Eyed Water Sitting***, or ***Glassy Eyed Lake***. See the story "The Arapaho at Paradise Valley Lake" on how this lake acquired its name.

PASS ON MYTOGE MOUNTAIN EAST OF FISH LAKE This is the pass located in the northeast quarter of Section 29, Township 26 S, Range 2 E. The Indian name is Tawsee´un Toam Poats ***Early Morning Winter Trail***. This is the time of morning when the Morning Star appears. Jimmy Timmican, Koosharem, note

198. This pass might have derived its name because early in the morning in the winter the lake was frozen sufficient to allow the Indians to cross the lake to Rabbit Valley. They couldn't do this in the summer or on milder winter days. It served as a winter shortcut so that the Indians wouldn't have to go around the lake. See map under Fish Lake.

PRAETOR CANYON This is the canyon on the east side of the valley due east of the Koosharem Reservoir dam. This canyon is called Yoo-oo´ Skuv´enuts Ooweeng´w ***Leg Cutoff Canyon***. This name was applied at a time when an Indian had his leg cut off in this canyon.

REFLECTION SPRING This spring, on the north end of Fish Lake, is called Pawkwun´aw Vawts ***Frog Water***.

ROCKY FORD This name refers to a narrow place on the Sevier River about two miles north of Sigurd, Utah, and immediately north of the Rocky Ford Dam. This narrow place was called Too´ Choogweetch ***Black Narrow***. This name was used in reference to Rocky Ford. This name comes from the words too ***black*** and nawchoo´kweech ***narrow flowing***.

SEVEN MILE CREEK The Indian name is Sawngwunts ***Rushing Water***. This creek makes a rushing sound as it plummets down its last mile before going into the Johnson Valley Reservoir. There used to be an Indian camp in a little tree cove just a few hundred yards west of where this creek enters the reservoir. It is located on the west side of Section 24, Township 25 S, Range 2 E, Fish Lake Quad. See map under Fish Lake.

SEVIER RIVER Jimmy Timmican says that the name of this river is the name of a large animal once seen at this river near Joseph, Utah. This animal was large with his head hanging down somewhat like a mammoth and had never been seen before. The animal was called "Mooyai sevee´u." Mooyai means ***to hang down the head*** and seevee´u was the name of the animal. The name of the river was shortened to Seevee´u, which sounded to the white man like Severo and Sevier.

It is doubtful that this name referred to the buffalo as the Paiutes were acquainted with this animal and called it moahoy´ kootch and tuhdu´ kootch. Anglo informants claim there were buffalo wallows and bones in the area in the 1870s therefore it is very doubtful that they had seen a wandering buffalo and named the river after it. Place names are often very old, therefore an animal other than the buffalo would be the most likely candidate for this name. There is a petroglyph nearby depicting a mammoth or mastodon that could account for this name.

SPRING IN RICHFIELD, UTAH This spring is called Yoomeen´ Choopeets ***Warm Springs***. This spring is located near 500 North and 600 West in Richfield.

TWIN CREEK This creek at Fish Lake is called Awsee´ Vaguhu ***Gray Fish***. Paiutes used to camp by this creek. See map under Fish Lake.

U M VALLEY This valley, north of Fish Lake, Utah, is called Yooveemp ***Ponderosa Pine***.

UNIDENTIFIED CREEK This creek runs from the Daniel's Pass area to Lost Creek. It is called Ungkaw Moouts ***Red Pass***.

UNIDENTIFIED VALLEY This valley is at the west foot of the mountain at Daniel's Pass. It is called Wawv´uh Koyo´koytch ***Wild Rye*** or ***Wheatgrass Valley.*** The word koyokoytch means a ***bowl-shaped valley*** or ***depression,*** and the word wawv is either ***wild rye*** or ***wheatgrass***. This might be Plateau Valley, but I'm no longer sure as this name was given to me long ago.

UNLOCATED SPRING There is a spring on the mountain straight west of Koosharem that is called Seu´ Suhpeech ***Aspen Spring***.

UNNAMED HILL There is a big black hill about three miles straight west of Venice, Utah, and about the same distance north-northeast of Glenwood, Utah. It has a large white "V" painted on its west side. The Indian name of this hill is Too´ Kawduhd ***Black Sitting*** or ***Black Hill***.

UNNAMED HILL This is the hill on the west side of Highway 24 south of the Koosharem Reservoir. This hill is located between mile posts 33 and 34. There is a gravel pit on this hill. The hill is located in Section 18, Township 29 S, Range 1 E. This site is called Tawvoon´ Koochun or Tawvoon´ Koochoo´ud ***Cottontail Droppings***.

UNNAMED RIDGE This mahogany-covered ridge on Boobe Hole Mountain is called Toonus´kee Awveech, Toonaw´ Awveech ***Mahogany Lying*** or ***Mahogany Ridge***.

UNNAMED SPRING This spring is located in the northeast quarter of Section 34, Township 26 S, Range 1 E. It is on the right side of Highway 25 going towards Fish Lake. There are several cabins located here and this spring is but a few hundred yards east of the radio facility on top of the knoll south of the highway. The Indian name is Oonun´to Pawts ***Badger Water***.

UNNAMED SPRING This spring is located a very short distance northeast of Highway 24, near milepost 25, between Sigurd and Koosharem, Utah. At this place the low wash that the highway passes through, opens up into Plateau Valley. This spring is located in the southwest quarter of Section 31, Township 24 S, Range 1 E, Boobe Hole USGS Quad map. This spring is called Ungkonun Tsuhpeech ***Ungkonun Spring***. Ungkonun refers to an unidentified grass that grows there. This spring has probably dried up. An informant stated that he heard a story where an older lady told a young lady to go to this spring to get a bucket of water but she couldn't find the spring.

UINTAH COUNTY

UINTAH The word Uintah comes From the Paiute/Ute word Yooveen´tuh ***Ponderosa Pine***.

UTAH COUNTY

GREAT SALT LAKE This lake was called O-aw´ Vaw ***Salt Water***.

SANTAQUIN In the 1905 Allotment Records of the Uintah Band at Fort

Duchesne, Utah, there is to be found the name of an Indian by the name of Santaquin. The same record shows his Indian name to be Saguanookweent which sounds very much like the word Santaquin. It is therefore very likely that Santaquin is a corruption of this name The book on Utah place-names says that this town was named after an Indian by the name of Santaquin. The name Sawwhaw Nookweent means ***Green*** or ***Blue Running*** referring to the stream there. The same word is used for green and blue among the Utes and Paiutes as well as among many other tribes.

TIMPANOGOS According to Jimmy Timmican, this word comes from the Indian name Tuhmpaw Nookweent ***Rock Water Running***.

UTAH This name comes from the word yootaw which could be of Ute or Hopi origin. Yootaw is the Hopi name for the Utes.

WASATCH PLATEAU The range of mountains from Manti to Salt Lake City is called Awvaw Awveets ***Shady Lying***. ***Shady*** is my interpretation. It could have another meaning.

WASATCH This name comes from Paiute and Ute Indian phrase pronounced Wuhu Seai meaning ***Frozen Penis***. Archie Rogers of Shivwits tells the following story about the origin of this name: "The Utes told me what the word "Wasatch" means. They said that one time many Indians lived there between Heber and Provo. One day the men were out hunting when a big blizzard came up and they lost one of the hunters. When they found him he was dead and his penis was frozen stiff. They therefore called the place Wuhu´ Seai ***Frozen Penis***." Francis McKinley, a Ute, tells the same story.

WASHINGTON COUNTY

ASH CREEK It was called Too´yoonuv ***Lava Flow***. It has the same name as Black Ridge.

BLACK RIDGE The black ridge north of Pintura, Utah, was called Kaw´uwhaim Awvee ***Ankle Lying***. This area is also called Too´ Yoonuv ***Lava Flow*** referring to the black lava flows to be found there. The area in general was also called Chuhngkawweep ***Rough Land*** due to the roughness of the area caused by the large lava field.

CANE SPRINGS This is a spring near the town of Central, Utah. It is called Pawhum´ Paw ***Reed Water***.

CASTLE CLIFF This site is near the Arizona border on old Highway 91 going toward Beaver Dam, Arizona. The Paiutes called the caves there Moou Tuhngkawn ***Owl's Cave***. See the legend Owl and the Skunk.

FIVE-MILE This is an area on the Santa Clara River on the east end of the Shivwits Reservation. It is called Toho´u Opawk´eev ***Rattlesnake Hole***.

HURRICANE The name of this town doesn't come from the English word "hurricane" as commonly thought. This name comes from the Paiute word

Awduhng´ Kawn ***Hot House*** referring to the cave there with the hot springs in it on the Virgin River between Hurricane and LaVerkin. Awdduh´ is a Paiute expression made when one gets burnt. This cave was a special place to the Paiutes. It was a cave where Indian travelers were welcome. They often left offerings there. Archie Rogers says that "The Paiutes used to drop money in the Hurricane Hot Springs and pray and it would heal them."

JACKSON PEAK This is the pointed peak west of Gunlock, Utah. The Paiutes called it Tseeoo´kwuts ***Sticking Out***.

KOLOB This name comes from the Paiute word Koduv´ ***Neck***. According to Carl Jake there is a geographical feature in the area with this name.

MOTOQUA This name is pronounced Mutoo´kwu ***Disappearing Under***. This name comes from the rolling hills that are crossed over for several miles while traveling northwest to Motoqua. Charley Greyman of Shivwits says that, "The name comes from watching someone traveling ahead of you. He will disappear from sight and come back into view several times as he drops down into the numerous low places on this route."

PINE VALLEY MOUNTAIN This mountain is called Mu-haw Kaiv ***Forested Mountain*** also Mu-haw Kawduhd ***Forested Sitting***.

SANTA CLARA RIVER The Paiute name is Too Nookweent ***Black Flowing***. The white man Anglicized this to Tonaquint.

SHINOB KAIB This is a hill just southeast of Washington, Utah. The words are correctly pronounced Soonungwu Kaiv ***Coyote Hill***. The name Soonung´wuv applied to anyplace, refers to mysterious things happening there.

SINAWAVA This name used for a geographical feature in Zion National Park comes from the Paiute word Soonungwuv. He is Coyote, the younger brother to the deity Wolf.

SOUTH BLACK ROCKS The lava flow crossing Highway 91 between Santa Clara and St. George, Utah, is called Toch´okwup ***Crushed Rocks***. The same flow just above this is shown as South Black Rocks on the USGS map.

SQUARE TOP MOUNTAIN This mountain is southwest of Jackson Peak. It appears to be just to the left of it looking north. It was called Kai´oowheef ***Mountain Lying This Way***.

ST. GEORGE The area below the temple where the Indians used to lived was called Seeveem´ Paw ***Sour Water***. (see Plate 8, page 194)

TAYLOR CREEK The creek by the Kolob exit south of Kannarraville (sometimes called Bear Creek) was called Awntawmooun Nookwee´tseech ***Brother-in-law Flowing***.

THREE CREEKS These are the creeks leading off Cedar Mountain into Zion National Park. The Indian name is Muow Ooweep ***Forested Canyon***.

TOQUERVILLE The first part of the name Toquerville comes from the word too´kwawd ***black***.

UNNAMED HILL This hill between the entrance to the Virgin Narrows near Littlefield, Arizona, and Castle Cliffs, Utah, is called Aiyu´ Kodu Kaiv ***Turtleneck Hill***. This name comes from the fact that this large hill resembles the

shape of a turtle when viewed from old Highway 91. It has a turtle-back hump and long curving neck with the head pointing southward. The tip of the head is almost due east of the Utah-Arizona border signs. This large hill is the westernmost extension of the mountainous area east of the old highway.

UNNAMED HILL The large red mountain point that juts southward straight north of Ivans, Utah, is called No´whunt. This word is similar to the word for pregnant, nou´hunt, but Archie Rogers says it doesn't have the same meaning. However, the hill does look like a pregnant lady when viewing it from the Shivwits Reservation.

UNNAMED HILL This hill is located on old Highway 91, 1.2 miles west of the main turn-off into the present Indian village (1990). At this place the highway goes up over a little rise just south of the Santa Clara River. This hill is called Mook´ which is short for Mookweech. This is the Paiute word for Hopi. This hill was given this name because there is an old Hopi (Anasazi) village situated there that the Shivwits discovered when they helped put the road though. Archie Rogers, Shivwits, note 227.

UNNAMED HILL This hill is the only hill on the west side of old Highway 91, 0.7 miles south of Castle Cliff, Utah, between mileposts 4 and 5, and 0.2 miles north of milepost 4. It is called Tsaw Kwetoots ***Skinny Buttocks***.

VIRGIN RIVER It is called Pawdoos´ by both the Kaibab and Shivwits which can have two meanings. One is ***Water Going Under*** from the words Paw udook, and the other is ***White Water*** from Paw Tosaw´kawd. The word white is often slurred to doos within a sentence structure. White Water would then refer to the white foaming water as caused by the many small rapids as this river traverses Zion Canyon.

ZION CANYON The Paiute name for this canyon was Ai Oogoon or Oo Koon´uv ***Quiver***. The name comes from the word arrow ***oo*** and koonuv ***sack***. The name is probably derived from the narrowness of this canyon.

ZION NARROWS The Indian name is Tuhmpeow Ooweep ***Big Rock Canyon***.

WAYNE COUNTY

BIG HOLLOW This wash drains into Rabbit Valley near Dab Keele Spring a little over one mile west of Bicknell, Utah. Indians camped here to be protected from the wind. This wash is called Sawkhwaw´ Ooweep ***Green Canyon***.

BIG ROCKS The outcrop southeast of Loa known as Big Rocks is called Mokov by the Paiutes. This place was Jimmy Timmican's birthplace. He said the word means the type of rock found there which appears to be granite.

BLACK RIDGE This is the long ridge running east and west for around three miles about one mile north of Highway 24. It is five to six miles east of Loa, Utah. The USGS map for Loa, Utah, gives the name of this ridge as Black Ridge. This ridge is called Wawu Awveetch ***Cedar Ridge***. The cedar trees on this hill give it a

black appearance from the highway therefore the Anglo name for it.

BLACK RIDGE This is the mountain on the east side of the road leading to the fish hatchery just as you leave Highway 24 a few miles southeast of Bicknell, Utah. This mountain is called O-aw´ Kaiv ***Yellow Mountain***. From a distance this mountain appears black due to the thick growth of trees covering its upper section. However, the base of this mountain on the west side is basically a shade of yellow with some red. This red and yellow section near its base is locally called "The Petrified Forest."

BOULDER MOUNTAIN This mountain was called Oahon´ Tuhkaw ***Pine Top.***

COCKSCOMB This is the prominent rock several miles east-southeast of Teasdale that can be seen as far away as Bicknell. This rock is called ai´suhpuneench ***Rock-Flat***. Ai denotes the type of rock and suhpuneench means "flat" referring to the rock's narrowness as it rises above the landscape.

GEYSER PEAK This is the peak northwest of Thousand Lake Mountain. The Indian name is Sewung Kwechoowunt ***Sand Peak***.

HENRY MOUNTAINS Untaw´dee. The meaning of this name is unknown. Florence Kanosh says, "The Indians from the Fish Lake area used to go out there and gather Indian rice grass."

PINE CREEK This is the creek west of Boulder Mountain that runs past the fish hatchery south of Bicknell, Utah. It is called Po-aw´ Tawkawvveeuts ***Bug Thigh***.

PINE CREEK SPRING This is the large spring about one-half mile southwest of the fish hatchery south of Bicknell, Utah. The Indian name is Awtawn´eogots ***Comes Up***.

POTTER SPRING This spring is located on the north side of Dry Valley about 2 miles northwest of Loa, Utah. It is called Kumoo´ Vaw ***Jackrabbit Water***.

RABBIT BRUSH SPRING This spring is located on the northwest side of Boulder Mountain. The Indian name is Kwe´kee Kawneevuhts ***Magpies House***.

RILEY CANYON SPRING This spring is in Riley Canyon a few miles east of Loa, Utah. This spring is called Soaveetoots or Soavee´ Pawts ***Cottonwood Water***.

RILEY CANYON This is the canyon south of Highway 24 just a few miles east of Loa, Utah. This wash is called Sawwhaw´ Tuhmpe Ooweep ***Green Rock Canyon***.

ROCK POINT This point is located on Pine Creek near Torrey, Utah. The Indian name is Pawchaw Tuhngkun´eevuhts, ***Bat Cave***. No cave is presently visible from the road in this area. There is a possibility that this cave was destroyed when the road went through that destroyed the base of the hill. The Indians used to camp in the cove on the north side of Rock Point and gather duck eggs in the large area of water that backed up at the base of this point. It was here that the battle with Paiutes and the white men took place. See the story of the "Battle with the White Man in Wayne County" in Chapter 2 on War and Historical Stories.

TERSEY'S NIPPLE The Indian name is Weeoo´ Koonu´vuhts ***Awl Sack***. This site is near Loa, Utah. Locally it is called "The Nipple" and "Elsie's Nipple." It is the nipple several miles straight south of Loa beyond the dump.

THOUSAND LAKE MOUNTAIN The Indian name is Sohod´uh Kaiv´u ***Damp Earth Mountain***.

UNIDENTIFIED PAINT SOURCE This paint site is located on the south side of Thousand Lake Mountain. This place is called Awveemp´ the name of a white gypsum type paint obtained there. The informant heard of this site and only knew the general location.

UNNAMED PEAK This is a small peak that resembles an ant hill when viewed from a distance as you approach Loa from the west. It is a small peak in a large pass as you look northeast. It is about one-half mile south of the crest of Geyser Peak and a little over one-eighth of a mile north-northwest of Riley Spring. This little peak is situated on the south line of Section 28, Township 26 S, Range 4 E, Geyser Peak USGS Quad. This small peak is called Tawsee´u Kawnee´vuhts ***Ant House***.

UNNAMED POINT This is the long red point that protrudes the furthest south from Thousand Lake Mountain. It is best viewed looking east on Highway 24 from Bicknell, Utah. The Indian name is Ungkaw Mookwun´eench ***Red Point***.

UNNAMED RIDGE This is the long gray ridge south of Highway 24 at milepost 50 about one and one-half miles northwest of Loa, Utah. This ridge is called Awsee Awveech ***Gray Lying***.

UNNAMED SPRING OR WATER TANK This source of water is located next to the road just south of Highway 24 between the junction to Fish Lake and Loa, Utah. There is a rocky section here surrounded by some trees that creates a short waterfall in the dry wash. It is a very noticeable and pretty location standing out amidst the sagebrush flats. This spring is called Peku´ Vawts ***Rotten Water***. Indians would camp here on their way back and forth from Rabbit Valley and Koosharem. This site is located near the center of Section 21, Township 27 S, Range 1 E.

ARIZONA

COCONINO COUNTY

CEDAR RIDGE This area is called Tono Weep ***Greasewood Canyon***.

COLORADO RIVER The Kaibab and Shivwits bands called this river Pawhaw ***Big water***. The Moapa band called it Chuhcheep.

KAIBAB Kai Awvahv ***Mountain Lying Down,*** from the words kaiv ***mountain*** and awvee ***lying down***.

KWAGUNT Kwagunt Rapids on the Colorado River was named after a Paiute who once lived there. His name was Kwawgunt ***Quiet***.

MAGUNTUWEEP This name means ***Mawgin's Land***. Mawgin was an Indian who lived in this area. He was a grandfather to Tony Tillahash.

NANKOWEAP This name comes from the words Nengwoo´ koahoyp ***Indians Killed*** and probably refers to the time a group of Kaibab Indians were killed by Apaches referred to in Chapter 2 on War and Historical Stories.

NAVAJO MOUNTAIN An informant from the area said it was called Nengwoo Kaiv ***Paiute Mountain***. Later upon being re-questioned he just called it Kaiv ***Mountain***.

PARIA PLATEAU This plateau is called Paduh´eu Kaiv ***Elk Mountain***.
SAN FRANCISCO PEAKS These peaks are called Noovu´ Hawduhd ***Snow Sitting***.
TOROWEEP This name means ***Cattail Canyon*** and is pronounced Toyo´ Weep.

MOJAVE COUNTY

MOUNT TRUMBULL This mountain is called Yooveen Kawduhd ***Ponderosa Sitting***.

PAHCOON From the words paw ***water*** and koonaw´ meaning ***fire***.

PARASHONT This word comes from the Paiute name Pawtuh´ee oasoant ***Elk Hide Softening***.

RIGGS SPRING This spring is located on the Kaibab Paiute Reservation near Fredonia, Arizona, and is called Skoom Pawts ***Rabbit Brush Water***. It is southwest of Six Mile Village.

SIX MILE SPRING This spring is located on the Kaibab Paiute Reservation at the Six-Mile Village. It is called Suhuh´ Vawts ***Squaw Bush Water***.

TASSAI This place name in the Grand Wash on the Arizona Strip comes from the Paiute word Taws, the ***Corky-seed Pincushion Cactus***.

UINKARET This word comes from the word Yooveen Kawduhd ***Ponderosa Sitting***.

WOLF SPRING This spring is located on the Kaibab Paiute Reservation near Fredonia, Arizona, and is called Tono´ Vawts ***Greasewood Water***.

NEVADA

BAKER MOUNTAIN This mountain is in White Pine County. The Paiute name is Tuhngkunt.

EAGLE VALLEY This Valley is located in Lincoln County. The Paiute Indian name for this valley is Nopaw´ Sawkwayuv ***Egg Belly***. The valley is called Nopuv for short.

FURNACE CREEK This creek in Death Valley was called Tuhmpees´ by the Paiutes. The meaning refers to a type of rock.

MOAPA This is the name of a town and Paiute Band in Clark County. This name is correctly pronounced Moou´ Paw ***Mosquito Water***.

MOUNT CHARLESTON This mountain in Clark County is called Noovu´uhunt signifying ***Has Snow***. This mountain was a sacred mountain to all the Paiutes and the location where those who survived the flood were saved.

PAHRANAGAT From the word Pawdun´uhguhts ***Sticking Your Feet in the Water***. This name undoubtedly comes from the abundance of water in this area of Lincoln County.

PAHRUMP This name comes from the word pawhump ***common reed*** *Phragmite*, or from the words paw and tuhmp ***rock*** and ***water***..

PANACA From the word Punu´kawd meaning anything that ***shines***, including

metal, gold, and silver. This name was probably given to this town in Lincoln County due to the mining activities there in the early days.

TONOPAH This is the name of a town in Nye County. The word comes from the words tonup´ ***chokecherry*** and paw ***water***.

UTE PLACE-NAMES

UTAH

BOTEN SPRINGS This spring on the Ute Reservation in Uintah County is called Oodoom´ Ma-hawpuhts ***Lodge Pole Sanding Place***. There are some grooves on top of bedrock sandstone there that Ouray McCook says were used in smoothing and shaping tipi poles.

DUCHESNE RIVER The Duchesne River in Duchesne County, Utah, is called Sawkhwaw´ Nookweech ***Blue Running***.

GREEN RIVER Awvaw´ Paw ***Big Water***.

HILL CREEK Tonee´ooweep ***Greasewood Creek***.

WILLOW CREEK This river in Uintah County, Utah, is called Peku´ Pawts ***Rotten Water*** because of the slew-like swamp there.

COLORADO

ANIMAS RIVER This river running though the Southern Ute Reservation is called Sawkhwaw Nookweetch ***Blue Running***.

BLUE MOUNTAIN This mountain in Moffat County, Colorado, is called Sawkhwaw Kawduhd ***Blue Sitting***.

COLORADO RIVER Peuvaw Nookweetch ***Mother Water Running***.

DENVER The city is called Teu´puhts.

DOLORES RIVER The river in Southwestern Colorado is presently called Todoos. This is the Ute way of pronouncing the word Dolores. Molly Deer a Ute from Towoac, Colorado, says that the original Indian name referred to some settlements by the river burnt by the Utes long ago. Allen Neskahai, a Navajo, says that the Navajo translation of their word for this river is "Place Where People Burned" after the Ute name.

FLORIDA RIVER This river in La Plata County is called Tuhduh´dongweetch ***Running Through a Meadow***.

SAN JUAN RIVER Supaw ***White Water***.

UTE MOUNTAIN The highest peak on Ute Mountain in Montezuma County is called We´sevee Kawduhd (an unidentified plant ***Sitting***).

WHITE RIVER This is the river that runs though Rio Blanco County in Colorado and Uintah County within the state of Utah. It is called Kwou´paw ***Smoke Water*** due to the swirling silt in it that makes it look like smoke.

KANSAS

TOPEKA The word Topeka is a Ute word given to that place one time "when the Utes raided that far east. It was here that they ran out of arrows and so they named this place Toopeek ***All Gone***."

PLATE 7

Kanosh, Utah, 1900. Photograph by G. E. Anderson. Courtesy of Rall G. Francis, Heritage Prints, Springville, Utah.

PLATE 8

Shivwits Indians camping in St. George, Utah, near the Dixie Sun Bowl,1899. The photograph was taken by Mrs. Starr, the white lady in the photograph. The only surviving copy was given to me by Bessie Tillahash who identified the people in the photograph. Left to right 1. Matt Spute 2. unidentified 3. Frank Snow 4. Frank Fisher 5. Paul Jake 6. Lloyd Napa Tom (5 and 6 are the two little boys in the foreground) 7. Will **Kawngwuhnts** (man on wagon) 8. unidentified little boy on Will's left 9. unidentified tall boy on Will's left, (10-13 are the four little kids below the two boys on Will's left)10. unidentified 11. unidentified 12. Rosie Pinkie 13. Bessie Simon 14. Ivy Foster (child in ladies arms) 15. Mrs. Starr 16. unidentified white man 17. Ruth Empey 18. Sadie Pinkie 19. Jennie Mokiac 20. Sue Mokiac (Jim Mokiac's daughter), 21. Susie (Susie is the lady standing behind the four little girls. She is Bessie's mother) 22. Simon (Bessie's father) 23. Ta wa wa **Tavaw´awvee** 24. unidentified 25. unidentified 26. unidentified 27. unidentified.

CHAPTER 12

THE SOUTHERN PAIUTE LANGUAGE

All honorable men belong to the same tribe.

People who have never studied Indian languages may suppose that the Indians are at the bottom of the scale in their ability to express a wide range of thoughts like the English language, because of the so-called "savage" nature of the American Indian. Since the very first contact between Europeans and Indians, certain elements of the European population always deemed themselves superior to the Indian. History books are filled with their statements classifying American Indians as "savages" not worthy of the same status and human rights as the rest of humanity. The conquerors used this lower status as an excuse to give them the moral right to run rampant over the Indian in taking away their land.

There is still an attempt to belittle the intelligence of the American Indian concerning their language, picture writing, and sign language. However, there are those scholars who have made in-depth studies and come up with findings that present a clear picture of the intelligence of the American Indian. Scholars at the Smithsonian have written: "Suffice it to note that the American Indian languages, as finished systems, can express fully as wide a range of thought as can the languages of Europe" (Kopper 1986, p. 62).

If you were to make a word count of words presently in use in the English language, as compared to those in an Indian language, English would far exceed Indian in word count, but not in the ability of expression. The reason for this higher word count in English is that English has borrowed a very large amount of words from numerous other languages, including American Indian languages, but more particularly from the Latin and Greek. Deduct all these borrowed words from English, and then watch the word count diminish. It is the quality of expression of any language that really counts, not quantity.

I have devised the Southern Paiute Dictionary to make it easier for those without a college degree to read and write Paiute. This dictionary is designed

especially for Indians. I've avoided using special characters that aren't found on a typewriter so that this language could be typewritten. Therefore, I've confined the expression of the Paiute alphabet to the 26 letters of the English alphabet.

The dictionary is in alphabetical order, according to the English translation of the words, to make it easier for the reader to find the words he's looking for. I've chosen the English word closest to the Paiute equivalent to make it easier to look up. This choice might not always be entirely grammatically correct but is more as an Indian would interpret the word into English. It would be much simpler to compile this dictionary using the Indian word first, in alphabetical order, but this would make it extremely difficult for anyone who doesn't understand Paiute to find anything.

In most Indian languages many words are seldom used alone but rather combined with other words, such as mooun´ (***my father***). You never hear an Indian say moo´ for father; it sounds foreign. The structure of Indian languages and their use of verb phrases with hundreds of prefixes and suffixes, means that there are very few fixed and rigid separate words in the language. To write the full conjugation of one Paiute word would be very time consuming. The language is copious, flexible and expressive. Because of this it is sometimes difficult to break up Indian sentences into their various word elements as some of them never stand alone. I do break them up with a space in many of the more apparent examples. However, I'm not always consistent in breaking up the same word as it tends to make the reader want to read it in a choppy manner with a slight break between syllables. The reader shouldn't do this. The syllables and short word elements all should be spoken together in a smooth flow. What I try to do is to keep the sentences decently short, and break them up where it might be the most beneficial to the reader who has no access to actually hearing Paiute spoken.

The reader will often find several variations in the way a word is said. Sometimes these variations occur due to language structure and other times they are normal variations as those found in English. When I include variations, they are not guesses as to how they are pronounced. I do speak the language and one must remember that present-day Paiute is a conglomerate of several minor dialects, which also accounts for some of the variations.

I could attempt to pattern this dictionary after Sapir's 1930 book *Southern Paiute, A Shoshonean Language*, with a complete breakdown of the words with all their aspirations and numerous special characters. Then, as with his book, you would have to speak Latin, German, Gaelic, and French to know the key to the sounds. He also breaks up the words into so many small pieces that it becomes difficult for the non-linguist to grasp. The Paiute language is constructed this way, but I believe it is easier to grasp such examples in sentence form. His book is good in this respect but is limited in usefulness to a few of the best linguists. I have written this for the Indian and the average student. Those who want Sapir's type of work may refer to his book, if they can find a copy. Although it analyzes the language from a linguist's viewpoint it has its faults, wrong translations, omitted initial sounds, and other mistakes since he didn't speak the language. However, it

is a very good work despite these shortcomings, and far exceeds mine in understanding linguistic principles. He based his work on legends and therefore omits many of the common everyday words. I have designed my work to fill in much of that gap, although I didn't take the time to point out his mistakes. Perhaps I could do so in a future work.

This dictionary isn't complete nor are all the tenses of each word given. To do this would be very time consuming. I basically only recorded my language notes as my own personal memory aid which I first started when I began learning the language in the 1940s. My pencil notes were getting faded, worn, and smeared, and were inconsistent in pronunciation keys (as I improved them over the years). This work is therefore an editing of my pencil notes, making them consistent so that others could understand them.

Many of the words in this dictionary come from much older Paiutes born in the last century and forgotten by the present generation, most of whom only speak a pidgin Paiute. One of the purposes of this dictionary is to preserve many of those words never before published and even forgotten by the present generation. Today no one younger than fifty speaks the language; of those that still do, many of them speak in a pidgin fashion. Those who do speak it very fluently find very few to converse with. Therefore they've forgotten many of the old words that there is no occasion to use today. I would especially like to thank the following individuals who are among the most fluent speakers today for their help in going over portions of this dictionary: Smith Bushhead, Warren Bushhead, Eunice Tillahash, and Marilyn Jake (Shivwits), Vera Charles (Koosharem), and Earl Pikyavit (Kanosh).

The accents of yesterday have pretty well blended into one due to intermarriage between bands and the constant intermingling. Remnants of band accents and words peculiar to certain bands (which I note when they occur) still exist, but the difference in accents is very minimal today. I've noticed that Kanosh and Koosharem seem to use the sound "ts" often in place of "ch" so common at Kaibab, Cedar City, and southward. To say this is the rule would be wrong as the Shivwits and other bands often use both sounds, as does Kanosh and Koosharem. The "ch" sound is more common at Kaibab, Cedar City, and Indian Peaks, and southward. I give the different variants of many of the words but due to the extent of intermarriage and intermingling I make no attempt to distinguish band origins of some of these words as I would only be guessing. When I do assign band differences then I have observed them or they were told to me by other Paiutes. In some cases these variants are pidgin Paiute incorrectly pronounced by the younger bilingual generation where English took precedence.

I started learning Paiute from members of the Cedar City, Indian Peaks, and Shivwits bands living at Cedar City in the 1940s and early 1950s. When I married Doris Kanosh of the Koosharem Band I learned a lot more from her. She spoke the Koosharem dialect with a very noticeable "ts" accent since she was raised by her grandmother Florence Timmican Kanosh from the Koosharem Band. However, Doris's mother was of the Indian Peak Band so some blending of accents had oc-

curred. Many of the sentences with the "ts" sound in the section on Paiute sentences were given to me by my wife, Doris.

The Koosharem accent is more akin to Northern Ute than to Shivwits although they have no trouble in understanding each other. The Koosharem accent lacks the occasional "r" and "f" found among the Ute. The Willow Springs, Arizona, accent is closer to Paiute than Ute.

I give sentence examples in many places to help those who want to study the language more thoroughly.

Words that are peculiar to one band are noted with the band name following the word. When a Moapa word or accent is given then in most cases it also applies to Las Vegas and Chemehuevi. When Chemehuevi is given then in most cases the word also applies to Moapa and Las Vegas.

With all the intermarriage it is sometimes hard to tell which words are peculiar to certain bands since they are often borrowed by others as the old Paiute diminishes in the wake of pidgin Paiute. In many cases where a word is peculiar to one band I have found they know and use the more common words for the same thing as used by other bands. When I list two ways of saying one word and one of the words is assigned to one band then it should be assumed that the other word is common to all the bands. However, there could be some exceptions to this.

DICTIONARY

— A —

ACCIDENT, WRECKED
1. (to be killed in a car wreck, shooting, fall, etc.) nawvuk´ai, nawvuk´aing ***he killed himself*** nawvuk´ung
2. ***wrecked*** poong´kwunt
ACCUSTOMED TO IT wee´unee
ACHE (see ***pain***)
ACROSS (see ***over*** and ***other side***)
ACT (see ***do***)
ACTING SMART naw´hawvus
ADD (see ***put with***)
ADOBE tawvus´oop weuv (dry mud)
AFRAID, FRIGHTENED, surprised
1. yaw´vawghai
I'm afraid yaw´vawghaiun
2. suhdee´u
I'm afraid sudee´unchun
you scared me suhdee´u tuhchunee
AFTERWHILE see ***later***
AFTER, BEHIND, IN BACK OF awvee´nungk, awvee´nawp
after New Year's New Year's awvee´nawpawchuhk
the one that always sits behind the post office post office awvee´nungkwup kawduh´meent
AGAIN, REPEAT -wuhsuh´
do it again ooneng´wuhsoouk, ooneng´oos (a shortened baby talk way of saying the same thing)
AGAVE *Agave utahensis* eyunt´, nunt (shortened from eyunt´)
Agave canyon nuntaw´ ooweep
AGE (see ***winter***)
AHEAD, IN FRONT (see ***leading***) wawmee´tuh
don't get ahead of us kawtch nuhm´ee wawmee´tuh whawvungwai
don't get ahead of me kawtch nuh wawmee´tuh whawvungwai
AID (see ***assist***)
AIM (to) waw´vuhnee
aiming waw´vuhnekai
AIR, BREATH soowup´
ALDER (THINLEAF) pawwhay´uv
ALIGHT (see ***hit***)
ALIKE, SAME KIND toahoy´ nudoo´ai
same amount toahoy´nawvai
same kind toahoy´ nawdoo´ud
ALIVE (see ***living***)
ALKALI mawsump
ALL BROKEN UP poaduh´duhkwaip
ALL THE TIME (see ***always***)
ALL munok´, muno´nee, muno´kos
everything, everybody puaw´ munok
ALLUVIAL FAN (see ***base of mountain***)
ALMOST, NEARLY soowaw´
I almost fell soowaw´ kwepu´chun
ALONE, SEPARATELY, EACH, EVERY, ONESELF nonohs´, nawnohs´
ALONG pa-hai
eating along tuhkaw´ pahai
ALREADY, PRIOR, EARLIER, JUST PAST
1. ono´
I just arrived ono pee´chukunt
2. ***I'm already dancing*** oowee´tus (from wee´tuhmp ***old***)
ALSO, TOO -khai´nee
me too nuh´ khainee
you too emee´ khainee
ALWAYS DOES -meent
it always does like that muneng´oomeent
always does like me nuh´pu ooneng´oomeent

it always stops tuhdus´ukoa meent
ALWAYS, CONTINUALLY, ALL THE TIME
1. tuh´sump
they keep asking tuh´sump tooveeng´woont
keeps telling it tuhsump tuhneunk´oomeent
2. nahduh´vee
AMEN, LET IT BE, SO BE IT
1. *let that which I said go through* oo´puk oodoo´awvaw umpaw´haw nunuhd
2. *let it come true* tooveets´eek oodoo´awvaw
3. *let it turn the way I said* oo´puk tuhkai´vaw ai´nun uhd
AMERICAN, WHITE MAN (Eng. American)
1. mawdeeng´kun, mawduh´kawts
2. haiko (Moapa and Las Vegas; of Mojave derivation)
AMONG THEM awmuh´ukawv (see *some*)
among the rocks tuhmpee´ awhawv
AMOUNT
1. -ee´tuhnee, -ee´tuhmuhnee.
2. *this amount* e´vaiunee (from ee´vai *here*)
3. *that amount* oo´vaiunee (from oo´vai *there*)
Numbers 2 and 3 are normally used with pointing gestures as one would say in English, "Fill it *to here*."
AMPHITHEATER *cliffs in a broad semi-circular shape* awvoo´uv
ANCESTORS ee´nuhng (lit. *long ago Indians*)
ANCIENT (see *old*)
AND, WITH (see *with*) -engwu
Austin and the Navajos Austin ung pu-hawng´weets engwu
with the Navajos pu-hawng´weets engwu
ANGLE (see *uneven*)
ANGRY, MAD, TO SCOLD nungai´ai
he's/she's angry nungai´ai ung
he's/she's scolding me nungu´mai ungun
angry at me nuhnai nungu´mu
ANIMAL puawv´
ANKLE
1. tawweench´
your ankle tawngwen´chohom
2. *your ankle* kaw´uhoym
3. *your ankle* tawsuhmp´echum
hoatomp´awchun is the back bone at ankle level
ANOTHER (see *different*)
ANTELOPE wunts, wuntsee´puhts
ANTLION LARVAE, DOODLEBUG *myrmeleontidae* kuhuh´toanoyntch
ANTS (collectively) tawsee´uv
ANY paw-
any amount paw no´pai
any time paw nok´
ANYPLACE, ANYWHERE paw hu´vawntuh
I'll see you anyplace paw´huvu nawvuh´nekaivum
ANYTHING paw haw´duh
ANYTIME, SOMETIMES naaw´kawnos, naaw´tuhmpu
APACHE PLUME *Fallugia paradoxa* meah´puh oonup´
APPEAR, EMERGE INTO VIEW
For any celestial body to emerge from beneath the horizon, for an animal to emerge from its den, or for someone to come into view over the horizon or from around a bend mungwee´see
sunrise tahvai´ mungwee´see
he's appearing mungwee´suchung
APPLES (Eng. apple) aw´pawdoos
APRON pekwun
APRIL tawmu´muhunts (lit. *spring moon*). Spring begins in March in the St. George and Las Vegas areas so the

spring moon could vary according to the area.
ARAPAHOE Sawdeets´ekuts (lit. ***Dog Eaters***)
ARBOR, SHADE HOUSE awvaw´ kawnee
ARGUE (to) QUARREL nunu´ai
nawvu´chungwai
nawvu´tsuwee (Kanosh)
arguing nawnaw´ung wuhchung
ARIZONA (Eng. Arizona) awdu´so
ARM (from shoulder to wrist)
1. puhd-, puhdu-
your arm puhdum´
2. ***upper arm*** unguv
ARMADILLO punu´tuhmpee nahdo (lit. ***iron rock clothes***)
ARMPIT
1. kuhtsuhk´, kuhchuh´eets
2. awsoam (lit. ***salty***)
ARMPIT ODOR kunchuh´eets pono´ai
AROUND
to go around something aaw´ketuhk
ARRIVE pechuh´, peech´
arrived peech´ukunt
arrived (past tense) pechuh´puhkunt
when did you arrive? eem hunok´u peech?
he/she never arrived yet kawchung´ pechuhng´wais
when are you arriving? hunok pechuh´ vawntus?
when does he arrive? hunok´ oa pechuh´mee?
ARROGANT peunk´
ARROW WRENCH kuh´eyok
ARROW hookwee´oo, oo´
ARROWHEAD wunup´
ASH TREE *Fraxinus* wawmpeep´
ASHES kootsup´ (Kanosh), koochup´ (Shivwits)
ASK tooveeng´ee
ask him tooveng´eyung
ask for it tooveech´oouk
ask me tooveeng´een
ASSEMBLE (animals) kwuhchoomp´
they assembled
kwuhchoomp´ekainum
ASSEMBLE, MEETING, POW WOW, GATHERING
(for people to assemble for a meeting or some event)
1. soo´pawdoy, soo´pawdoai
they will have a gathering soo´pao vawnahdoong,
when are they going to meet?
huhok´u soopadoovawnee?
2. na-hawd´uhee
ASSIST, HELP, AID mawduh´ai
help him/her mawduh´ai ung, mawduh´aing, mawduh´aing wung
ATTACKING
1. ***a group going towards to do***
mamoon´wuntoowun ooneen
2. ***coming to do*** unekunguduhm
AUGUST (lit. ***fall moon***)
yoovun´umuts
AUNT
1. paaw-´
his or her aunt paawng´
your aunt pawawm´
niece (reciprocal) paawts´
my aunt paawn´
aunts pauv´eng
2. nuhmpee´uts
AUTOMOBILE (Eng. automobile)
1. awdum´peid
2. aiyum´ooveep (Moapa)
AUTUMN, FALL yoovun´
it's getting fall yoovun´uteuk
AWAKEN (see ***wake up***)
AWFUL (see ***ugly***)
AWL weeoovb
AXE
1. kwepu´nump (lit. ***hitting thing***).
2. tavee´nump (lit. ***hitting thing***)
These words can mean anything used to hit with, even a stick.

— B —

BAPTIZE (to)
1. ***to go under the water*** paw´enaw yowk´w
2. ***washed*** paduh´kekunt
3. ***baptize him*** paw dook´wetook´wung (lit. ***put him under the water***)

BABY
1. ***new born*** kengaw´peets
2. ***a little bigger than a new born*** pee´sots, pe´shoats
3. pe´veets. (Eng. baby)

BACK
1. o'-awv´
your back o'-awm´
2. ***humped portion of back*** saiyu-

BACKBONE
o'-oh´um

BACKWARD pe´meetook

BAD, NO GOOD uhvuh´, uhvuh´nee
whiskey uhvuh´upaw (lit. ***bad water***)
you're no good eem vuh´upuhwuhnee

BADGER oonum´puhts, oon
badgers oonum´puhtsengw

BAG (see ***sack***)

BALD
1. yuhnuh´kunt
2. tuh´du hawd

BALD EAGLE pawngwu´

BALL paw´ko-oonump (Koosharem)

BANK punu´ kawdee kawn (lit. ***money house***)

BANNOCK punaik´kee

BARELY ABLE, CAN'T HARDLY muhsuh´, mootsoo´
barely able to do it oonee´ muhsoo´ee
can't hardly nurse it pechuh´ muhsoo´ee ook
can't hardly carry it yungwee´ muhsoo´ee

BARK (from a juniper tree) moawhup´

BARK (of a tree) awsee´uk (from ***awsee´*** skin)

BARKING (of a dog) o'-oh´hoy, ko-oh´gwai
don't bark ko'-oh´gwaiup

BARREN, NAKED, DESOLATE, DESERT, IN THE OPEN, OUTSIDE tuh´du
flat desert tuh´du yooawv

BASE OF CLIFF kawnuh´guts

BASE OF THE MOUNTAIN
1. pengwuv
at the foot of the mountain pewaw´
further down (on the alluvial fan) pewuv´
2. tuhung´w
at the base of a mountain tuhung´wu vaiuk
3. ***foot of the hills*** kawnuh´guts

BASHFUL tookwee´ai

BASKET (bowl shaped cooking basket) yuh-up´

BASKET CAP suh'uh´ kaichuhots (lit. ***squawbush hat***)

BAT
1. pawchuts´,
bat who once was pawchuv´ookaip
2. pawtsuts´ (Kanosh)

BATHE (see ***wash***)

BE (to) -e´kai
will be -ekai´vu
when its getting to be sundown tahvai´ yowk ekhaik

BE QUIET ai´nekai

BEADS tchoy, tsoy

BEANS muhdee´, modee´, muhdee´vees (not used at Koosharem)

BEAR kweuts´ kweyu´hunt

BEAR DANCE maw´kon

BEARD (see ***whiskers***)

BEATING (to beat a drum) kwepum´weai

BEAVER paoons´
BECAUSE oonee´ku
BECOME, TO TURN INTO, CAUSE TO HAPPEN, TO TAKE PLACE (to) -tuhkai´ -tuhkaw'oong, -tuhkungw, -tuhkaik
became -tuhkung´wepuhku
it turned out no good uhvuh´ tuhkung´uhpuhku
he's becoming crazy unoo´pee tuhkaw´oong
BED awvee´tu, awvee´nump (lit. *lying thing*)
BEE whawtsuv´
BEER (Eng. beer) be´u
BEFORE (see *first*)
BEHIND (see *after* and *late*)
BELIEVE, OBEY, FAITH, TRUST tooveets´ekai
believe him, have faith in him, trust him tooveets´ekaiung
I believe it tooveets´e kaiuhkwun nuh
don't believe him tooveets´e kawngwaim
believe him tooveets´ ekaioom
believe in Jesus tooveets´ekung Jesus ee
believe in Him tooveets´ekawd oong
BELLY BUTTON sekoo´, sekoots´
your belly button segoom´
BELLY, STOMACH sawkoy´u
your belly sawkway´awm
BELONGING TO (suff.) -udun´
BELOW, UNDER udoo´kwut
To go under the water paw udook´we toovai
BELT *belt* naw´ whechup (lit. *self-wrap*)
BEND OVER *to bend over while on your knees* poong´kwai toovu (from poo´kwai, *to stoop*)
BENT soayaw´-
bent soayaw´kai
it's bent soayaw´e chuk, soayaw´etsuk
BERRIES (from serviceberry bush) toowump´eev
BESIDE -u´vai
beside him/her mung u´vaiook
BET (see *wager*)
BETWEEN, MIDDLE, CENTER, CLEFT nuduh´yu, naduh´euk
BEWARE (see *watch out*)
BIG DIPPER tosaw´kawm (lit. *white jackrabbit*)
BIG SAGE kawhup´
BIG TOE taw´to
BIG
1. peow´
big person peow´ vuhwuhnee
big ones (plural) pevee´owvuhnee
2. *big* awvawt
BIGGEST awvaw´tuhmus, awvaw´tuhm
BILLY GOAT savaw´toots
BIRDS (collectively) wetseech´, wecheech´
BIRTH (see *parturition*)
BITE (to) kuhuh´ee
bite into it kuhee´vu
BITTER (in a distasteful sense) mou´kawmunt, mou´kawmai
BLACK
1. too´, too´kwawd
black one too´kwawdum
black toopaw´hawdum (Chemehuevi)
2. *a dirty greasy black* yoovees´u hawd
BLACK BEAR too´kwawdum kweyu´hunt, too´ kweyu´hunt
BLACK SAGE *Artemisia nova* ungkaw´po sawngwuv
BLACK WIDOW SPIDER too hoo´kwump (lit. *black spider*)
BLACKBIRD, RED-WINGED *Agelaius*

phoeniceus pawhaw´chukup, pawhawn´tsukup (Koosharem)
BLADDER
1. pukwee´
2. se'-ee´ koonuv (lit. ***urine sack***)
BLANKET, QUILT
1. muhdoo´ee
2. moahoy´
BLAZINGSTAR *Mentzelia albicaulis* koo-oo´
BLESS (see ***fan with feathers***)
BLIND pooee´ait (lit. ***no eyes***)
BLOATED (see ***round***)
BLOOD (that has jelled or thickened) kuhchawng
BLOOD VEIN pao´tawngweem
BLOOD paop´ee, pauhp´
BLOODSUCKER suhum´ohots
BLOOMING suh'uh´enawk, suheech´
BLOSSOM, FLOWER
1. saeent´, suheenk´uhee, suhng´uhee
yellow blossom o-aw´saeent
2. nanaw´kawdout
BLOW, PANT (to) pookwee´
to tell someone to blow pookweeng´oa
BLUE, GREEN (many Indian tribes have the same name for ***blue*** and ***green***) sawkhwaw´kai, sawkhwaw´-
green/blue one sawkhwaw´ hawd
BLUEBIRD *Sialia* nawnchoots´
BOARD, STICK, WOODEN oveemp´
BOAT awvee´sok (lit. ***lies flat on the water***)
BOBCAT tookoo´puhts, took´
BODY nengwoo´uv
your body nengwoom´
BOIL
just starting to boil noanoa´yok
going to boil sa'ai´
boiling koanoa´oycoy
boiled sa'awp´
BOLT
to bolt as a horse does in fright or in a race pontsee´nai
it's bolting, it's taking off pontsee´nawm
BONE o'-ohv´
BORN (see ***parturition***)
BORROW (see ***copy***)
BOTH (see ***together***)
BOTHERING, TEASING ma-whus´senkuhee
BOTTOM tuhnawv´
it's bottom tuhnawk´
BOUNCING
to bounce up and down and back and forth in a stationary position yuhntsuh´khai
bouncing along yuhntsuh´kawhai (an example is bouncing up and down on horseback while riding along)
BOW STRING pakaw´way
BOW awtch, awts
your bow awchuhm´
BOWL
1. ***basketry bowl used for food*** koats (Smaller ones had another name)
your bowl koatseem´
2. ohots´
BOXELDER *Acer negundo* pawhoy´uv, pawkhoy´uv
BOY SCOUT soeets´ echuh´kwunt
BOY ai´puts
boys (plural) ai´putseng
BRAID (see ***weave***) sekwaw´ai, segwu´ai
BRAINS chuhpeek´, chuhpeek´eev
BRANCH, LIMB papaw´duhngkai
BRAVE, STRONG, SUPERIOR, GREAT, TOUGH, INVINCIBLE, ABLE suhpee´ait, supee´tseup
one who is great supee´ait uhm
BREAD (Span. pan) pawn´udoop, pawn´u
bread maker pawn´udoots
BREAK

1. ***to break a stick in two or to break off a limb*** moahup´enuk
broken in two kopok´w
broken pupawng´,
2. ***to break one piece at a time*** spoad´oawuk, tsispoad´ouk
3. ***to break into many pieces or to rip or break apart as something is forced through*** tapuhk´, tapuhts´, tapuhts´een
I broke it open tapuhk´eenupun
it ripped tapuhk´enuk
BREATH soowup´
breathing sowaw´kai
BREECH CLOTH kwusee´ugup
BRIDGE paw avawk´enump (lit. ***water crossing thing***)
BRIDLE tuhmpai´ukhup
BRIGHAM TEA *Ephedra* ootoop´
BRIGHT tavai´oonee
BRING IT, GET IT yah´vai oongwuk (compare ***take it back***)
went and got it yah´vai engwuhts
BROAD CHESTED, THICK (a person or animal) hoacoan´tuh muhnee (lit. ***thick one***)
BROOMRAPE *Orobanche fasciculata* too-oo´
BROTHER
1. ***elder brother*** pavee´, paveets´
2. ***younger brother*** chukaits´
BROTHER-IN -LAW
1. nawntaw´ mooun, yutaw´ mooum
2. tawn tungwuv´
BROTHERS nawvuv´ets eengw, nawvuv´ewu
BROWN BEAR undo´ kweuts (lit. ***brown bear***)
BROWN undok´kwawd, undok´
brown one undo´kwawdum
BRUISE (see ***purple***)
BRUSH, WEEDS, THINGS, PLANTS mu'uv´
my things mu'uv´ uhn
BUCK DEER tuheu´goom, tuheu´koom
BUCKBOARD ooweem´buhk
BUCKET pampuhn´
BUCKING
a bucking horse ponpoh´tsenai (plural of pontsee´nai ***to take off running***)
it's bucking ponpoh´tsenung
BUCKSKIN
tanned deer hide tuh´euv
BUD SAGE *Artemisia spinescens*
1. koochup´o sawngwuv (lit. ***ash sage***)
2. mawkaw´chuh sawngwuv´vuhts (lit. ***horned toad sage***)
BUFFALO
1. moahoy´ kooch (lit. ***blanket cow***) Kaibab
2. tuh´du kooch (lit. ***desert cow***) Kanosh
BUFFALO BERRY ungkawp
BUFFALO GOURD *Cucurbita* onook´weemp
BUFFALOBERRY BUSH *Shepherdia argentea* opeev´
BUG (see ***insect***)
BUILD (see ***make***)
BULL SNAKE, GOPHER SNAKE, BLOW SNAKE
Pituophis melanoleucus koahom´puhts
BULLETS wai´u
BUNCH GRASS *Muhlenbergia* noou´veev
BUNDLED
1. oatom´puhnawkunt
2. whechoo´kookunt (from whechai´uh ***to tie***)
BURDEN BASKET (large, cone-shaped) aws, aoos´
BURDOCK *Arctium* avaw´tuh kaw´menuv (lit. ***big kaw´menuv***)
BURN, FIRE na'ai´
burnt na'aip´

make a fire na'ai´tee (lit. ***make it burn***)
BURNT THROUGH
1. kwepoo´doonk
2. wa-haw´dok nawaid
BURST patawk´
BURY (to) tookoo´ee, koo´ee
going to bury tookoo´oongpawnt
buried kookwunt
BUTCHERING (cutting up meat) skuh´dai
BUTTERFLY
1. aw´sevuhts
2. awsee´voadonts (Kanosh)
BUTTOCKS kwetoomp´ kwetoo´
BUY, BARTER, PAY nahdong´w
buy it nahdo´uk
bought nawdoo´ai
BUZZARD, TURKEY VULTURE *Cathartes aura* wekoomp´uhts, week´w
BUZZING toongwu´vuhawn uk (lit. ***making noise-it***)
BY THIS TIME ee´vaiuk, ee´vaiook

— C —

CACTUS, THORN munuv´
CALF OF LEG (used to denote the calf of the leg and also the tibia bone) whetchu
my calf whechun´
your calf whechu´um
CALL, INVITE pawvai´
to call him/her pawvai´teung
call the doctor poowu´hunt oong pawvai´
CAMP kawnee´kai, kawnee´vu
CAN'T SHOOT STRAIGHT wee´nait
CANAIGRE, DOCK, WILD RHUBARB *Rumex hymenosepalus* kwevuv´
CANARY (caged) o-aw´ we'tseech´ (lit. ***yellow bird***)
CANE (for walking) poado´
your cane podom´
canes (plural) poadots´
CANNOT kawchoo-
I can't do it kawchoo´kwun
CANVAS sechaw´hawv
CANYON
1. ***a dry canyon or wash*** weep, ooweep
2. ***a canyon between two mountains*** wee´wuk
3. ***a canyon with water*** ooweng´w
4. ***crack*** sekuv´
CARBORUNDUM koongwu´denump, koowaw´denump (lit. ***edger***)
CARDS paw´soonump
CARRY, LOAD
1. no´-, noy´
to carry in the mouth (as a cat carries its young) kuh´noy
carrying along in the mouth kuh' no´meai
load it up nou´tengwuk
2. yungwee´
carrying along yungwee´mee
carrying separately nawai´ yungwee´ uk
many carrying yuyung´weukum
CAT
1. kedeets´ (Eng. kitty)
2. moos´uts
CATCH UP wachuh´kee, watsuhng´
going to catch up wachuhng´paw
have to catch up watsuhng´oompawk
caught up with me wachuhng´ wechuk´un
I'm going to catch up with you (plural) wachuhm´ pawmum
I'm going to catch up with you (beat you) wachuhm´ pawngwun
CATCH (see ***hold*** and ***seize***)
to catch something that has been thrown mawnchawk´, mawntsunk´ (from muntsaw´ ***upraised hands***)

one who catches something thrown mawntsunk´aiung
CATCLAW ACACIA *Acacia greggii* sechuh´uhdump
CATTAIL *Typha domingensis* toa'oyv´
CAUSE (see ***happen***)
CAVE tuhng kawn´ (lit. ***rock house***)
CEDAR CITY INDIANS Suh´duts
CEDAR CITY Suh´du (Eng. Cedar)
CEDAR TREE (see ***juniper***)
CENTER (see ***good*** and ***between***)
CENTIPEDE
1. tuhmpee´ tohouv (lit. ***rock snake***)
2. suhng´ump (Shivwits & Koosharem)
CHAIR kawduh´nump
CHANGE COLORS (as tree leaves turning yellow) takov´eeng
CHANGE IT, FLIP IT, TURN IT munuh´ee kwunk uk
CHAPPED SKIN
chewung´w
tsewung´w (Kanosh)
CHAPS peku´koosuts (lit. ***leather pants***)
CHARGING
running a horse at full speed tawngwus
making a horse go full speed tawngwus´u teung
CHASE (to), PURSUE, FOLLOW mawduhn´ai
chasing him/her mawno´koung
chaser mawduh´nuts
CHEEK sovuv´
your cheek sovuv´um
CHIEF, BOSS neahv´
War Chief Nawhoo´kwee Neahv
CHEMEHUEVI Tawntuh´vaits
Chemehuevis (plural) Tawntuh´vaits eng
CHERT, FLINT kawntuhmp´
CHEST yoonguv´
your chest yoonguv´oom

CHEW koatsok´
chewing kuhtsok´o-ai, kuhcho´okwai
CHICKADEE wetsee´geets
CHICKEN (Eng. chicken) tsee´kununts, tsee´kenunts
CHILDREN pee´suhcheng, pee´soats eng
his/her children pee´soa ung
CHIN kawnok´
my chin kawnok´on
CHIPMUNK The following animals were not fully identified. The first three could be chipmunks or ground squirrels.
1. tawvawts´ (with two stripes)
2. onchop´
3. oyoy´chuts (two stripes)
CHIPPED se'-ee´chai, seu´keku
a chip seuk´
CHISELER (a rodent)
1. kuhmp´pawts (Kanosh)
2. spees, sepees´
3. chuhpeesh´(Koosharem)
CHOKE
1. pegweech´, pechung´
he's choking pechung´engchung
I'm choking pehoo´eun, pechung´aiun
repeatedly choking pepee´kwengkwunt
2. pekhoy´eyung (Kaibab)
CHOKECHERRY *Prunis virginiana* toanup´
CHOOSE ***to take the one you like out of several*** awmun´tuh kuh owsuhn´teneeum
CHOP, CUT (from kuh´du ***to cut***)
go chop it kuh´du whaiuk
CHUCKWALLA *Sauomalus obesus* chukwawd´
CIGARETTE, TOBACCO, SMOKE kwoup´, kwou´
give me a cigarette kwou´ muhawng´ wuhn

CIRCLE (see ***cove***)
CIRCLE DANCE kwenok´ oowee´kai
CLAPPING HANDS
mawvee´chuhkee (from mawvee´chuhkeengk ***smash***)
clapping hands while sitting mawvee´chuhkee kawdee
CLAW (see ***fingernail***)
CLEFT (see ***between***)
CLEVER (see ***smart***)
CLIFF tuhmpee´ paiu´dook (lit. ***rock wall***)
CLIFFROSE BARK suhnup´
CLIFFROSE *Cowania stansburiana* peow´ oonup
CLIMAX (see ***orgasm***)
CLIMB
to climb a tree, mountain or anything
awdoo´kwununkw
climbing the mountain kaiv´u awdoo´kwununkw
climb it! awdoo´kwunung oa!
I'm going to climb it nuh awdoo´kwunu pawnee
CLING (see ***stuck***)
CLOSE, NEAR chu-haip´
CLOSED (see ***shut***)
CLOSED EYES oochoom´eku
going along with closed eyes (plural) oonchoom´ ekaimee´
all close your eyes muno´neuk oochoom´eku
CLOTH
1. sawdup´eev
2. pawn´uhsuhv
CLOTHES, DRESS, SHIRT (see ***things***)
1. tow-uh-
2. -nahdo
CLOUD pawkuhn´uv (lit. ***water sack***)
CLOVER *Trifolium* koosawd´
COAL ***a burning coal*** kookhweev´, okhweev´u
COAL MINE kweuh´dutu
COCKLEBUR *Anthium strumarium* kaw´menuv
COCOPAH Wekuh-upaw (Chemehuevi)
COFFEE
1. too´pawts, too´paw (lit. ***black water***)
2. kapee´ (Eng. coffee)
COIL, WRAP wuhkween´tuh
COLD (sickness) wavai´ yuai (lit. ***cold-die***)
COLD (weather)
1. seyai´
I'm cold seyai´un
it was cold seyai´puhkunt
2. (referring to the atmosphere) stoo´ee
it's cold stoo´eook, stoo´euk
3. spuhd´ai
it's cold spuhd´aiuk
I'm cold spai´ai un, nuh spai´yai, nuh spuhdd´ai
that object is cold mudd spuhddai
4. uhvuh´vuh.
COLLARED LIZARD (Black) *Crotaphphytus insularis* chungunts´
COLLECT (see ***gather***)
COLOR There is no word for color as used in English. Colors are verbs, not adjectives. The suffix -kawd is used to say ***in kind*** at the end of the various colors and in this usage approaches the word color.
COLORADO COLUMBINE *Aquilegia coerulea* whechee´ungkopenump
COLORED ROCKS peko´nukai
COME HERE hukai´, hukhaink´ee, hukhaing´oa
come sit closer wakhain´eu kawduh
come in vuh´u wakhaik
COME UP, COME IN tuhnunk´w
COMMANCHE koomunts´ (lit. ***different***)

COMMAND (used at the end of a sentence to tell someone to do something) -oa
wake up puhneng´oa
drink it eveeng´oa
COMPANION (this word is much stronger than tuhkoo´vun *my friend*. The relationship is more like a brother. The word comes from ai´vum *young men*, hence the implication of comradeship)
my companion aivai´yun
COMPARABLE (see *same way*)
COMPETE naveech´unkuhee
CONCEAL (see *hide*)
CONDUCTING (see *guide*) *to lead someone by the arm* tsungkaw´waing, chungkaw´waing
CONFLICTING VIEWPOINTS *a state where one person wants to do one thing while the other wants to do something altogether different* nudu´tsou
CONFLUENCE (of two rivers) nawvung´kweetoo nookwee (lit. *running together*)
CONICAL koovoo´, koovoo´u
CONSUME
to finish eating or drinking something soowu´-
consume it all soowung´wuk
CONTINUALLY (see *always*)
COOK (Eng. cook) kook
COOKED (see *ripe*)
COPY, BORROW tuhup´
one who always borrows tuhuv´ (from the idea that one who borrows is a copier)
CORKY-SEED PINCUSHION *Mammillaria tetrancistra* taws
CORN
1. ung-weev´
2. komee´
CORNER (see *cove*)
COST nahwhaw´hai.
how much does it cost? hunop´ai nahwhaw´hawd?
COTTON TAIL *Sylvilagus* tawvoot´s
COTTONWOOD (Fremont) *Populus fremontii* soa´veep
COTTONWOOD (narrowleaf) *Populus angustifolia* sawghawv´, sawhup´
COUGAR, MOUNTAIN LION peu´dook, peu´ tookoop (lit. *big cat*)
COUGH hoakoy´
coughed okhweeng´w
COULD, WOULD, SHOULD -koop
could stay over night (lit. *lie-could*) awvee´eng koop
should sit here evahn kawduh´ koop
what would happen? what would you do? uhun´engkoo?
I could kill you if you do that pukawng´koom mun´ekoom
COUNTRY, LAND, EARTH tooweep´, tooveep´
COUSIN (see *relation*)
COVE, CORNER, CIRCLE peko´uv, pekoan´euk
red circle, or *cove* ungkaw´ pekonump
COVER OVER (to) wuhkum´ee
cover it up wuhkum´euk
COW
1. kooch, kwechoom´puhts
a herd of cows kwechoom´puhts evw
2. wanggus´ee, wangguz´ee (used from Moapa south. From the Spanish vaca or Hualapai waksee´)
COWBOY (Span. vaquero) pakay´do
COWHIDE koochoomp´
COW HORN koochoo´ awp
COYOTE
1. soonuv, suhnuv
2. yoho´vuhts (one who always has intercourse. This term applies to Soonungwuv)

3. Soonung´wuv (a legendary deity who was once human)
CRACK (see ***cut***)
CRACKED youk´, yoaw´keku
CRACKED LIPS
1. oapoa´domp (name of a white man)
dried out lips tuhmpu´ kwusee´oonuh tawvus´ee
CRADLEBOARD koan´, koanonts´
CRADLE VISOR moompu´chuts
CRANK IT chukoyn´noakwee uk
CRAWL, CREEP mungwuv´ai
CRAZY, FUNNY unoop´ekunt (lit. ***has a ghost, possessed***)
going crazy unoop´ee toowee
CREATE (see ***make***)
CREMATE, BURN kwechee´kee
CREATE (see ***make***)
CREATURES (any small living thing including insects) pauv´
CREDIT nahwhawv´
CREEK paw´ nookweent (lit. ***water running***)
CREEP (see ***crawl***)
CREOSOTE BUSH *Larrea tridentata* yutump´, yutuv
CREST OF A HILL (see ***summit***)
CREVICE (see ***cut***)
CRICKET
1. chuhduhts
2. tsuh´duhts (Kanosh)
3. skedeets´ (Shivwits)
CROOKED (see ***curve***)
CROSSWAYS (see ***sideways***)
CROTCH (the inner thigh area between the legs) tahaw´vai
your crotch ta-haw´veum
CROW, RAVEN
1. yutaw´puhts, awtaw´puhts
2. yataw´kots
3 hataw´konts (Kanosh)
CROWN OF THE HEAD (where the hair swirls to the center at the back) kweyoon´
CRUSHING, GRINDING whechuhn´tooai
CRY OUT IN PAIN (to) kwawdu´vai
CRYING yaghai´
mourning ceremony yawhup´
CRYSTAL (crystals are thought to be left in the ground where lightning strikes; therefore, they are called ***the rain's arrow***) oongwud´uh oowai´uk, oongwud´uh oowuk, oongwud´u oo'-oo´
CUP see ***bowl***
CUPPED HANDS (to hold something in the cupped hands) mantsoon´ovawk
CURLEYGRASS *Pleuraphis jamesi* wuhkuh´ moasoa (lit. ***vagina hair***)
CURRANT (Golden) *Ribes aureum* poahomp´eev
CURVE, BEND, CROOK noakoa´mee
big bend in a river noakov´enawk
little bend in a river meah´pee noakov´ekainawk
little curve noakoa´mee
big curve noapoa´nee
crooked noapuhn´ench
CUT some of the following words can also mean rip. (see ***rip***)
1. ***cut it in two, split it*** takaw´penuk
2. ***cut it in two equal halves*** skup´enuk naw´vai
3. ***cut it off, slice it, cut the cards*** chukup´enuk, tsukaw´penuk (lit. ***to cut one object in one quick cut***) Kanosh
4. (applied to card games)
cut a card, take a card chunuv´enu, ***take a card and turn it over*** chunup´enuk. or chunuv´enuk, tsunuv´enuk (Koosharem)
5.***cut it*** (using a large knife) wuhkup´enuk
6. ***cut it*** (using a small knife that

takes several motions and more time to cut something off, or in two. Also, to rip something slow in several pulls of the hands) tsakaw´venuk, skuv´enuk
7. ***to rip in two with one quick motion of the hands*** tsakaw´penuk
8. ***cut it*** (using scissors) suhkuh´uk, sekoo´uk (Kanosh)
CUT, SLIT, CREVICE, RIP, SPLIT, FISSURE, CRACK sekawv´,sekuv´ee, seuk´
cracked it seuk´ekai uk
CUTE (see ***pretty***)

— D —

DAMP EARTH soahod´
DAMP pasoap´
DANCE oowee, oowee´kai
let's dance oowee´ vawdum
DANDELION *Taraxacum officinale* o-aw saweent (lit. ***yellow flower***)
DANGEROUS (see ***ugly***)
DARK (see ***night***)
it's getting dark tookwud´eng wuhchuk
DAUGHTER pawchuh´
your daughter pawchoom´
DAWN
1. tawsee´u
2. ***coyote morning*** suhnu´ tawsuh´ai (coyote dawn, about 3:00 a.m. when the false dawn occurs before it darkens again)
DAY tavai (from tavaw´puhts ***sun***)
DAY AFTER TOMORROW penu´ tuaik, penu´ echuhk
DEADWOOD oavee´ yuaip (lit. ***wood-dead***)
DEAL THE CARDS mawmun´uvoytseuk
pull a card munuv´enuk
DECEMBER Toopoodookweech or Paaw´toaumuh, puaw´tom (lit. ***long moon***). The informant Carl Jake gave Toopoodookweech as December and Paaw´toaumuh, Puaw´tom as January. However, December is the longest month but early January would seem almost as long to Indians who never had a watch to time the length of each day so I'm not really sure which months to assign these Indian names. The informant was somewhat confused with English equivalents.
DECORATE (see ***to paint***)
DEEP tookwawd´, took´w
it's deep tookwai´oouk
DEER (mule deer) tuh´euts, tuh´ee
the biggest of the two point bucks soowees´
DENT, DEPRESSION (in metal ,or a low place in the land) koyokwawk´u
DESERT (see ***barren***)
DESERT VELVET, TURTLEBACK *Psathyrotes ramosissima* wuh´pa-whawts
DESOLATE (see ***barren***)
DESTROY, DAMAGE (to) madok´emawnuk
DEVIL (see ***ghost***)
DEW punu´kwun
DIAPER
1. pesoam´, pesoan´ee
2. peshoam´ (Kanosh)
DIARRHEA
1. naw whee´chu (lit ***excrement on oneself***)
2. paw kwechup (lit. ***water excrement***)
DIE, INFECTED yuai´
going to die yuai´vawnt
died, dead yuai´kunt
infection from a thorn munai yuaing´wuhts (lit. ***sticker-dying***)
plural, chowwuh´

many dying (continuous tense) chowwuh´kee
many died off (past tense) chowwuh´kaw puhkunt
DIFFERENT, ANOTHER, STRANGER, STRANGE, WRONG ONE, ENEMY koomunts
that's the wrong one koomung´us
it's yet another one koomus
he's different, he's a stranger koomun´ung
wrong one koomus´
DIG oadai´
DIGGING STICK chewu´kainump
DINNER, LUNCH (mid-day meal) tavaw´ tuhkai (lit. ***day-eat***)
DIP (see ***valley***)
DIRECTION (from) -nungkw
where from? hu´mununungkw?
DIRECTION, TOWARDS -tuhk
towards engwee´tuhk
the other way enee´tuhk
this way, that way emee´tuhk
DIRT tooweep´
DIRTY tuhdooch´ukai, toochaw´hai, toochaw´haw
DISAPPEAR (into thin air like a whirlwind does) choo´paw
DISCOVER (see ***find***)
DISCUSS (see ***talk***)
DISGUSTING utump´unee
to say something disgusting utump´unee aik
DISLIKE, HATE kaw ows´uhntewait
maybe she/he hates me soov kawchoon ows´uhntewait oong
DISOBEDIENT (see ***stubborn*** and ***doubting***)
DISTANT RELATIVE nawai´yoogwee
DISTRUSTFUL, JEALOUS tuh´aiu hawd
DIVIDE (in equal halves or portions) nawvai´
DIVORCE, ESTRANGED (see ***forget***)
nuhsuhm´upeuk, nusuhm´u-hu
DIZZY aw´kwechuhduhee
DO ***to do as indicated, to do in a prescribed manner*** mun
don't do like that, kawchoo mun´eup
doing like this muneek´
DO (to), HAPPEN, ACT oonee´
done that oonee´pukunt
you have already done it ooneng´kwainum
do it for me ooneenk´kuhukun
does it every time ooneeng´oomee
do it well ows´unee
do it like this mun´euk ooneng
I'm going to do that oonee´umpawnt
I've done that nuh´nee oonenk´ookwain
you've done that emee oonenk´ookwain
I don't want to do it nuh kawchuk´ oonees´umpaw, nuh kaw oonees´ umpaw
I'd like to do it nuh oonees´umpa-hai
you're going to do it oonee´ umpawnum
it will happen after while penunk´wunee oonee´um pawnt
what happened to him? (where did he go?) aitaw ooneets´ oong
Bill does that Bill ooneed´
DOCTOR poowu´hunt (lit. ***has supernatural power***)
DODGE
1. naw´ kawduhngkee (from kawduhngk´ee ***to miss***)
I'm dodging naw´ kawduhngk´uchun
2. ***I'm dodging*** awtawd´ung kuchun
DOE tuheuv´ee, tuheu´veup (lit. ***deer mother***)
little doe tuheuv´veuts
DOG

1. sawdeets
2. sawdee´voongkoo (lit. ***dog pet***)
3. suhnuv´, soonuv´
4. poongkoots´ (Moapa) this is also the word for ***horse*** with some Utes

DOG MINT toowee´seev
DOGWOOD, RED OSIER *Cornus sericea*
ungkaw´ kawnuv (lit. ***red willow***)
DOING THAT -uhdu´puhku (suffix)
DOLL keyu´tenump (lit. ***plaything***)
DOMESTICATED (see ***pet***)
DON'T kaw-, kawchoo-, -up
don't do that kawchoo mun´eup, kawchuk oonee´up, kaw mun´eup
don't say that kawchoo mai´up
I don't have any kawchoon´ oodooung´wai
DONKEY moasuhmp´oavoy
DOODLEBUG (see ***antlion larvae***)
DOUBTING, DISOBEDIENT, SUSPICIOUS kaw tooveets´ eku´ (lit. ***not believe***)
DOUBTLESS (see ***yea because***)
DOUGLAS FIR (and other firs) *Pseudotsuga* sumu´ oahomp (lit. ***blanket pine***)
DOWN toovai, toovu´
DOWNWARD pechoo´um
going downhill pechoo´um toovu
come down pununk´w
DRAG (see ***pull***)
DRAGONFLY saw´duhveengkuhts
DREAM nonoh´see
DRESS kwawsuhmp´
DRILL toodoo´enump
DRINK evee´
what is drunk eveep´
DRIPPING pawtso´tsokwai, poachoa´choahoy
DRIVE waus´
DROP ***to accidently drop something or for it to slip out of the hand*** mawvuhts´uskeenk
dropped it mawvuhts´u skeengku chuku
I dropped it mawvuhts´u skeengku chukun
DROP-SEED *Sporobolus cryptandrus* moanomp´eev
DRUM kwepoy´unump
DRUNK
1. awmuh´u
he's drunk awmuh´aiung
2. yuai´ ung (lit. ***dying***) Las Vegas

DRY tawvus´oop
dry it tawvus´ uteuk
dried up tawpus´kai uduk´
is it dry? tawpus´kai uduk u´?
DUCK (Lesser Scaup) too´ koochoomputs
DUCK (all kinds)
(singular) chuhk
tsuhg (Kanosh and Koosharem)
(plural) chuhkuts, chuhkung
tsuhguts (Kanosh and Koosharem)
DUMB kaw toosoo´ait (lit. ***smart-no***)
dumb person kaw toosoo´ ait uhm
DUPLICATE ***to do it the same way*** awpus, awps´unee
DUST okoomp´
blowing dust okoong´kwai
floating dust too´seev
DWARF JUNIPER *Juniperus depressa* sumu oahomp´ (lit. ***blanket pine***)
DWELL (see ***sit***)

— E —

EACH (see ***alone***)
EDGE (see ***sharp***)
EAGLE, GOLDEN kwuwnunts´
EAR nungkuv´
your ears nungkaw´vum
my ears nungkaw´vun
EARTH tooweep´, tooveep
EARTHQUAKE tooveep´ nuhnuhn´tseek

EAST WIND suhkwee´um
EAST tahvai mungwee´see engwee´tuhk. (lit. ***sunrise direction***)
EASY TO DO, OVERCOME peyungk´uhee
EASY, NOTHING TO IT
1. nawvus´ tuhmpee
2. soee´nepuhts
EAT tuhkaw´
to go eat tuhkaw´vaw
come and eat tuhkaw´hai
let's eat (plural) tuhkaw´kavaw tdungw
I'm through eating tuhku´muk oochun
EDGE koong-wawv´, koo-waw´
EGGS nopuv´
laying an egg nouv´uteung
setting on the eggs nouv´ee
EIGHT wa'ong´ wachuhng´wee (lit. ***two fours***)
ELBOW keep, kepoom´, keem´poh
ELDER BROTHER pawveets´
ELDER SISTER pawtseets´
ELDERBERRY BUSH *Sambucus* koanoak´weev, koonook´w
ELK paw duh´ee (lit. ***water deer***)
EMERGE (see ***appear*** and ***exit***)
END (of town or board, etc.) kawtso´uk
the end of it kawtso´u vawntuk
ENEMY (see ***different***)
ENGLISH SPARROW *Passer domesticus* yuhuhng´kawhunt. (lit. ***stealer***)
ENOUGH
1. -sump, -hump
that's enough mun´ehump
enough of doing oo´nesump
finish what your doing oonee´sump´ uk
that's enough of that mu´du sump uk
2. toahoyng´wai, toahoy´sump
that's good enough toahoy´sump uk
3. ***now*** aw´oovus
ENTER (see ***exit***)
ERECTION wuhu´ nungai´ai (lit. ***penis-angry***)
ESCAPE (see ***run away***)
ESCORT (see ***guide***)
EVENING
1. ***before sunset*** taw´pook, tawsuh´pai.
2. ***after sunset*** soo´puk
3. ***evening, sundown*** suhup´uh
EVENING STAR (a modern term) tawsuh´puk poot´seev
EVERYTHING, EVERYONE (see ***all***)
EVIL EYE
to witch someone by looking at them kwesunk´uhd
they who use the evil eye kweshunk´eoom
EVIL SPIRIT, EVIL OMEN, EVIL ***a big person or giant found in legends*** oddo´souts, oddo´soai
EXACTLY (see ***good***)
EXCEPTIONAL, REAL GOOD petsee´ai, petsee´
EXCREMENT, FECES kwechup´
I'm going to go defecate kwechu´ whai vaw´neun
to defecate in one's pants naw´ whechun
I'm about to (I have to) defecate kwechung´ wuhseng kunt
EXIT, COME OUT, EMERGE, MOUNT, CLIMB ON suhpe-, suhpeng, speng
get out! suhpeng´oa!
came out easy nawvus´ spengkwunt
a spring paw tsuhpee´tseech (lit. ***water coming out***)
went out of office office sepeeng´uhpuhkunt
enter (the word suhpe- can be used for ***enter*** if refering to entering or mounting a car)

EXPLODE (see ***pop***)
EYE BROW puhtuhnk´ kawneev (lit. ***eyeball house***)
EYE LASH puhtuh´seev
EYE pooeev´
your eyes pooeem´

— F —

FACE kov´
your face kovum´
FAINT tawpus´
FAITH (see ***believe***)
FALCON kawsuv
FALL (to) (see ***hit***) we'-eek´
it's going to fall we'-eek´oovaw
it's almost falling we'-eng´ weuk
it fell we'-ee´chuk
FALL (the season, see ***autumn***)
FALL OVER moompuk´
FALL SHORT ***for something to fall short of where it was intended to go*** eyu´tuhus, eyu´tuhk
FAN WITH FEATHERS (to), TO BLESS mawvoo´kwee
FANCY (see ***pretty***)
FAR
1. meo´nee
I'm going a long ways away meon´ wuhnchun
Lets go drink someplace evee´ meyu´ vawdungw
2. eev
sounds like someone eating way over there eev´uts tuhku toowuv´ugai
3. wawn
way over there wawn´tuh
FARMERS (see ***plant***) uhu´ nuhwunts (lit. ***planting Indians***)
FART oo´pee
FAST (see ***keep on***)
FAT, GREASE, LARD yoo-oo´
to be fat yoo-oo´kwunt
grease bread yoo-oo´ vawnu

FATHER moou-´
my father mooun´
FAVORITE PLACE to´tsee (a phrase used in a legend song)
FAWN
1. tuheu´ toowuts (lit. ***deer's son***)
2. meah´pee tuheu´ toowuts (lit. ***little deer's son***)
FEATHER ROACH muhnchuhn´ookweemp
FEATHER wuhsee´uv
FEBRUARY (see ***March***)
FEELING (with your hands) mawvee´kunee
FENCE kweeup´
FENCE POST kweyu´nuk
FERNBUSH *Chamaebatiaria millifolium* Moo-oon´ Tuhuv
FIERCE (see ***mean***)
FIFTY CENTS (Eng. four bits) poa´veets
FIGHT
1. nunump´ukai
you might fight nunump´ukavaw
2. ***always wanting to fight*** too-oo´kunt (a term applied to the Yavapais and Apaches)
FILE, RASP wuhnuhd´unump
FILM (Eng. film) fil´um
FIND, DISCOVER mai, maee´
he found them main´chuk ung
FINE (see ***good***)
FINGERNAIL, CLAW maw sechung
his or her fingernail sechoo´ ung
your fingernail sechoom´, chechoom´
FINGER mawsuh´
fingers (plural) mawmaw´suh
FINISHED, ENDED awvuhs
1. ***are you finished?*** awvuhs´tudu? awvuhs´u tsudu?
I'm finished awvuh´stun, awvuh´suts un
2. -muk

I'm finished doing oonemuk´oots un, oonemuk´wuhchun
do it after you eat tuhkaw´ mookoots oodoo´ai
3. ***I'm finished*** toahoyng´ wuhnchun (from toahoy´ ***good***)
FIRE, MATCH (see ***burn***) koonaw´, koon
FIRE MAKING KIT (fire by friction)
1. kootoon´ooee nump.
2. koonu takaw´suhnump
FIRST, PRECEDING, BEFORE nahmuh´
FISH pawkuh´uts, pawguh´uts
FIT (see ***good***)
FIVE mawnuh´kee
FIX, REPAIR (to repair something) mawduhngk´, mawdung´kai
I'm going to fix it nuh mawduhngk´u vawnt uk
their going to fix it mum mawdungk´u vawnt uk um
she's going to fix it mung mawduhngk´u vawnt uk
FLASH punuk´wesai
FLAT sipun´awkaw, spun´ee, sipun´ee
it's flat spun´inch
went flat spun´aw puhku
FLAT LAND (see ***plain***)
FLATTER ***to make someone feel good*** soowai´ ungkoopee, soowai´ unkuhkaw
FLEX THE BICEPS (to) mootsoong´wuk
FLICKER, RED-SHAFTED *Calaples cafer* kwunu´wunts
FLINT (see ***chert***) tuhseep
FLIP (see ***change it***)
FLIP OVER HEADFIRST un´ee kwetook
FLIRTATIOUS, SILLY sawm´ekunt, saw´meents
FLOOD weech
the start of a flood ooweech´
it's flooding ooweng´ wuhchuk
it's going to flood oowee´oom pawneu
FLOP DOWN to ***flop down in a limp manner as you sit down***
1. so-wawk´
2. pawngkoyn´ekai
FLOUR
1. puhduv
2. tooweev´
3. toosoop
FLOWERS (see ***blossom***)
FLOWING (see ***running***)
FLUTE oy´yo
FLY (to)
(singular) nontsee´ku
(plural) yontseek´
going to fly yontseek´oovawnt, yontsee´kawvaw
several flying yaius´ yaius´echung
flying yontsee´ kawd
the kind that fly yusuhd´uh muh´nee
flapping wings to take off weentseek´, weetseek´
trying to take off weetseek´ oomee´haieku
took off weetseek´uhpuhku
FLYING SQUIRREL oahon´ tawvawts (lit. ***pine squirrel***)
FLIES (insect) moo´pechuts
FOG
1. ***a dark blue smokey colored fog*** kwe-ee´kai (from kwe-eep´ ***smoke***)
2. pawkuhn´u kawduhk´ai (lit. ***cloud sitting***)
FOLD mawsup´
folded mawsu´pakaw
to fold over and over mawmus´upuk
FOLLOW (see ***next***)
FOLLOWING IN A ROW nunu´penungk pakhai (lit. ***follow-next walking***)
FOOD tuhkup´

FOOLING (see ***teasing***)
FOOT numputs´, nump´
coyote foot suhnu´ numputs
FOOTPRINT (see ***track***)
FORASMUCH AS (see ***yea because***)
FORD (lit. ***water crossing***)
1. pawdov´
2. paw´awvawk (Kaibab)
FOREHEAD mootaw´kaw
your forehead mootawk´um
big forehead pa´awngk´ow
FORGET, DIVORCE, LEAVE ***to let go from ones mind something learned or someone once known*** suhmuh´u, suhmuh´gahaw, nawsuhm´uhai
I'm going to leave them suhmuh´kwai vawneum
I'm going to leave you suhmuh´u whaivawm, suhmuh´u vawneum
left her/him suhmpai´ empai´ayung
forget them nawsuhmai´um
FORGETFUL suhmpu´tuhkwai
FORMER, HAVING BEEN, USED TO BE -kaip
he who was in the past nengwoo´ kaip
Cottontail who once was tawvoom´ puhkaip
FOREST muhaw´ kawduhd. (lit. ***all kinds sitting***)
FORT nawhoo´kwee kawn (lit. ***war house***)
FOUR wachoo-oonee, wachuh´ee, wachuhng´wee
FOUR-WING SALTBUSH, WHITE GREASEWOOD
Atriplex canescens moodoo´nuv:
FOX onchee´uts, ontsee´uts
FREMONT SCREW BEAN sechuh´uhdump (from sechoo´ ***claw***)
FRIEND (see ***companion***) tuhkoov´
my friend tuhkoov´un
FRIGHTENED (see ***afraid***)
FROG
1. pawkwun´, pawkwun´uv (larger than waw´hots and smaller than a bullfrog)
2. waw´hots (a small green frog that makes a sound like "waw´ho")
3. pawkots´ (Willow Springs)
4. sakhwaw´hawduhm wawhots (lit. ***green frog***) Kaibab
FRONT (see ***ahead***)
FRONT QUARTER OF A DEER unguv (lit. ***upper arm***)
FROZEN tuhus´kunt
I'm frozen tuhus´eun
FRY wesaw´ weshaw´
FULL pono´ai
I'm full pono´unchun
it's full poochu´kunt
fill it up poochu´teuk
FUNNY (see ***crazy***)
FUR, FURRY HIDE puhoov´
it's furry puhoo´ung
horsetail hair kuvaw kwusee poo-ook
FUTILELY (see ***vainly***)
FUZZ (see ***stickers***)

— G —

GALLOP hawpoa´nai
galloping along hawpoanai´menai
GAMBLE (to gamble with cards)
1. paw´see (Span. pasar)
gambler paw´seets, paws´ekunt
2. tuhun´ee (Moapa)
GAMBEL OAK, SCRUB OAK *Quercus gambelii* kweuv´
GATHER, COLLECT chouk´
gathered chou´kunt
gather it choung´wuk
GEE uhun´
GENTIAN *Fresera* kaiv´u okoonump (lit. ***mountain okoonump***)
GENTLE (see ***soft***)

GET OFF
1. wa-aing´oa, oeng´oa
2. weuk´evu
GET UP kuhduh´kee, kwuhduh´kee
I got up kuhduh´ke chun
GET, TAKE kuh'uh´
get it kuh'uh´ee ook
GETTING, BECOMING, ABOUT TO -wuh´seengk
I'm about to urinate se'-ee´ wuhseeng kunt
GHOST, EVIL SPIRIT, WHIRLWIND, DEVIL, MONSTER
1. unoo´peets (whirlwinds are considered ghosts so the word unoo´peets is used for ghost and whirlwind)
2. ***whatever scares a person*** uhdduhts´
GIANT
1. peow´ noong (lit. ***big person***)
2. kwetoos (the name of a legendary giant. His name is therefore synonymous with the word giant)
GIFT nuhngwu´haw
let's give it nuhngwu´havawdum
GIGGLING kekee´ungk (plural of keyunk´ee ***to laugh***)
GILA MONSTER, BANDED *Heloderma cinctum* etseev´
GILA MONSTER *Heloderma suspectum* hawtsee´mo
GIRL (adolescent age) nawain´seets
GIRLFRIEND kuh´dee (Eng. girl)
GIVE IT HERE hukai´uk, hukaik´ (shortened form of hukai´uk)
GIVE IT TO ME
1. nuhdoo´gwuk, nuhdoo´kwaiook
give me that one mud´u nuhdook´kwuk
give it to him ungud´owuk
2. ***in the sense of giving to keep*** muhawng´wuhn
GLAD (see ***happy***)
GLASS (see ***transparent***)
GLASS CUP suhguh´ ohots (lit. ***transparent bowl***)
GLASSES punu´pooeem (lit. ***shiny eye***)
GLOBEMALLOW *Sphaeralcea* kuh´eyokomp
GLOVE maw´ koonuv (lit. ***finger sack***)
GNATS
1. ungeev´
2. moapuhmp´ (different type of gnat) Koosharem
GO
1. ***to tell someone to go to, or move towards, in a direction away from the speaker*** kwaw
go on, go away kwawng´oa
(plural) podo´, podoy´
shall go away podo´kwai-
2. oovuh´nee, vuh´
go ahead and do it uhvuh´ukaw
I'm going uhvuh´tsun
shall we go? vuh´dum u'?
go on (by yourself) oovuh´eyuk
3. ***to go away*** oodoo´-
we're going away oodoo´ whawmpawn´eunum (dual)
I'm going away oodoo´ whawm pawn´eun
GO GET IT yow´khwaingwuk, yow´whaingwuk
GO HOME paiyuh´kwai
GOD (Wolf, the older brother) Toovuts´
GOD (Coyote, the younger brother) Soonung´wuv
GOING TO GET HIM (I'm) chungkaw´whaim pawneun
GOING UNDER, TO SINK (as one does in the water, or as the sun sets beneath the horizon) yowk´w
GONE (all used up) toopeek´w
I'm all out of it toopeek´wuhchun
it's all gone toopeek´wuhtsuk,

toopeek´wuhchuk
GONORRHEA ko´chuv
GOOD ONE uup´uoonee
GOOD, CENTER, JUST RIGHT, HALF, MIDWAY, FITS, ENOUGH, THANKS, FINISHED, ALL, EXACTLY, STRAIGHT
toahoy´ (this word has a very broad range of meanings that seems to be based on the idea of ***center***. If something is centered then it is ***just right***, it's ***good***, it's ***enough***, it ***fits***, it's ***finished***, ***it's directly overhead*** and so on).
the same amount toahoy´nawvai
thanks toahoy´uk (lit. ***good-it***)
midday toahoy´ tavai
midnight toahoy´ tookwun
haven't you got enough kawchuhd, u toahoyng´wai
does it fit? toahoyng´wuhnchuduk?
GOOD, WELL, FINE, ALRIGHT, THANKS, PATIENT, HAPPY, FAIRLY
1. aw´tai, ai´ee
it's real good tooveets´ ai´euk
I'm very fine, I'm very well, I'm happy tooveets´ aiun
that's alright, it's okay ai´hump uk
be patient ai´munekai
thanks ai´uk (lit. ***it's good***)
2. ***good in the sense of being still or quiet*** soo (see ***happy***)
lie still soo´ awvee
GOOD-BYE puhnekay´vawsoom (lit. ***I'll see you again***)
GOOSE *Branta* kaov´
GOPHER *Thomomys* muheyuhm´puhts
GOURD, BUFFALO-GOURD *Cucurbita* onoo´kweemp
GOURD, RATTLE kuhsud´uhai nump, wuhsawd´uhai nump
GRAB (see ***seize***)
GRANDDAUGHTER
1. ***paternal*** wheechech´een
2. ***maternal*** kawhoots´, kawgoots´
GRANDFATHER, GREAT GRANDFATHER, GRANDFATHER'S BROTHER
1. ***paternal*** koonoo-,
your grandfather koonoon´
grandson (reciprocal) koonoonts´
2. ***maternal*** tokon´
grandson (reciprocal) tohots´
GRANDMOTHER, GREAT GRANDMOTHER, GRANDMOTHER'S SISTER
1. ***maternal*** kawgoo-
your grandmother kawgoon´
grandmother of many kawkaw´huhvoom (Kaibab) kawkaw´goom (Koosharem)
granddaughter (reciprocal) kawhoots´, kawgoots´
2. ***paternal*** wheetsee´ee
granddaughters (plural) wheechech´een
GRANDSON
1. ***paternal*** koonoonts´
2. ***maternal*** tohots´
GRANITE moakov´
GRASS, HAY oogweev´
GRASSHOPPER awdung´kupeets, awdung´kawts
GRAVE
1. nengwoo´ goop
2. nengwoo´chungwup (Kaibab)
GRAY
1. awsee´ awsee´ku
gray one se´kawdum
2. ***a dirty white*** (of a different shade than awsee´) yooveen´kawd, yoovee´shuhai
gray hill yooveen´ kawduhd (this word could also mean ponderosa hill)
3. ***ashen color*** koochu´kawd (lit. ***ash kind***)

GRAY SQUIRREL ung´kuchawn
GREASE (see *fat*)
GREASEWOOD, (black) *Sarcobatus vermiculatus* tonov´
a piece of greasewood toneev
GREAT AUNT whechee´
GREAT (see ***brave***)
GREAT UNCLE'S SON hoakoy´cheen
GREEDY
1. nuhnchov´
one who is greedy nuhncho´kwawdum
one who has greed nuhnchov´ekunt
2. ***one who doesn't give*** noomu´hait
GREEN FLAGSTONES ai´tuhmpetsee
GREEN (see ***blue***)
GRINDING (see ***crushing***)
GRIZZLY BEAR tosawk´ kweuts (lit. ***white bear***)
GROUND SQUIRREL (see ***chipmunk***)
GROW nunai
full grown nunuk
GROWL, ROAR oaddong´wai
GUARD ta-ong´waikup
GUIDE, CONDUCT, ESCORT, LEAD, HELP (see ***conducting***) ***leading a person by the hand, to help along*** toovuhn´uhawk
conducting him/her toovuhn´uhawng
GUITAR ka-haw´tee nump (lit. ***singing instrument***)
GUM (see ***pitch***)
GUN (see ***rifle***)
GUN MEDICINE MAN (a man with supernatural power to heal bullet wounds) tuhmpeoo´ poowu´hunt (lit. ***gun-medicine-has***)
GUN toompeoots´
GUNPOWDER koochung´wawk
GUYS tu'uts´

— H —

HAIL pa-omp´
HAIR
1. pauhk´ee
2. totsee´vuhum
HALF BREED
1. sunu´ mawduh´kawts (lit. ***tan colored American***)
2. yoovees´u hawdum (a term used for someone who is half Negro (see ***black***)
HALF, SIDE
1. nawvai´
exactly half toahoy nawvai
2. tuhdu´kwouk (lit. ***to halve it; to cut something down the middle into two equal halves***)
half full, full to the middle tuhdu´kwoupawk
3. sengkwun´na-haik, singkwun´uv (one of the halves after it has been cut down the middle (lit. ***side half***)
HALT (see ***stop***)
HAND GAME naiyung´weep
HAND mo'-oh´
your hand mo'-ohm
HANDLING ROUGH mamaw´duhoy
HANG
1. koaduk´
hang it up koaduk´ainuk
2. oowai´
to hang up many times (plural) oo-oo´waingwuk
to hang lots up oongwaing´wuk
hang it up oongwai´uk (this sentence is almost identical with ***it's raining*** and would be spelled the same).
hung up oongwai´kunt
hanging up oowaing´wuk
one hanging oongwaing´
HANGING HEAD DOWN WHILE WALKING muheyaing´wai
HANGING ON (to hang, to swing at the end of a rope, or to cling at the edge of something) puhduh´dai, puhntuh´ai,

puhnduhk´uhmee, puhntuhk´ee
HANDKERCHIEF (Eng. handkerchief) haing´kechup
HAPHAZARDLY (to do something any way it suits you without regard to what's right) pawhun´
does it any way pa-hun´ oonee´tee
HAPPEN (see *do*)
HAPPY, (see *good*)
HARD, LEATHERY (like a cloth that is made stiff when a liquid has dried on it, or rawhide after it dries) pegu´gai, peku´hai
HAS -hunt, -kunt, -uhunt, -ugunt, -ekai
I have a brother nuh chukaits´ekunt
I have a baby nuh pesoa´hunt
HAT kai´chuhots
HAT BAND kai´chuho whechup (lit. *hat-wrap*)
HATCHET tawvee´nump toowuts (lit. *axe child*)
HATE (see *dislike*)
HAVEN (see *nest*)
HAY (see *grass*)
HEAD totsee
your head totseem´
the one with the head (a horse's name) totsee´vuhuts
HEADACHE totsee´pukawngkee (lit. *head-hurt*)
HEAD OFF kwuhtok´weuveung (*to intercept*)
HEAR, LISTEN nungkaw´, nungkai´
hear me nungkaw´kaichun
not listening nungkaw´vait (lit. *no ears*)
HEART, SPIRIT, SOUL
1. mookoo´uv
your spirit mookoo´um
2. peyuhp (the physical heart)
HEARTBEAT
1. tawveen´weai
2. toowuv´ugai (this word for *noise* or *sound* can also be used in referring to a heartbeat)
HEAT WAVES (see *vapor*)
HEAVEN (SKY) toohoom´paiahv
HEAVY, WEIGHTY puhtee´ud
it's heavy puhtee´uhunt (has weight)
HEEL tawmpeep
your heel tawmpeem´
HELD FAST, STUCK chukaink (from chu'ai´ *to hold*)
it's stuck chukaw´uchuk
HELLGRAMMITES *Corydalidae* pawsuh´kawmeents
HELLO maik´w
hello sir maik oongwus´
HELP (see *assist* and *guide*)
HER (see *him*)
HERBS (see *medicine*)
HERE (a location) ee´vai, evahnt´
beginning from here evai´yuhs
about here evai´uhnee
right here, to here evahnt´uh
HERE (to give) eyun´
here (take it) eyun´
here it is eyun´ uk kawdee (lit. *here it sits*)
HERMAPHRODITE tungwu´mumowm (Lit. *man-woman*)
HERMIT THRUSH *Hylocichla guttata* sawngwuv´ ooet (lit. *sage sparrow*)
HIDE, CONCEAL, SECRETE
1. awhaw´-, awgaw´-
hidden awhaw´pukaw
hidden person aw´hawvuhts
2. *to hide or cover self in fright, cringe, shrink* paw kaik´
to hide out of fright awhaw´ pawkai´eku
HIGH (see *tall*)
HILL
1. kaiv´uts
2. kawduhd (this word for *sitting* is

used concerning people or stationary objects such as hills, mountains, and lakes)

HIM, HER, HE, SHE, THAT ONE (can be either sex)
1. ***that one*** (visible, animate) mung
2. ***that one*** (not present, animate) ung, oong´w
3. ***this one*** (present, animate) eng

HIND QUARTER to'-oh´vum

HIP seump´, cheump´
my hips cheim´puhn

HISTORY, CHRONICLE nawduh´gwenup (events told by witnesses, compare ***legends***)

HIT, STRIKE, PUNCH, STAB (to hit by thrusting with the hand) tonu´
stabbed with a knife we-ee´ tonu´puhku
beat him up! toch´okwawngw!
he's going to hit you toch´ung kuhneung oong

HIT, STRIKE, WHIP, FALL kwepu-´
hit him, whip him kweep´ung
spank him kweep´oongwung
fell to the ground kwepu´puhku

HIT, ALIGHT, LAND, STEP tawvee´
alight tawvee´ veech´ookwaw

HOARSE
1. tsoakoad´
he/she's hoarse tsoakoad´ung
2. kawnu´doai
3. yogwud´unwuhtsuk (***throat mucus*** from yogwuv´)

HOBO
1. cha-haw´vuhts. (lit. ***one who sews because he has ragged clothes***) from cha-haw ***to sew***. This word also applies to anyone who sews, such as a seamstress.
2. tawhaw´puhts (lit. ***poor***)
3. wunts from wuntsee´puhts (lit. ***antelope***) used at Cedar City for an Anglo hobo.
4. toodump´

HOIST (to hoist something up at the end of a pole) sichunk´aiuk
hoisted me sichunk´aiunk

HOLD, CATCH chu'ai´
hold it chu'aik´ayuk
let me hold you chu'ai´nevum
catch it chu'ai´uk

HOLE opuk´ai

HOLLER (see ***yell***)

HOME (see ***return***)

HOPI Moo´kweech, Moo´kwee

HOPPING wuhwuh´tuh hainum

HORIZON paiu´dosee toohoom´pai

HORN (from an animal) awp

HORN BELLY (on a wooden bow) awtawk
to have a horn belly awtaw´ukunt

HORN SPOON (used nowadays for a metal spoon) meenchoak´, meencho´kwuts

HORNED LARK *Eremophila alpestris* sechoo´nunts

HORNED TOAD, SHORT-HORNED LIZARD *Phrynosoma* mukaw´chuts

HORSESHOE kuvaw´ pawtch

HORSE
1. kuvawts´ (Span. caballo) kuvaw´oong (plural)
2. kuvaw´ voongkoo´ (lit. ***tame horse***)
3. o-waw´dov (Moapa)

HORSETAILS, SCOURING RUSHES *Equisetales variegatum* pawhaw´ wuhchuh´choogwee nump

HOT
1. ***hot*** (inanimate) kuhchuhng´ee
2. (weather) tawdo´ee
it's hot tawdo´e ook

HOUSE, kawn´, kawnee´
houses (plural) kawngkawn´
little house kawneents´

HOW?
1. u-hun´?

how do you do it? u-hun´engchuk uneng?
how are you? (singular) u-hun´ee udoo´ai?
how are you? (plural) u-hun´ee moodoo´ai?
2. hawd?
how is it? haw´doai ee´neuk?
how are you? haw´do een´eu?
HOW ABOUT YOU? eem´ oovai?
HOW DID HE DO IT? WHAT DID YOU DO?
awkhuhn´?
HOW MUCH? huno´pai?
HUGGING aiun´ookwai
HUMAN (see ***Indian***)
HUMMING BIRD moo´toonchuts, moo´toontuts
HUNCH BACK saiu´
had a hunched back saium´puhkunt
hump backed one sawv´ oongwawdum
HUNGRY
1. tuhkuh´ee, tuhguh´ee
are you hungry? tuhkuh´e aiay´du?
I'm hungry tuhkuh´e aiun
2. ***starving*** tuhguh´e yuai (lit. ***hungry-die***)
she's starving tuhkuh´eai chung
HUNT (to hunt)
1. tuhnu´
let's go hunting (plural) tuhnu meu vawdum
lets'go hunting dual) tuhnu´ whaimpawdum, tuhnu´ whaivawdum
2. yuahng´kwai, yahngk, yahng
let's go hunting yuahng´kwai vawdum
HUNTER tuhnunts´
HURRY UP
1. toowin´eu, toowin´ee tuhngwin´eu
2. uhvuh´neu oon
shall we hurry? vuh´neudungw?
HURT (see ***pain***)
HUSBAND koomu-´
my husband koomun´
to have a husband koomu´hunt
to have husbands (plural) kookoom´uhunt

— I —

I AM, I'M -aiun
I'm hungry tuhkuh´e aiun
I, ME nuh', nuhk'
that's me nuh´vuhts
ICE pawus´kup, paw kuhup
frozen water paw tuhus´ku
ILLEGITIMATE
kaw moo´ait (lit. ***no father***)
IMAGE nawvuhn
IMITATING nengwoo´ nawvus
INDEED uhngkuh´(adv)
INDIAN CABBAGE, PRINCE'S PLUME
Stanleya pinnata tuhmu´duh
INDIAN PAINTBRUSH *Castilleja*
1. moo´tuntu sueep´ (lit. ***hummingbird's flower***) Koosharem
2. toho´ oaho´ suent (lit. ***snake tongue blossoms***)
INDIAN POTATO *Orogenia linearifolia* whechuhn´
INDIAN RICEGRASS *Oryzopsis hymenoides* (and related species) wai
INDIAN, PERSON, BODY, HUMAN
nengwoo- nengwoonts´, nengwoo´vuhts (singular)
Indians, people (plural) nengwoonts´eng, nengwuhng´ nuhng´w
INDISCRIMINATE ***one who speaks indiscriminately and says things he shouldn't say*** pawnee´
to say everything pawnee ai´tee
don't say everything pawnee ai´teup

one who says everything pawnee´ ainch oong (this sentence refers to someone you're talking about who is absent)

he who says everything pawnee´ ung usunee (this sentence refers to someone you're talking about who is present)

INDIVIDUALLY (see ***separately***)

INFECTED (see ***die***)

INSECT, BUG pa'awts´

insects, bugs (plural) pa'awts´eev

INSERT (to insert, like threading a needle) chuhnuhk´euk

INSIDE, IN

1. awvung´way
2. inawk´ inaw´tuh

it's inside inaw´etuhk.

get in here inaw´haiktseep

INSTRUMENT (see ***thing***)

INTELLIGENT (see ***smart***)

INTUITION, SENSING (***to sense something is going to happen or has happened***)

1. aik´unee

I sense it aik´unin

2. soontoo´wee

INVINCIBLE (see ***brave***)

INVITE (see ***call***)

IRON OXIDE, OCHRE oampee´, oamp

IRON WEED koav´

IRON, METAL, STEEL punu´kawd (lit. ***shining***)

IS IT SO? u'?

is it true? tooveets´ u'?

IT (see ***that***)

ITCH (to) peyuh´hungkuhee

—J—

JAB (see ***poke***)

JACKRABBIT kumoonts´

JAIL (see ***locked***, also ***shut***)

JAM, JELLY peuv

JANUARY Pa'aw´toaumuh, Pu'aw´tom (lit. ***long moon***) or Kawng´wu (lit. ***squeak-made-by-walking-on snow-moon***). (The long moon would probably be December. The informant, Carl Jake, was somewhat confused on the English equivalents as have been other informants.)

JAPANESE (Eng. Japanese) chupun´ee

a Japanese person chupun´evuhts

JAY, ARIZONA *Cyanocitta woodhousei* choeng´kee

JAY, STELLER'S *Cyanocitta stelleri* chaiu´kutch

JEALOUS (see ***distrustful***) koodaw´doo-whu, koodaw´dookwunt (lit. ***neck?***)

JERKED MEAT eyung´

one who is drying meat eyu´num

JERUSALEM CRICKET, COPPERHEAD *Stenopelmatus fuscus*, tuhgoo´tuh neahv (lit. ***burying chief, grave chief***)

JIMSON WEED, SACRED DATURA *Datura meteloides* moamop´

JOINT REED pawhaw´ wuhchuh´choogwe nump

JOKING, MAKING FUN

1. uhjuhts´
2. ***I'm just saying that*** nawvus´ un aik (from nawvus´ ***nothing***)

JOSHUA TREE *Yucca brevifolia*

1. osaw´dumpeev
2. choowaw´duhmp

JUMP (to jump down, over, or off)

1. tawpook
2. wuhvuhk´ee

to jump in response wuhvuhk´umee

JUMPING MOUSE *Zapus princeps* paiyuhm´puhts

JUNCO, SLATE COLORED *Junco hyemalis* noovu´ toampoa´koytch (lit.

snow toampoa´koytch)
JUNCTION (of roads)
1. poa´ nawvung´utookenaw
2. povo´uhunt (plural)
JUNIPER, CEDAR TREE *Juniperus utahensis* and *osteosperma* wawup´
JUST, ONLY, EXCEPT, BUT, ALTHOUGH, IN SPITE OF, EXACTLY, SUITABLE
-sump
in spite of what he said aikuh´sump ung
let it be exactly like that munee´sump
just stay there mu´vu sump unee´ku, mu´vu sump ooni´nee
go ahead and bite me kuh'uh´ee sumpun
only me, just me nuh´sump
If you want to oonee´sump pa-hai

—K—

KANGAROO RAT *Dipodomys* tawwee´uts
KEEP ON (to), PERSISTENTLY, STUBBORNLY, QUICK, FAST, HARD (to continually do, to do hard or fast) puhngku´nee
keep going puhngkun´eng oa
keep doing it puhngku´onee
KEY chukwee´nump (lit. ***twisting thing***)
KICK tungai
he's kicking tuntdung´ai ung
I'm kicking nuh tuntdung´aiun
KIDNEY pesup´ov
your kidney pesup´om
KILL, WIN
(singular) pukaw-
I'm going to kill you nuh pukaw´ompawm
(plural) koahoyp´
killed them all koahoy´kaium
I killed them all nuh koahoy´kaiun
KILLDEER *Charadrius vociferus* pawntuh´keets
KIN (see ***relation***)
KIND (see ***soft***)
KING SNAKE suhng, suhng´uv, suhng´ump
KISS
1. kees (Eng. kiss)
2. pechee´ (suck)
will kiss you tuhmpai´um pechuhng´umpaw (lit. ***mouth-suck-will***)
KNEAD (see ***squeeze with fingers***)
KNEE tunguv
your knee tungu´voom
KNEELING tawn´udoy kawdee
KNIFE we'-eets´, we'-eech´
his knife mung´ai we'-eets´
my knife nuh´nai we'-eets´
KNOCK (to) mawvoan´toahoy
KNOCKED OUT woachok´ween
knocked him out woacho´kwe ung
KNOTTED STRING: tawpee´chup
KNOW (to) (see ***understand***)
1. tooveech´
doesn't know how kaw toovee´ait
doesn't know how to do it kaw oonee´tooveait
I'm learning to be smart toosoo´ai tooveech´oowaiun
2. -skway, -vaius
I don't know oodoo´skway
I ***don't' know about it***, (***I don't think so***) oodoo´vaius
I ***don't know about him***, (***it's up to him***) oongwu´vaius, oongwu´skwai
you know, it's up to you, (ask yourself) emee´skway
it's up to you (plural) muhmuh´evaius
it's up to them oomuh´skwai

— L —

LADY (see ***woman***)
LAKE paw´ kawduh (lit. ***water sitting***)
LAMBS QUARTERS, PIGWEED
1. ***Chenopodium fremontii*** koav´ (Koosharem)
2. ***Chenopodium album*** pee´gee nungkaw´vawm (lit. ***pig's ears***) Cedar City
LAME (to limp) sawngkuhd´
one who limps, lame sawngkuhts´
LAND tooweep, tooveep
LARD (see ***fat***)
LAST ONE (the last one following along) nengwoo´venunkw
LATE, BEHIND nengwoo´venu pawchuhk
LATER, AFTER WHILE
1. kai´uhsoon
he hasn't arrived yet kaiuhs´ pechuhng´wais
2. pee´kai
3. (see ***next***) penunk´
LAUGH keyunk´ee
always laughing keyunk´oomeent
LAVA ROCKS, LAVA FLOW too´ yoonuv
LAY (to lay with the hands)
to lay an object on with the hands mawkuh´ nunump
laying on of hands mawkuh´nai
administer (lay on hands in prayer) mawvoo´kweep
LAY, LIE
(singular) awvee´
lying, ridge awveech
lying around awvee´nee
staying over night awveng´wee
(plural) kwawvee´
LAZY nahdum´muh-ai
LEAD (see ***guide***)
LEADER mooeed´
your leader mooeen´chum, mooeen´tum
man leader, boss mooeen´tungwung
LEADING, IN FRONT, AHEAD mooweep
I want to go ahead nuh mooee´vaw
LEAF, EAR nungkuv´, nungkawk´
LEAKS pawcho´cho whaiuk
LEARN tooveech
LEATHER peghup´, pehup´
LEAVE (see ***forget***)
LEFT HAND kwee-
left handed kwe'-ee´kunt
LEG yoo'-oo´
your leg yoo'-oom´
water legs pai yoo'-oots´
bloody legs paop´ee yoo
LEGENDS, MYTH, STORY tookwee´nup (these stories are basically fairy tales that are designed to show some evidence of legitimacy by showing analogies in nature.
LEGGINGS, PANTS koos´, koosuts´ (plural) kookoo´suts
LEGS UP IN THE AIR WHILE LYING DOWN (as a baby does) tawchai
LET (see ***make***) -vu
don't let it fall kaw oowee´vungwu
LET GO (to) mungoop´
let go of it mungoop´uk
LET IT BE, NEVER MIND empai´uk oonee´vu, empai´uk oodow´vu
LET ME GO WITH YOU nuh´ muheng´kwaivaw, nuh emeeng´whaing
LET'S GO
let's go vuh´dum (dual)
let's go then vuh´dum eku
let's go dance oowee´ vawdum
let's go home paiay´kwai vawdum
should we go? vuh´dum oo´vai?
let's go to the meeting vuh´dum soopawd´oupawntookwum
let's go to town town´e kwai vawdum

let's go (plural) vuh´dungw
let's go (more than two) uhvuhts´udung
LEVEL (see ***plain***)
LICK
1. kweu´pee, kweuk´
lick yourself kweuv´um
2. ***lick it*** a-ho´dovee (from a-ho´uv ***tongue***)
lick it a-ho´doveuk
LID toowup´
LIE, UNTRUTHFUL toovuhs´uddai (lit. ***it's a lie***)
LIFT (to) kwuhuhk´
LIGHT, SHINING punai´, punu´kaw
LIGHTNING punuk´wees, punuk´wuhs
LIKE, LOVE, WANT, NEED, WISH ow´suhntuhee
I really love you tooveets´ ow´suhntuheun
I want that one ow´suhntuheuk mud´uhn
LIKENESS (see ***resemble***)
LINED UP, IN A ROW nawvee´cheku
hanging in a row oongwai´ nawvee´chekunt
one after another unee´nawveecheku
lined up behind nawvee´ nawpawchuhk
lots lined up behind nunu´penuk
LIP (upper lip or mustache area) tuhmpu´kwusevum
LIPS (see ***mouth***)
LIQUOR (see ***wine***)
LISTEN nungkaw´kai
LITTLE BIT meunts´, meunts´unee
LITTLE BOY ai´puts, ai´pu, aip´
LITTLE, SMALL, TINY meah´puhts, meah´pee meu´peech
LIVER nengwoomp´
LIVING, ALIVE nengwoo´kain
I'm living nengwoo´kaiun
LIZARD (collective name for most lizards) sekoo´peets
LOAD (see ***carry***)
LOCKED tsukwu, chukwee´
locked up chuhkwee´kaivu
he's locked up, in jail kechoong´wung
LOCOWEED *Astragalus purshii*
1. chuhkwee´kaivu (Koosharem)
2. pataw´kai nump (lit. ***poping thing***)
3. sawdu´ganump (lit. ***rattling thing***)
LOCUST *Robinia neomexicana* peu´ sechump´eev (lit. ***sweet scratcher***)
LOCUST, CICADA *Cicadidiae* kuhv, kuhoov´
LONESOME
1. nuhnuhnts´tsungaiee
2. ***to miss someone or something*** soowaw´duhkuheun
LONG (in length) puawn´tuh muhnee, puawn´tuhnee
LONG TIME AGO ees, wee´tuhs
LOOK puhn´nee, puhnee´ku, ni´ku (a shortened version).
looking puhnee´kai
LOST mu'ung´
I'm lost mu'ung´engchun
LOTS (see ***much***)
LOUD pu'aw´nee (from pu'awn´ ***high***)
LOUSE pouv´
lice tseuv´
LOVE (see ***like***)
LUNCH (carried in a bag) tookwus´
LUNGS soav
your lung soam
LYING IN WAIT mawntsuh´ai awvee´ (lit. ***to catch while lying***)
LYING ON YOUR BACK pawdu´metook

— M —

MAD (see ***angry***)
MAGPIE maw´kwaiuv, maw´kwaiuts

(kwaiuv´and kwaiuts´ are shortened forms)
MAHOGANY (CURL-LEAF) *Cercocarpus ledifolius* toonump´, toonup´
MAKE, CREATE, BUILD
1. -echooum, -ekwoai
let's go build a house kawneents´ekwai vawdum
2. mawduhngk´
in the name of He who created the earth Oongwai neu´pawtuhk tooveep´uh mawdo´koym mawpuhkunt´uh
3. -do
make some bread pawn´u dong oa, pawn´u do
make a cradle board koano´dong oa, koanod´do
to make a bow awchuh duh´
MAKE, LET -tee
make a fire nawai´tee
make her cry ya-haw´teung
let me do it nuh oonee´teng
let (make) him do it himself mungu´tus oonee´teng
MAKING BELIEVE (see ***pretend***)
MALLARD achuh´
MAMMOTH, MASTODON mooyai sevee´u
MAN tungwuts´
MANNER (see ***way***)
MANO, MEALER moouts´
MANY (see ***much***)
MANZANITA *Arctostaphylos* awdu´dumpeev (Kaibab)
MARCH sovawdum muduhwuts, so´vai muhunts (lit. ***meanest moon***). (There was some confusion with the informant, Carl Jake, as to the English equivalents. This month could be either February or March)
MARE peup´
MARROW pekoo´hoom
MARRY (to)
1. pengwud´u (from pengwu´ ***wife***)
I'll marry you nuh pengwu´ doongpawm
they got married pengwu´ doong kwuntum
2. ***married*** nawhoom´
MARSHHAWK *Circus cyaneus* maaw´vu chukuts
MASTURBATE wuh'u´ keyu´teku (lit. ***penis-playing***)
MAT, RUG (this word can be used for anything that is spread out including a blanket, tablecloth, etc.) sumup´
MATCH koonut´ (see ***fire***)
give me a match koonaw´ muhawng´wuhn
MATCHBRUSH, BROOM SNAKEWEED *Gutierrezia sarothrae*
1. yoowaw´dump, yoowu´unump
2. koo´kwunump (this last word is only used by the Kaibab band; however, they also use yoowu´unump)
MAYBE soov´
ME (see I)
ME TOO nuh´kainee
MEADOW LARK *Sturnella neglecta* ee´toowuts
MEAN, FIERCE, ANGRY
1. nawngung´kunt
2. ***always wanting to fight*** too-oo´kunt
3. so´vai
mean month so´vai muhunts (an undetermined winter month; see ***March***)
MEASURE tuhkai´
MEAT tuhkoo´uv
MEDICINE ROCK poowu´duhmp
MEDICINE, HERBS, PILLS moosoo´tookweev
MEDICINE MAN (he who uses his supernatural powers to do either

good or bad) poowu´hunt oong (compare ***witch doctor***)
MEDICINE MAN, HERBALIST moosoo´tookwe hunt (lit. ***one who has medicine***)
MEETING (see ***assemble***)
MELTED su'ung, su'aing´
MENSTRUATE
1. na'aw´hawdee, na'aw´hawduh (lit. ***sitting alone***)
2. moounts´ee hawduh (lit. ***moon-sitting***)
she's menstruating mooun´ung (lit. ***she's mooning***)
you're menstruating mooun´um (lit. ***your mooning***)
MESA (see ***top***)
MESQUITE, HONEY MESQUITE *Prosodis* opeemp´
METAL, MONEY (see ***iron***) punu´kawd (lit. ***shining***)
METATE
1. mawd´
2. moouts (Koosharem)
MEXICAN hookwuts´
MIDDLE (see ***half*** and ***between***)
MIDGET nahduh´veets
MIDNIGHT toahoy´ tookwun
MILK
1. mooeev´
2. tawuv´
3. pe-ee´
4. mee´deek (Eng. milk)
MILKWEED *Asclepias* pe'-ee´ whawvoo´kwunump (lit. ***milk squirter***)
MINE, MY nuh´nee
it's mine nuh´nee udun, nuh´nai oodoo´un
my father nuh´nee mooun
MIRAGE
1. nawduh´ku (a phrase from a song)
2. too´see kawduhd (lit. ***floating dust sitting***)
MIRROR, nawvuhn´e nump (lit. ***image thing***)
MISS (to) kawduhnk´
keeps missing it kawduhnk´ oome kaiuk
MISSIONARY, PREACHER, PRIEST Soonung´wuvee umpaw´hawd (lit. ***Coyote Talker***)
MISTER (see ***sir***)
MIX
mixing liquids pawdoo´pee
mix it pawdoo´euk
MIXED nawnaw´hawninee oonee´kunt
MOCCASIN nengwoo´ pawtch, nengwoo´ vawchuts. (Moccasins were originally called "pawtch" but since they have become a rarity due to the modern shoe, moccasins are now called ***Indian shoes.***)
MOCKING BIRD yump
MOJAVE INDIAN
1. Aiut´
2. Ma-uhkaw´uhveech
MOLASSES (Eng. molasses) mudus´
MONEY
1. punu´kawd (lit. ***shining***)
2. muhnee (Eng. money)
3. tuhmpeem´ (used at Moapa, from tuhmpee´ ***rock***)
MONSTER (see ***Ghost***)
MOON, MONTH
1. muhyu´tohots, muhunts´
2. maw´tohots (Koosharem)
3. ***month*** (Eng. month). -umuts´
September yoovun´umuts (lit. ***fall month***)
MOOSE paiyoo´kwutch
MORMON (Eng. Mormon) Moa´mun, Moa´munee
MORNING STAR tawtsee´untsaw pootseev, tawsuh´untoo pootseev, tawsuhn´too pootseev
MORNING, TOMORROW ee´chuhk

in the morning ee´chukoos, wee´chukoos
this morning aw´wechuhk
MOSQUITO moouv´
MOTH
1. moo´sevuhkots
2. wuhsee´u vuhkuhts. Wawseev´ are the fine scales that come off the moth's wings (see ***stickers***).
MOTHER peyu-´
his/her mother peyung
my mother peun´
MOUNT (see ***exit***)
MOUNTAIN GOAT kai´tos (Moapa and Las Vegas)
MOUNTAIN LION (see ***cougar***)
MOUNTAIN SHEEP, DESERT BIGHORN nawk´, nawghaw´
MOUNTAIN kaiv
mountain lying down kai´awvahv
MOURNING DOVE
aiyov´
MOUSE pooee´chuts
MOUTH OF CANYON
1. tuhuk´, tuh´
2. sekai´uk toompawk (lit. ***a crack's mouth***)
MOUTH, LIPS tuhmpum´
One Who Doesn't Talk (a personal name) Tuhmputs´
MOVE OUT OF THE WAY
emee´tuhkwaw
MOVE (to move or to travel far away) meyawv´ughai.
let's move away meyowm´padum
I moved away meyaw´vuhai koochun
MOVEMENT (of the body), MOVE ABOUT, STIR ABOUT
to move the entire body munai
to move one part of the body munung´oomee
MOVIE, SHOW (Eng. show)
1. soo´
2. punun´tseets (Chemehuevi)
MUCH, LOTS, MANY awvawn
lots of it awvawn´ooud, awvawn´oot
many awvawn´utuhnee
MUD weuv´
watery mud pawng´weuv
MULBERRY *Moraceae* moakov´
MULE mooduts´ (Eng. mule)
mules mooduts´engw
MUSCLE, STRONG suh'uh-´
MUSH, SOUP sa'awp´ (lit. ***boiled***)
MUSKRAT pawdung´wunt
MUSTARD WEED oaw´suent
MUSTACHE (see ***whiskers***)
MYSELF, JUST ME nuh´sump

— N —

NAKED (see ***barren***)
NAME neud
to have a name, named nineu´hunt
your name neum´
what is your name? unineu´hunt uhm?
NARROWS (where a river narrows down) nawchook´weech
NASAL FLUID moopeek´ee, moopeek´
NASTY (sexually) nawai´suhunt
NAVAJO
1. Pu-hawng´ Weets (lit. ***Cane Knife People***)
2. Wee´ Kwuseets (lit. ***Knife Tail people***) Kaibab
NAVEL CORD
1. sekaw´vee
2. sekoo´soodung
NEAR (not quite there) eyu´tuhs, eyun´uhs
NEARLY (see ***almost***)
NECK koduv´
hugging around the neck koodai´um aiun´ookwai

NECKLACE kawk
NEED (see ***like***)
NEEDLE chawhaw´nump (lit. ***sewing thing***)
NEGRO
1. Too´ Mawduh´kawts (lit. ***Black American***)
2. Ni´kuhts, Ni´keets, Negeets (Eng. Negro)
3. Too´ Negeets (lit. ***Black Negro***)
NEPHEW
1. (brother's son) koo´uv
your nephew koots´eem
2. (sister's son) suhnunts´
my nephew suhnunts´un
(suhnunts may also refer to a ***maternal uncle***, or ***parallel cousin***)
NERVOUS
1. mawsuhng´ekee
2. nawguh´tsai (Moapa)
NEST, HAVEN, PREPARED PLACE
1. Sonee´ung. (This word refers more to the inner part of a nest; a soft, comfortable, warm haven where one is safe from harm. It is also a place prepared by someone for those who depart this life. The Pleiades has this name, for it is there that Coyote's wife and daughters fled to safety from him.)
sonee´ vuhdookwai (lit. ***to prepare a place for someone so that it will be ready when he arrives***)
2. ***nest*** nouv´u teung (a bird's nest)
NEVER MIND (see ***let it be***)
NEW MOON aw´ muhyu´tohots´, aw´ moounts
NEW aw´uhkawd, aw´-
new house aw´kawnee
NEXT, NEXT TIME, LATER, AFTERWARDS, FOLLOWING
penunk´w
next day penu´tawv
next summer penu´tawtch
next winter penu´tom
a little while later penunk´wunee
following him oongwu´venungkw
NIECE
1. pa'awts´
2. nuhmpee´uts
NIGHT, DARK tookwun´
it's getting dark tookwu´deuk
NIGHTHAWK, COMMON *Chordeiles minor* peum´oanoaupuhts
NIGHTHAWK, LESSER *Chordeiles acutipennis* pee´yoots
NINE soowaw´ toaho mawsuhng´wee
NIT cheeu´peech (the eggs of a louse or a small louse itself. This word is diminutive of tseuv´, the word for ***lice***)
NO kawtch, kaw-
NOBODY, NO ONE kaw nengwoo´ait
NOISE (see ***sound***)
NOISY, CLAMOROUS padaw´dai (this word means making a great deal of noise and can be used when refering to a baby or even a car)
NONE, NOTHING
there isn't any kawchuk´
I have none kawchun´, kawchoo´un
NOON toyhoy´tavai (lit. ***middle-day***)
NORTH WIND, COLD WIND kweum
north wind blowing kweum´ai, kweu´munt
NOSE
1. mooveep´ee
your nose mooveem´
2. muhnchuhv´, moonchoov´
NOT, NEGATIVE kaw-, kawchoo-
I'm not mad kawchoo nungai´aingwu
no arm kaw puhdait
NOT PAYING ATTENTION
I wasn't paying attention kawmus´un ainee wainee
NOTCHED weuhd´ukunt
NOTHING, JOKING, EASY nawvus´

nothing to it nawvus´tuhmp
NOW ai´oov, aw´oov´
NUMB (when a portion of your body goes to sleep) tawsuhng´ee
sleeping hand mawsuhng´ee
sleeping leg tawsuhn´eng
NUMB, PARALYZED (lack of feeling and ability to move) toongkoont´towng
NURSING pechuhng´, pechuh´vung

— O —

OBEY (see ***believe***)
OBSIDIAN toop
OBSTINATE (see ***stubborn***)
OCHRE (see ***iron oxide***)
ODOR, SMELL kwunu´meent
OFF (to come off, such as a ring from a finger) to-awk´
take it off toopuk´
OLD, ANCIENT (inanimate) ee´tuhmpuhts, wee´tuhmp
OLD MAN naw´poo, naw´poots
OLD WOMAN
1. mows´uhoych, maw´puhts
2. punaints (Koosharem uses the above, plus punaints´)
ON, UPON awvawn´
on that one mud´awvawn
on top of a person nengwoo´vawn
ONE EYED, TO WINK onchok´
ONE MORE TIME, AGAIN soo´tus
ONE PLACE soo´kopaws
ONE soo´ee, soo´kos, soo´yus
ONION sevoy´u (Spanish ***ciebolla***)
OPEN
1. mawduhng´, mawduhng´ween
2. too´wenuk.
opening it tawtoo´wenuk
OPEN YOUR MOUTH kuhpuk´ai
OPENLY, UNFEIGNED, TRUTHFUL (not done in secret) ow´wainee
OREGON GRAPE *Mahonia repens* weump´eev
ORGAN PIPE CACTUS, (or saguaro) haawv´ (Chemehuevi)
ORGASM, CLIMAX (male)
1. awveem·tawngwuk´enu (lit. ***semen shooting***)
2. kookwee´ (lit. ***to shoot***)
ORION'S BELT (the three stars in the constellation Orion) nawhung´ (lit. ***mountain sheep*** [plural])
ORPHAN
1. kaw moo´ait (lit. ***no father***)
2. tuhduh´ hawd, tuhduh´heets (lit. ***barren***)
OTHER SIDE
1. munungk´ (visable)
on the other side munungk´opawk. munung´kwup
coming back from munungk´wuhai
2. munawp´ (Blanding)
OUCH uddee´, uddow´, unow´
OUR (see ***we***)
OUTSIDE
1. awvee´nawp
2. tuh´duvaw (see ***barren***)
laying outside tuhd´uvaw awvee
it's blowing outside nuh'ai´uk tuh´duvawnt
OVER THERE wawn
OVER, ACROSS awvawk´
OVERCOME (see ***easy to do***)
OWE nahwhawv´
OWL, BURROWING *Speotyto cunicularia* mookoo´hoots
OWL (GREAT HORNED) moo'-oom´puhts

— P —

PACK UP, GATHER UP naw´vai
pack it up naw´vai tengwuk nawvaing´wuk
PACK RAT kawts
PAIN, ACHE, PAIN, HURT

pukawng´kee
I'm hurting pawkai´un
PAINT (earth pigments of different colors found near Overton, Nev.) toodoov´
PAINT (to), DECORATE mawu- (lit. *to rub on*)
paint it mu'ung´wuk
PAIR nawvuh´u (from nawvuhn´ *image*)
PAIUTE Paiyuhts
PALM (of the hand) mawpai´awvoon
PALMER PENSTEMON *Penstemon palmeri* toho´u sawdu´ganump (lit. *rattlesnake rattler*)
PAN punu´ohots (lit. *metal bowl*)
PANT (see *blow*)
PANTS (see *leggings*)
PAPER (Eng. paper) pawpee´duv
PARALYZED (see *numb*)
PARTURITION, GIVING BIRTH
1. toowung´w
she had her baby toowung´oonung
having a baby toowai´unee
2.we'-ee´puhkunt (lit. *fell out*)
PASS (to)
1. *to pass another going in the same direction* aw´paong
let's pass him ungu´ paom´ padum
it passed us tdum´e paon´tsuk
2. *to pass someone who is going the opposite direction* naw´opung
PASS OUT (to pass out from drinking)
1. awmuh´u kwepuk´u (lit. *to fall drunk*)
2. pai yai´, pai yai´eku (lit. *water die*)
3. pawhoy´puhku (Shivwits)
PASS, DIVIDE, SADDLE (in a mountain)
1. muhuv´, muhuk´
2. mawdo´enawk (lit. *in the opened place*)
3. mawduh´uk (lit. *it's open*)
PATCH (closing something up or covering a hole) wuhtoo´noo nanawk´u
PATIENT (see *good* and *silent*)
PAY (see *buy*)
PEACE nawhoo´kwee kawduhk (lit. *war stopped*)
PEACEFUL (see *happy*)
PEAK
1. *a conical peak or object* kwevoo´awmawk
2. kwe´choovunt
PEAS wechee´ nupuv (lit. *bird's eggs*)
PEEK, PEEP sootsee´
peeking out sootsee´nee
PEEL (see *skin*)
PENCIL po'-oh´nump (lit. *writing instrument*)
PENIS wuh'u´pee
erect penis wuh'u´ nungai´ai (lit. *angry penis*)
PEPPERMINT pawkoa´nunump, pawwhaw´nunump
PERSON (see *Indian*)
PERSONAL SONG nunu´kaw awv´oouv
my own singing nawno´ kawnun
PET, DOMESTICATED, TAMED poongkoots´, -voongkoots
pet dog sawdee´ voongkoots
pet horse kuvaw´ voongkoots
we have a pet bear nuhm kweyu´kuntuh voongkoo´ kwuntuhm
PETROGLYPH, PICTOGRAPH (a written message, in any form, upon a rock)
tuhmpee´po'-ohp´ (lit. *rock writing*)
PHEASANT
1. ungawd, (lit. *red one*)
2. chupun´ee wetseech´ (lit. *Japanese bird*)
PHOTOGRAPH, PICTURE, PORTRAIT naiahv´uteep
PIERCED EAR nuhngku´vawm

mawcheu´pawk
PIG
1. kwecheen´ (Span. cuchina)
2. pe´keets (Eng. pig)
PILLOW toachung´eep, toasung´eep
PILLS (see ***medicine***)
PINCH HIM
1. tsi'tsuh´meung (Koosharem)
2. sechoo´meung
he's pinching me sechoom´ee chungun
I'm going to pinch you sechoom´evum
PINE (fir and spruce) oahomp´
PINE CONE kawvoo´uv
PINE GUM sunup´ee, sunup´
PINE HEN, BLUE GROUSE *Dendragapus obscurus* kaom´puhts
PINE (probably limber pine *Pinus flexilisis* or bristlecone pine *Pinus aristata*) pawnaw´ oahomp
PINENUT
1. (large Nevada and Western Utah variety) toovuts´
(plural) toov´
2. (small southern Utah and Arizona variety) pawduhv´
PINK, REDDISH ungkaw´seukawd
PINTO, SPOTTED sai´kudum
PINYON JAY *Gymnorhinus cyanocephala* ungunts´
PINYON PINE *Pinus edulis* and *monophylla* toovup´
PIPE chuhmoo´, kwou moochoo´ung
smoking a pipe kwou moochoo´kwai
PISTOL pee´stonu (Eng. pistol)
PITCH, RESIN, GUM sunup, sunup´ee
PLAIN, FLAT LAND, LEVEL yoo-wawv´
PLANT (to), TO FARM uhu´
going to plant uhu´vawts
I'm going to plant uhu´vawnt
PLANTS (see ***brush***)
PLAY keu´
game keup´
go play keu´te kwai
PLEIADES Sonee´ung (see ***nest*** for an explanation of this word)
PLUME wusee´udook (lit. ***feather-under***)
POINT OF A HILL mookwun´
has a point mookwun´ekunt
pointed mookwun´eench
POINTED HILL weoom´ookweuhunt (from weeoovb ***awl***)
POINTING ***pointing a finger*** ma-hoo´kwenum
POKE, JAB (to poke or prick with something pointed and sharp) sehee´ton, segee´tonaw (from tonu´ ***to hit with a thrust***)
POKER, FIRE STICK
1. ***stirrer, stirring instrument*** chikood´oonump
2. kwetsee´toa
POLE, POST uhduv´
POLICEMAN tawpee´chuts (one who ties)
I'm going to be a policeman nuh tawpee´chuts ekaivaw
PONDEROSA *Pinus ponderosa* yooveemp´
POOR ta-haw´puhts
POP, EXPLODE patawk´
PORCUPINE yoongoom´puhts, yuhnguh´puhts, yuh'uhm´puhts
PORCUPINE QUILL yoo'-oo´munuv (lit. ***porcupine thorn***)
sewing on quills, doing quill work yoo'-oo´ munuveem cha-hai
sewn with quills, quill work yoo'-oo´ munu´veem cha-haw´kunt
POSITIVELY (see ***sure***)
POTATO
1. ***Indian potato*** *Orogenia linearifolia* whechuhn´
2. (Eng. potato) tuh´dus

POUND IT IN
1. taio´kwunkuk
2. kweep´oanoy uk
POUR chawm
to pour in squirts, to shake out chawchawm´
POW-WOW (see ***assemble***)
POWDER HORN koochung´wu awp
PRAIRIE DOG aiah´vuhts
PRAY tooveech´uh kuhn´u moou´ vawchuh´num (lit. ***asking-I'm-father-towards***)
praying for it umpawhawng kuhuk (lit. ***talk-gets***)
PRAYING MANTIS
1. tuh´euts
2. nuhmu´hawpeev (Shivwits)
PREACHER (see ***missionary***)
PRECEDING (see ***first***)
PREGNANT nou´kwunt
PRETEND, MAKING BELIEVE
1. ***making believe*** nawsuhmp´
2. ***pretending*** oonee´tee (lit. ***just doing that***)
PRETTY, GOOD LOOKING, CUTE, FANCY
1. u'up´uchoonee, up´usuhwuhnee
2. peyuhn´ai
you're looking nice peyuhn´unchechum
it's cute peyuhn´ud
PRICKLY PEAR *Opuntia engelmannii* yoowuv´
PRICKLY PEAR FRUIT yoomuv
PRIOR (see ***already***)
PROPHET, SEER pawdoo´koots
PROUD, SHOWING OFF, ADMIRING YOURSELF
naw suh´denkuhee (lit. ***afraid of yourself***)
proud of you suhduh´enkuheum
PUBIC AREA penu´seku
PUBIC HAIR
penis hair wuh'u´ moasoa
vagina hair wuhkuh´ moasoa
PULL, DRAG peyo-´, peyo´hong
pull it peyo´hongwuk
PULL OUT (to) ootoop´
pull it out ootoop´eenuk
they pulled it out ootoo´veets´ ukwum
PUNISHING, HURTING pukaw´pee (from pukawng´kee ***pain***)
PURGE ***to push intestinally*** moomoo´chooungkuhee
PURPLE, BRUISE toa-whawd´ (the word for ***bruise*** is also the word for ***purple*** because a bruise is purple)
PURSUE (see ***chase***)
PUS pekeep´
PUS THAT COMES OUT OF EYES pawsok´
pussy eyes wekeev´oowemees
PUSH
too´kweuk
PUT IT ON, WEAR IT (to put on an article of clothing) tawnuh´kee
put it on tawnuhk´euk
wear it around tawnuhk´eeneuk
try it on nawhaw´kaiuk
PUT IT TOGETHER numai´uk wawch
PUT YOUR HANDS UP mawntsaw´kai
PUT, SET
(singular) wawchuh´
put it away wawchoong´wuk
it's put away wawchuh´kunt
(plural) yoonuk´
put them away for me yoonu kuhuk´un
let me keep them yoonu´kai vawkwun
many put away yoonu´ nawvee´chekunt
PUT WITH, ADD puhu-´
add it puhud´evuk (lit. ***put it with it***)
put five cents with it puhud´evuk

five cents ee
with him -puh ung

— Q —

QUAIL awkaw´dumpuhts
(plural) awkaw´dumpuhts eng
QUAKING ASPEN *Populus tremuloides* suhuv´ seuv
QUAKING ASPEN SAP suhngu´veuv (lit. ***aspen-sweet***)
QUARREL (see ***argue***)
QUARTZITE poantsee´tuhmp, poantsee´
QUICK, FAST (see ***keep on***)
QUIET (see ***silent***)
QUILT (see ***blanket***)
QUIVER oogoon´, hookoon´ (lit. ***arrow sack***)
QUIVERING BREATH (to take a deep quivering breath like a person does when he cries) yawhaw´ soowu´kuheun (lit. ***I'm cry breathing***)

— R —

RABBIT BLANKET kumoo´ muhdoo´ee
RABBIT BRUSH *Chaysothamnus nauseosus* skoomp, spoomp
RABBIT BRUSH GUM skoo´ sunuk´oh
RABBIT HEAD GAME
tawsuhng´uhmp
instrument used in game tawsuhng´unump
RACE nontsee´ku (this word means ***flying*** and as in English may refer to racing)
RACCOON yumus´uts
RAG pawnuh´seev (Koosharem)
RAGGED, WORN OUT (see ***wearing out***) pekweep´
ripped up puhguh´kekwaip
RAGWEED *Ambrosia* pawwhu´munump
RAIN oongwai´
RAINBOW pawdo´kwawveech, pawdoo´kwawv
RASP (notched stick used as a musical instrument in the Bear Dance) wuhnuhd´uhnump
RATTLE SNAKE
1. toho´uv
2. kweuts (Moapa)
RATTLE sawdu´gai (this word can also represent a death rattle in the throat of someone who is about to die)
RATTLESNAKE WEED *Euphorbia albomarginata* tooveep´uh kawhaiv (lit. ***earth's necklace***)
RAVEN (see ***crow***)
RAW (see ***unripe***)
RAWHIDE awtup´
READING po'-oh´puhnee (lit. ***writing-see***)
REALLY, TRULY, VERY
1. tooveets´ (see ***true***)
it's very good tooveets´aiuk
2. tuh, tuhnk, teenk (possibly an abbreviated form of tooveets)
it's very good tuh´ aiayuk, tuh´ ai
3. kuhvee´uts (used by the Shivwits in sentences where you might have ***really*** hurt someone or ***really*** done it)
4. nukuh´ (Moapa)
RED ANT ungkaw´ tawsee´uv
RED BEANS ungkaw´ muhdee´
RED BIRCH, WATER BIRCH *Betula occidentalis* kai´soov, kai´shuhduhts
RED CEDAR *Juniperus virginiana* spawngwup´
RED OSIER DOGWOOD *Cornus sericea* ungkaw´ kawnuv (lit. ***red willow***)
RED PENSTEMON moo´tuntutsee pechuh´meen (lit. ***the one the hum-***

mingbird sucks)
RED RACER nuntuh´nuv
RED ungkaw´, ungkaw´hawd
red one ungkaw´ hawdum
RED-TAILED HAWK *Buteo jumaicensis* sunu´kwununts (lit. ***pitch eagle***)
REDO (to do it over) nawvee´nawonenawkum
REED (*Phragmites communis*) pawhump´
RELATION, RELATIVE, KIN, COUSIN (the following term has a closer application than among the Anglos. It implies not only a relative or cousin but in the sense of a dear friend) puhu-
my relative puhun´
your relative puhum´
he's related puhung´
RELUCTANTLY, UNWILLINGLY, NOT WANTING TO kaw ow´suhntuhee waisump (lit ***not-like-enough***)
REMAINDER, LEFT OVER peai´
save me some peaing´kuhn
REMEMBER, TO HAVE IN MIND soomai´eku
can't remember kawsoomaing´wu
I can't remember kawchu´kun soomaing´wai
REMOVE, TAKE AWAY, COME OFF
to remove a stain from cloth totseng´wu
it never came off kawchuk´ totseng´wu
the paint never came off paint ud kaw totseng´wu
it will come off to-awk´aivawnt
REPAIR (see ***fix***)
REPEAT (see ***again***)
RESEMBLANCE, LIKENESS, SEEMS
1. nai-ah´vai
it looked like him to me nai-ahv´ unchun
it looks like Bob Bob´ee nai-ahv´awtseek
2. tuhuh´ee
RESIN (see ***pitch***)
RESURRECTED yu'ai´ puhduh´suts (lit. ***to die and wake up***)
RETARDED tuhnuh´kwechuts
RETURN, TO CIRCLE BACK kon´ekai
I will return nuh pekon´evun
RETURN TO, GO BACK (to) paiyuh-´
go home paiyuh´kwai
I'm returning home paiay´kwai vawneun, paiay´kwai vawnin, nuh paiyuh´kwaing
go home (several) moonis´kwai
go home (more than two) pawnaw´kwaiuk
where have you been? hu´vaichu paiyoong´? (lit. ***where are you returning from?***)
are you going home? uhm paiyuh´kwai vawnt u´?
REVOLVE (see ***turn around***)
RIB awngwu´tump
RIDGE awveech´ (lit. ***lying***)
RIDING kawduh´nee
doing nothing but riding around nawvus´ kawduh´ vuhduhkwaw
RIFLE, GUN toompeoots´
RIGHT HAND, RIGHT SIDE podu-´
your right side podum´ukwut
my right side podun´ukwut
RINGTAIL CAT *Bassariscus astutus* moosoon´ tookoopuhts
RIP, TEAR, SPLIT see ***cut***)
1. chupu´kainuku (lit. ***to rip by pulling apart***)
rip it chupuk´enuk
2. ***accidently gives way*** puhkuh´kee, pawkawk´
RIPE, COOKED, DONE kwusuhng´wuhchuk
RISING (see ***emerge***)
ROAD (see ***trail***)

ROADRUNNER
1. soonung´wuvee toowuv´ukaip (lit. ***Coyote's son who once was***)
2. soonung´wuvee toowung (lit. ***coyote's son***)
3. oachuv´ookaip
ROAST UNDER THE GROUND (to) toomu´-
roasted toomung´woochuk
ROBIN senk´o kwunuv, tsek´wunkwunuv, tse´konung
ROCKCHUCK yu'um´puhts
ROCK SLIDE (the kind that slides down beneath your feet as you seek to climb it) sawveev´
ROCK, STONE tuhmp
ROCKING
1. ***to rock a baby in your arms*** mawnuhnts´chuhkee
2. ***rock her*** chumuh´eung
ROCKY EARTH tuhmpee´ tooveep
ROCKY MOUNTAIN BEEPLANT *Cleome serrulata* soa´kwunuv (lit. ***armpit odor smeller***)
ROGUE, RASCAL (a person who is considered no good) ee'ai´chum, yu'ai´chum
ROLLED UP uhduhmp. mawdomp´enawk
I'm going to roll a smoke kwou´ mawdoo´paw oompawn
ROLL OVER moompu´
rolling over moompuv´oodoo
roll over! moompuk´oa!
roll it over noompai´uhuk
ROOT, STUMP (the base of anything) tuhnuv´, toonawk´
ROPE
1. tuhsuv, tawsuv´
2. uhdoomp
ROTTEN
1. moeep´
2. pekeep´
ROUGH chongkaw´hawd
rough country chongkwaw´ ooweep
ROUGH ROCK (an unidentified type of rock common at Indian Peak, Utah) chongkwaw´ duhmp
ROUND, SPHERICAL, SWOLLEN, BLOATED
1. ***to swell up and become round and hard as one's stomach does when a person overeats*** poaton´, poaton´ee
I'm full poaton´ekain (lit. ***I'm round***)
2. utawp´odo
RUBBING ALCOHOL wheechuv´, whechu´koduv
RUG (see ***mat***)
RUINS Moo´kweech ee kawnee´ kaip (lit. ***Hopi-house-used-to-be***)
RUN
1. tohok´wee
2. tuhduwai (Chemehuevi)
RUN AWAY, BURST INTO A RUN, ESCAPE kawkawd´uh
ran away, escaped kawkawd´uhpuhku
ran away (plural) meento´nee
RUNNING, FLOWING (liquid, people or animals) nookwee´
he's running nookwe´nung
flowing, river stream nookweent´
RUSHING WATER sawngwunts´
RUST
1. oaw´tsawv, ous´seintu
2. nawsawnts´spengwuchuk (lit. ***rust coming out***)

— S —

SACK, BAG koonuv´
SADDLE kawduh´nump (lit. ***sit-thing***)
SADDLE HORN kawduh´nump totsee (lit. ***sit-thing head***)
SAGE HEN *Centrocerus urophasianus* sechu´
SAGEBRUSH (big) *Artemisia tridentata* kawhup´

SAGEBRUSH (collectively)
sawngwuv´
SAGUARO or ORGAN PIPE CACTUS
Cereus ha'awv´ (Chemehuevi)
SALIVA kuhtseep´
to spit out kuhtsee´oonai
SALT
1. ouv´
2. awsoap´
SALTGRASS *Distichlis spicata*
awsoamp´
SAME (see ***alike***)
SAME ONE uhdu´tuhs
SAME PLACE oovus´
SAME WAY, ALIKE, COMPARABLE
1. ***to copy or to do the same thing again*** ow´pus, oop´us, up´suhnee
just like Colleen Colleen ung up´suhnee
don't do like I do nuh oop´sunee oonee´vungwu
2. ***to do the same old thing or do it the same way*** oonee´soonee
SAND
1. ***fine sand*** awtuv´
2. ***course sand*** sewump´
3. too'goo´ (Koosharem)
SAND HILL
1. too'goo yooweech (Koosharem)
2. sewu´ toonoo´keed
SANDSTONE ungkaw´ tuhmp
SAP (soft runny sap from any tree)
pavoats´
SAY
to say ai, mai
saying ainch
did he say that? maik´udung?
says it every time, always says it aing´oomee
saying it all along ai´meu
say some more aiuh´suh
that's what I say mai´nookwaik
say it ai´tee
he says anything pawnee ai´tee oong
said aik
said that ai´puhkunt
as those two said aik´ooum
that which you said aik´ainumee
I said ain, ai´kunt nuh
those two said ai´puhkaim
they said hai´mee
spoke out aing´puhku
when you say it maing´oots
you're saying it maik´waik
after it was said maing´uhmuhuts
did he say that? maing woonts´udung?
to say something to someone mai´ ungwee
I'm going to say something to you aing´kuhpum
isn't it so? aing´oa (used like the English phrase ***ain't it***)
tell him that ai´vung kwai
what do you want (say)? empuh´u aik
many speaking (lit. ***many making noise***) wai´kawdum, wai´ekai
SCALP totsee´um wetoyn´uvu
SCARLET BUGLER PENSTEMON
Eatonii moo´tuntutsee pechuh´meen (lit. ***what the humming bird sucks***)
SCATTER (see ***spread***). (People scattering)
going individual directions nawnee´nee nungkwetuhk
they travel their individual ways poodoo´kwawchum nawnee´nunkwetuhk
SCATTER (see ***spread***)
chuhkuh´ekaivu
SCAUP, LESSER *Aythya affinis* too´ koochoomputs (lit. ***black koochoomputs***)
SCOLD (see ***angry***)
SCORPION
1. kwawsee´ kwepump (lit. ***hits with the tail***)

2. podo´tsekunt (lit. ***has a cane***)
SCOULER WILLOW *Salix scouleriana* kwechum´paw kawnuv (lit. ***ugly willow***)
SCRAPER (made from the foreleg of a deer for scraping hides and aspens for juice) muntseev´
SCRAPING A HIDE took´oonai
SCRATCH ***to scratch an itch*** chow´nai, tsaw´nai
SCREECH OWL waw´nawkweech
SCROTUM chukaiv´oweem koonuv´ (lit. ***testicle sack***)
SEA GULL noovu´dos
SEAMSTRESS cha-haw´vuhts
SEARCH (to) puhsaw´haik
SEE (see ***look***)
SEED BEATER whuhstu´senump
SEEDS puhee´uk, poowe´uk
SEEMS LIKE IT ow´wainee, ow´waiuhnee
SEEPING OUT whawvook´wu, kwawpook´
SEER (see ***prophet***)
SEGO LILY, MARIPOSA LILY *Calochortus nuttallii, C. nuttallii* seko´, segoo´
SEIZE, GRAB, CATCH chu'ai´ uk (from chu'ai´ ***to hold***)
SELFISH mooud´
SELL nahdo´u tuhdu´vee, nahdong´wai tuhdu´vee
SEMEN awveem´
SENSING (see ***intuition***)
SEPARATELY, DIFFERENTLY, INDIVIDUALLY
(see ***alone***) na'aw´, nawnee´
individual directions nawnee´nunkwetuhk
individually, one apiece nawnee´sooyus
SEPTEMBER yoovun´umuts, yoovun muhunts (lit. ***fall moon***)
SERVICEBERRY BUSH *Amelanchier* tuhuv´ (the berry is called tuhngwump, toowoomp)
SET (see put)
SET THE TABLE tuhkaw´ sumai (lit. ***eat-spread out***)
SEVEN navaik´uvawt (lit. ***over six***)
SEW cha-haw´
one who sews, seamstress cha-haw´duhm
SEXUAL INTERCOURSE
1. yoho´-
let me have intercourse with you yoho´vum
2. (this word for ***shoot*** can refer to inseminating) kookwee
let me shoot you kookwee´vawkwun
SHADE awvuv´
shade house awvaw´ kawnee
SHADY CANYON awvaw´uweep
SHADOW awvaw´um (lit. ***your shade***)
SHADSCALE *Atriplex confertifolia* kawnguhmp´
SHAKE ***to shake out an object with the hands***
1. mamawn´e chuh´keuk
2. kwetoan, whecho
shake it wheton´euk
SHAKING, TREMBLING, SHIVERING
1. suhnuh´gai
2. tasuhn´ukee, tasuhn´uhgweek
SHALL, WILL -vawnee, -pawnee
I shall go home, nuh paiay kwai vawnee, nuh paiay kwaim pawnee
will you marry me? nuh´nee udu pingwud´ oo vawnee?
SHAME ***to hang the head down*** muhyai
SHAMPOO (see ***soap***)
SHARP, EDGE koong-wu
to be sharp koong-wu´uhunt (lit. ***to have an edge***)
sharpen it koong-wu´deuk (lit. ***edges it***)
SHARPSHOOTER wenunts,

wenu´hunt
SHE (see ***him***)
SHEDDING HAIR oavee´
SHEEP (Eng. sheep) see´peets
SHEET BLANKETS kweneev
SHIELD awtup´
SHINE (see ***light***)
SHINNY STICK kwepu´nump
SHIRT tow-uhts´
SHIVERING (see ***shaking***)
SHIVWITS See´veets
SHOE puawtch´, pawtch, -vawchuts´
SHOOT
1. ***shoot a weapon*** or ***male orgasm*** kookwee´
2. tawngwuk´enu
SHORE OF A LAKE, WATER'S EDGE pawgoo´u, pawkoong´wu
SHORT tawvay´
short one tawvay´puhts
short one standing tawvay´puhtsuh wuhnee
SHOSHONI (Wyoming) Soa´hots
SHOULD (see ***could)***
SHOULDER ***your shoulder*** chouv´uhm
SHOUT wa'ung´eng
SHOVEL (Eng. shovel) soa´vuhd
SHOWING OFF (see ***proud***)
SHUT, CLOSED toongwu-´
close it toongwuk´
closed, shut, in jail toongwu´kunt
did you shut it? toongwung´ wuh´chuduk u?
SIAMESE TWINS, RESEMBLE nuhntuh´eku
SICK na-hu´mee
I'm sick na-hum´eun
SIDE (see ***half*** and ***wall***)
SIDEWAYS, CROSSWAYS wa-hee´chuhk
put it side ways wa-hee´chook wuk uneng´oa
SIDEWINDER tawnu´keets, tawnu´kuhts
SILENT, QUIET (from ai´ee ***good***)
be silent ai´nekai
SILLY moa-hup´
she's silly moa-hup´uhkunt ung
SINEW, THREAD tawmoov´
SING kaw, ka-haw´
your singing kaw´num uhd
SIR, MISTER oongwus´
SISTER
1. ***elder sister*** pawtseets´
2. ***younger sister*** numeents´
your younger sister numeem
SISTERS nawvuts´eng
SISTER IN LAW nain´ pengwun (lit. ***younger sister wife***)
SIT, DWELL, STAY
(singular) kawduh´
sitting kawduhd, kawdee
just sit right there mu´vusump oonee´ kawd
will stay kawduh´vawnt
sit still aw´kawduh
sit up straight tuhnk´kawduh
for more than one to sit or stay yookwee´, yoogwee´ (plural)
set them down yookwee´uk
SITTING CROSS LEGGED tungu´choy kawduhd
SITTING ON THE GROUND WITH LEGS STRAIGHT OUT mootawk´hawduhd
SITTING WITH LEGS SPREAD APART tawhaw´saw kawdee
SIX navai´
SKIN, BARK, PEEL awsee´-
bark awsee´uk
your skin awsee´um
peel it off awsee´guk
SKINNING AN ANIMAL tuh-un´ee
SKINNY, BONY
1. ***skinny to the extreme that your bones show*** oy´yu'ai (lit.

boney-dying)
he or she's boney oy´yu'aip oong
2. (not as extreme as oy´yu'ai) tsaw´, chaw
skinny one cheu´kwawdum
SKIRT, APRON pekwun´, pekwun´ee
SKULL
1. o'-oh´ totsee´kaip (lit. ***bone-head-used to be***)
2. totsee´ o'-ohv´ (lit. ***head bone***)
SKUNK poanee´
SKY toohoom´paiahv (lit. ***above-slope***)
SLANT EYES weoo´ vooeets (lit. ***awl eyes***)
SLAP
1. moa'hoyp´
2. mawvee´chuhkeengk
SLEEP
(singular) awpuh´ee
I'm going to sleep awpuh´ee whaivawn´eun
John is sleeping John awpuh´eed
(plural) hoa'koy´
SLIP (to slip and fall) petuv´
SLIP OF THE TONGUE (saying something you don't really mean)
1. suhvuh´ maiku
2. tookhoomp´ai
SLIPPERY (see ***smooth***)
SLIT (see ***cut***)
SLOPE (see ***wall***) sevu´vai (Kaibab, not used by Shivwits)
you guys smooth the slope paoo´ sevu´vai tevawkum
SLOW suneev´
SMALL (see ***little***)
SMART, WISE, INTELLIGENT, CLEVER
1. moohoo´uhunt. (lit. ***sense-has*** from the word for heart)
2. ***smart, intelligent, wise*** toosoo´ai
he's smart toosoo´aiudum
maybe he doesn't know anything soov toosoo´ait oong
he's not smart kawchoo´ ung toosoo´aingwai
SMASH, CRUSH, CLAP, SLAP (to press the hands together to crush or applaud)
mawvee´chuhkeengk
SMEAR (to spread something like butter) muawk
smeared muaw´kunt
SMELL (to), SNIFF ookwee´
smell it ookwee´uk
it smells like sagebrush sawngwuv´ oo´kwunuk
SMILING kuhsuh´eku
SMOKE ***to smoke a cigarette*** kwou´ tuhkai (lit. ***tobacco-eats***)
do you smoke? emee´chudu kwou´ tuhkai u?
SMOKE FROM A FIRE kwe'-eep´
SMOKING A DEER HIDE koop´seev
SMOOTH, SLIPPERY pa'awng´kai, paung´kuhee
it's slippery pa'awngk´kaiuk
SNAKE (the word for any snake at Moapa) wauhts´
SNAKEWEED (small) *Gutierrezia microcephala* kuh´kwunump (Kaibab)
SNEEZE ungwee´see
sneezes ungwee´sengoomee
SNORE oso´doway
SNOW
1. noovuv´
2. ***first snow of the year*** oo´noovuv (lit. ***nothing snow***)
SNOWBERRY *Symphoricarpos* awvaw´koonump (lit. ***thing that goes over***)
SNOWSHOE RABBIT tosaw´ kawm (lit. ***white jackrabbit***)
SOAP, SHAMPOO oos (this name comes from the soap found in the roots of the *Yucca baccata*)
SOBERING UP ahmuh´u puhduh´suts (lit. ***waking up from being drunk***)

he's sobering up ahmuh´u puhduh´sutsung
SODA POP spuh´eveep (lit. ***cold drink***)
SOFT SPACE IN FRONT OF NEW-BORN BABY'S HEAD soangwu´kunt
SOFT, TENDER, KIND, GENTILE (refers to meat, cloth, skin, etc.)
1. paiyook´, paiyoo´kwai
always gets soft paiyuh´dung omeent
gets soft paiyuh´dung ont, paiyuh´du'ung
2. yoomee´kai (this word for ***weak*** can also mean ***soft*** in certain instances)
SOFTENING IT
1. soy´yuhk
2. -oasont, usunt
softening an elk hide paw duh´ee oasont
SOLDIER (Eng. soldier) soeets
SOLID (see ***stout***)
SOME, AMONG, IN
1. emun´tuh
It's snowing in the mountains noovu´waiuk kaiv´emunt
2. ma'awk´
SOMEPLACE
1. soo´vawnt
2. ma'aw´tuhk, ma'awn´
SOMETHING soo´kopeet
SOMETIMES (see ***anytime***)
SON (young adolescent years) toowuts
your son toowu'um
big son peah´toowai
his or her son toowung´
SON-IN-LAW moonuts
your son-in-law monuts´eem
my son-in-law moonuts´een
SORE (see ***pain***)
SORE, WOUND peku´, peku´du
pussy, infected peku´du awkaw
SORREL tseentuh´kawdum
SORRY
1. ***I didn't mean to do it*** nawvus oonee´ kuhdaik
2. ***I didn't mean to do it*** soo´moane wuhnchun
I didn't mean to say it soo´moaneuk wainun, soo´moa maing wuhnchun
3. ***I'm sorry*** uhtuh´aiunee
SORT OUT chuhu´vawcheuk
SOUL (see ***heart***)
SOUND NOISE toongwuv´ugai
SOUP (see ***mush***)
SOUR suhuhngk´ai
to taste sour suhuhng´kawmai
it's sour suhhung´kaiuk
SOUTH WIND petun´um
SPANK (see ***hit***)
SPARROW HAWK, AMERICAN KESTREL
Falco sparverius kuhdee´ nungkuts (lit. ***cut neck***)
SPARROWS (collectively) o´euts
SPEAR sekees´, chegees´
SPEARHEAD (this word applies to a stone spear point as well as a stone knife) teep
SPECIAL ow´tsees
SPECIES, KIND (noun) -muh´nee
the kind that flies yuhsuhd´uh muhnee
this kind echu´tuhnee.
turned out to be your kind eem edooud´uhmuhnee
like unto him ungud´u umuhnee
SPIDERS (collectively) kookwump´
SPILL oaw´koo-
spills it oaw´koomeent
SPIN (see ***turn around***)
SPIRIT (see ***heart***)
SPIRIT HELPER, FAMILIAR toohoo-
his guardian spirit too´hoo ung
SPLIT NOSE mooveets´ekee´
SPOON mentsee´ohots, mencho´ohots

horn spoon awp´ mencho´ ohots
SPOTTED too´enee nawvee´cheku (lit. ***black spots***)
SPOTTED podo´se-eku (lit. ***having spots like an Appaloosa***)
SPREAD OUT (to spread something out flat) sumu´
spread out sumu´kunt
what is spread out (blanket, tablecloth, etc.) sumup
saddle blanket kuvaw sumup (lit. ***horse blanket***)
SPREAD, SCATTER, STRETCH (to spread something out beyond its normal limits hence the extensions of scatter and stretch) chupuhd´, tsupuhts´
it's scattered chupood´ooekainuk
I'm scattering it chupood´ooenawkun
scattered chupood´ukweenkuk
2. mumum´ookwawk
SPRING (season)
1. tawmun
it's getting spring tawmu´deuk
2. ***it's getting green*** sawngwud´eook
SPRING (water) paw suhpee´tseech (lit. ***water coming out***)
SPRUCE *Picea engelmannii* and *pungens* munu oahomp (lit. ***sticker pine***)
SQUAW BUSH BERRIES ee´see, e'-ees´
SQUAWBUSH *Rhus trilobata* suhv, suh'uhv´
SQUEAK pinchoa´choy
SQUEAK MADE WHEN WALKING ON FROZEN SNOW kawng´wu
SQUEEZE IT, SMASH IT mawnchoo´kwenuk
SQUEEZE WITH FINGERS SEVERAL TIMES, TO KNEAD maio´cho
SQUIRREL, FLYING *Glaucomys sabrinus* oahon´ tawvawts (lit. ***pine squirrel***)
SQUIRREL, GRAY *Sciurus griseus* ung´kawchawn
SQUIRREL, RED *Tamiasciurus hudsonicus* ungkaw sekoots´ (lit. ***red squirrel***)
SQUIRREL, ROCK *Spermophilus variegatus* sekoots´
SQUIRREL, WHITE-TAILED ohon´ tawvawts (lit. ***pine squirrel***)
SQUIRT kwawpook´
STAB (see ***hit***)
STACK UP maw-huhn´ai (lit. ***to put weight upon***)
STALLION, STUD naw´uhkuhts
STAND ***to stop or stand while walking*** (singular) wuhnuh´
I'm standing wuhnai´un
stand right there mu´vusump ooneng´wuhn
to stand up from a sitting position wuh'wuh´nuh
to tell someone to stand up from a sitting position wunuhng´oa
to stand up for a cause wuhnuhnk´ai
(plural) wungwee´
for many to stand up from a sitting position wungwee´weuk
standing in a row nunup´aioo wungwee
many were standing wungwee´puhku
STARS pootseev´
START UP toongwu´vawghai (the word for ***sound*** and ***noise*** also refers to any engine or device that makes a noise when it starts up)
it wont start kaw toongwu´vawghai (lit. ***it wont sound***)
STAY (see ***sit***)
STEAL (to) yuh'uhngk´ee
stolen yuhngk´ukunt
STEAM (see ***vapor***)

STEEL (see ***iron***)
STEEP paiyaw´hunt (lit. ***wall-has***)
STEP tawngwun´chuhvaw, tuhdung´wachoovu
missed a step tawseech´oogweenk
STEPBROTHER (older) tuhdung´wuchuh pawveets´een (can add sister, mom, dad, etc.)
STERILE awveem´ tawpo´hunt
STICK (see ***wood*** and ***board***)
STICKERS, FUZZ (the very fine stickers on prickly pear fruit or the fuzz [scales] on a moth's wings) wuhsoov´, wuhsee´uv, wawseev´
STICKING UP, PEEKING OUT sootsee´
STIFF
1. hookwu´kai
2. chuhkwaw´kawd
3. tuhntsee´chouk
STILL, PLACID, MOTIONLESS, CALM, QUIET, PEACEFUL
1. aw´-
sit still aw´hawduh
2. soo
be good, sit still, be quiet soo´ninee
STINGING NETTLE *Urtica dioica* kwawsoo´ kwepump (lit. ***sting hitter***)
STINKBUG hookoo´vechuts
STINKING FEET putaw´kawv
STINKS
1. pono´ai
2. kwunai
STIR skwun
stir it sikwun´owuk
STOCKINGS, SOCKS
1. tawpup´
2. tawsuhngk´
3. taw´kenu (Eng. stocking)
4. tai-een´keets (Kanosh)
STOMACH sawwhay´awm
STONE (see ***rock***)
STOOP (to) poo´kwai
stooped over poo´kwunt
STOP, HALT
1. tuhdus´u kwaw
stop it here tuhdus´ kwou´teuk
stopped again tuhdus´kwupuhkais
2. kawduhk´ (lit. ***sits***)
STORE (Eng. store) stoo´u
STORY, LEGEND (see ***legends***)
STORY TELLER (one who relates stories) nawduh´kwaynuts
STOUT, SOLID tuhntsee´ku
stout horse toongkoo´kwawdum
STRAIGHT mookoont´
straight ahead toahoy´mookoont
STRANGER (see ***different***)
STRIKE (see ***hit***)
STRONG suh'uh´kunt
STRUTTING peow nengwoo´ukai (lit. ***being a big Indian***)
STUBBORN, OBSTINATE, DISOBEDIENT (see ***keep on***) nungkaw´ vait (lit. ***ears-no***)
STUCK, FASTENED, CLINGING (see ***held fast***) pawchaik´eku, pawtsai´eku, pawchaik
it's stuck pawchai´ekuk
clinging on the edge pawtsu´ kawdee
STUD (see ***stallion***)
STUMP (see ***root***)
STUNNED tapaw´see
I blacked out tapaw´sechun
SUCK, KISS pechee´, pechuh´ee
suck it pechuhng´wuk
SUDS sudonts´eev, sawduhnts´eev
SUFFOCATED soowaw tuhmaw´ukunt
SUGAR (see ***sweet***)
SUMMER tawts, tawtch
SUMMIT, CREST, HILLTOP wuhkawm´
SUN DANCE tawgoo´ wuhnee, tawhoo´wuhnee (lit. ***thirsty standing***)
SUNRISE tahvai´ mungwee´see

SUN, DAY tavaw´puhts, tawv
SUNDAY, SUNDAY SCHOOL (Eng. Sunday) Sawn´tay
SUNFLOWER *Helianthus annuus* huhkuhmp´, kawngoomp
SUNSET tahvai´yowk (lit. ***sun disappearing***)
SUPERIOR (see ***brave***)
SUPERNATURAL POWER (to have) poowu´hunt
SURE, POSITIVELY uhun´ovai
SURELY (see ***yea because***)
SUSPICIOUS (see ***doubting***)
SWAINSON'S HAWK *Buteo swainsoni*
1. kwununt´seets (lit. ***little eagle***)
2. undo´kwununts (lit. ***brown eagle***)
SWALLOW (to), DRINK yuh'uhk´ee
swallow it yuh'uhk´keuk
drink from me yuh'uhk´e vawts nuh´vuchuh
SWALLOW (unidentified bird of the swallow family) paw´su dokupeets
SWALLOW, BARN *Hirundo rustica* paw´su toakoytch
SWAMPY nawsoo´uduh tooweep (lit. ***sinking ground***)
SWEAR sengkwu´see
SWEAT tawkai´yai
I'm sweating tawkai´aiun
SWEEP IT whechoon´uk
SWEET, SUGAR peuv
SWEETCLOVER *Melilotus officinalis* peu´ whawnunump
SWIM nawvuk´uh nawvuck´ (from nawvuk´ ***wash***)
SWINGING
1. aiyoy
2. puhduh´duh
SWOLLEN pawngwuk, pamawk´wechuk (see ***round***)
SWORD (spear) chegees´
SYPHILIS
1. oko´pee
2. mookoo´pe yu'ai (Shivwits and Moapa)

— T —

TAIL kwusee´
TAKE (see ***get***)
TAKE IT BACK yah´kwaingwuk (compare ***bring***)
TAKE IT OFF, REMOVE IT tookween
take it off tookween´awk
taking it off chukwee´nai
TAKE, GET, ACQUIRE, BRING kuh'uh´, kuh´uk, kuh'uhk´, kwuh'uhk´
take it kuh'uh´uk
TALK, DISCUSS, CONFER umpaw´hai
speak up, say something nunum´pawhaw
to hear talking umpaw toongwu´vawghai
TALL, HIGH, LOUD, LONG pu'awn´
tall one pu'awn´tuh muhnee
singing loud pu'awn´e kai
long pu'awn´tuhnee, pu'awn´tuhd
TALLEST pa'aw´tuhmus, pa'awn´tuhm
TAMARISK, SALT CEDAR *Tamarix pentandra* spawngwup
TAME (see ***pet***)
TAN sunu´- (from the word for ***pine gum*** sunup, and its color after it has been chewed as chewing gum)
TANGLED na'aw´hawvuk
TANSY MUSTARD *Descurainia* awk
TANTRUM (kicking while lying down, like a baby does while crying) taiun´oogwee
TARANTULAS kawngeng´chohots
TASTE kawmud´
taste it kawmuk´engwuk
TATTOO
1. sawkhwaw´ nawvoa´up (lit. ***blue***

image)
2. sawkhwaw´ pooee´wu
3. nawvoa´ai (lit. ***image***)
4. too´munenum (lit. ***what you made black***)
TEAL (green-winged) Anas carolinensis oampee´ koonu´vuhts (lit. ***ochre sack***?)
TEAR (see ***rip***)
TEARS ya-hawp´ pooee´ nookwee. (lit. ***cry-eyes-running***), ya-haw´pooeem
TEASING, FOOLING (see ***bothering***)
1. sechung´wai
2. nawvus´
I'm just saying it (just joking) nawvus´ unaik
TEATS
1. pe'-eets´
2. pechuhp´ee
TIPI kawneev´, pawde'u kawneev (lit. ***elk skin house***)
TIPI POLES uhduv´
TELL (to) tuhn´neu
told it tuhneu´puhkunt, tuhneu´puhkaikw
I'm telling you tuhneunk´eoom
(plural) tuhntuhn´eu
TEN toahoa´ mawsuhng´wee
TENDER (see ***soft***)
TENDERLOIN (the meat on each side of the backbone) oontook´oov, oontook´
your tenderloin oontook´oom
TESTICLES chukaiv´oweem, chukweets
THANK YOU (see ***good***)
1. toahoy´uk (lit. ***good***)
2. ai´ee uk (lit. ***it's good***)
THAT'S ALL oo´nesump
THAT, IT, THOSE
1. (inanimate visible) mud, mud´u
like that one mud´u'tunee
2. (inanimate invisible) uhd´u, uhd, -u´du, -ud
that which I said uhd´u ai´kainun
it was like that uhduhru´kunt
3. -uk
what are you going to do with it? hun´euk?
give it to him ungud´owuk
here it is eyun´uk
THIGH
1. puhngku´voo
2. to'-oh´vum
THEM, THEY, THOSE mum, mauhm, -uhm
THEN -eepuhn
THERE
1. (visible) mu´vu, mu´vai
2. (invisible) oo´vai
THEREUPON, THEN, AT THAT TIME
1. oo´vaiuk
it happened then oo´vaiuk uneets
real soon, immediatley oovai´ukos
2. ai´tawng
THICK, BROAD (see ***broad chested***)
THIN
1. (pertaining to paper, string, etc.) tawkai´ nawpeets, tawkee´ nawpuhts´unee
2. (referring to string only) tseu´putsuhnee
THIN-LEAFED ALDER *Alnus tenuifolia* pawwhay´uv
THING, INSTRUMENT -nump (instrument or material with which or by which something is made or done)
axe tawvee´nump
THINGS, CLOTHES (see ***brush***)
1. mu'uv´
my things ma'awv´uhn
his things ma'awv´ oong ud
your things mu'uv´oom
2. mud´oowuv
THINK (to),
1. ai´kainee
I think it's that way uhduk´hunee

I wasn't thinking about anything kawmus´un ai´newainee
I was thinking it could be done nuh´udu maim´pai unee´uk
2. soomai´
I'm not thinking about anything kawchoon´ soomain´ewainee
sitting thinking soompaw'hawduhd
what I'm thinking nuhn´ee soomai´kain

THIRSTY tawkuh´ee, tawgoo´
THIS eench
I said this one echuh´unaik
this was the water pai´eench udu´puhku
THIS HIGH, THIS LONG, THIS SIZE evay, evay´tuhmuhnee
THIS ONE AND THAT ONE (from a song) ee´vee ai´vee
THIS PERSON (present, visible) eeng
THIS SIDE enunk, enunk´opawk, enunk´wup
THISTLE paw´tsengupeev
THORN munuv´
THREAD (see ***sinew***)
THREE pu'ai, paik, pu'ai´oonee
three of them pai´umuhnee
THRESH (to thresh out by stomping). This word is extended to mean ***shake out*** and ***wring*** in the sense that what is unwanted is done away with hoakoy´, mawhoy´choy, hoakotch´ uhoynawk´u
THROAT
1. pawkoym´
2.pawngween´ (Kaibab)
THROAT MUCOUS
1. yogwuv´
2. kuhchuv´
THROUGH
pass through there (telling another where to pass through, visable) mawpaw, mawpoo´
pass through over there, that way, through there oo´paw (invisable)
I'm coming through there oo´paw ompawn
pass through here ee´paw
come through here, this way yoo´pu, yuh´pu

THROW (to), tuhduv´ee
throw it tuhduv´euk
to throw something over yourself nawvaw´kai tuhduv´
THROW DOWN OR AWAY (to) (singular) wuhnai´
throw it down wuhnai´uk
throw them away (plural) chungwee´nuk, tsungwee´nuk
go throw it away chungwee´no-whaiuk.
THUMB mawtoa´hom
THUNDERBIRD (a modern term since Paiutes didn't have a thunderbird deity) oonoo´noo wetseech
THUNDER onoon´ooweench
TICK, WOOD TICK
1. mutuv´, mutaw´kitch
2. touv´ (lit. ***rabbit tick***) Shivwits
TIE, WRAP
1. ***to tie up*** tawpeech´
2. ***to wrap or tie a band or ribbon around something to hold it together*** wheechai´uh
what is wrapped around, band, cinch whechup´
belt naw´ whechup (lit. ***self-wrap***)
TIGHTENED huhkuhm´ukunt
it's tight wukuhm´ungkuk
TIRE, (Eng. tire) tai´u
TIRED
I'm tired kawchoo´unchun
I'm getting tired kawchoong´wuhnchun
TOBACCO *Nicotiana trigonophylla*
1. sakhwaw´ kwoup (lit. ***green smoke***)
2. tawmo´nump

TOE tawsuh´u
your toes tawsoom´
TOGETHER, BOTH, TWO
1. (referring to two others) nungwai´, nungwais´
both of them nungwaw´kos, nuwai´koos
2. (referring to yourself and another) mumais
TOILET kwechu´ kawn (lit. *excrement house*)
TOMAHAWK nengwoo´ kwepu´nump (lit. *Indian axe*)
TOMATILLO, WOLFBERRY *Lycium* suhnu´ oop (lit. *coyote berry*)
TOMORROW
1. tu'aik´
2. ee´chuhk
TONIGHT aw´tookwun
TOO (see *also*)
TOOTH tawngwump
your teeth tawngwum´
TOOTHPICK tawngwu´ scood´oonump
TOP, MESA, FLAT TOPPED tawkawk´, tuhkawk´
on top tawkaw uvawn
TOUCH mawpeek´
touch it mawvee´kuk
to touch you mawpeek´uvum
TOUGH (see *brave*)
TONGUE a-ho´uv
your tongue a-ho´um
TOWARDS -vawchuh (see *direction*)
towards you emee´ vawchuhk
towards him ungu´vawchuh
I'm looking at you emee´ vawchuhs puhnin´ee
looking at me nuh´vuchuhs puhni´nee
TOY keu´tenump (lit. *plaything*)
TRACK, FOOTPRINT nungwud´eku
TRADE na'aw´tuhkwung, naw'oo´tookwai (lit. *to pass each other*)
let's trade naw'onk´ ootoo´kwai vawdum
TRAIL, ROAD poa
roads povo´uhunt
TRAIN koonaw´ waikenu (lit. *fire wagon*)
TRANSPARENT, GLASS suhguhng´kai, suhhuhn´kawd
TRAVEL (see *walk*)
TRAVELING ALONG (plural) -meu
singing along kaw´meu
TRAVOIS uhduv´
TREE TRUNKS tawvus´ukoo wungwee (lit. *dry-standing*)
TREMBLING (see *shaking*)
TROTTING mawvoy´ungkwai
TROUT ungkaw´ pawguh´u (lit. *red fish*)
TRUE, TRUTH tooveets´
I'm telling the truth tooveets´unaik
is it true? tooveets´ u'?
TRUST (see *believe*)
TRUTHFUL (to speak the truth) tooveech´ aintch
TRY IT munuk´engwuk
TRYING, CAN HARDLY -muhsoo´ee
can hardly do it oonee´ muhsoo´ee
TULE, BULRUSH *Scirpus* sawmpeev
TUMBLEWEED *Salsola iberica*
1. mawntee´nu munuv
2. noopu´nump (lit. *rolling bush*)
TURKEY (Eng. turkey) tuh´keets, tuh´kee
TURN AROUND (to move in a circular direction as you turn around, like turning around in a car) noy´yaw, noyu´
I'm turning it around noyun´chuk
TURN AROUND, REVOLVE, SPIN (to turn around while standing in one place)
1. kweno´
to command to turn around

kwenoong´oa
he's/she's spinning kwenoong
2. komee´ (a shortened or slang form of kweno´)
turn it around komee´ unee´teuk

TURN OVER (to be turned on ones belly or side; animate and inanimate) oy´metuhk
turn it on its belly, put it face downward oy´metuhk wukwuhts
lying on one's belly oy´metuhk awvee

TURTLE, DESERT TORTOISE *Gopherus agassizii*
1. aiyuv´, aiyu´vuhts
turtle who used to be aiyahv´ookaip
2. pekai

TWENTY FIVE CENTS (Eng. two bits) too´veets

TWINS numunk´ooseng

TWISTING IT, TURNING IT chukoyn´o kweenkuk
I'm twisting it (used when twisting a hide) chukwee´unuk

TWO wa'ai´uhnee, wa'ai´oonee, wa'ai´, wawk´

— U —

UGLY, AWFUL, DANGEROUS
1. yah´vuhnee, yahv´eeng
getting ugly yahv´eeng
toowud´uhnee (this word can also mean ***dangerous*** in the same manner as ***ugly*** in English)
2. ***not pretty*** kaw peun´ungwu

UNCLE, GREAT UNCLE
paternal uncle ain
maternal uncle kootseen, koots, hoakoyn, oakween

UNDER, UNDERNEATH (see ***below***)

UNDERSTAND, KNOW, LEARN poochoo´chookwai, pooch´ukwai
I don't understand kawchoo´kwun poochoo´choo kwawngwai
what do you know? empuh´uk poochoo´ukwai?

UNDULATING, ROLLING (as in rolling hills) tsoakoam´, soakoam´

UNEVEN, NOT LEVEL, AT AN ANGLE skeemp´took, sekeem´etook

UNFAMILIAR (something you haven't seen for a long time and do not recognize) wuhgai´ook, wuhkai´ook

UNFEIGNED (see ***openly***)

UNLOAD mumowm´ engkwuk´w, mumum´ekwuk

UNRIPE, RAW sawngkawd

UNTANGLE
untangle it chupuhn´ekeen kuhuk

UNTIE, UNDO, TURN LOOSE (to) sitoop´, sitoop´ungkwai
untie him or her sitoop´ungwung, sitoop´ung

UNWRAP mawduh´penup

UP toohoon´toh, tuh´

UPON (see ***on***)

UPRAISED HANDS muntsaw´

URINATE se-ee´
I haven't urinated yet kauh´suh se-eeng´wais
I'm going to go urinate se-ee´ whaivaw´neun
urinated on himself nawsee´ku

URINE se-eep´

US, WE (speaker and hearer) nuhm´ee, tdum
you and I tum´evuhts

UTAH (Eng. Utah) yoo´tu

— V —

VAGINA
1. wuhhump´ee, wuhguhts´, wuhkuh´
2. tompo´kweev (the badger's way of saying vagina in a legend)

VAINLY, FUTILELY, UNAVAILING,

UNYIELDING
uh-´
to futilely get mad uh´ nungai´etseek
VALLEY (big valley with mountains on each side) paw´noouhunt
VALLEY, HOLE, DIP, DENT, DEPRESSION
(any bowl shaped depression) koyyoa´koytch
VANILLA too´kwawcheech
VAPOR, STEAM, HEAT WAVES
awsoa-
the heat waves of fire na'aip´awsoa´kwaiv, na'aip´ oahoa´hoy
VARIOUS (see ***separately***)
VERY (see ***true***)
VICKS spuh´eyunts
VIRGIN yoho´nait (lit. ***never had intercourse***)
VIRTUOUS aw´tai peyung (lit. ***good mother***)
VISOR ON CRADLEBOARD moopu´chu
VOMIT pevee´tunee
I'm vomiting pevee´tuneun
VULTURE (turkey vulture) wekoomp´uts, wek´w

— W —

WAD SOME PAPER UP INTO A BALL
(to) mawmun´tsoho-aw mawmun´chohouk
WAGER, BET too´kwu
WAGON (Eng. wagon) wai´kenu
WAIL toodoo´ekee ya-haw´num
WAIST, LOWER BACK pechok´wee
hairy waist poo-oo´whechok
WAIT
1. mawnchoo´aikai
wait for me munchoo´aikayn
wait for him mawnchoo´aik ung
2. ***not yet, still not*** kawchoos´
WAKE UP, AWAKEN
1. tawpuhn´ee
wake up again tawpuhn´esu
woke up again tawpuhn´e kuntus
2. ***wake up*** puhneng´oa
WALK, TRAVEL, GO pakhai´, pa-hai´nee
I'm walking pa-hai´un
walking pakhaing´oowai
I'm going to travel pa-haing´ kwayvaw´nin
I'm going to go away nuh pa-hain´ee kwayvawnin, pa-hai´ne kwayvawnee
walking around on foot numpaw´ va-hai´nee
a walker pa-hai´chum
WALKING AROUND DOING, MOVING ABOUT DOING
chasing around or going all over from place to place -vuhduh´ee
going about doing oonee´vuhduhee
WALL, SIDE, SLOPE paiyaw´, paiuv´ (this word can refer to any kind of a wall such as a cliff, the sky, etc.)
house wall kawnee´paiyahuhk
WANT (see ***like***)
WAR BONNET wuhsee´u kai´chu-hots (lit. ***feather hat***)
WAR PAINT oampee´, oamp
WAR nawhoo´kwee (lit. ***to shoot reciprocally***)
WARBLER, MYRTLE *Dendroica coronata* toanchoa´noych
WARM yoowaw´dai
make him warm yoowai´utee mung
WART chuhuts´
WASH, SWIM, BATHE
1. nawvuk´
washing up nawvu´chuhaw
2. (Eng. wash) waw´see
WASHAKIE wuh´saikeek

WASHBASIN
1. moa′-oh´ vawduhge nump (lit. ***hand washing thing***)
2. nawvu´duhge nump (lit. ***washing thing***) Koosharem
3. nawvu´duhge ohots (lit. ***washing bowl***) Koosharem
4. nawvuck´enump (lit. ***washing thing***)

WATCH OUT, BEWARE yah´ puhnekaik´
WATER paw, paw´su
WATER BABY (a mythical water being the size of a baby) paingu´peets
WATER CRESS *Nasturtium officinale* pawmuhmp´
WATERFALL pawsodo´do
WATER HOLE, RAIN TANK (a catch basin in a rock)
1. peku´voats
2. paw enaw´hawdee (lit. ***water-in-sitting***)

WATER JUG oachuts´, oatch´, oats´
my water jug oachawn´
WATER MELON (Eng. melon) maw´dunts
WATER SNAKE paw´ toho´uv
WAVE YOUR HAND (to), mawntsu´vai, mawnchaw´vai
waving your hand mawnchaw´doy
WAY, PATH, MANNER, THIS WAY poo´paw
that's the way it's done poopawk´tuhkain
WE, US, OUR
1. nuhm´ee
2. (dual) tdum´
3. (three or more) tdung´w

WEAK, SOFT (see ***soft***)
1. yoomee´kai
one who is weak yoomee´kawduhm
2. ***not strong*** kaw suh′uh´ait

WEAN pechuh´mup
WEAR (see ***put it on***)
WEARING OUT, RAGGED (see ***ragged***) waing
it's wearing out waing´wuhchuk
WEASEL pawvee´tseets
WEAVE, BRAID (to weave a rug, basket or hair) sevo´kawdo
WEIGHTY (see ***heavy***)
WELL DONE (to cook something well done) koapuh´chu-haik´u
cook it well done koapeech´ukaikeuk
WEST tahvai´yowk engwee´tuhk (lit. ***sunset direction***)
WEST WIND paw´num
WESTERN YARROW *Achillea millefolium* oychu´ kwawseev (lit. ***squirrel tail***)
WET pawchuk´weku
is it wet? pawchuk´we kaiuduk?
WHAT
1. hunee´, unee´
what are you doing? hun´eku?
what are you going to do? hun´evuts? hun´evu?
what did he do to you? huneng´wuhchungum?
what did you say? hun´eaik?
what did he say? hun´eung aik?
what did I say? hun´eun aik?
what happened? hun´engkwunt?
what are you thinking? huneuk´eunu? huneuk´ kaweneu?
what do you say? what do you say about it? what do you want to do? huneevut´seaik?
what should we do? hun´ee vawdum?
2. eempuh´? eemp´?
what is that? eempuhdai´?
what do you say (want)? eempu´u aik?
what is it? eempuh´uhd?

WHAT IS THE NAME? unineeu´hunt?

what is your name? unineeu´hunt uhm?

WHAT KIND? WHAT SORT? WHICH? WHO?
eneents´? (animate)
what kind are you? een´udain?
whom? which ones? eneeng´?
what kind? een´udai?
maybe it's some kind, it might be something soov enee´sump
2. hawd´o udu? (inanimate)
what kind of car does he have? hawd´o udu awdum´peid uhunt?
3. haw´tunee? (Koosharem)
What kind are you? haw´tainum udai?

WHAT SIZE? HOW BIG? huvai´tuh muhnee?

WHAT'S HIS NAME, WHATCHA-MACALLEM
uhng´kwai

WHAT'S THE MATTER? hun´eng?
what's the matter with you? hun´eng wuhchu?
what's the matter with it? hu´neng wuhchuk?

WHAT'S ON YOUR MIND? huneud´onee eem?

WHEN? hunok´w?

WHEEL yoo'-oo´uk (from yoo'-oo´ *leg*)

WHERE?
1. hu´vu?
where? hu´vawnt?
where? hu´vawntuh?
where is he? hu´vawngw?
where are you? u-hu´vaw ninee?
2. ai´tawk (to ask where something or somebody went after they disappeared suddenly)
where did it disappear? aitawk´?
where is it then? aitawk´oovai?
where did he disappear? aitawng´ wuhchung?
where is he? ai´tawng oong wus´oong?
3. oovai?
wheres your pair? nawvuh´um uhd oo´vai?

WHERE ARE YOU GOING?
1. haw´do kwainik´?
2. haw´pawchaw?

WHICH? (see *what kind*) awhaw´duh? haw´duh? hawd?
which side? hu´nunkwup?
which way? haw´paw?
which one? awhawd oodoo´ai?

WHIP (see *hit*)

WHIP-POOR-WILL OR COMMON POOR-WILL
Caprimulgus ridgwayi or *Phalaenoptilus nuttallii*
pawnu´hoytch

WHIRLING koodoo´doo

WHIRLPOOL wekweenk´oopaw

WHIRLWIND, GHOST unoo´peets

WHISKERS, BEARD monchov´ monchok´
your whiskers moncho´um

WHISKEY (Eng. whiskey) wee´sekee

WHISPER
1. oku´soa mai
2. awk´so umpawhai

WHISTLE (a musical instrument) koosoo´kwee nump

WHISTLE (to whistle with the mouth) koosoo´kwe

WHITE EARTH PAINT oaveemp´

WHITE INDIAN Nengwoo´ Mawduh´kawts (lit. ***Indian-American***)

WHITE MAN hai´ko (of Mojave derivation and only used at Moapa, Pahrump, Las Vegas and among the Chemehuevis). (See ***American***)

WHITE SPINED CLARET CUP HEDGEHOG *Echinocereus melanacanthus* ovu´gawv

WHITE TAILED DEER chigoos´, chegoop´, chegoots´
WHITE TAILED SQUIRREL (found in the Kaibab mountains) ohon´ tawvawts
WHITE tosaw´hawd
white one tosaw´hawdum
WHITTLE weuhd´u
WHITTLED STICK (a personal name) Taioo´soov
WHO? (see ***what kind***) ung? ung´ai?
who is it? ung uhdai´?
WHY? hun´ehu?
WIDE, BROAD ungwaw´no
wide one ungwu´nud
it's wide ungwawn´tuhnee
WIFE pengwu-´
my wife pengwun
to have a wife pengwu´hunt
WIGGLE pekweech´ookoy
WIGGLE THE PELVIS IN SEX (to), HUMPING wayno´mee
WILD ONION *Allium*
1. koongkuv´ (Koosharem)
2. kwechus´eev
WILD PARSLEY *Ligusticum porteri* pawkoov´, pawgoov´
WILD PEPPERMINT *Mentha piperita* and *canadensis* pawkoa´nunump, pawwhaw´nunump
WILD RASPBERRY *Rubus idaeus* nuhaw´ wunawtump (lit. ***mountain sheep penis***)
WILD ROSE *Rosa woodsii* seump´eev, cheump´eev
WILD RYE *Elymus triticoides* wawv´
WILDCAT tookoo´puhts
WILLOW *Salix exigua* kawnuv´
WILSON SNIPE *Capella gallinago* koeet´
WIN, BEAT (see ***kill***) kwawng´w, kwaw-oong´
WIND, BLOWING nuhud´
starting to blow nuhu´deent
WINDBREAK kwuhtok´weuveung (lit. ***to head off***)
WINE, LIQUOR uhvuh´upaw (lit. ***bad water***)
WING we'kee´vu, we'keev´
WINK, ONE EYED onchok´
looking with one eye onchok´we vuhneku
WINNOWER, ROASTING TRAY
1. tawkoy´oa
2. poowu´nump
WINTER, AGE tom, to'-om´
how old are you? huno´paiuk toamuhnk´ee? (lit. ***how many winters are you?***)
how old is he? huno´paiuk toamuhng´kawduhm?
WINTER-FAT, WHITE SAGE *Eurotia lanata* pawvee´cheev
WIPE IT CLEAN wawtuh´chuk, wawtoo´tsuk
WIPE mawduhts´, maw'o´nai
wipe it mawduh´chuk
what you wiped maw'un´um
wipe the snot moopee´kee mawd
wipe my snot moopeek´ee mawun´
WIRE (Eng. wire) wai´u
WISE (see ***smart***)
WISH (see ***like***)
WITCH DOCTOR (one who uses his supernatural powers to do evil to others) nuhntuh´ku (Moapa)
WITH (see ***and***)
1. emuk´ (inanimate)
with this eenchuh´ awmuhuk
2. -ungwu, -engwu
with the dog sawdeets´ ung ungwu
with whom? eenee´ eng´wu?
WITHOUT, NOT HAVING -ait
without a home kaw kawnee´ait
not having school kaw school´e kawngwait
WITHOUT RELATIONS tuhduh´ukuhts, tuhduh´ukuhts

kaieng´wait
a person with no relations tuh´duhaits
WOLF
1. kwetoo´unuv (lit. ***master wolf***)
2. peah´suhnuv (lit. ***big coyote***)
3. ***God*** (the wolf is associated with God among the Southern Paiute) Toovuts
WOLFBERRY *Lycium andersonii* or *Lycium torreyi* oo-oop´
WOMAN, LADY mumowts´
women mumowm
WOOD, FIREWOOD, STICK kookwup´
WOODPECKER (collectively) oavee´ toapoa´neench. (lit. ***wood pecker?***)
WOOD TICK (see ***tick***)
WORK (Eng. work) wuh´ukai
WORM toowee´ toho´uv (lit. ***earth snake***)
WORN OUT (see ***ragged***)
WOULD (see ***could***)
WOUND (see ***sore***)
WRAP (see ***tie*** and ***coil***) mawhoan´tuhvuk
WRECKED (see ***accident***)
WRINGING IT OUT (see ***thresh***)
1. moahoy´chengwuk, moahoy´cheoo´wengwuk
2. wekweech´oonaiuk (lit. ***wringing the water out by twisting with a stick***)
WRINKLED (to sit on something and wrinkle it) tawsu´mungkuhk
WRINKLED FACE tsaw´kovuku
WRIST mungwee´chohom
WRITE (to) po'-oh´
what is written po'-ohp´
he is writing mung po'-ohd´
WRONG ONE (see ***different***)´

— Y —

YAMPA, WILD CARAWAY *Perideridia gairdneri* yump
YEA BECAUSE, FORASMUCH, SURELY, DOUBTLESS
(An expression used in affirming something that someone else might have had doubts about or expressing something that should have happened.)
tihdee´yung, tuh´deyungw, tuhdee´yung whaiyuh
surely! make him sit down tuhdee´yung kawduh´teung
doubtless you were going to say something aing´oompawtsaing tuhdee´yungw
YEARLING DEER yuhkoots´
YELL, HOLLER, SHOUT
1. t*o cry out in fear* kwawdu´vai
2. ***to shout*** wawung´ee
YELLOW o-aw´kawdu, o-aw´
YELLOW JACKET whechun´ukawmoont
YES
1. uh'-uhng´, uh'-uh´
2. huhvuh´ (Moapa)
YESTERDAY kuh'ung´
YOU
1. eem, uhm
your turn emee´ kwin
2. huhm (Moapa)
YOUNG MEN (in the teens) ai´vum
YOUNGER BROTHER chukaits´
YOUNGEST, LAST
last daughter penu´pawchoom
youngest daughter penu´puhts
YOUR (see ***you***)
YOURS oodoo´unum
YOURSELF, JUST YOU emee´sump
YUCCA, NARROW-LEAF *Yucca utahensis* and probably *baileyi.* chumuv´eep
YUCCA *Yucca baccata* oos´eev
stalk of the yucca ovweep´

IDIOMS

Webster's dictionary classifies an idiom as "an expression in the usage of a language, that is peculiar to itself either in grammatical construction or in having a meaning that cannot be derived as a whole from the conjoined meanings of its elements." The following examples do not have any English equivalents and are therefore easier to list with the Indian word first, followed by an explanation of it's meaning.

TOOMEE´
: A woman's child will cry a lot when the mother is expecting another baby. This condition is called Toomee´.

MUNUH´KEE
: This word describes a healing practice wherein the index finger is stuck down a baby's throat to depress a lump of mucus. This practice is explained under beliefs.

TOOMU´KUNT
: This word refers to being roasted under the ground if discussing meat or plants, but concerning women it refers to a practice that Paiute women followed after delivering a baby. They would lie upon a protecting layer of sand over a heated bed of rocks to stimulate blood circulation. This practice is discussed under Paiute beliefs.

PAWTAWNG´
: The noise made when a falling object lands.

CHUHNGUD´
: For a smell to stick with you.

TAWKOY´VOOP
: For another to press down on a pregnant woman's belly, from behind, to aid her in giving birth.

KWOEEM´UHNG, KWOEE´ TUHMAI´UNG
: A practice wherein a disobedient child is placed in some thick smoke to induce him to mind.

PAWNOA´WENG, PAWNAW´OWAY
: A practice wherein a disobedient child is placed in the snow to help induce him to mind.

TAWVUT´SEKAIU, TAWVUTS´EAI
: The feeling that a two- to three-month-old baby has when it senses its mother has been unfaithful. As a child gets older it becomes stronger and no longer cries in such circumstances. This word doesn't apply when the father is unfaithful.

EXPRESSIONS

Expression of ***appraisal***, ayyyyk, (a drawn out sound).
Expression of being ***afraid***, uhddow´.
Expression of ***fear*** peculiar to the Shivwits, uhduh´duh.
Expression of ***pain***, uddow´, unow´.
Expression of being ***cold***, uh yuh´.
Expression of being ***burned***, uddee´, awdduh´.
Expression of ***surprise***, aik´kookwai.
Expression given as a result of being ***teased***, utump´unee.
Expression of ***repulsiveness***, uhk.
Expression used with children and babies to warn them of something ***repulsive*** like a messy diaper, kuh.
Expression similar to the English ***oh oh*** and ***whoops***, uhvuhs´, uhvuh´skway.
Expression of ***wonderment*** and sometimes ***fear***, muh´ee, uhmuh´cc, uhmuh´eyu, uhmuhee´kway.
Expression of the ***wonderment of something very cute***, muheyuhn´kuhts.

COUNTING

Many people believe that American Indians were limited in their ability to count. Anyone familiar with Indian languages knows this limitation to be a fallacy. W. C. Eels in his *Number Systems of the North American Indians* studied many North American and Eskimo languages and demonstrated that most could count higher than many people thought. On page 208 he states:

> *The Indians of the eastern United States who stand comparatively high intellectually, could use their numerals to 10,000 and their systems were such as to admit of indefinite expansion, one billion for instance being expressed as 1,000 x 1,000 x 1,000. The Winnebagoes are said to use their numerals as high as one million. Indefinite and countless numbers they represent by the terms "leaves on the trees," "stars of the heavens," "blades of grass on the prairie," "sand on the lake shore." The Crows do not count above a thousand, as they say honest people have no use for higher numerals.*

When the following Southern Paiute counting system is studied it will be seen that this system is also designed so that numbers beyond 1,000 could be used if necessary. I never asked if this was done and now no one is left alive with the knowledge to answer this question. In the natural world of the Paiutes where they had no money they would seldom have the need to count very high, but they could if the need arose.

1. Soo´ee, soo´kos, soo´yus.
2. Wai, wawk, wa-ai´oonee (lit. ***two of them***).
3. Pai, paik, pu'ai´oonee (lit. ***three of them***).
4. Wachuhng´wee.
5. Munuh´kee (lit. ***all***) referring to all five fingers of one hand.
6. Navai´.
7. Navaik´ uvawt (lit. ***over six***).
8. Wa'ong´ wachuhng´wee (lit. ***two fours***).
9. Soowaw´ toaho´ mawsoo´weinee (lit. ***nearly all the fingers***).
10. Toaho´ mawsoo´weinee (lit. ***all the fingers***).

On all numbers ending from 11 to 19 either of the following words may be used on the end of the number: speeng´wuhunt, or speengk´oowuhunt. This word means ***to stick out, to be over, above,*** or ***beyond,*** and refers to numbers beyond ten to the number nineteen. These words also refer to numbers from one to nine following twenty, thirty, forty, and so on. Another word that is sometimes used instead of speengk´oowuhunt is puhu´hunt (lit. ***put with it***). For example one hundred and ten is is sooko moa´ toaho mawsuh puhu´hunt (lit. ***one hand and all the fingers put with it***).

11. Toaho mawsoo´weinee soo´kos speengk´oowuhunt (lit. ***all the fingers and one beyond***).
12. Toaho mawsoo´weinee wawk speengk´oowuhunt (lit. ***all the fingers and two beyond***).
13. Toaho mawsoo´weinee paik speengk´oowuhunt (lit. ***all the fingers and three beyond***).
14. Toaho mawsoo´weinee wachuhng´wee speengk´ oowuhunt (lit. ***all the fingers and four beyond***).
15. Toaho mawsoo´weinee munuhk´ee speengk´oowuhunt (lit. ***all the fingers and five beyond***).
16. Toaho mawsoo´weinee navaik speengk´oowuhunt (lit. ***all the fingers and six beyond***).
17. Toaho mawsoo´weinee navaik uvawt speengk´oowuhunt (lit. ***all the fingers and over six beyond***).
18. Toaho mawsoo´weinee´ wa'ong´ wachuhng´we speengk´oowuhunt (lit. ***all the fingers and two fours beyond***).
19. Toaho mawsoo´weinee soowaw toaho mawsoo´weinee speengk´oowuhunt (lit. ***all the fingers and nearly all the fingers beyond***).
20. Wa'u´ mawsoo´weinee or wa-ai mawsoo´weinee (lit. ***two tens***).
21. Wa'u mawsoo´weinee sookos speengk´oowuhunt (lit. ***two tens and one beyond***).
22. Wa'u mawsoo´weinee wawk speengk´ oowuhunt (lit. ***two tens and two beyond***).
23. Wa'u mawsoo´weinee paik speengk´ oowuhunt (lit. ***two tens and three beyond***).

24. Wa'u mawsoo´weinee wachuhng´wee speengk´ oowuhunt (lit. ***two tens and four beyond***).
25. Wa'u mawsoo´weinee munuhke speengk´oowuhunt (lit. ***two tens and five beyond***).
26. Wa'u mawsoo´weinee navaik speengk´oowuhunt (lit. ***two tens and six beyond***).
27. Wa'u mawsoo´weinee navaik uvawt speengk´oowuhunt (lit. ***two tens and over six beyond***).
28. Wa'u mawsoo´weinee wa'ong wachuhng´we speengk´oowuhunt (lit. ***two tens and two fours beyond***).
29. Wa'u mawsoo´weinee soowaw toaho mawsoo´weinee speengk´ oowuhunt (lit. ***two tens and nearly all the fingers beyond***).
30. Pai mawsoo´weinee (lit. ***three tens***).
31. Pai mawsoo´weinee soo´kos speengk´ oowuhunt (lit. ***three tens and one beyond***).

From one to nine in the thirties to the nineties is the same as shown above for the twenties.

40. Wachuhng´wee mawsoo´weinee (lit. ***four tens***).
50. Munuhk´ee mawsoo´weinee (lit ***five tens***).
60. Navaik mawsoo´weinee (lit ***six tens***).
70. Navaik uvawt mawsoo´weinee (lit. ***seven tens***).
80. Wa'ong wachuhng´wee mawsoo´weinee (lit. ***eight tens***).
90. Soowaw toaho mawsoo´weinee mawsoo´weinee (lit. ***nine tens***).

The word for ten (toaho mawsoo´weinee) becomes the word for one hundred when preceded with a number from one to ten (soo´ee toaho mawsoo´weinee). A much shorter way of saying one hundred is to say soo´ko moa (lit. ***one hand***). This is sometimes abbreviated to soo´ moa. I once heard the word soo´yus mawsuh (one finger) used for one hundred but it doesn't seem to be well known today. This might have come from the Ute sign language where one dollar (one hundred pennies) is made by placing the right extended index in the palm of left hand. In expressing numbers beyond one hundred, like one hundred and one, give the number for one hundred and then the word for one.

I didn't ask for the word one thousand when I had the opportunity, but it would probably be a ***hundred hundreds*** unless the Utah and Arizona Paiutes had their own word like the Chemehuevis.

100. Soo´ee toaho mawsoo´weinee (lit. ***one and all the fingers***). Soo´ko moa (lit. ***one hand***).
200. Wawk toaho mawsoo´weinee (lit. ***two and all the fingers***). Wawk´o moa (lit. ***two hands***).
300. Paik toaho mawsoo´weinee (lit. ***three and all the fingers***).

400. Wachuhng´wee toaho mawsoo´weinee (lit. ***four and all the fingers***).
500. Munuh´kee toaho mawsoo´weinee (lit. ***five and all the fingers***).
600. Navaik toaho mawsoo´weinee (lit. ***six and all the fingers***).
700. Navaik uvawt toaho mawsoo´weinee (lit. ***over six and all the fingers***).
800. Wa'ong wachuhng´wee toaho mawsoo´weinee (lit. ***two fours and all the fingers***).
900. Soowaw toaho mawsoo´weinee toaho mawsoo´weinee (lit. ***almost all the fingers and all the fingers***).

MOAPA, LAS VEGAS, & CHEMEHUEVI COUNTING

These bands counted the same except for seven, eight, nine, ten, and one hundred.

1. Soo´ee
2. Wa-ai
3. Pa-ai
4. Wachuh´
5. Munuhk´
6. Navai
7. Mookwis
8. Na'awnts´yoogwee
9. Yooweep
10. Mawsuh´
100. Mawsoo´weinee mawsuh
1,000. Chawpeed´eun

Sentences

The following sentences were recorded by me in the 1950s to help understand sentence structure. They are presented here to help the reader do the same thing. The majority of these examples were given to me by my wife, Doris Kanosh.

That's the way it is uhdu´vuhts
Forget them naw suhmai´um
I'm not going to do it kawchoo´ oonee´vungwainee
I'm just asking nawvus´oon tooveeng´oongwu
Where are you going? eem haw´pawmpawnt?
I can't do it kawchuh´koon oonee´vungwainee
I'm not going to do it kawtsuk´un oonee´vungwainee
What are you sitting there thinking about? hun´eu kawdee´neu?
Where do you think you're going? haw´pawm pawneudu?
How do I sing? hun´eun kai?
Are you going to be here? evahn evaw´neudu?
Let me kiss you pechuh´upawm
Will you be my wife? nuh´nee udu pingwud´ oo vawnee?
Where does your mother live? (where is your mother's land?) hu´vu peum tooveep´uh ugunt?
Where is your father's house? hu´vu mooum´ kawnee´gunt?
You say that because you're going to get mad nungai´evuts aing´oomee
Do it just like this munee´sumpuk
Do it like this munee´uk
Still sitting here evai´unees unee´unee kawdee
That's what I said mai´nuhgwaik
Doing nothing but walking around nawvus´ pawhai´negu
What are you thinking about? hunuk´eunu?
I'm not thinking kawchoon´ soomai´newainee
Are you tired? kawchoo´unchudu?
I do not drink nuh kaw eveeng´wait
I'm sick nawhum´ee unchun
Is it hot? kuhchuhng´euduk u'?
I'll do it oonee´umpawn
Those two are cussing each other (dual) nunung´umai uhm
They're cussing each other (more than two) nunung´umai kaioom
Those two are arguing nawvuch´umai oom
More than two are arguing nawvuch´umai kaioom
I never saw him kaw puhnee´u wupawn
Maybe he's around here soov evu oonin´eech
That's what you're going to eat tuhkaw´vawnum
A car's coming down awdum´peid pununk´wawhai
Do you want a drink? evee´oom pawd u'?

His name oong´wai neum´
God our father God mooun´um
In Jesus's name oongwai Jesus neu´vawntuhk
To see what he could do puhnee´kai whaingwuhts´ee
Get me some water pai´nun kuhkain
Strangers are not there koomunts´ee kaw awvung´ wu
Joe has blue eyes Joe sawwhaw´ pooee´kunt
I have blue eyes nuh´ sawwhaw´ pooee´kunt
Joe has big feet Joe peow´ numpaw´hunt
I have big feet nuh´ peow numpaw´hunt
I have a big head nuh´ peow´ totsee´kunt
He has a big head mung peow´ totsee´kunt
It's his house mungai udu 'kawn
My house nuh´nai kawn
Our house (dual) nuhmuh´ee kawn
Our house (three or more) tdung´we kawn
Our house (dual) tdum´ee kawn
Their house mawmuh kawn
Your house uhmuh´ee kawn
She's his daughter mung´ai pawtsuh´ung
She's my daughter nuh´nai pawtsuhn´
She's their daughter mawmuh pawtsuh´ung
Our daughter (dual) tdum´ee pawts
Our houses tdung´wee kawng kawn
Their houses mawmuh kawng kawn
I have a cat nuh kedeek´ee voongkoo´kwunt
I have a horse nuh´ kuvaw voongkoo´kwunt
I have some horses nuh´ kuvaw´ voongkoong´ookwunt
I have some babies nuh´ pe´soang´ookwunt
I have a knife nuh´ we-eets´ekunt
I have a lot of knives nuh´ awvawn´utuhnee weets´ekunt
I have two knives nuh´ wawk´w we-eets´ekunt
He has two knives mung wawk´w we-eets´ekunt
I have a hat nuh´ kai´choho kwunt
Get my purse kuhuhnk´kuhukun purse´enud
Get your purse kuh´uk purse´ eem ud, purse´eem ud kuhuh´
Get our purse kuh´uk purse´ee tdum ud
Get his purse kuh´uk purse´ee ung ud
Get their purse kuh´uk purse´ee um ud
Go get my purse purse kuhuhnk´kuh kwaing oan, purse´een ud kuhuhnk´kuh kwaingwu
Go get your purse purse´ eemud kuhuh´kwaingwu
Go get his purse purse´ee ung ud kuhuh´kwaingwu
Go get our purse purse´ee tdum ud kuhuh´ kwaingwu

Go get my shoes pawtsun´ud kuhuh´kwaingwu
Go get my scissors scissors een´ud kuhuhnk´kuh kwaingwu, scissorn kuhuhnk´ kuh
It's getting dark tookwud´ eoompawn´euk
It's getting noon toahoy´ tahvai eoompawn´euk
I'm getting tired kawtsoong´oom paw´neun
Are you getting tired? kawtsoong´oom paw´neud u'?
Are you getting old? naw´poodekee udu?
Are you getting sleepy awpuh´eng wuh´ee udu?
Are you getting hungry? tuhkuh´eai aydu?
Go home! paiay´kwaing oa!
They're going home (dual) paiyuh´kwaium
Go home! (more than two) pawnaw´kwaiuk
I'm going home nuh paiyuh´kwaivawnt
Let's go home (dual) paiyoo´kwai vawdum
Let's go home (more than two) pawnaw´ok kwai vawdung, pawnaw´kwai vawdum
We're going home (dual) nuhm paiyuh´kwai vawntuhm
We're going home (more than two) nuhm panaw´ok kwai uhmpawnt´uhm
Let's go home vuh´dum paiyuh´kwaivu
Go get me some water puain´kuhuhnk´ kuh kwaing´oan
Here's your water you asked for eyun´uk paain´ eem ud
When are we going home? huhnok´o tdung panaw´ok kwaivawnee?
One man soo´yus tungwuts
Two men wai´yuhnee tungwuts´eng
Make her cry yawhaw´teung
Don't make her cry kawtsung´ yawhaw´teup
Just let her cry yawhaw´vawsump ung
Let her stay kawduh´vung
Just let her stay kawduh´vawsump ung
Let her eat tuhkaw´vungw
Let her play keyu´vung
Feed her, make her eat tuhkaw´teung
Let her sleep awpuh´evung
Where have you been, was it Cedar? hu´vaichu paiyoong, Cedar vai u'?
Is she asleep? awpuh´eudung u'?
Nothing, just standing listening nawvus´ nungkawng´ wuhnee´ku
She's going to eat tuhkaw´ whai vawnee ung
I'm going to eat nuh tuhkaw´whai vawnee
They're going to eat mum tuhkaw´ whai vawnee um
I'm going home nuh paiay´kwaim pawnee, nuh paiay´kwai vawnee
She's going home mung paiyoong´ pawnee, mung paiyoo´kwai vawnee
I have younger brothers nuh chukaits´eng ookwunt
I have younger sisters nuh numeents´eng ookwunt

I have a head nuh totsee´kunt
I have a daughter nuh pawtsuh´kunt
I have some daughters nuh pawtsuhng´oo kwunt
We have daughters nuhm pawtsuhng´oo kwunt uhm
They have daughters mauhm pawtsuhng´oo kwunt uhm
We have cats nuhm kedee´kee poongkoong´ oo kwunt uhm
We have horses nuhm kavaw´ poongkoong´oo kwunt uhm
We have a house nuhm kawnee´ kunt uhm
We have a knife nuhm we-eet´sekunt uhm
We have a baby nuhm pesoa´u kunt uhm
We have some babies nuhm pee´soangoo kwunt uhm
They have a house mauhm kawnee´ kunt uhm
They have a knife mauhm we-eets´ekunt uhm
They have a daughter mauhm pawtsuh´ kunt uhm
You have a knife uhm we-eets´ekunt
You have a house uhm kawnee´kunt
You have a horse uhm kuvaw´ voongkoo´kwunt
We have a horse nuhm kuvaw´voongkoo´ kwunt uhm
We have some horses nuhm kuvaw´ voongkoong´oo kwunt uhm
We have a pet bear nuhm kweyu´huntuh voongkoo´ kwunt uhm
We have pet bears nuhm kweyu´huntuh voongkoong´oo kwunt uhm
Your father uhmuh´ee mooum´
Your fathers muh´nee mooung´wuh um
Our fathers (both of our fathers) tdum´ee moou´dum
Our fathers (the fathers of three or more of us) tdung´wee moo´
My kitty nuhn´ee kedee´kee voongk
My kitties nuh´nee kedee´kee voongkoong
My friends nuhn´ee tuhkoov´oong wuhn, nuh´nee tuhkoov´
My grandfather nuh´nee tohots´een
My shoe nuh´nee pawtsun´
Your shoe uhmuh´ee pawtsum´
We have a house (three or more) tdung kawnee´gunt
We (three of us) ***have*** (two) ***cats*** tdung kedee´kee poongkoong´oo kwunt uhm
Let's go to sleep (plural) hoakoy´ vawdungw, hoakoy´kwai vawdum
Let's go then uhvuh´dung weku
I'm done toahoyng´wuhnchun
Not that way mun´eup
When he eats chili chili tuhkung´oots
I'm saying it again nuh ai´uhs (this sentence can also mean ***it's blowing again***)
He's there oo´vu ninee
Where is George now? hu´vaw onin´ee George oong?
Almost frozen soowaw´ seai´puhku
Are you going to school? eem school eed u'?
Are you working? eem wuh´ukawd u'?

He said mai´puhku
Doing it again ooneng´oomee
Got mad again nungai´puhkuntus
He's riding the horse kuvawng kawduhk´ai nung
Wash it wash engoom´pukhai
Didn't go home paiyuh´nait
Where is it at? u-hu´vawk oonee´tseku?
He's a cowboy cowboy oonin´ee
Kenneth is going to work Kenneth wuhu´kawwhai
Take your shoes that way shoes munee´tuh kuhuhts´
After you're through washing wash emuk´wuhchum
Got scared when you said it yah´pawk aing´oots
I'm going to drink it when I get mad nungaits´ evee´oompawn
Don't eat it when you drop it kawchuk´ tuhkup oowee´tseuk
He doesn't do it kawtch ening´wu
A Mormon was doing it also Mormon ung oonee´puhkais
That's what he said aimee´ung
They had blankets moahoy´uhd oodoo´aw puhkunt
They had wagons wagons uhduh´duhs
How should it be? How is it going to be? hun´eek uh´dawvaw?
He's got hair totsee´ vuhu kunt
Some Indians do it also nengwoo´ oonee´puhkuntus oong
Go take it off chukween´aw kwaingwuk
Is that what you mean (said)? uh´du udaik?
Went through again poo´paw puhkais
On the water paw´ awvawn
Rough skin chongkwaw seu´gunt
That's what he said to him oongwus´ mai´puhkais
Didn't come kaw pechuh´puhu
All getting gone mawno´nee toopeng´wai
Maybe that's alright soov oonee´sump
Just let it be, leave it the way it is oonee´sump uk, oodoo´awvaw
Are you going to do it again? oonee´umpawsuk u'?
It doesn't start kawchuk´ start´ engwu
Always sitting in the car car´ enaws kawdee
You ask him aioompaw
Say the same to him ungus´ ai´kos
He's sick mung nawhu´meent
Started breathing soowawk´aw kuh´puhkunt
He got his breath soowaw´ kuhuhts´ ung
Listening around nungkaw´ vuhduh´ee
Gathered together in one place soo´pawnee nawneech´eku
He likes Indians Indians´ee ow´suhntee kawduhm
All of them eating mawnoh´nee tuhkawts´eng

Always asks to be carried uh´ yungwee tooveech´ee
Coyote had a daughter soonuv´ee pawtsuhm´ udu´puhku
They're drinking now aiuhv evee´kawdum
Do you mean him? oong´wu hai?
He was saying oong ai´meung
They went through oo´pa-haw
Where did you get that one? mu´du hu´vawntu ooneep´?
She has a boyfriend boy friend ee´tseku
Hasn't eaten yet kawchoo´ tuhkaw´nai sump, kaw tuhkaw´nais
Lot of people pick up something kuhkuh´ee ukum, chouk´ai
Doesn't say that kaw maing´wait
I was saying aing´oomee nuh
Say it the way he says it ungu´pus ai´vaw
Which way will it be u-hun´eek uhdu´vu
Go chop (plural) chop´ee meyung´weuk
Do it for me ooneeng´kuhuk´un
Don't write in those books mudu book´ eum kaw po-ohk enawk
Are you both ready ready engwoon´chudum
Are you ready (plural) ready´ ekow-oong´chudum
That's all I'm going to say uh´du sump mai´vawnee
I'm asking again maik´usoon
Does Joe sleep alone? Joe nawnoh awpuh´eseech u'?
Tell him no kawtch´ aiung
More than you emee´haw awvaw´nee
Never did anything kaw hun´engwait
Sleeping with mom mom eng´wai awpuh´ee
By the water pai koo´awvai, pai koongwu´vu
Bring her here hukai´ ung kuhuh´
How dirty are your shoes? hun´euk dirty shoes´ eemud?
Will say ai´vawts
She says that ai´kooung
While he is sleeping awpuh´ekoom
Do you get cold? uhm spai´uhmeent u'?
She's going to get cold mung spai´ayvawnt
I'm going to get cold nuh spai´ayvawnt
Or is it a week? week udoa´?
Don't' sit on that one mud´u awvawn´ kawduh´vungwu
Did you get hungry? uhm tuhkuh´ee yuai´kunt u'?
Be good aw´tai oonih´nee
Johnny is working for Kenneth Johnny oong Kenneth´ee wuh´ukawng kuhkwaing´kwunt oong
Don't do anything pawhun´ unee´kwoup
Should I get it? kuhuh´ vawduk´un?
Say it only once soot´us ook aing´oomeengpu

Going with us tdung´we whaingpawnt
Comes back again ow´pusump paiay´kee
I have no pair kawchun ´nawvuh´u'
Is the same guy still walking around? eng´udu toahoy´pawhain´eus?
To you uhmuh´ee dookw
Give me the salt and pepper salt and pepper´ud nuhdook´
That one also udoo´tus
Water Baby's house paingu´peetsee kawneng´
Joe is going to look like that when he gets old, huh? Joe naw´poodeech mun naiah´vai aing´oa?
Can I have it? nuh´uk uduv u'?
Say "Cowboy" in Indian vuh "Cowboy" Nengwoo´ aingoots
As they always say ai´kaimenum
As you always say uhm´ee ai´meen
Say it like me nuh´pus ai´vaw
Where is Lorraine at? hu´vawng oonih´nee Lorraine oong´wai?
Just leave it like that munee´sumpuk unee´kaivu
I'm not good at finding things anymore kaw tooveets´ maingwait´us nuh
Took it from me kuhunhk´utuhee chukwun
Go and get some from him yow´whai ungu´vawchuh ooneets
I'm going to Cedar Cedar engwee´took paiyuhm´pawnt
I'm going to the movie nuh soo´ee kwaivawnt, nuh soo´ee kwaing´uhmpawnt
Are you going to the movie? uhm soo´ee kwaivawnt u'?
Are we going to the show? tdum soo´ kwaing´uhmpawntuhm u'? Tdum soo´ kwaivawnt u'?
What would you do? uhm hun´eeng koop?
What could I do? hun´eng kooun?
What could (would) you do? uhm hun´eng ookoo?
What could they do? hun´eng oongkoo´um?
What could we do? hun´eng oongkoo´ tdum?
What should I do? hun´eng oompawn?
What would we do? hun´eng oompaw´ tdum?
Where are you? u-hu´vaw ninee?
Where did it go? ai´tawk uhdus?
Giving to him oongwu´dook
He killed me pukawng´oong chungunee
Killed him pukawng´oong chungung
Lets all push it push´ ee kaompaw´ekawdum
Until we reach the house kawn´ee emun´tuh kwawnee
I got it from this guy eng´hai ung-un´took
He said aik´ooung, aik´oong
What happened to it? ud´u hun´eeoo´puhkunt?
It was green sakhwai´enee´ku
Where do you have your house at? eem hu´vu kawnee´kaingoomee?

What have you got? empuh´ uhdoo´ai?
What did he do to you? hun´engwuh´chungum?
What did they do to you? hun´engwuh chungwum?
What happened to you? what's the matter with you? hun´eng wuhchu?
I'm still doing it, I'm at it again oonee´kuhsoon
It's alright ai´u whaihump
I guess it's the right size toahoy awvai´tuhnee uhdus´
What else from there? hun´ uhduv´ oovai?
While you're doing that muneeng´oopai
Going to sit alone naaw´hawduh´vawnt
When he threw it on her munchung´wenunts
What did you go do? hun´evai´uhgu?
He arrived back home paiyuhk uhmuhv peechuh´puhku
You're saying it now eem ai´oov ai´muk
When I shave shave´ engwoot
I'm a banana eater banana tuhkud ungus nuh
What does it say? hun´eukawk´?
It doesn't say anything kawchuk´ hunee´ungwu
I came from there walking oo´vaiun nawnee´kee pawhainkeku
I won't let you nuh kawtchuh´ muheneengwhait´evungwainee um
You will be alright in a few minutes ai´umpaw few minutes ekaik

A SAMPLE LETTER

I'm writing to you this day, Po-oh´ eun emee´vawchuhk ai´oo tawvawm´.

I'm fine. I'm thinking about you. How are you? Ai'uhku. Soomai´kai emee. Hawdo´aienee?

How are the Indians now? Are they all right? Aioov Nengwoong haw´doawkai? Ai´uhkai u'?

What is Bob doing? Bob uhdu´vu huneench?

Is he doing something? Maybe he went up town to drink, huh? Soo´kopenee nikudung´ u'? Soov town´ evahnt evee´kwaikunt u'?

It's snowing in the mountains. Noovu´wai uk kaiv´emunt.

Here, they went to the movies. They have lots of money. But me, I haven't any money. Evahnt´uhm soo´meai. Tooveets awvawn tuhmpee´kunt uhm. Nuhsu ungus, tuhmpee´aw.

Sometimes I have a little money, Naaw´kawnos tuhmpeets´ee kaingwuhts.

I buy flour, I buy potatoes, I buy pig meat. Tooween´ nahdoy, whechuhn´ai nahdoy, kooseen tookoo´uv ee nahdoai.

CHAPTER 13

THE OLD ONES

He that boasts in the glory of his ancestors
lacks that quality that made them great.

When I first began to compile this genealogy in 1956, I only had it in mind to record all the ancestors and relatives of my wife Doris Kanosh. When she died and I married Evalina Mae McFee, from the Shivwits Reservation, I did the same with her family. Much of the information I received from the Old People was sometimes only scanty but I did record whatever they told me even if the relationship was distant. In some cases I never did find the time to pursue the more distant Nevada relations to get more information. On the more recent families of my own time I did little work since most of this information is available. I basically wanted to get as much of the older material while there were still a few people left who could remember it. When more recent information was volunteered I recorded it, but because of other involvements I did not generally pursue it.

In Section 1 of this work is the material relating to the ancestors and other relations of my first wife, Doris Kanosh of the Koosharem Band. Most of this information was acquired from about 1955 to the early 1960s. Section 2 consists of the ancestors and other relations of my second wife, Evalina Mae McFee of the Shivwits Band acquired in the 1960s. In some cases these relationships cross. In fact if one goes back a little in time it appears that almost everyone from Koosharem, Kanosh, Kaibab, Cedar City, Shivwits, and Moapa are distantly related. All the names in this work are related to my children from both marriages.

Many times when an Indian informant gives a name of a relative it is seldom a maiden name. When an Anglo wrote down an Indian name they hardly ever wrote it down the same way twice as they didn't speak the language. I write them down as I find them in census records and also as they are correctly pronounced. Indian names that are typed in **bold** are the correct pronunciation and are put into

the records by me. Indian names not in bold are copied exactly as found in census and other records.

Whenever I could, I asked how to spell certain English names. However, with the older people who did not speak English very well, and who had little education, I spelled them as I thought they might be. This does not mean that they are the way the person with that name spelled them. English names have a variety of spellings.

When the name Greenwich, Utah, is used it refers to the Koosharem Indian Reservation near there. The names are listed in alphabetical order beginning with "A" in each section. If the husband's name isn't known then the wife's last name is used. If both husband or wife are unknown then the name of the first child is used. Sometimes I group a family name according to families; therefore, the names might not be in alphabetical order in such cases.

Because of cultural differences, the art of acquiring Indian genealogy requires an entirely different approach than in soliciting Anglo genealogy, especially from elders whose first language is Indian and who still adhere to many of the ancient beliefs. It is always best not to ask any leading questions, but rather to let the informants volunteer what they know and want to give. There is always the possibility of the Old People misunderstanding because of their inability to speak English fluently, and if the informants don't like the white man very well they will be prone to giving false information.

Indian elders have generally kept good track of even distant relationships since it was not considered good for any relations to marry, no matter how distant. They might not know the exact relationship, in the more distant cases, but they always knew there was a relationship. The younger generation is losing these traits.

One important difficulty in Indian genealogy is getting an older informant to mention the name of the dead. This is because of the belief that if the dead hear their name mentioned they will come to you at night, as a ghost, and bother you. The elders I asked did break this taboo but didn't like to make a habit of it.

Another difficulty is getting the date that an Indian was born. Indians in general never kept track of their age, and about the only thing they might remember is the place and time of year they were born, spring, fall, etc. Some of the older people had little knowledge of the calendar and often the only date they had heard spoken of much was the famous "4th of July" date they had learned to celebrate with the white man. This date therefore, became a favorite date to give as a birth date. It is also very difficult to guess the age of Indians by looking at them. Many of them often look a lot younger than they really are. This is one reason Indian agents were often wrong in recording birth dates. Agents were also not that concerned about accuracy in birth dates as long as they had something approximate to go by. There was also a language barrier in acquiring many of these early birth dates. Records made by Indian agents are better than nothing, but very poor because they really didn't care that much.

Another Indian belief to be aware of is that Indians had but one name; they didn't have a given name and a surname. Among the Paiutes it was very common

for them to receive their Indian name from some little childish action noticed when they were very young such as Rolls His Snot Up in Balls, Skunk, and even names with sexual connotations and organs. Such names often stuck with them throughout life. This gave no embarrassment to the Indians as this naming practice was well understood, fitting well into the concept of Indian humor. However, as the Paiutes became more civilized and aware that some white men were a little too prudish to hear such names, they would sometimes become reluctant in divulging the English translation of their Indian name.

Some Paiutes were lucky enough to gain a second name in life due to some noted action such as **Tosaw´ Kuvaw Neahv** (White Horse Chief) and **Nawhoo´kwee Neahv** (War Chief). Others, no matter how famous they became in their war exploits, never escaped their childhood name. Chief Walker was probably one of these. His name **O-aw´kawd** (yellow, or brass colored) Anglicized to Walker, could well have been given to him as a child from being covered in yellow dirt or ochre. Yellow does not have a connotation of cowardice as among the whites. Another famous chief, Quannah Parker of the Comanches, a tribe linguistically related to the Paiutes, appears to have been stuck with his childhood name **Kwunu´** (Smells). The Anglo name of Jenny seems to have been popular among early Paiute women, maybe because they could pronounce it easily and possibly because they were reluctant in giving their Indian names. Paiute names were preferred and used more often among themselves than their English names.

Paiutes had no orphanages, nor the need for them, since Indian people were always very eager to take in anyone who lost their parents. They would raise them as their own and call them their own children, and sometimes it takes extra questioning to dig out such adoptions. The name Kanosh is a good example of this. The Kanosh family of Paiutes today are not direct descendants of Chief Kanosh, but of an orphaned boy raised by Chief Kanosh who was given the name of John Kanosh.

It was also a custom for a Paiute man to marry the oldest sister in a family first and then the younger ones. This was his right, if he chose to do so, and was a good enough hunter to support them. Examples of this will be found in the accompanying genealogy. The last known example of Paiute plural marriage was as late as 1943 with Crockett Kanosh who married two sisters, Florence and Nancy Timmican.

In acquiring Indian genealogy it is important to understand the terms of relationship used by the Paiutes. Their terms are a lot more explicit with grandparents and brothers and sisters than among the white man. The name for a paternal grandmother, **wheetsee´ee**, is different from the name, **kawgoon**, which is used for a maternal grandmother.

The same is true of paternal and maternal grandfathers. To complicate this, a grandparent will use the Indian name applied to her as a grandparent and apply it to a grandchild in a reciprocal manner. For example a paternal grandmother, **wheetsee´ee**, will call her son's daughters **wheecheech´een**. Therefore, to those who do not speak Indian and who do not understand this relationship, it is always best to ask "Who was your father's father, mother's father?" etc. Another thing to

remember in this respect is that great aunts and great uncles use the same relationship term as the grandmother or grandfather who would be either a brother or sister. For example, the name for a paternal grandmother, **wheetsee´ee,** would also be applied to her sisters.

Paiutes always refer to brothers and sisters as older brother **pawveets,** younger brother **chukaits,** older sister **pawtseets,** and younger sister **numeents**. First and second cousins are also called brothers and sisters; therefore, if one does not understand this it is best just to ask for the names of the children and not for brothers and sisters. This is a practice common to many American Indian tribes.

Sometimes there can be difficulty in obtaining information about twin births if it would embarrass the informant. It is believed by some that twins are the result of two different fathers and therefore unfaithfulness.

The material included in this chapter consists of extracts from a larger collection of Paiute genealogy that I have distributed seperately. That original collection has more recent information much of which is available in public and church documents. My purpose in this book is to make older genealogy available to the public that cannot be found in such records. Most of this older information came from the mouths of Paiutes born in the last century.

I include but one census record in this work, the 1898 Shivwits Census. It gives the reader a good idea of early English names and also Indian names and translations.

SECTION ONE

HUSBAND Walker Ammon.
Born about 1854.
Died 16 April 1920 at Koosharem Reservation, Utah.
Father Chief Walker. **O-aw´kawduh, O-aw´kawduhm** is the correct pronunciation of his name which means Yellow. As the whites attempted to pronounce this name it got anglicized to Walker. It is said that Walker Ammon had a house in Teas Valley, Utah.
Mother **Ungkaw´hawduhm,** a sister of **Pee´weech.** **Ungkaw´hawduhm** means Red One.
WIFE Dora.
Born 1860.

CHILDREN
1. **Alma** (male) born about 1900.

INFORMATION SOURCE: Minnie Kanosh.

HUSBAND Charlie Arrowgarp.
Other wives (1) Millie Arrowpane. Charley Arrowgarp and Millie Arrowpane had a child Dela Arrowcup born August 1912 at Greenwich, Utah, Died 4 March 1917. Buried in Richfield, Utah.
WIFE (2) Amy Emma Timmican.
Born Dec.1886 or 1897 at Lyman, Wayne County, Utah.
Died 9 Jan. 1961 at Richfield, Utah.
Buried 12 Jan. 1961 at Richfield, Utah.
Father John Timmican.
Mother Rose.
Other husbands (2) Tom Parashont (3) Jesse Jim.

CHILDREN
1. Unnamed (male) born Greenwich, Utah, died about 1916 at Greenwich, Utah. Lived 2 years.
2. Unnamed (male) born Greenwich, Utah. Died about 1915 at Greenwich, Utah. Lived nine months.
3. Unnamed (female) born Greenwich, Utah, died about 1916 at Richfield, Utah. Lived 1 year.
4. Dell Arrowgarp (male) born 20 Sept. 1917, at Greenwich Utah, died 13 Oct. 1988, Richfield, Utah. Married Mabel Provo.

INFORMATION SOURCE: Emma Timmican.

HUSBAND unknown (Benson?).
WIFE Lily Tom.
Father Panaca Tom.

CHILDREN
1. Joe Benson (male) married to Mable.
2. Lila Benson (female) married to (1) Baker (2) Ted Pikyavit (3) Archie Rogers.
3. Bessie Benson (female).
4. Margie Benson (female).
5. Daniel Benson (male).

INFORMATION SOURCE: Carl Jake.

HUSBAND unknown.
WIFE unknown.

CHILDREN
1. Name not known (female) died Wayne County, Utah, married to Tom.
2. Bob (male) died and buried at Lyman, Utah (note says that Bob and Charley [Roberts?] raised by Joe and Sally).
3. Name not known (female) died at Greenwich, Utah "She was Frank Woody's mother's paternal grandmother."

INFORMATION SOURCE: Jimmy Timmican and Minnie Kanosh.

HUSBAND Black Hawk (John W. Mountain.) Ute tribal records states that Black Hawk has a nephew and wife (Walkers) who live in Grass Valley, Utah (the Koosharem Reservation at Greenwich, Utah).
Born 1851.
Died 24 May 1942.
Father Mountain.
Mother Sumbitzh.
WIFE Quinn.
Born about 1856 (age 49 in 1905).
Died 26 May 1922.
Father John Skyro.

CHILDREN
1. Happy Jack (#2), (Jack Mountain) born 1890, died April 1961?
   Happy Jack had a half-brother John Merrycats of Kanab, Utah; Quinn was his mother.

Many Paiutes from southern Utah would visit Happy Jack at his old log cabin near Whiterocks, Utah, during Sun Dance and Bear Dance times and stay with him as they recognized him as a relation. I visited him once myself with Foster Charles and Edward Rice in 1949, and later with Jimmy Timmican.

INFORMATION SOURCE: Ute tribal allotment record of 1905, Fort Duchesne, Utah.

HUSBAND	(2), (Old) Bob.
Birth	of Wayne County, Utah.
Died	Wayne County, Utah. Killed by a horse
Buried	Lyman, Utah.
WIFE	Sally Timmican. Sally lived to be very old and became gray and blind .
Birth	of Wayne County,Utah.
Died	Greenwich Utah.
Buried	Greenwich, Utah.
Other husbands	(1) **Pawguh´ Neahv** (Fish Chief). He married Sally when she was very young.

CHILDREN
1. Little Bob (male) born Wayne County, Utah. Married and had one boy.
2. Joe Bob (male) born Wayne County, Utah, died Richfield, Utah, married **Pawmunts** (a Ute from Whiterocks, Utah). They had a boy who lived two days.
3. Lemuel (male) born in Utah. Died at about age 16 at Lyman, Utah.

INFORMATION SOURCES: Jimmy Timmican and Minnie Kanosh.

HUSBAND	Little Bob.
Born	Wayne County, Utah.
Died	Greenwich, Utah, when his son Charley was a baby.
Buried	Greenwich Utah.
WIFE	unknown.
Born	**of** Kanosh, Utah.
Died	Kanosh, Utah, when her son Charley was a baby.
Buried	Kanosh, Utah.

CHILDREN
1. Charley Roberts (male) died at Cedar City, Utah, married Virginia Wall.

INFORMATION SOURCE: Jimmy Timmican.

HUSBAND (Tom Quakanab's brother.)
Born Henry Mountains, Utah.
WIFE unknown.

CHILDREN
1. Dick (male) born 1866 Escalante, Utah. Died 27 June 1948. Died and buried at Kanosh, Utah. Married (2) Tappy. Dick is Dorothy Dick's father.
2. (Male.)
3. (Male.)
4. Sally Ann (female) born Escalante, Utah. Died at Kaibab, Arizona. Not married.

INFORMATION SOURCE: Jimmy Timmican.

HUSBAND Dick.
Born 1866, of Wayne County, Utah.
Died 27 June 1948 at Kanosh, Utah.
Father Tom Quakanab's brother of Henry Mountains.
Married (2) Tappy.
WIFE unknown.
Born of Escalante, Utah.
Died Near Escalante.
Buried Near Escalante.

CHILDREN
1. Dorothy Dick (female) born about 1902 Greenwich, Utah. Married (1) Toby John (2) Lonnie Kouchomp.

INFORMATION SOURCES: Dorothy Dick, and 1940 census for Kaibab.

HUSBAND Johnny Dick (his Indian name was Paw´ooksawts)
Born 1875.
Died 8 May 1942, 5:00 a.m at Kaibab, Arizona.
Buried May 1942 at Kaibab, Arizona.
Other wives (1) ? (had no children). (3) Maggie (had no children).
WIFE unknown.

CHILDREN
1. Clara Dick, (female) born 1902, married Roy Tom. 1940 census calls # 1 "Clara Johnnie a daughter of Johnnie Indian."
2. (Female) died and buried at Kaibab. Died young.

INFORMATION SOURCES: Jimmy Timmican.

HUSBAND	Hunkiter, **Ungkaw´ Tawkawd**.
Died	1851 (81?).
Buried	Kanosh Mountains, Utah.
WIFE	unknown.
Died	Lived 40-50 years, died at Milford, Utah.

CHILDREN

1. Joe (**Cha-haw´vuhts**), (male) of Milford, Utah. Died when an old man at Greenwich, Utah. Married **Cheng´uvuhts** from near the Nevada border. They had no children.
2. Rosey (**Mawn´taw, Mawn´tai**), (female) of Milford, Utah. Lived about 40 years. Married (1) **Nawhoo´kwee Neahv** (War Chief).

INFORMATION SOURCE: Minnie Kanosh.

HUSBAND	unknown.
WIFE	unknown.

CHILDREN

1. Jake (Jake Moroni) married Lucy .
2. Charlie Pete (married Queen).

INFORMATION SOURCE: Carl Jake.

HUSBAND	Jake Moroni. Carl Jake referred to him both as Jake Moroni and Moroni Jake. When I asked who Jake Moroni's father was I got a similar answer, so I was left unsure about who Carl's paternal grandfather was. Once he just said Moroni. Moroni was Chief near Shoal Creek and Clover Valley. This would be Jake Moroni or his father. Carl said his father was from that area.
Died	Eagle Valley, Nevada.
Buried	Eagle Valley, Nevada.
WIFE	Lucy.
Died	Cedar City, Utah.
Buried	Cedar City, Utah.
Father	John Manarra.
Mother	Jenny (Jeannie).

CHILDREN

1. (Female) died at Kanosh Utah. Not married. Lived about 11 years.
2. Ed Jake (male) born in Utah. Died at Cedar City, Utah. Not married.

3. Carl Jake (male) born 1895 at Hamilton's Fort, Utah. Married Minnie John.

INFORMATION SOURCE: Carl Jake.

HUSBAND	Indian Jake (Watermelon Jake). Morris Jake says his name should have been "Tum."
Born	1874.
Died	1959.
Buried	Kaibab, Arizona.
WIFE	Minnie Pikyavit.
Father	Joe Pikyavit Sr. of Kaibab.

CHILDREN

1. Andrew Jake (male) born 7 August 1910 at Kaibab, Arizona. Died 23 September 1925. Buried at Cedar City, Utah.
2. Morris M. Jake (male) born 28 May 1913 at Kaibab, Arizona. Died 1970? He married Lucille Tom.
3. Emma M. Jake (female) born 1915.
4. Hattie Jake (female). Died January 1937.
5. Woodrow Jake (male).
6. Margie Jake (female).
7. Francella Jake (female) born 20 October 1925.

INFORMATION SOURCE: Morris M. Jake.

HUSBAND	unknown (probably Joe?).
WIFE	**Moogoo´uts** (Minnie Ankerpont?).

CHILDREN

1. Grant Joe (male) died 14 January 1924 at about the age of 23. Married **O-aw mumunts´u** (Ute Indian). Ute records state that Grant Joe (Ska-putz) died 14 January 1924. His mother was Minnie Ankerpont. Grant's brothers were Capson Ankerpont and Moroni Ankerpont (a half-brother). Grant's wife was Sa-waw-nantz who died 13 October 1912.
2. Bill Joe (male).
3. **Koapoa´doahoynt** (male). Married **Weem´eup**.
4. (Female.)
5. (Female.)
6. (Male) lived 6 months.

INFORMATION SOURCE: Minnie Kanosh and Florence Timmican.

HUSBAND Bill Joe.
Mother **Moogoouts.**
WIFE unknown. The Ute 1905 Allotment Record page 110 lists Bertha Chimburas as the mother of the children listed below. The Ute record lists Bertha as dying 15 Dec. 1918. Minnie Kanosh stated that Bill Joe was the father and she didn't know who the mother was; therefore, Lawrence Yump listed on the Ute record as father is probably a step-father. B.I.A. records commonly make this mistake. Koosharem Paiutes have always recognized the Yumps as relatives and vice versa.

CHILDREN
1. Carrie Yump (female) born 15 April 1908. Married (1), (2), (3) Chicora.
2. Oscar Yump (male) born 3 March 1915.
3. Jack Yump (male) born 1 December 1906.
4. (Male) no wife.
5. (Female) died Fort Duchesne Utah. Married (2) **Tookoo´puhts.**

The children listed above (not the dates) were given by Minnie Kanosh. Ute Records give the following information which is not always reliable concerning blood parents:

Carries brothers:
Willie Yump born 10 April 1911, died 14 June 1924.
John Yump born 12 February 1913, died 16 February 1913.
Oscar.
Jack.
Stella.
Stewart Yump, a half-brother, born 19 May 1920, died 11 August 1921.

Carrie's husbands: (1) Frank Cheum, married 1902, (2) Ben Mountain. Carrie's father was Lawrence Yump born 1879. Lawrence's mother was Maimie Ankerpont. Carrie's mother was Bertha Chimburas born 1893, died 15 December 1918.

INFORMATION SOURCE: Minnie Kanosh and 1905 Ute Allotment Records.

HUSBAND Kanosh John. Kanosh John was a medicine man. His Indian name was **Pook.**
Died April 1947 at Shivwits Reservation, Utah.
Other wives (2) Ida Toab.
WIFE Eliza Menarrow (Manarra).
Born 1864, of Hamilton Fort, Utah.
Died about 24 July 1931.
Father John Manarra.
Mother Jenny.
Other husbands (1) Quist John.

CHILDREN
1. Julia John (female) born near Newcastle, Utah, married (2) Jack Nort.
2. Ada (female) married Georgey George. Ada was one year older than Hannah.
3. Hannah, (female).

INFORMATION SOURCE: Julia John.

HUSBAND	Quist John.
Other wives	(1) Eliza Manarrow (Manarra).
WIFE	Mattie (Eliza's sister).
father	Manarrow.
Mother	Jenny.

CHILDREN
1. Jim John, (male).
2. Levi John, (male) born 1892, married Alice.
3. Meddie John, (female) married Charlie Chassis.
4. Joseph John, (male) born 1901 Orderville, Utah, died 17 October 1947. Married Ada Snow, 5 Sept. 1924.

INFORMATION SOURCE: Julia John, and Joseph John's marriage license application.

HUSBAND	Levi John.
Born	1892.
Died	1951.
Buried	at Kaibab, Arizona.
WIFE	Alice.
Born	1894.
Died	1960.
Buried	at Kaibab, Arizona.

CHILDREN
1. Leta, (female) born 15 February 1925.
2. Reuben, (male, born 6 April 1930, married Lilly Tillahash.
3. Finley, (male) 14 March 1933, married Nevada Smokey.
4. Larry, (male) born17 June 1935.
5. Hamblin, (male) born 14 February 1938.

INFORMATION SOURCES: Julia John.

HUSBAND Quist John.
Other wives (2) Mattie.
WIFE Eliza Manarra.
Born 1864, of Hamilton's Fort, Utah.
Died about 24 July 1931.
Father John Manarra (Manarrow).
Mother Jenny.
Other husbands (2) Kanosh John.

CHILDREN
1. Jody Roe (male) married Wilhemina (a Ute Indian).
2. (Female.)

INFORMATION SOURCE: Julia John.

HUSBAND Toby John.
Born of Kaibab, Arizona.
Died Iron Springs, Utah.
Buried at Kaibab, Arizona.
Father John.
WIFE Dorothy Dick.
Born about 1902.
Father Dick.
Other husbands Lonnie Kouchomp.

CHILDREN
1. Unnamed, (female) (stillborn) born in Kanab, Utah, died and buried in Kanab.
2. Unnamed, (female) born in Kaibab, Arizona, died and buried in Richfield, Utah. Lived two years.

INFORMATION SOURCE: Dorothy Dick.

HUSBAND Willie John.
Born Eagle Valley, Nevada.
Died about 1898 in Eagle Valley.
Buried at Eagle Valley.
Father Pete.
Mother Phoebe.
WIFE Maimie (her Indian name was **Wuhsee´udok**, Plume)
Born Sharp, Nevada.
Died Caliente, Nevada.
Mother Jennie died at Caliente, Nevada.

Other husbands Los Leon.

CHILDREN
1. Ellis John, (female) died and buried in Nephi, Utah, married a Mexican (no children).
2. Ada John, (female) died and buried in Modena, Utah.
3. Minnie John, (female) born 1898 Eagle Valley, Nevada, married Carl Jake.

INFORMATION SOURCE: Minnie John (Jake).

HUSBAND unknown.
WIFE of eastern California.

CHILDREN
1. Chief Kanosh (male) born February 1821 eastern California, died 4 December 1884.
2. Chief Walker **O-aw´kawduhm** (male) born about 1815 eastern California, died 29 January 1855, Meadow, Utah. Some historians have stated that Walker was born on the banks of the Spanish Fork River, whereas Kate B. Carter in *Heart Throbs of the West* Vol. 1, Page 101, says he was born in eastern California. Minnie Kanosh, born in 1884, the Paiute Informant on this family, says the three brothers were born in eastern California.
3. Hunkiter (correct pronunciation is **Ungkaw´ Tawkawd,** Red ?) born Eastern California. Died 1851 or 1881.

INFORMATION SOURCE: Minnie Kanosh and the book *Heart Throbs of the West*.

HUSBAND Chief Kanosh.
Born February 1821, of eastern California.
Died 4 December 1884 at Kanosh, Utah.
Buried Kanosh, Utah.
Other wives (2) Betsykin (3) Mary Voreas (4) Sally (no children).
WIFE (1) Julia.
Died Kanosh, Utah.

CHILDREN
1. (Male) lived about 15 years.
2. (Male) lived about 5 years.

INFORMATION SOURCE: Minnie Kanosh and misc. histories.

HUSBAND unknown.
Died when John was a baby.
WIFE unknown.
Died when John was a baby.

CHILDREN
1. John Kanosh (male) died at Fillmore, Utah, buried at Greenwich, Utah. Married Peaweeds (**Pee´weech**). John was raised by Chief Kanosh when his parents died, therefore, he was given the last name of Kanosh.
2. (Male) married **Moogoo´uts** (who died at Myton, Utah).

INFORMATION SOURCE: Minnie Kanosh.

HUSBAND John Kanosh. His Indian name was **Kaiv´u wuhnuh´** (Mountain Standing).
Died at Fillmore, Utah.
Buried Greenwich, Utah.
WIFE Peaweeds, **Pee´weech.**
Born 1842.
Died 19 September 1929 at Greenwich, Utah.
Father **Poawhaw´dawveech.**
Buried Greenwich, Utah.
Other husbands (1) Chief Walker.

CHILDREN
1. (Male) died Kanosh, Utah.
2. (Male) died Kanosh, Utah.
3. Rosey Kanosh (female) born Greenwich, Utah, died Greenwich, Utah. Married Tommy Utes (had children).
4. (Sex unknown) died Greenwich, Utah.
5. **Ke-eh´taw** Kanosh (female) born Greenwich, Utah. Died Greenwich, Utah, married **Pooeech**, he died when about 25 years old (no children).
6. Crockett Kanosh (male) born Greenwich, Utah, died 16 April 1943 at Whiterocks, Utah. Married (1) Nancy Timmican.
7. Minnie Kanosh (female) born December 1884 at Angle, near Antimony, Utah. The Indian name of this place is **Sawwhaw´ Hawduhd**, Green Sitting. Died 20 March 1961. Married George Timmican. Minnie was one of my main infor-

mants on much of the older genealogy included in this work.

8. (Female) born near Antimony, Utah. Died at Greenwich, Utah. She was married and had 1 child.

INFORMATION SOURCE: Minnie Kanosh.

HUSBAND	Crockett Kanosh (There is a story that Crockett was shot and wounded by a policeman in Salina, Utah.)
Born	1881.
Died	16 April 1943 at Whiterocks, Utah.
Buried	Greenwich, Utah.
Father	John Kanosh.
Mother	Peaweeds (**Pee´weech**).
Other wives	(1) Nancy Timmican (Indian plural marriage).
WIFE	Florence Timmican.
Born	about June 1889 at Fish Lake, Utah.
Died	9 January 1986, 6:30 a.m. at Richfield, Utah.
Buried	13 January 1986 at Richfield, Utah.
Father	John Timmican.
Mother	Rosey **Wawn´uvuhts** (Quakanab).

CHILDREN

1. John Kanosh (male).
2. Deere Kanosh (male) born 20 October 1911 at Greenwich, Utah. Died 9 December 1971. Married (1) Annie (Peaches) Toney a Ute Indian. Her father was White R? Jack and her mother Utchea. (2) Edurine Jake.

INFORMATION SOURCE: Florence Kanosh.

HUSBAND	Crockett Kanosh.
Born	1881.
Died	16 April 1943 at Whiterocks, Utah.
Buried	Greenwich, Utah.
Father	John Kanosh.
Mother	Peaweeds, **Pee´weech.**
Other wives	(2) Florence Timmican (Indian plural marriage)
WIFE	(1) Nancy Timmican.
Died	5 August 1953 at Richfield, Utah.
Buried	9 August 1953 at Richfield, Utah.
Father	John Timmican.
Mother	Rose **Wawn´uvuhts** (Quakanab).

CHILDREN
1. Female) born 1905.
2. Fred Kanosh (male) born December 1906, died 12 March 1925.
3. (Female) born 1907, died 1909.
4. (Male) born 1908, died 1908.
5. (Male) born 1910, died 1910.
6. Lyman Kanosh (male) born 2 September 1912 at Greenwich, Utah. Married Emily Baker.
7. Woodrow Kanosh (male) born 15 April 1914-15, died 31 October 1933. Died of tuberculosis.
8. Reed Kanosh (male) born 1919, died 20 December 1925.
9. Edward Kanosh (male) born 5 July 1922 at Sigurd, Utah.
10. Archie Kanosh (male) born 1924, died 10 July 1925.
11. Nellie Kanosh (female) born 1 September 1926, died 31 January 1927.
12. Ilene Kanosh (female) born 11 December 1929, died 2 December 1930.

INFORMATION SOURCE: Some births obtained from the records of Petrear Larson Koosharem, Utah. The rest of the information from Florence Kanosh and Nancy Timmican.

HUSBAND **Koapoa´doahoynt.**
Mother **Moogoouts** (Minnie Ankerpont?).
WIFE **Weem´eup.**

CHILDREN
1. Mary Ungapont (Ankerpont?). Her Indian name was **Kuhv´us.**
2. (Female) died at the age of about 25.
3. (Male.)
4. Francis Collero, (male) of Bridgeland, Utah.

INFORMATION SOURCE: Minnie Kanosh.

HUSBAND unknown.
WIFE Curley Annie (she had another brother named Jake).
Born Kanosh, Utah.
Died Kanosh, Utah.
Buried Kanosh, Utah.

CHILDREN
1. Lonnie Kouchomp Sr. (male) married Martha. Martha's mother was Jean of Shivwits. Lonnie died and buried in Kanosh.

INFORMATION SOURCE: Dorothy Dick.

HUSBAND	(1) Lonnie Kouchomp Sr.
Died	at Kanosh, Utah, when his son Lonnie was 3 years old.
Buried	Kanosh, Utah.
Mother	Curly Annie.
WIFE	Martha.
Born	Kanosh, Utah.
Died	Kanosh, Utah.
Buried	Kanosh, Utah.
Mother	Jean (from Shivwits, Utah).
Other husbands	(2) Alec.

CHILDREN
1. <u>Lonnie Kouchomp</u> (male) born 15 April 1892, married Dorothy Dick.

INFORMATION SOURCE: Dorothy Dick.

HUSBAND	Lonnie Kouchomp.
Born	15 April 1892 at Kanosh, Utah.
Father	Lonnie Kouchomp Sr.
Mother	Martha.
Other wives	(1) Julia John (2) Harrine.
WIFE	(3) Dorothy Dick.
Born	about 1902.
Died	at Fillmore, Utah (car accident).
Father	Dick.
Other husbands	Toby John.

CHILDREN
1. <u>Dean Kouchomp</u> (male) born 1927 Kanosh, Utah, died and buried at Kanosh 1930.

INFORMATION SOURCE: Dorothy Dick.

HUSBAND	Los Leon (Mexican).
WIFE	Maimie (**Wuhsee´udok**) of Sharp, Nevada.
Mother	Jennie.

CHILDREN
1. <u>Mike Leon</u> (male) died August 1952 at Cedar City, Utah.

INFORMATION SOURCE: Carl and Minnie Jake.

HUSBAND	(2) Joe Levi (a cousin to Crokett Kanosh).
Born	Kanosh, Utah.
Died	Kanosh, Utah.
Buried	Kanosh, Utah.
Father	**Tungaw´pawsoov**, died at Kanosh, he had two brothers.
Mother	**Pooee´chuts,** (Mouse).
WIFE	Annie.
Born	of Boulder, Utah. ("Taken away".)
Died	Kanosh, Utah.
Buried	Kanosh, Utah.
Other husbands	(1) ?

CHILDREN
1. (Female) born Kanosh, Utah, died at Kanosh as a child.
2. Mary Ann Levi (female) born Kanosh, Utah, married (2) Eddie Jake.
3. Milford Levi (male) born Kanosh, Utah, died Kanosh, lived about 25 years.
4. Ida (**Mooweech**) Levi (female) born about 1885 at Kanosh, Utah, died 12 June 1960, buried at Richfield, Utah, married (1) John Manarra (2) Frank Woody.
5. Andy Levi (male) born Kanosh, Utah, died Kanosh, Utah, married (1) Aimie (2) Lucy Manarra. (Andy is the father of Johnson Levi.)
6. Wess Levi (male) born 1888 at Kanosh, Utah, married (1) Aimie (2) ? (3) ? (4) ?
7. (Male) born Kanosh, Utah, died at Kanosh as a child.

INFORMATION SOURCE: Minnie Kanosh.

HUSBAND	Manarra (Pau-wow-a-woots). Carl Jake says the word Manarra, Monnaro, Menarrow, comes from the Spanish name "Manel," pronounced by Indians **Munyawd´** as the Paiute language has no "L's" or "R's." This name was Anglicized to Manarra, Menarrow. The Indian name of Pau-wow-a-woots is an Anglicized word also. Johnny Jake says Manarra was a Mexican who came from Mexi County. Isabel Kelly in her *Southern Paiute Ethnography*, Anthropological Papers of the University of Utah, number 69, May 1964, page 177, mentions a man from the Panguitch Band with the name of "Minari, meaning legs stretch over; referring to his walk."
Born	about 1838, of Hamilton Fort, Utah.
Died	about 1872 near Hamilton Fort, Utah.
WIFE	Jennie (Jeannie) Wearament.

Born	about 1840, Virgin, Utah.
Died	30 January 1925, near Hamilton Fort, Utah.
buried	Cedar City, Utah.

CHILDREN

1. Wint Menarrow (male) born about 1858, of Hamilton Fort, Utah, died at Panguitch Lake, Utah about 1938.
2. (Female) born about 1860, of Hamilton Fort, Utah. Died as an adult.
3. Big John Menarrow (male) born about1862, of Hamilton Fort, Utah, died at Cedar City, Utah, 24 July 1931, buried at Cedar City. Married Ida Levi, no children.
4. Eliza Menarrow (female) born 1864, of Hamilton Fort, Utah, married (1) John .
5. Anna Mennarrow Hamilton (female) born 15 October 1866 (70), of Hamilton Fort, Utah, died about May 1958.
6. Lucy Mennarrow (female) born 1868, of Hamilton Fort, Utah, died in Cedar City, Utah, married (1) Jake Moroni (2) Andy Levi, no children from Andy Levi.

INFORMATION SOURCE: Anna Mennarrow Hamilton and Carl Jake.

I became acquainted with Anna M. Hamilton before she died. She was living in Salt Lake City and had been raised by white people. She had little contact with her own people. She spelled her last name Mennarrow. There is a story about her entitled "Purchased from Slavery" in the Church Section of the Deseret News, week ending May 17, 1958.

HUSBAND	(1) **Nawhoo´kwee Neahv** (War Chief).
WIFE	Rosey (her Indian name was **Mawn´taw, Mawn´tai**).
Other husbands	(2) Jake Wiggits (Wichetts).

CHILDREN

1. (Female) born Greenwich, Utah, died Uintah County, Utah, married (1) a Ute Indian.

INFORMATION SOURCE: Minnie Kanosh.

HUSBAND	Nick (Little Nick).
Died	Bridgeland, Utah.
Other wives	(2) Maggie John (Toby John's Sister). Maggie died and buried at Lyman, Utah.
WIFE	unknown.
Born	of Wayne County. Utah.

CHILDREN.

1. Shah-kom (**Tosaw' Kawm,** White Rabbit), (male) born in Wayne County, Utah, died at Duchesne, Utah. Married a lady of Duchesne, Utah.
2. Charlie (male) born 1887? in Wayne County, Utah. Died Near Gusher, Utah, 20 December 1929? Married Ida May Antach a younger sister to his brother Shah-Kom's wife. Ida May born 1892, died 26 June 1916. They had a son Joseph Nick, a half-brother to Fred Nick.

INFORMATION SOURCE: Jimmy Timmican.

See "Nick, The Moqui Captive" in Chapter 3 where Malan Jackson says that Nick was a Moqui captured as a child by the Paiutes. He was very short. Ute Allotment records of 1905 list a John Nick (age 39 in 1905, died 30 March 1912) with the Indian Name of Nan-nah- mo-qua which sounds like "Growing Hopi." Both Utes and Paiutes call the Hopis **Mookweech** (Moqui.) John Nick could be a son of Little Nick?

HUSBAND	(2) Jack Nort.
Died	Ibapah, Utah (car accident).
Father	Jack.
Mother	Annie.
WIFE	Julia John.
Born	near Newcastle, Utah.
Father	Kanosh John.
Mother	Eliza Manarra.
Other husbands	(1) Nathaniel Joe of Kaibab, Arizona, (3) Lewis M. Snyder, a Chemehuevi, (4) Albert Rice.

CHILDREN

1. Jackson Jack Nort, (male) born 9 July 1923, at Cedar City, Utah, married (1) from Yuma, Ariz, (2) Mexican (3) Kooseta.
2. Jessie Nort, (female) born 8 March 1925, at Cedar City, Utah, married (1) Jackson Bow.

INFORMATION SOURCE: Julia John.

HUSBAND	Tom Parashont. Tom Parashont's Indian name was **Sekoots´** (Squirrel).
Died	at Cedar City, Utah.
Buried	at Cedar City, Utah.
Father	Tom Parashont.
Other wives	Maimie Snow (had no children).
WIFE	Amy (Emma) Timmican (she went by the name Emma).

Born December 1886, at Lyman, Utah.
Died 9 January 1961, at Richfield, Utah.
Buried 12 January 1961, at Richfield, Utah.
Father John Timmican.
Mother Rose.
Other husbands (1) Charlie Arrowgarp (3) Jessie Jim (who died about 1942).

CHILDREN
1. Unnamed (female) born about 1924 at Greenwich, Utah, died about 1925 at Richfield, Utah. Lived 1 year.
2. Unnamed (female) born about 1926 near Salina, Utah, died about 1926 at Cedar City, Utah. Lived 3 months.
3. Unnamed (male) born about 1927 at Cedar City, Utah, died about 1927 at Cedar City, Utah. Lived 2 months.
4. Viola (female) born about June 1928 at Richfield, Utah, died 1929 at Cedar City, Utah. Lived 1 year.
5. Captola (female) born about June 1928 at Richfield, Utah, died at Richfield, Utah, in 1930. Lived 2 years. Viola and Captola were twins. Emma says that, "Viola Hansen, a white lady, gave the twins their names."
6. Stillborn (male) born about 1930 at Cedar City, Utah, died about 1931 at Cedar City, Utah.

INFORMATION SOURCE: Emma Timmican.

HUSBAND Peanump (**Peu´nump**) Big Foot. See the article *One Indian's Vengeance* by James Sharp published in the "Improvement Era" February 1936. There is a story about him.
WIFE unknown.

CHILDREN
1. Culbert Peanump (male).
2. (Male.)

INFORMATION SOURCE: Carl and Minnie Jake.

HUSBAND unknown.
WIFE unknown.

CHILDREN
1. (Female.)
2. Pete (male) died at Indian Peak, Utah. Married Phoebe. They are the parents of Willie John.

3. John Syme (male).
4. Gima (Jones).
5. George Swallow? (male). He had a son named George Swallow Jr.

INFORMATION SOURCE: Carl and Minnie Jake.

HUSBAND	Pete. (See "Pete the Medicine Man" in Chapter 2 on War and Historical Stories.)
Died	Indian Peak, Utah.
Buried	Indian Peak, Utah.
WIFE	Phoebe.
Died	At Baker, Nevada.
Buried	At Baker, Nevada.

CHILDREN
1. Willie John (male) born at Eagle Valley, Nevada, died at Eagle Valley about 1898. Married Maimie.
2. Tappie also known as Sarah Tappie (George). Born about 1879 at Eagle Valley, Nevada, died 11 January 1953 and buried at Shivwits, Utah. Married Benjamin Avov and Brig George.
3. Panaca Tom (male) died at Milford, Utah. Married Clara.

INFORMATION SOURCE: Carl and Minnie Jake.

HUSBAND	Jimmy Pete. Jimmy Pete was raised by Captain Pete. His real father was Coal Creek John. Coal Creek John was Tau-gu according to Page 91 Southern Paiute Petition before Indian Commission, Docket numbers 88 and 330.
Born	about 1892.
Father	Coal Creek John.
Mother	Flo.
Other wives	(1) Shivwits marriage license says he married Adelse Rice 6 January 1915. Adelse Rice was a daughter of Tom Rice and Anna Seaman according to the license. (2) Josephine.
WIFE	Lilly Bell Timmican.
Born	Greenwich, Utah.
Died	February or March 1943 at Moapa Valley, Nevada.
Father	John Timmican.
Mother	Rose.
Other husbands	(2) Willy China of southern Nevada.

CHILDREN
1. Ella (Helen) Pete (female) born 12 September 1926.

INFORMATION SOURCE: Florence Timmican Kanosh.

HUSBAND unknown.
WIFE unknown.

CHILDREN
1. Phoebe (female) died at Baker, Nevada, married to Pete. They are the parents of Willie John.
2. (Female) she married the father of Peahnump.

INFORMATION SOURCE: Carl and Minnie Jake.

HUSBAND **Poawhaw´dawveech.**
Born at **Toopaw Hawduhd** (a mountain on the other side of Bryce Canyon, Utah).
Died about 1889.
WIFE unknown.
Died about 1885.

CHILDREN
1. **Ungkaw´hawduh, Ungkaw´hawduhm** (Red One), (female). Married Chief Walker (**O-aw´kawd, O-aw´kawduhm**). This name meaning "Yellow" was Anglicized to Walker.
2. (Female) married Peterson.
3. (Female) married Chief Walker.
4. Peaweeds, **Pee´weech** (female) married (1) Chief Walker, had no children (2) John Kanosh.
   Walker was married to all three sisters in Indian plural marriage.

INFORMATION SOURCE: Minnie Kanosh (Timmican).

HUSBAND unknown.
WIFE unknown.

CHILDREN
1. Tom (Tom Quakanab) male, born Henry Mountains, Utah, died Greenwich, Utah.
2. **Kwe-eep´** (male), **Kwe-eep´** was Anglicized to Kurrip. Kwe-eep´ was the father of Lester Kurrip a Ute.
3. (Male) Dorothy Dick's grandfather.
4. (Male) traded to Mexicans.

INFORMATION SOURCE: Jimmy Timmican.

HUSBAND	Tom Quakanab. Tom was also known as Chicken Shootum Tom. His Indian name was **Kwee´kunuv** which means Foggy. This word was Anglicized to Quakanab and other spellings. He seems to have also been called **Wawn´uvuhts**. Jimmy Timmican remembers that Tom was still alive in 1911.
Born	about 1814 in the Henry Mountains, Utah. (See Indian depredations in Utah P 342 by Gottfredson.)
Died	after 1914 at Greenwich, Utah.
Buried	Greenwich, Utah.
WIFE	unknown.
Died	Wayne County, Utah.

CHILDREN
1. Liza Quakanab (female). Rosey and Liza were married to John Timmican in Indian plural marriage according to Indian custom.
2. Rosey Quakanab (Rosey **Wawn´uvuhts**) married John Timmican.
3. **Pooeetch´** (male) died Greenwich, married **Ke-eh´taw**.

INFORMATION SOURCE: Jimmy Timmican.

HUSBAND	unknown.
Father	Tom Quakanab's brother.
WIFE	Lucy.
Born	of Cannonville, Utah.
Died	at Kaibab, Arizona.
Buried	Kaibab, Arizona.
Other husbands	Dick?

CHILDREN
1. Maggie (**Tuh´dus,** meaning Potatoes), (female) died Greenwich, Utah, married Ben Sampson.
2. Johnny Dick (male) died Kaibab, Arizona. Married Maggie, she had no children. Maggie's Indian name was **Tawk**. Maggie's mother's name was Tappy. The Indians of Kaibab state that Maggie was a great runner when she was young. She could outrun the men in a footrace. She was sometimes called "Antelope" in Paiute because of her speed.

INFORMATION SOURCE: Jimmy Timmican, Stanley Samson.

HUSBAND	Charley Roberts.
Died	Cedar City, Utah.
Buried	Richfield, Utah.
Father	Little Bob.
WIFE	Virginia Wall.
Father	Fred Wall.
Mother	Mable John.
Other husbands	(2) Georgey George.

CHILDREN
1. Hilda Roberts (female) married (1) ? (2) Smith Bushhead.

INFORMATION SOURCE: Jimmy Timmican.

HUSBAND	Ben Sampson.
Born	"In the ledges near Kanab, Utah."
Died	about 1902 "in the ledges near Kanab, Utah, when Stanley was a baby"
Buried	"In the ledges near Kanab, Utah."
Father	Sampson.
WIFE	Maggie (**Tuh´dus**).
Born	near Cannonville, Utah.
Died	at Greenwich, Utah after Stanley was married.
Buried	Greenwich, Utah.
Mother	Lucy.
Other husbands	Bullets. (Fred Bullets and Dan Bullets are Stanley Sampson's half-brothers. They had the same mother. Dan Bullets had the Paiute name of **Chuhku´ Numpuv** meaning Duck Feet).

CHILDREN
1 Snow Sampson (male) older than Stanley. Drowned on the other side of Johnson, Utah when he was an adult.
2. Stanley Sampson (male) born 1 January 1901, near Fredonia, Arizona, married (1) Amy Jim. Amy Jim died 21 June 1935, and buried at Kaibab. Stanley Sampson and Amy Jim had two children: 1. Stanley Sampson Jr. (male) born at Kaibab. 2. Evelyn Sampson (female) born at Kaibab, she married Arthur Tillahash. (2) Margerite McQueen (Shoshoni).
3. Mable Sampson (female) born 1891, married (1) **koavok** (2) Frank Dry.

INFORMATION SOURCE: Jimmy Timmican, Stanley Sampson, and 1965 census.

HUSBAND unknown.
Born of Wayne County, Utah.
Died "When his children were very young."
WIFE unknown.
Born of Wayne County, Utah.
Died "When her children were very young."

CHILDREN
1. John Timmican (male) born Wayne County, Utah, buried Lyman, Utah, married (1) Liza (2) Rose.
2. Sally Timmican (female) born Wayne County, Utah, died Greenwich, Utah, married (1) Page Neab, **Pawguh´ Neahv** (meaning Fish Chief), (2) Bob. John and Sally were raised by Tewok. Tewok and John Timmican's father were brothers? Tewok died and buried in Lyman, Utah.

INFORMATION SOURCE: Jimmy Timmican.

HUSBAND John Timmican.
Born Wayne County, Utah.
Died "May," about 1906 near Bicknell, Utah.
Buried Lyman, Utah.
Other wives Rose.
WIFE (1) Liza Quakanab (Rose's sister).
Died Greenwich, Utah.

CHILDREN
1. George Timmican (male) born 10 Oct. 1868, died 1 Nov. 1953, Richfield, Utah, married Minnie Kanosh.
2. Eliza Timmican Jackson (female). Eliza was raised by old man Jackson of Lyman, Utah. She lives in Salt Lake City, married Paul Cheser or Chese, had three children and then divorced. (Paul Chese's last name probably not correctly spelled.)

INFORMATION SOURCE: Jimmy Timmican.

HUSBAND George Timmican.
Born 10 Oct. 1868.
Died 1 Nov. 1953 at Richfield Utah, (ulcer).
Buried 3 Nov. 1953 at Richfield, Utah.
Father John Timmican.
Mother she had the last name of Quakanab.
Other wives Minnie Kanosh.
WIFE Ruth (Timmican?)

CHILDREN
1. Young Timmican (male) born 9 September 1910, married Ruth Sobquint.

INFORMATION SOURCE: Minnie Kanosh.

HUSBAND	Young Timmican.
Born	9 September 1910.
Father	George Timmican.
Mother	Ruth.
WIFE	Ruth Sobquint.

CHILDREN
1. Shirley Timmican (female) born 14 Oct. 1936.

INFORMATION SOURCE: Minnie Kanosh.

HUSBAND	John Timmican.
Born	Wayne County, Utah.
Died	"May," about 1906 near Bicknell, Utah.
Buried	"Lyman cemetery, Utah" according to Florence Timmican.
Other wives	Liza (Indian plural marriage).
WIFE	Rose Quakanab (**Wawn´uvuhts**). Rose Qwakanab's Indian name was **Kweyu´hunt** (Bear).
Died	5 April 1942 at Greenwich, Utah.
Buried	Greenwich, Utah.
Father	Tommie (Tom).

CHILDREN
1. (Male) born about 1880 at Teasdale, Utah, buried at Teasdale.
2. (Male) about 1881 at Teasdale, Utah, buried at Frying Pan.
3. Unnamed Timmican (male) born about 1882, in Utah, died and buried at Fish Lake, Utah.
4. Nancy Timmican (female) born "When pinenuts opened" October 1883 at Frisco, Utah, died 5 August 1953, married Crockett Kanosh.
5. Florence Timmican (female) born about June 1889 at Fish Lake, Utah, married Crockett Kanosh.
6. Jimmie Timmican (male) born about 1895 at Loa, Utah (by the shearing corral), died 1972, married Annie.
7. Amy (Emma) Timmican (female) born December 1886 (97?) at Lyman, Utah, died 9 Jan. 1961, married (1) Charlie Arrowgarp.
8. Lilly Bell Timmican (female) born Greenwich, Utah, died April 1943, married (1) Jimmy Pete.

9. Martha Timmican (female) born Bicknell, Utah, died young.
10. (female) born Greenwich, Utah, lived one week.

HISTORICAL NOTE: The name Timmican comes from the Indian word **Toomu´kunt** which means "Roasted." It was a Paiute custom that after a woman gave birth she would lie upon a layer of sand placed over some heated rocks in a shallow pit big enough to lie in. "This made the women's blood circulate a lot better and helped in childbirth."

INFORMATION SOURCE: Jimmy Timmican, Florence Timmican, Emma Timmican, Vera Timican.

HUSBAND Panaca Tom.
Died Milford, Utah (killed with shotgun).
Buried Milford, Utah.
Father Pete.
Mother Phoebe.
WIFE Clara (**Aiuv´ee**).
Died 1964 at Cedar City, Utah.
Buried Cedar City, Utah.
Other husbands Zuniga (Mexican), Buckskin Joe.

CHILDREN
1. Roy Tom (male) born 1898 at Panaca, Nevada.
2. Albert Tom (male).
3. Lilly Tom (female) born Milford, Utah, died Cedar City, Utah.
4. Eva Tom (female) born Kanosh, Utah, died Cedar City, Utah.

INFORMATION SOURCE: Carl Jake, Arthur Richards.

HUSBAND **Tungawpawsoov.**
Died Kanosh, Utah.
WIFE **Pooee´chuts** (a Paiute name meaning Mouse).

CHILDREN
1 Joe Levi (male).

INFORMATION SOURCE: Minnie Kanosh.

HUSBAND	(2) Jake Wiggits (Wichetts) His last name comes from the Paiute word **Wuhguhts´** meaning Vagina.
Born	of Indian Peak, Utah.
WIFE	Rosey (**Mawn´taw** or **Mawn´tai**).
Other husbands	(1) **Nawhoo´kwee Neahv** (War Chief).

CHILDREN
1. Eddie Wiggits (male) born 1892.
2. (female).
3. (female).
4. (female).

INFORMATION SOURCE: Minnie Kanosh.

HUSBAND	Willy.
Born	of Wayne County, Utah.
Mother	Mary of Wayne County (Mary's mother was **Noakoa´sawvuhts**).
WIFE	Minnie.
Father	**Wawu´puhts.**
Mother	**Kaikoaduts** (of Indianola, Teas Valley).

CHILDREN
1. Frank Woody (male) born 4 Sept. 1902, died 2 May 1973, married Ida Levi.

INFORMATION SOURCE: Minnie Kanosh.

Section Two

HUSBAND unknown.
Death before 1897.
WIFE Annie.
Birth about 1858.
Died 1 January 1946.
Other husbands (1) Peter Harrison (2) Yellowjacket.(not sure of sequence).

CHILDREN
2. Johnnie (male) born 1887.
1. Clara (female) born 1889, died about 1909 at Shivwits, Utah, married about 1903 to Max Tai-u-su (2) Jannie Rogers (Foster).

INFORMATION SOURCE: Bessie Tillahash, Mable Yellowjacket and Shivwits Death Roll.

HUSBAND Rex Asket.
Died 20 April 1966 at St. George, Utah.
Buried 23 April 1966 at Shivwits Indian Reservation, Utah.
Father **Poo-oo´ Weechok** meaning Fur Back.
Mother Tai-u-su (Ti-usa) correctly pronounced **Taioo´soov** (Whittled Stick).
Married 13 June 1961 (legally).
WIFE Nora George.
Born about 75 years old in 1962.
Died 18 Sept. 1962 at Caliente, Nevada.
Buried at Shivwits Indian Reservation, Utah.

CHILDREN
1. Lester Asket (male) married to Lilly Tillahash.

INFORMATION SOURCE: Shivwits marriage records and Nora.

HUSBAND (1) Big George.
Father Railroad George.
WIFE Ida Toab.
Birth about 1879, at Tassai, Mojave County, Arizona.
Death 20 may 1959, at St. George, Utah.
Buried at Shivwits Reservation, Utah.
Father Toab.
Mother Ta wa wa, la wa wi, Chipmunk. The name is correctly pro-

	nounced **Tavaw´aw Vee** meaning Chipmunk Mother.
Other husbands	(2) Indian Jake (Watermelon Jake), (3) Jim Snow (4) Frank Snow (5) Kanosh John (6) Jim Hooveutz.

CHILDREN

1. Dolly George (Snow), (female) born 1894, died 23 July 1946, married Seth Bushhead on 31 December 1911.

INFORMATION SOURCE: Stewart Snow, Edrick Bushhead, Bessie Tillahash.

HUSBAND	(2) Indian Jake (Watermelon Jake). Indian Jake's real name should have been "Tum" according to Morris Jake.
Born	1874.
Died	1959.
Buried	Kaibab, Arizona.
Other wives	(1) Minnie Pikyavit.
WIFE	(2) Ida Toab.
Born	about 1879 at Tassai, Arizona.
Died	20 May 1959 at St. George, Utah.
Buried	May 1959 at Shivwits, Reservation, Utah.
Father	Toab.
Mother	Ta wa wa, la wa wi, Chipmunk. The name is correctly pronounced **Tavaw´aw Vee** Chipmunk Mother.
Other husbands	(1) Big George (3) Jim Snow (4) Frank Snow (5) Kanosh John (6) Jim Hoviutz.

CHILDREN

1. Serena Jake (Snow) born 1900, died 2 Aug. 1967, and buried 6 Aug. 1967, at Kaibab.

INFORMATION SOURCE: Serena, and Bessie Tillahash.

HUSBAND	Coal Creek John "Chief of Coal Creek Band of Cedar City, Utah".
Died	Minersville, Utah.
Other wives	Flo (Indian plural marriage). Coal Creek John and Flo had a child, Jimmy Pete of Cedar City Utah.
WIFE	Rena.
Born	1878 of Panguitch Lake, Utah.
Died	Shivwits.
Buried	Shivwits Indian Reservation, Utah.
Other husbands	Squint. Squint married Rena and had: (1) Annie (female) died

at Cedar City, Utah at about age 9. (2) (female) died shortly after birth.

CHILDREN
1. Mabel John (female) born about 1890 at Minersville, Utah. Married (1) Fred Wall (2) James Yellowjacket. James born 3 July 1898, died 2 July 1963.
2. Jennie (female). Died at Silver Reef, Utah.
3. (Male.)

INFORMATION SOURCE: Mabel John and 1940 census.

HUSBAND	Mack (Max) Tai u su. His Indian name is **Moovee´tsekee** (Split Nose). The family Indian name Tai u su is correctly pronounced **Taioo´soov**. It means Whittled Stick.
Born	about 1884.
Died	"Died at Five Mile on the Shivwits Reservation from some kind of sickness while he was still a young man" (about 25 years old).
Father	**Poo-oo´ Wechok** (Fur Back).
Mother	Tai-u-su (Ti-usa) correctly pronounced **Taioo´soov.**
Married	about 1903.
WIFE	Clara.
Born	1889.
Died	about 1909 at Five Mile, Shivwits Reservation, Utah.
Mother	Annie.
Other husbands	Jannie Rogers (Foster).

CHILDREN
1. George McFee (male) born 25 May 1904 at St. George, Utah, died 22 April 1962, buried at Shivwits, Utah, married Marie Snow.
2. Martha (female) born 1906 at St. George, Utah, died 12 January 1935, buried at Shivwits Reservation, Utah.
3. Died young.

INFORMATION SOURCE: Bessie Tillahash, Rex Asket, and tombstone inscription for child number 2.

HUSBAND	**Poo-oo´ Wechok** (Fur Back).
Death	about 1895.
WIFE	Ti usa, Tai u usa, **Taioo´soov** (Whittled Stick). Also called Sally.
Born	about 1843.

Died about 1900.
Father Tai-u-su. This name is shown on the 1898 census as being born about 1828. It is normal in Indian census taking for a child to take the father's name for a last name.
Other husbands Big Jim.

CHILDREN
1. Jannie (Janey) Rogers (Foster), (male) born about 1875-79. Died 7 August 1957. Married (2) Clara, wife of Mack Tai u su (**Taioo´soov**), (3) Sue Mokiac at St. George, Utah, 1911. Janie's Indian name was **Saikumee´do**.
2. Rex Asket (**Iscawts**), (male) born 1884 in Grand Wash, Mojave County, Arizona, died 20 April 1966. He married Nora.
3. Mack (Max) Tai-u su (**Taioo´soov**), (male) born about 1885, died about 1909. Married to Clara.

INFORMATION SOURCE: Archie Rogers, Rex Asket, Bessie Tillahash, Jannie's marriage license and 1897 census.

HUSBAND Sa-ap, Old Snow, Snow. Sa-ap is correctly pronounced **Sawup´** meaning "Mush." Stewart Snow gives the following information on his father: "Snow was the owner of the deer and mountain sheep in his area and helped people be more successful by telling them where to go hunt them. He also had power to heal and at one time he healed me of a serious dog bite by sucking on the wound. He could prevent infection and after effects and did at this time."
Born about 1840 at **Sunup** Mountain on the Arizona Strip, Arizona.
Death Shivwits Indian Reservation, Utah.
Buried Shivwits Indian Reservation, Utah.
WIFE Pa-wans, Lucy (**Pa-wunts´** means "Swollen")
Born about 1848 at **Weow´deev**, Arizona (on the Arizona Strip).
Died Shivwits Indian Reservation, Utah.
Buried Shivwits Indian Reservation, Utah.

CHILDREN
1. Frank Snow born about 1871 in Arizona, died July 1931 Shivwits Utah, wife (1) Nancy John.
2. Jim Snow (male) born about 1879 at **Sunup** Mountain, Arizona, died 10 Oct. 1928. Married Ida Toab.
3. Edwin Snow born about 1890.

INFORMATION SOURCE: Stewart Snow, 1898 census, and tombstone inscription.
HUSBAND Frank Snow.

Born about 1871 in Arizona.
Died July 1931 at Shivwits Reservation, Utah.
Father Snow.
Mother Lucy.
WIFE Nancy John.
Born of Long Valley, Kane County, Utah.
Died about 1921 at Kaibab, Arizona.
Father Jim John.
Mother Molly.
Other husbands Brig George.

CHILDREN

1. Nannie Snow (female) born 1899 at Gunlock, Utah, died 1920, buried at Shivwits, Utah, married 2 May 1918 to Tom Parashont.
2. Stewart Snow (male) born 5 November 1905 at Mount Carmel, Utah, married 1929 to Mary Bushhead.
3. Agnes Snow (female) born about 1907 at Shivwits Reservation, Utah, died about 1922, buried at Shivwits Reservation, Utah, married 1919 to Glen Pinkie, a son of Old Pinkie. Glen Pinkie was born about 1903 and died about 1923. Glen Pinkie married Agnes Snow; they had a child Amy Pinkie who married Archie Kay. They had no children. Amy born about 1921 at Shivwits, died 13 June 1965.
4. Richard Snow (male) born about 1909 at Shivwits Reservation, Utah, died March 1921.

INFORMATION SOURCE: Stewart Snow, marriage licenses, and tombstone inscriptions.

HUSBAND (3) Jim Snow.
Born about 1879 at **Sunup** Mountain, Arizona.
Died 10 October 1928 at Shivwits Reservation, Utah.
Buried Oct. 1928 at Shivwits Reservation, Utah.
Father Snow.
Mother Lucy.
WIFE Ida Toab.
Born about 1879 at Tassai in the Grand Wash, Mojave County, Arizona.
Died 20 May 1959 at St. George, Utah.
Buried May 1959 at Shivwits Reservation, Utah.
Father Toab.
Mother Ta wa wa, La wa wi, Chipmunk. The name is correctly pronounced **Tavaw´aw Vee** Chipmunk Mother.
Other husbands (1) Big George (2) Watermelon Jake (4) Frank Snow (5) Kanosh John (6) Jim Hoviutz.

CHILDREN
1. Ada Snow (female) born 1907, married 5 Sept. 1924 to Joseph John, died 11 March 1959.
2. Louise Snow (female) born 15 June 1910, married Willie Fisher.
3. Lee Snow (male) born 1912, married Madilene Chassis, died 12 January 1956 at St. George, Utah.
4. Marie Snow (female) born 15 October 1915 in New Harmony Mountains, Utah, married George McFee 7 June 1930.
5. Jessie Snow (male) born about 1918.
6. Nellie Snow (female) born 1924.
7. Lucy Snow (female) born 1926.

INFORMATION SOURCE: Marie Snow, Edrick Bushhead, Stewart Snow, marriage licences, census records and dated photographs.

HUSBAND	unknown.
Born	Kaibab Mountains, Arizona.
Died	Killed by a white man near Pipe Springs, Arizona.
WIFE	**Koavuv´.**
Died	near Orderville, Utah.
Father	Mahgin.
Mother	**Tuhdu´heets,** meaning Orphan, she died when Tony about 5.

CHILDREN
1. (Female) traded to Navajos in Arizona or New Mexico by an uncle.
2. Tony Tillahash (male) born 1886 at Mount Carmel, Utah, married Bessie Simon.

INFORMATION SOURCE: Tony and Bessie Tillahash.

HUSBAND	(John) Toab (**Touv'** meaning Rabbit Tick).
Born	about 1839.
Other wives	Susan.
WIFE	Ta wa, La wa wi, Chipmunk. **Tavaw´aw Vee (**Chipmunk Mother).
Born	about 1842 (1848) Parashont Mountain, Arizona Strip.
Died	at Shivwits Reservation, Utah.
Buried	at Shivwits Reservation, Utah.
Father	Quetoos (**Kwetoos'** meaning Giant).
Other husbands	Charley.

CHILDREN
1. Jack Toab (male) died in Uintah County, Utah.

2. <u>Foster</u> Toab (Foster Charles), (male) born about 1880 near Tuweep, Arizona, died 1957. In about 1900 several young Indians including Foster Charles, Thomas Mayo, Brig George, Seth Bushhead, Tony Tillahash, and Minnie Rice were sent to attend the Carlysle Indian School. The first four studied agriculture and became members of "Pop" Warner's famous football team the Redskins. They were guests at "Teddy" Roosevelt's Thanksgiving dinner at the White House.
3. <u>Ida Toab,</u> **Etsoov´** (female) born about 1879 at Tassai, Arizona, Died 20 May 1959, married (1) Big George (2) ? (3) ? (4) ? (5) ? (6) ?

INFORMATION SOURCE: Bessie Tillahash, and Foster's history.

1898 SHIVWITS CENSUS

INDIAN NAME	ENGLISH NAME	SEX	RELATION	AGE
1. Quee tus	Burning Fire	m	father	90
2. La wa wi	Chipmunk	f	daughter	50
3. Ma-git-tsuk	Charley	m	husband	50
4. U-tsuk	Little Eyes	f	granddaughter	20
5. Waw-sai-ak	John	m	husband	25
6. Foster	Foster Charley	m	grandson	22
7. Quai-tsee-ut	Jack in a Box	m	grandson	24
8. Ye-anap	Mrs. Jack in a Box	f	wife	22
9. Sai mon		m	nephew	55
10. Uwee-we	Susan Simon	f	wife	50
11. Puny kub	Ruth Simon	f	daughter	7
12. Pee Kattets	Jim Mokeak	m	nephew	55
13. Pu yas	Blowing Wind	f	wife	45
14. Pa u an tuh	Sallie Wallace	f	daughter	26
15. Sa quai win ti	Winnie Wallace	f	granddaughter	12
16. Pai wip	Harry Wallace	m	grandson	7
17. Ai-o-wa	Susan Jake	f	daughter	23
18. Tut-tsa-wit	Jake	m	husband	35
19. A-a-mud	Mandic Jake	f	daughter	12
20. Sang-an	Lester Mokiak	m	son	13
21. Pai yen am	Sue Mokiak	f	daughter	9
22. Mo pits av am	Jeanie Mokiak	f	daughter	6
23. Mo-win ok	Jim	m	nephew	60
24. Sa-ap	Snow	m	nephew	58
25. Pa-wans	Mrs. Snow	f	wife	50
26. Bran bi dop	Frank Snow	m	son	24
27. Ban ki duk	Jim Snow	m	son	18
28. Mas sus	Edwin Snow	m	son	8
29. Po romp	Limpie	m	nephew	50
30. Mu ya sob	Gopher Cheek	f	wife	50
31. Mo que a sa munts	Billy Limpie	m	son	17
32. Tsai na	Mary Limpie	f	daughter	14
All of the above belong to the family of Chief Quee-tus				
33. Tom-mo-lo	Peter Harrison	m	father	35
34. Mai-mi eno	Waving Hands	f	wife	35
35. Doc	Doc Harrison	m	son	13
36. Mo kot	John Rice	m	father	65
37. Me naip	Sallie Rice	f	wife	55

INDIAN NAME	ENGLISH NAME	SEX	RELATION	AGE
38. Nang amp	Minnie Rice	f	daughter	11
39. Yo ok	Mrs. Janey (Dora)	f	niece	30
40. Quee tuts	Dick Gillespie	m	brother-in-law	30
41. Moq nee a	Tom Moqwa	m	brother-in-law	25
42. Tsam mo	Priscilla Moqnun	f	wife	20
43. Toab		m	father	65
44. Ma wa	Susan Toab	f	wife	50
45. Pa glin-o-wow-amp	Joe	m	brother-in-law	55
46. Sang a nim	Wind Blows the Sand	f	sister	35
47. Keep				
48. Po le on	Napoleon Bonapart	m	father	25
49. Mary	Mary Bonapart	f	wife	25
50. Ta kam		m	Mary's father	60
51. David		m	Mary's brother	23
52. Kom pa-se	Mrs. David	f	wife	18
53. Jack	Jack Takem	m	brother	18
54. Sai ka vak	R. R. George	m	father	50
55. Sa quantwim	Sarah George	f	wife	45
56. Pee ap	George R.	m	son	21
57. Wee mi wi ka	Susan George R.	f	wife	20
58. To ko nit ap	Heber R. R. George	m	son	6
59. Tai-u-su	Bout?	m		70
60. Avav	Big Jim	m	father	55
61. Tai-u-su	Bout	f	wife	55
62. Ra nants	Janey Foster	m	son	30
63. Ai ask it	Jack Tai-u-su	m	son	19
64. Tammat	Benjamin Franklin	m	son	15
65. Pa-rak wa wa	Max Tai-u-su	m	son	15
66. Pots ee	Star Tai-u-su	m	son	8
67. Ma quet tsup	Chipmunk	m	father	70
68. Taylor	Taylor Chipmunk	m	son	18
69. Pa nai ak	Barley	f	sister	67
70. Bird	Bird	m	nephew	33
71. Dick	Dick Bird	m	nephew's son	13
72. Tai mon	Taimon	m	nephew	30
73. Kap puts	Susan Taimon	f	wife	35
74. Ta raip	Brig George	m	nephew	22
75. Tom pup-wu	Beacham George	m	nephew	18
76. Tacwac um	Annie Yellowjacket	f	niece	40
77. Pa wit	Yell Yellowjacket	m	husband	40
78. Tsop wup	John Yellowjacket	m	son	12
79. Sai wat am big	Clara Yellowjacket	f	daughter	8

Indian name	English name	Sex	Relation	Age
80. Sa wah wimp	Tony	m	father	45
81. Ya as	Pine Bark	f	daughter	14
82. Se en a win	Waddy	m	husband	26
83. Min ne nas	Ned Tony	m	son	11
84. Lap pa	Lloyd Tony	m	son	6
85. Tsa wu	Lime	m	cousin	43
86. We wunka	Pretty Neck Lime	f	wife	35
87. Wah mank	Greyman	m	brother	42
88. Mo wel la	Mrs. Greyman	f	wife	30
89. Pak wee sap	Jack Greyman	m	son	15
90. Ka ram pits	Ida Greyman	f	daughter	8
91. U tsuk	Fanny Greyman	f	daughter	6
92. K'sa be	Susan Spute	f	sister	35
93. On to tots	Edith Spute	f	daughter	9
94. U win a rip	John Spute	m	son	6
95. O arh	Nappa Tom	m	father	65
96. Ko romp	Mrs. Nappa Tom	f	wife	40
97. O wai nons		m	son	7
98. Sin nap	Teweep	m		50
99. Saquant wi nuk	David	m	husband	55
100. Mo bi a		f	wife	50
101. Mai o	Jacob	m	father	30
102. Mak sip	Annie Jacob	f	wife	26
103. Pa kai do	Tommy Jacob	m	son	7
104. Quee tum pequip	Roman Nose	m	father	50
105. Inu sak rek		f	wife	50
106. Hi kats a ret		f	daughter	35
107. Mot tar ra wek	Pagumpagets Joe	m	husband	50
108. To rots	Sandy Pagumpagets Joe	m	grandson	10
109. Ta wonts	Jim Pagumpagets Joe	m	grandson	8
110. Pa na qua	Nick Moroni	f	daughter	22
111. Tai akh rum	Moroni Mary	m	husband	22
112. Tom pits	Fred Roman Nose	m	son	10
113. Tsam ber	Pete	m	brother	48
114. Ban ger	Buffalo Bill	m	father	55
115. Pang ee a	Mrs. Buffalo Bill	f	wife	40
116. Pab wees	Will Buffalo Bill	m	son	18
117. Tawin ap		m		75
118. Grai wits		f	sister	80
119. Ta wul	John Tawul	m	father	45
120. U sirik	Sallie Tawul	f	wife	40
121. Keno	Keno Tawul	m	son	18
122. Se ee mod	Minnie Tawul	f	daughter	16

Indian name	English name	Sex	Relation	Age
123. Tsop bid	Charley Tawul	m	nephew	15
124. Wai bos	Ray Tawul	m	son	10
125. Quin se da	Monday Tawul	m	son	10
126. Waw ai bor	Carrie Tawul	f	daughter	7
127. Dai sits ur		f	mother	90
128. Ai ab uts	Annie Tuutuksank	f	niece	22
129. Tun tuk saik		m	husband	24
130. Mo sa bib	Pinkie	m	father	65
131. Maw kats ats	Mrs. Pinkie	f	wife	40
132. To quai tse	Theodore Pinkie	m	son	12
133. Saidee	Saidee Pinkie	f	daughter	6
134. To quo kung	Wild Cat	f	wife-mother	70
135. Tso ink ee	Flowing Hair	f	aunt	68
136. Tsl mar ro	Monday	m	uncle	70
137. Ko ob	Mrs. Tsimarro	f	wife	65
138. Ko nop guip	Charley Blow the Fire	m	father	50
139. Ko rak wek	Mrs. Charley	f	wife	50
140. Skump		m	father	48
141. Sai gats	Mrs. Skump	f	wife	45
142. Ai ots	Theodore Skump	m	son	18
143. Pai sit	Bessie Skump	f	daughter	12
144. Tai ral lots	Little Jim	m	father	50
145. Na nak ka	Mrs. Little Jim	f	wife	45
146. Smoki	Smoky Little Jim	m	son	10
147. Dimmis	Dimmis Little Jim	m	son	10
148. Wah sivenungs	Albert Little Jim	m	son	8
149. Sun ban wee wits	Shem (Sam)	m	father	55
150. Mar ro wits	Susan Shem	f	wife	55
151. Waw pai ko	Nora Shem	f	daughter	17
152. Tim buts	Sammy Shem	m	nephew	9
153. Kar rok	Frank	m	wife's brother	30
154. Wu ruts		f	wife's brother	30
155. Waw ai wa		f	mother	80
156. Do ming go	John Domingo	m		30

SOUTHERN PAIUTES

BIBLIOGRAPHY

CONETAH, FRED A. *History of the Northern Ute People*. Uintah-Ouray Ute Tribe, Salt Lake City, Utah: University of Utah Press, 1982.

CURTIN, JEREMIAH. *Myth of the Modocs: Indian Legends of the Northwest*. (1st edition 1912.) New York: Benjamin Blom, Inc., 1971.

EELS, W. C. *Number Systems of the North American Indians*. "The American Mathematical Monthly" Vol. XX, December 1913.

GIVON, T. *Ute Traditional Narratives*. Ignacio, Colorado: Ute Press, 1985.

GOTTFREDSON, PETER. *Indian Depredations In Utah, 1919*. Salt Lake City, Utah: Merlin G. Christenson, 1969. (Second edition—private printing.)

KELLY, ISABEL T. *Southern Paiute Ethnography*. Anthropological Papers No. 69, May 1964 (Glen Canyon Series Number 22). Salt Lake City: University of Utah Press.

KOPPER, PHILIP. *The Smithsonian Book of North American Indians before the Coming of the Europeans*. Washington D.C.: Smithsonian Books, 1986.

MC KENNAN, ROBERT and others. *Walapai Ethnography*. Memoirs of the American Anthropological Association, No. 42, 1933.

PALMER, WILLIAM R. *Why the North Star Stands Still and other Indian Legends*. (1st edition 1946.) Springdale, Utah: Zion Natural History Association, 1973.

PALMER, WILLIAM R. *Two Pahute Indian Legends: "Why the Grand Canyon was Made" and "The Three Days of Darkness."*. (Research supplementary information and editorial commentary by Dr. Thomas Keith Midgley.) St. Cheney, Washington: Lighthouse Publishers, 1987.

PALMER, WILLIAM R. *Forgotten Chapters of History*. Vol. 2, Radio Scripts 1951-1954. Southern Utah State College Library.

POWELL, J. W. and G. W. INGALLS. Report on the condition of the Ute Indians of Utah; the Pai-Utes of Utah, Northern Arizona, Southern Nevada, and Southeastern California: the Go-si-Utes of Utah and Nevada; the Northwestern Shoshones of Idaho and Utah; and the Western Shoshones of Nevada. Commission of Indian Affairs for 1873, Washington, 1874.

SAPIR, EDWARD. *Southern Paiute, a Shoshonean Language*. Proceedings of the American Academy of Arts and Sciences. Vol. 65, No. 1, June 1930.

SHARP, JAMES P. and GLYNN BENNION. *One Indian's Vengeance*. Salt Lake City: Improvement Era, February 1936.

THOMAS, ALFRED B. *The Plains Indians and New Mexico 1751-1778; A Collection of Documents Illustrative of the History of the Eastern Frontier of New Mexico*. Albuquerque: University of New Mexico Press, 1940.

UNITED STATES SENATE. *Walapai Papers*. Senate Doc. 273, 74th Congress, 2nd Session. Washington, 1936.

VOGEL, VIRGIL J. *American Indian Medicine*. Norman, Oklahoma: University of Oklahoma Press, 1970.

WILKERSON, CRAGUN and BARKER. *The Southern Paiute Nation vs. the United States of America*. Docket Nos. 88 and 330 before the Indian Claims Commission, 1963.

WILSON, E. N. *The White Indian Boy, The Story of Uncle Nick Among the Shoshones*. New York: World Book Co., Yonkers on Hudson, 1919.